Contexts for Learning

Contexts for Learning

SOCIOCULTURAL DYNAMICS IN CHILDREN'S DEVELOPMENT

Ellice A. Forman

Norris Minick

C. Addison Stone

New York   Oxford
OXFORD UNIVERSITY PRESS

Oxford University Press

Oxford   New York
Athens   Auckland   Bangkok   Bogota   Bombay
Buenos Aires   Calcutta   Cape Town   Dar es Salaam
Delhi   Florence   Hong Kong   Istanbul   Karachi
Kuala Lumpur   Madras   Madrid   Melbourne
Mexico City   Nairobi   Paris   Singapore
Taipei   Tokyo   Toronto

and associated companies in
Berlin   Ibadan

Library of Congress Cataloging-in-Publication Data
Contexts for learning: sociocultural dynamics in children's development
edited by Ellice A. Forman, Norris Minick, C. Addison Stone,
p.   cm.   Includes bibliographical references and index.
ISBN 0-19-510977-5 (Pbk.)
1. Learning, Psychology of—Social aspects.
2. Constructivism (Education).
3. Cognition and culture.
4. Cognition in children.
I. Forman, Ellice A.
II. Minick, Norris.
III. Stone, C. Addison.
LB1051.C6782   1993
370.15′2—dc20   92-5058

1 3 5 7 9 8 6 4 2

Printed in the United States of America
on acid-free paper

In memory of Sylvia Scribner,
whose continuing presence can be
felt throughout this book.

CONTENTS

CONTRIBUTORS

Alexandra Belyaeva
The Velikhov-Hamburg Collective
at The Institute of Psychology
Moscow, Russia
and The Laboratory of Comparative
    Human Cognition
San Diego, CA

Ann L. Brown
Education in Mathematics, Science,
    and Technology
Graduate School of Education
University of California, Berkeley
Berkeley, CA

Joseph C. Campione
Education in Mathematics, Science,
    and Technology
Graduate School of Education
University of California, Berkeley
Berkeley, CA

Courtney B. Cazden
Teaching, Curriculum, and Learning
    Environments
Harvard Graduate School of Education
Cambridge, MA

Gen Ling M. Chang-Wells
Toronto Board of Education
Toronto, Canada

Paul Cobb
Peabody College
Vanderbilt University
Nashville, TN

Michael Cole
Laboratory of Comparative Human
    Cognition
University of California, San Diego
La Jolla, CA

Ellice A. Forman
Department of Psychology in
    Education
School of Education
University of Pittsburgh
Pittsburgh, PA

Ronald Gallimore
Department of Psychiatry and
    Biobehavioral Sciences
University of California, Los Angeles
Los Angeles, CA

Claude Goldenberg
Department of Psychiatry and
    Biobehavioral Sciences
University of California, Los Angeles
Los Angeles, CA

Artin Göncü
Department of Educational Psychology
College of Education
University of Illinois at Chicago
Chicago, IL

Jacqueline J. Goodnow
School of Behavioral Sciences
Macquarie University
Sydney, Australia

Peg Griffin
The Velikhov-Hamburg Collective
at The Institute of Psychology
Moscow, Russia
and The Laboratory of Comparative
    Human Cognition
San Diego, CA

Fran Hagstrom
Frances L. Hiatt School of Psychology
Clark University
Worcester, MA

Giyoo Hatano
Faculty of Liberal Arts
Dokkyo University
Saitama, Japan

Bonnie E. Litowitz
Department of Psychiatry
Rush Medical College
Rush-Presbyterian–St. Luke's Medical
  Center
Chicago, IL

Jean McPhail
Program in Educational Studies
School of Education
University of Michigan
Ann Arbor, MI

Norris Minick
Program in Learning Disabilities
Department of Communication
  Sciences and Disorders
Northwestern University
Evanston, IL

Jayanthi Mistry
Department of Child Study
Tufts University
Medford, MA

Luis C. Moll
College of Education
Language, Reading, and Culture
The University of Arizona
Tucson, AZ

Christine Mosier
Department of Psychology
University of Utah
Salt Lake City, UT

Ageliki Nicolopoulou
Department of Education and Child
  Study
Smith College
Northampton, MA

Martin J. Packer
Program in Educational Studies
School of Education
University of Michigan
Ann Arbor, MI

Annemarie Sullivan Palincsar
Program in Educational Studies
School of Education
University of Michigan
Ann Arbor, MI

Barbara Rogoff
Psychology Department
University of California, Santa Cruz
Santa Cruz, CA

Robert Serpell
Psychology Department
University of Maryland, Baltimore
  County
Baltimore, MD

Galina Soldatova
The Velikhov-Hamburg Collective
at The Institute of Psychology
Moscow, Russia
and The Laboratory of Comparative
  Human Cognition
San Diego, CA

C. Addison Stone
Program in Learning Disabilities
Department of Communication
  Sciences and Disorders
Northwestern University
Evanston, IL

Roland Tharp
Board of Studies in Education
University of California
Santa Cruz, CA

Peeter Tulviste
Department of Psychology
Tartu University
Tartu, Estonia

Gordon Wells
Joint Centre for Teacher Development
and Department of Curriculum
Ontario Institute for Studies in
    Education
Toronto, Canada

James V. Wertsch
Frances L. Hiatt School of Psychology
Clark University
Worcester, MA

Kathryn F. Whitmore
College of Education

Language, Reading, and Culture
The University of Arizona
Tucson, AZ

Terry Wood
Department of Curriculum and
    Instruction
Purdue University
West Lafayette, IN

Erna Yackel
Department of Mathematics
Purdue University, Calumet
Calumet, IN

Contexts for Learning

INTRODUCTION

Integration of Individual, Social, and Institutional Processes in Accounts of Children's Learning and Development

NORRIS MINICK, C. ADDISON STONE,
and ELLICE A. FORMAN

Over the past 10 to 20 years, scholars concerned with human development have shown increasing interest in the social and cultural foundation of developmental processes. A recognizable piece of this complex fabric of theory and research consists in attempts to apply, extend, and develop the work of what is now widely known as the Soviet sociohistorical school—the work of L. S. Vygotsky, A. N. Leont'ev, A. R. Luria, and their colleagues and students. This volume continues the tradition by offering examples of theoretical and empirical attempts to extend and enrich the evolving framework. Though their ideas differ in many ways, the authors of the chapters included in this book share the view that early attempts to apply the Soviet sociohistorical framework to issues of development and learning had serious limitations. These limitations represent in part failure to capitalize on existing aspects of the framework and in part failure to integrate other frameworks into a more inclusive sociocultural theory of human development.

When we refer to the Soviet sociohistorical school, we are referring to more than Vygotsky's work on language and thought. Although Vygotsky was indeed very much concerned with the links between modes of discourse and modes of thought, his discussion of the links between these phenomena constituted only one element in a much broader conception of the relationships between the social and the psychological that he was working to develop. Though little of this material has been translated into English, Vygotsky's writing dealt not only with cognition but also with the emotions, motives, and personality. Moreover, his conception of the social extended well beyond social interaction and discourse to include both cultural and social-institutional levels of analysis. It is also important to understand that though Vygotsky's scholarship and leadership were critical to the emergence of the Soviet sociohistorical school, it makes little more sense to equate the two than it would to equate "cognitive-science" with the early work of Miller, Galanter, and Pribram (1960). Vygotsky's colleagues—A. N.

Leont'ev, A. R. Luria, D. E. El'konin, A. V. Zaphoroshets, P. I. Zinchenko, and others—made distinct and important contributions to the development of this tradition, and both Soviet and non-Soviet scholars have continued to do so over the ensuing decades.

We would also emphasize that the Soviet sociohistorical school did not develop in isolation from related theory and research elsewhere. Within the Soviet Union itself, what we are referring to here as the Soviet sociohistorical school is simply one expression of an extensive tradition of Russian and Soviet scholarship concerned with the links between psychological development and its societal context. The Vygotskian group, the Bakhtin circle, and even certain Pavlovian scholars represent various expressions of this tradition. Furthermore, this broader Soviet tradition of theory and research was only one expression of the widespread concern with social and cultural issues in the European scholarship of the late nineteenth and early twentieth centuries. Here we refer not only to such social theorists as Durkheim, Weber, and Marx but also to such psychologists as Buhler, Janet, Binet, Wundt, and Freud. Finally, it is worth noting that scholars working within what we are calling the Soviet sociohistorical school have continually sought to draw on existing theory and research outside the Soviet Union, from the early work of Piaget during the 1920s and 1930s to the American cognitive science of the 1970s and 1980s.

Although these Soviet scholars have struggled against considerable odds to remain aware of major developments in relevant European and American scholarship, their own tradition of theory and research was little known in the West until recently. There was some awareness of the work of Vygotsky and his colleagues in the United States during the early 1930s, with several articles published in translation in prominent American journals (Luria, 1931; Vygotsky, 1929, 1934). However, there was no coherent attempt to apply and develop these ideas until the mid-1970s and early 1980s.[1] This more recent and systematic interest in the Soviet sociocultural school in the United States emerged in connection with two interconnected lines of empirical work. On the one hand, cross-cultural research informed by Soviet sociocultural theory—such as that carried out by Cole, Scribner, and their colleagues (Cole & Scribner, 1974; Cole, Gay, Glick, & Sharp, 1971; Scribner & Cole, 1981)—challenged existing notions about mental development by suggesting that cognitive functioning is bound to specific contexts of social practice and that development is based on the mastery of culturally defined modes of speaking, thinking, and acting. On the other hand, scholars such as Bruner and Wood (Wood, Bruner, & Ross, 1976) and Wertsch (1979) applied and developed key concepts reflected in Vygotsky's writing in an effort to explore how children learn through collaborative interaction with adults. This work has served to provide concrete examples of how to "operationalize" certain important concepts within this theoretical framework. These empirical studies were supplemented and supported by selected translations of key works (Leont'ev, 1978, 1981; Luria, 1976,

1981; Vygotsky, 1962, 1978, Wertsch, 1981b) and by important theoretical and conceptual work (Cole & Bruner, 1971; Wertsch, 1979, 1981a).

Though it played an important role in introducing important aspects of the work of the Soviet sociohistorical school to the American scholarly audience, this early American work was limited in two important respects. For example, Scribner and Cole's groundbreaking work on literacy (Scribner & Cole, 1981) provided empirical support for the argument that literacy and cognition need to be studied in connection with the social practices that organize them. Along similar lines, Wertsch's early work on the development of cognition in dyadic interaction (Wertsch, 1979) provided plausible empirical support for the kind of relationships among social interaction, thought, and speech that Vygotsky had suggested. However, like much of the other empirical work completed during this period, these studies were less an effort to carry out full-scale investigations of psychological functioning and development in social context than an effort to establish the plausibility and necessity of such an enterprise. On the theoretical and conceptual side, the material that appeared in translation and in secondary analyses during this period tended to present a rather one-dimensional representation of the theory and research of the Soviet sociohistorical school, limiting the discussion primarily to the relationship between cognition and language (or "cognitive tools").

During the 1980s, a broader and richer picture of the Soviet sociohistorical school began to emerge in the work of English-speaking scholars, including those instrumental in the early efforts. In part, this was a function of increased access to the early works of the Soviet group, through their publications in Russian (El'konin, 1984; Iaroshevskii, 1984; Luria & Iaroshevskii, 1982; Matiushkin, 1983; Vlasova, 1983; Vygotsky, 1987) and their translations into English (Leont'ev, 1978, 1981; Vygotsky, 1987, 1993). It was also a function of the emergence of secondary source materials that conveyed a richer picture of the Soviet sociohistorical tradition to the American audience (Minick, 1985; Valsiner, 1988; Wertsch, 1985a,b; 1991). Equally important, however, were efforts to apply the central concepts of this tradition to the study of cognition in social context. These empirical investigations have played a critical role in forcing us to develop richer notions of the relationship between cognition and other psychological functions and more sophisticated understandings of sociocultural and linguistic theory. Research that begins with the concept that mental functions develop as a result of the child's appropriation of modes of speaking, acting, and thinking that are first encountered in collaboration with adults or more capable peers almost inevitably leads one toward the recognition of increasingly complex links between the domains of psychology, anthropology, sociology, linguistics, and education (Moll, 1990; Newman, Griffin, & Cole, 1989; Rogoff & Lave, 1984; Rogoff & Wertsch, 1984; Scribner, 1984; Tharp & Gallimore, 1988).

Many of the contributors to the present book have been heavily involved in developing, explicating, and applying the broader picture of Soviet soci-ocultural theory that emerged during the 1980s. All of the contributors have found aspects of the theory useful for the study of teaching, learning, and development in a variety of educational contexts. As a result of their shared experience in the application of sociocultural theory to educational research, a new and enriched conception of that theory is emerging. This new conception has a number of components.

First, it has become increasingly clear that the development of a socio-cultural theory of mind demands careful attention to the institutional con-text of social interaction. Culturally specific institutions such as schools, homes, and libraries systematically structure the interactions that occur among people or between people and cultural artifacts such as books or computers. One cannot develop a viable sociocultural conception of human development without looking carefully at the way these institutions develop, the way they are linked with one another, and the way human social life is organized within them.

Second, it is not "language" understood as a generalized or abstract semiotic system that mediates activity, interaction, and thought but lan-guage as a multitude of distinct speech genres and semiotic devices that are tightly linked with particular social institutions and with particular social practices. In scientific laboratories, courtrooms, homes, and schools there are many speech genres that mediate specific forms of social and psycholog-ical life in distinct ways.

Third, educationally significant human interactions do not involve abstract bearers of cognitive structures but real people who develop a variety of interpersonal relationships with one another in the course of their shared activity in a given institutional context. Within educational institutions, for example, the sometimes conflicting responsibilities of mentorship and eval-uation can give rise to distinct interpersonal relationships between teachers and pupils that have important influences on learning. For example, appro-priating the speech or actions of another person requires a degree of identi-fication with that person and the cultural community he or she represents. Educational failure, in this perspective, can represent an unwillingness to subordinate one's own voice to that of another rather than an inability to learn.

Finally, our various efforts to study the development of mind in its soci-ocultural context have forced us to alter our notions of cognition by recog-nizing that modes of thinking evolve as integral systems of motives, goals, values, and beliefs that are closely tied to concrete forms of social practice.

In brief, we have begun to move beyond the rather decontextualized, universalistic representations of social interaction, language, and cognition characteristic of much educational and psychological research of the recent past (as well as of the earlier interpretations of Soviet theory) toward a theory that highlights the rich interconnections between cultural institutions, social practices, semiotic mediation, interpersonal relationships, and the devel-oping mind. In our view, this emerging theory and the research associated with it involves a fundamental reconceptualization of the sociocultural theory that emerged during the 1970s. To say that social interaction and cognition are defined and organized in concrete social practices or that cognition develops as part of an integral system in connection with motivation, affect, and values does not merely imply the need for an addendum to earlier theoretical formulations. A fundamental reconceptualization of mind and its development in social practice is implied. We believe that this reconceptualization has profound theoretical, methodological, and pragmatic implications that we are only just beginning to understand and address.

Overview of the Book

The goal of this book is to offer a representative sample of work within the emerging sociocultural research paradigm as we have described it. Although theory development in the domain of developmental psychology is our primary goal, the book also strives to connect theory and practice. To accomplish this goal, a common empirical focus has been emphasized—that of educational contexts and the teaching/learning process. Each of the chapters presents a theoretical or empirical analysis (or both) of some aspect of the educational enterprise. The aggregate strives to illustrate how a sociocultural framework can enrich our understanding of both human development and the teaching/learning process.

The book is organized into three parts. Chapters in the first part focus on the traditional educational setting, the classroom, and the ways that activity, discourse, and modes of thinking are organized there. In the second part the chapters deal more specifically with the role that interpersonal relationships play in the teaching/learning process. Finally, the chapters of the last part address the broader issue of the relationship between the institutions of the educational system such as schools or after-school programs on the one hand and the processes and outcomes of learning on the other.

Each part is followed by an integrative commentary chapter. The purpose of these commentaries is twofold. First, they serve to highlight common issues across the individual chapters. Second, because they are written by scholars working within various theoretical frameworks (Robert Serpell, a cross-cultural psychologist, Giyoo Hatano, a cognitive psychologist, and Martin Packer, a hermeneutic psychologist) they provide a broad-based, multidisciplinary commentary. In a final general commentary, Jacqueline Goodnow places the issues raised in the volume as a whole in a historical context and sketches an agenda for future work.

Part I: Discourse and Learning in Classroom Practice

The first part of the book focuses on the classroom as a sociocultural system. In one way or another, all the chapters in this section deal with educational reform and its effect on classroom practice. In several of the chapters (those by Cobb et al., Palincsar et al., and Griffin et al.), educational change is studied genetically and at several levels: classroom, institution, and artifacts around which interactions are focused. These analyses of change reveal the often implicit cultural, institutional, and interpersonal factors that operate to constrain the reform process.

Another common theme is how teachers create a zone of proximal development in group settings. All five chapters emphasize that learning is a social activity, and four of the chapters (those by Moll and Whitmore, Palincsar et al., Chang and Wells, and Cobb et al.) also discuss how learners actively construct their understandings. In addition, several authors (Griffin et al., Chang and Wells, Moll and Whitmore, and Cobb et al.) suggest that learning is not merely conceptual change but entails a reorganization of goals, task understandings, motives, and interests.

Moll and Whitmore describe a third-grade bilingual classroom serving monolingual and bilingual Mexican and Anglo children that is located in a working-class neighborhood. The authors illustrate how a talented teacher creates collective, interrelated zones of proximal development by changing classroom practices, discourse, and materials. Through interactive, dialogic teaching, this teacher communicates her respect for the children's learning capabilities and her interest in fostering students' active involvement in, and control of, their learning. As Moll and Whitmore argue, this kind of teaching is unusual anywhere but especially in classrooms serving low income students.

Palincsar, Brown, and Campione discuss a first-grade classroom in which a unit on animal survival is taught through reciprocal teaching. The instructional program described in this chapter involves two key components: teacher scaffolding and task materials employing analogous themes. Palincsar et al. show how teachers scaffold by helping students make connections between old and new knowledge, request elaboration, restore direction, and clarify their contributions to discussion. Analogous themes, they argue, encourage students to look for core conceptual similarities between problems.

Chang and Wells focus on how elementary school children acquire literate modes of thinking and communicating. They examine instructional conversations (Tharp & Gallimore, 1988) in several multiethnic classrooms. In their rich examples of classroom talk, they illustrate the teacher's crucial role in supporting children's ability to explain their ideas to others, define their own questions, overcome their fears of risk-taking, and work together despite differences in language, cultural background, and ability. These examples are used to demonstrate how teachers can scaffold children's construction of scientific knowledge.

Cobb, Wood, and Yackel address the issue of educational reform by showing how a second-grade teacher implemented an inquiry mathematics program. The authors found that she used two intertwined levels of conversation to change classroom practice: doing and talking about mathematics on the one hand, and talking about talking about mathematics on the other. During the early part of the school year, the teacher was explicit and directive in her requests that children listen to each other's ideas, express their own ideas fully, and cooperate with each other. These requests were part of talking about talking about mathematics. In contrast, when the children were doing and talking about mathematics itself, the teacher was much less directive. This change allowed the children to try out and reflect on their own ideas and validate each other's work. Over the course of the school year, Cobb et al. found that the classroom community was able to spend more time talking about mathematics and less time on renegotiating classroom norms and values.

Griffin, Belyaeva, and Soldatova discuss a formative experiment to study the impact of a computer software program on mathematics instruction in American and Soviet elementary school classrooms. The process of describing how the program was understood and used in classrooms in each country revealed the influence of the programmers' voices on instructional processes. Instead of accepting the limitations of the software, Griffin et al. asked the programmers to make design changes they believed would make the program more effective. The result of this activity was not merely an improved piece of software but also a number of insights into the "polilogue" (a "conversation" among programmers, teachers, and students) that constitutes an educational context.

In the commentary chapter, Hatano focuses on a key theoretical question raised by the other chapters in Part I: How can sociocultural and constructivist perspectives on learning be reconciled? He shows how each chapter contributes to a reinterpretation of Vygotskian ideas so that the active, constructive nature of learning is emphasized. He extends the argument by suggesting revisions in basic assumptions about the knowledge acquisition process that would make sociocultural theory consistent with contemporary psychological views of cognitive development.

More than in the other two sections, the chapters in Part I use examples from specific classroom settings to embody the theoretical constructs discussed throughout the volume. In each classroom examined, a community of learners was established despite differences in expertise, language, culture, and political background. Key components of the learning process included artifacts (texts, charts, software), people (students and teachers), and distinct forms of discourse. These components were interrelated in complex and subtle ways so that changes in one produced changes in all. Yet these classrooms were not closed systems. External forces constrained, supported, or subverted the processes and outcomes of learning that occurred. Finally, as Hatano's commentary and several chapters stress, learning is not socially determined. The multiple determinants of children's development in classroom contexts is the overarching theme of this section.

Part II: Interpersonal Relations in Formal and Informal Education

Part II deals more directly than Part I with the interpersonal dynamics involved in children's learning and development. Two general themes are stressed in the five chapters of this part. The first theme is the importance of communicational dynamics or semiotic exchange in the social construction of knowledge. This emphasis is evident in the chapters by Forman and McPhail, Stone, Litowitz, and Cazden. The second theme is the role of cultural norms and social relations in such exchanges. This theme is taken up in varying degrees in all five chapters, with the Rogoff et al. and Cazden chapters placing particular emphasis on cultural differences and the Forman and McPhail, Stone, and Litowitz chapters focusing on role relations and affect.

Stone stresses the need to consider the specific mechanisms of communication at work during the informal instruction of adult–child interactions. He presents his arguments in the context of a critique of the traditional metaphor of scaffolding. Borrowing from Rommetveit and Grice, Stone demonstrates the value of conversational pragmatics (both verbal and nonverbal) as a framework for making sense of the instruction/learning occurring in such interactions. In particular, he stresses the importance of prolepsis and implicature in motivating and creating (via inference) new understandings. This foundation in the semiotics of interpersonal communication leads him to stress the importance of considering social relations in the effectiveness of interactions within the zone of proximal development.

Litowitz also takes up the issue of the semiotic mechanisms at work in adult–child interactions. She stresses the role of specific linguistic devices such as pronouns in signaling social relations and self-identification. From this foundation, she goes on to develop an argument for the need to consider affective issues such as identification and resistance (rather than skill mastery) as major motivators of interactions between adults and children. In the process, she presents interesting examples of interactions that illustrate resistance and thereby raises the important question of why not all adult–child interactions embody the idealized view offered implicitly by Vygotsky of adults eager to instruct and children eager to learn.

Cazden deals with related issues. She begins with a discussion of the semiotic aspects of social interaction. In particular, she focuses on the limitations of traditional sociolinguistic constructs of dialect and register as a proper unit for semiotic analysis. She argues for the value of Bakhtin's notion of voice as an additional analytical unit that is simultaneously a unit of mind and a unit of social interaction. Working with this notion, she analyzes some examples of dialogue that illustrate the resistances accompanying individuals' attempts to take on the voices of others. She is thus led to consider potential problems of both inter- and intrapersonal conflict engendered in instructional/learning situations when voices are not in synchrony.

In the next chapter in this section, Forman and McPhail provide an analysis of the intricate interplay between the meaning of specific learning activities to individuals and the patterns of interaction engendered by those activities. Their analysis provides insight into how situational meanings are marked by individuals in their language (drawing primarily on the notion of register) and how the evolving social relations involved in ongoing collaborations may lead to redefinitions of the situation by the participants.

The final chapter, by Rogoff, Mosier, Mistry, and Goncu, sets a caution-ary tone by highlighting cultural differences in the goals and patterns of the informal instruction provided by parents in their interactions with their young children. The authors present data from a comparative study of par-ent–child interactions in the United States and among the Mayans of Gua-temala. Although they see some cross-cultural communalities in the "guided participation" through which parents enculturate their children, the authors focus primarily on differences between the two samples—differ-ences that point to the ethnocentricism of past discussions of the dynamics within the zone of proximal development. In particular, they stress variation in the extent to which instruction is an explicit goal of parent–child inter-actions and the relative frequency of explicit (largely verbal) versus tacit (largely nonverbal) interactions.

In a commentary on the five chapters of this section, Packer provides an interpretation of the strengths and weaknesses of the chapters from a her-meneutic or interpretive psychological perspective. This perspective shares with the sociohistorical perspective a view of human learning and develop-ment as grounded in social experience. Thus Packer is able to draw parallels between certain constructs in the interpretive framework and themes he found to be common across the five chapters, such as the dissatisfaction with a simplistic view of learning and development as a passive internalization of social tools. Instead, Packer endorses and elaborates a view of learning as social negotiation of meaning in practical activity. At the same time, he raises some concerns about specifics of the various arguments presented in the five chapters. At the root of his concern is a feeling that certain compo-nents of the arguments suffer from a "creeping dualism," that is, a tendency to speak in mentalistic and individualistic terms. Packer's discussion pre-sents a challenge to all concerned with a sociohistorical approach to human learning and development, a challenge to focus more consistently on social practices, to be wary of mentalistic and individualistic constructs, and to avoid decontextualized, quantitative analyses in their search for the general patterns underlying human behavior.

As a whole, the chapters in this section present a multifaceted argument against our traditional notion of interactions within the zone of proximal development as involving a simple imparting of new skills to children via a didactic process of temporary assistance and gradual weaning. The chal-lenge is to incorporate a more serious analysis of the subtle semiotic and interpersonal dimensions of these interactions. These issues, in turn, force us to consider seriously the larger sociocultural and social organizational issues that are the focus of the third and final section of the volume.

Part III: Sociocultural Institutions of Formal and Informal Education

The chapters in the final part are concerned with the ways that social inter-action, learning, and development are organized by the institutional con-texts in which they occur. In various ways, each of these chapters explores the nature and dynamics of institutions touching on the education of children. In doing so, the authors point out various ways in which the more localized settings where most analyses of children's learning take place are themselves embedded in and constrained by a broader set of sociocultural organizations.

Tharp begins by raising the questions of why schools are so resistant to change and, in particular, why it is so difficult to transform schools into "communities of learners" in which teachers act to assist students in learning. Tharp argues that teaching in most existing classrooms is based on an assign/assess model. Teachers assign tasks to students, students work to complete these tasks, and teachers then assess the quality of student performance. Building on more than 20 years' experience in educational research and development in the Kamehameha project, Tharp argues that one cannot understand why classroom activities are organized in the way they are by looking at teacher beliefs, teacher training, or the constraints of the classroom environment itself. He suggests, rather, that we must look to the nested systems of social activities and social institutions within which classroom activities are embedded. Ultimately, he argues, the pattern of assigning and assessing that defines the relationship between teacher and child is simply one instantiation of a much broader system of institutionally defined relationships that also defines relations between teachers and school administrators as well as between school administrators and local, state, and federal officials.

Nicolopoulou and Cole take a rather different approach in exploring a related set of issues concerning the relationships between learning, activity settings, and the organization of social practices at the institutional level. They describe a study in which they introduced computer-based educational tasks and games into after-school programs in an effort to explore how a single "task-activity system" is differentially shaped and assimilated in two institutional and sociocultural contexts—one situated in a library setting and one in a recreation-oriented "after-school club." Nicolopoulou and Cole discuss how the computer-based activity system evolved at the two sites, the impact it had on learning and development, and how well the system was assimilated into the two institutional settings. At each phase of the analysis, they explore the relationships between the local activities of the computer-based system and the broader institutional settings into which it was introduced.

Gallimore and Goldenberg extend this exploration of the relationships among learning, activity settings, and social institutions in yet another direction, focusing on the relationships between the institutions of home and school. These authors review a research project that involved the introduction into low-income Hispanic households of collaborative adult–child reading activities comparable to those found in schools and in middle-class households. The authors found that the introduction of these books and activities promoted important kinds of interaction and language use that were not promoted by the traditional reading-readiness "homework" that had previously been sent home by the school. They also found, however, that the Hispanic adults in this study tended to focus on decoding skills when they read with their children, rather than on the understanding and interpretation of text that is more prevalent in both school and middle-class homes. These findings illustrate the role of culturally based belief systems in defining the nature of tasks and of the social institutions in which they are embedded.

Wertsch, Tulviste, and Hagstrom explore the links between the individual and institutional levels of analysis through a discussion of the concepts of "agency" and "social languages." They begin with the argument that Western psychological theories have tended to assume that "agency" is a property of the individual. They go on to argue that a sociocultural theory of mind requires that the concept of agency be reformulated such that the "agent" is represented as extending beyond the skin of the individual. They note the collaborative nature of many human activities and the "interpersonal" or "intermental" form of "agency" that emerges in these contexts. They follow this section with a discussion of the role "cultural tools" (i.e., physical and symbolic devices that do not originate with the individual) assume in mediating the activities of the human agent. Having expanded the notion of agency in these ways, the authors move on to suggest that we need to develop systems of concepts that make it possible to explore the links between the "agent" and the concrete sociocultural systems in which it acts. In this connection, they discuss Bakhtin's notion of "social languages" as one means of thinking about how the symbolic tools of language—and the agents who use them—are linked with specific social groups and social institutions.

In his commentary on the chapters in Part III, Serpell begins by noting that one of the strengths of Vygotskian theory has been the attempt to build "two-sided" constructs that provide a single conceptual system bridging the psychological and the sociocultural aspects, a single system of constructs that makes it possible to discuss these two analytical dimensions with a single theoretical and conceptual language. He then identifies ways in which the concepts employed vary across the chapters of Part III. Having noted this rich diversity in current efforts to develop a socioculturally based psychological theory, Serpell draws a series of connections among the various accounts of the interface between the social and the psychological dimensions that appear in these chapters. In the process, he raises a concern regarding an uncritical reduction of the psychological to the sociocultural or vice versa.

As a whole, the chapters of this section serve the important function of heightening our awareness of the myriad ways in which social institutions create and constrain the patterns of interactions discussed in the earlier sections of this book. As noted above, it is our view that the construction of a viable sociocultural theory of psychological functioning and development depends on the development of conceptual and methodological means for exploring the links between social interaction and learning as they occur at the local level of observable behavior and the broad organization of social institutions such as schools, libraries, courts, hospitals, and governments— and indeed the interrelations among these institutions at the societal level. In a variety of ways, the chapters in this section enhance our ability to think about such connections between the social and the psychological.

Concluding Comments

Together, the primary chapters and the commentaries are intended to provide a rich and representative picture of an emerging framework for considering how the mind develops and functions in sociocultural contexts. As with any edited volume, there are diversities of opinion, differences in emphasis, and gaps in coverage. However, as a whole, the book serves to illustrate the complexities of a thoroughly sociocultural approach to the analysis of how children acquire knowledge in both informal and formal educational settings, one that goes beyond the more static, transsituational view of social influences on learning that has passed as Vygotskian in many recent treatments. As in any treatment of an evolving framework, the answers are not provided, but at least we can hope for a cogent framing of fruitful questions that will lead us eventually to a theoretical integration of individual, social, and institutional levels of explanation in our account of children's learning and development.

Note

1. It is important to emphasize that we are speaking specifically about the United States here. The history of this tradition in Germany, Britain, Italy, Japan, and the Scandinavian countries is different.

References

Cole, M., & Bruner, J. (1971). Cultural differences and inferences about psychological processes. *American Psychologist, 26,* 867–76.

Cole, M., & Scribner, S. (1974). *Culture and thought: a psychological introduction.* New York: John Wiley & Sons.

Cole, M., Gay, J., Glick, J., & Sharp, D. W. (1971). *The cultural context of learning and thinking.* New York: Basic Books.

El'konin, D. B. (ed.) (1984). *L. S. Vygotskii. Sobranie sochinenie: detskaia psikhologiia* (Tom 4) [*L. S. Vygotsky. Collected works: child psychology* (Vol. 4)]. Moscow: Pedagogika.

Iaroshevskii, M. G. (ed.) (1984). *L. S. Vygotskii. Sobranie sochinenie: Nauchoe nasledstvo* (Tom 6) [*L. S. Vygotsky. Collected works: Scientific inheritance* (Vol. 6)]. Moscow: Pedagogika.

Leont'ev, A. N. (1978). *Activity, consciousness, and personality.* Englewood Cliffs, NJ: Prentice-Hall (originally published 1975).

Leont'ev, A. N. (1981). *Problems of the development of mind.* Moscow: Progress Publishers (originally published 1959).

Luria, A. R. (1931). Psychological expedition to Central Asia. *Science, 74* (1920), 383–4.

Luria, A. R. (1976). *Cognitive development: Its cultural and social foundations.* Cambridge, MA: Harvard University Press.

Luria, A. R. (1981). *Language and cognition.* New York: Wiley Intersciences.

Luria, A. R., & Iaroshevskii, M. G. (eds.) (1982). *L. S. Vygotskii. Sobranie sochinenie: Voprosy teorii i istorii psikhologii* (Tom 1) [*L. S. Vygotsky. Collected works: Problems of the theory and history of psychology* (Vol. 1)]. Moscow: Pedagogika.

Matiushkin, A. M. (ed.) (1983). *L. S. Vygotskii. Sobranie sochinenie: problemy razvitiia psikhiki* (Tom 3) [*L. S. Vygotsky. Collected works: problems of the development of mind* (Vol. 3)]. Moscow: Pedagogika.

Miller, G. A., Galanter, G., & Pribram, K. H. (1960). *Plans and the structure of behavior.* Orlando, FL: Holt, Rhinehard & Winston.

Minick, N. (1985). L. S. Vygotsky and Soviet activity theory: new perspectives on the relationship between mind and society. Unpublished PhD dissertation, Northwestern University.

Moll, L. (ed.) (1990). *Vygotsky and education: instructional implications and applications of sociohistorical psychology.* New York: Cambridge University Press.

Newman, D., Griffin, P., & Cole, M. (1989). *The construction zone: working for cognitive change in school.* New York: Cambridge University Press.

Rogoff, B., & Lave, J. (eds.) (1984). *Everyday cognition: its development in social context* (pp. 9–40). Cambridge, MA: Harvard University Press.

Rogoff, B., & Wertsch, J. V. (eds.) (1984). Children's learning in the "zone of proximal development." *New directions for child development* (no. 23). San Francisco: Jossey-Bass.

Scribner, S. (ed.) (1984). Cognitive studies of work. *Quarterly Newsletter of the Laboratory of Comparative Human Cognition, 6* (1, 2), 1–46.

Scribner, S., & Cole, M. (1981). *The psychology of literacy.* Cambridge, MA: Harvard University Press.

Tharp, R., & Gallimore, R. (1988). *Rousing minds to life: teaching and learning in social contexts.* New York: Cambridge University Press.

Valsiner, J. (1988). *Developmental psychology in the Soviet Union.* Sussex: Harvester Press.

Vlasova, T. A. (ed.) (1983). *L. S. Vygotskii. Sobranie sochinenie: osnovy defektologii* (Tom 5) [*L. S. Vygotsky. Collected works: foundations of defectology* (Vol. 5)]. Moscow: Pedagogika.

Vygotsky, L. S. (1929). The problem of the cultural development of the child. *Journal of Genetic Psychology, 36,* 415–32.

Vygotsky, L. S. (1934). Thought in schizophrenia. *Archives of Neurological Psychiatry, 31.*

Vygotsky, L. S. (1962). *Thought and language.* Cambridge, MA: MIT Press.

Vygotsky, L. S. (1978). *Mind in society: the development of higher psychological processes.* Cambridge, MA: Harvard University Press.

Vygotsky, L. S. (1987). Thinking and speech. In L. S. Vygotsky, *Collected works*

(Vol. 1, pp. 39–285) (R. Rieber & A. Carton, eds.; N. Minick, trans.) New York: Plenum.

Vygotsky, L. S. (1993). *The collected works of L. S. Vygotsky. Vol. 2. Problems of abnormal psychology and learning disabilities.* New York: Plenum Press. [L. S. Vygotsky. Collected works (Vol. 2)]. Moscow: Pedagogika.

Wertsch, J. V. (1979). From social interaction to higher psychological processes: a clarification and application of Vygotsky's theory. *Human Development, 22,* 1–22.

Wertsch, J. V. (1981a). Introduction. In J. V. Wertsch (ed.). *The concept of activity in Soviet psychology.* Armonk, NY: M. E. Sharpe.

Wertsch, J. V. (ed.) (1981b). *The concept of activity in Soviet psychology.* Armonk, NY: M. E. Sharpe.

Wertsch, J. V. (1985a). *Vygotsky and the social formation of mind.* Cambridge, MA: Harvard University Press.

Wertsch, J. V. (ed.)(1985b). *Culture, communication, and cognition: Vygotskian perspectives* (pp. 94–118). New York: Cambridge University Press.

Wertsch, J. V. (1991). *Voices of the mind: a sociocultural approach to mediated action.* Cambridge, MA: Harvard University Press.

Wood, D., Bruner, J. S., & Ross, G. (1976). The role of tutoring in problem solving. *Journal of Child Psychology and Psychiatry, 66,* 181–91.

I

DISCOURSE AND LEARNING IN CLASSROOM PRACTICE

1

Vygotsky in Classroom Practice: Moving from Individual Transmission to Social Transaction

LUIS C. MOLL and KATHRYN F. WHITMORE

In this chapter we present a case study of a third-grade bilingual classroom.[1] The students in the class are primarily working-class Mexican children, and the school is located within their neighborhood in a southwestern city of the United States. We have selected this classroom for discussion not only because it presents a striking contrast to the rote-like, intellectually limiting instruction that characterizes working-class schooling (e.g., Anyon, 1980; Goodlad, 1984; Oakes, 1986) but because its activities do not fit well or easily into current discussions of "guided practice" or "assisted performance" derived from Vygotskian theory, especially from dyadic interpretations of his concept of the zone of proximal development. Hence this chapter demonstrates how practice can exceed, as well as inform and elaborate, our theoretical notions.

By presenting the classroom analysis we emphasize what we consider to be a more dynamic and encompassing notion of Vygotsky's zone of proximal development. We are, of course, not the first to suggest that current interpretations of this concept may be too narrow.[2] Griffin and Cole (1984), for example, have suggested that "English-speaking scholars interpret the concept more narrowly than Vygotsky intended, robbing it of some of its potential for enabling us to understand the social genesis of human cognitive processes and the process of teaching and learning in particular" (p. 45).

Valsiner (1988) has pointed out that Vygotsky's intent in his introductory explanation of the zone of proximal development was much broader, to "get across to his pedagogically-minded listeners (or readers) a more basic theoretical message: . . . the interdependence of the process of child development and the socially provided resources for that development" (p. 145). Vygotsky used this concept to emphasize the importance—in fact the inseparability—of sociocultural conditions for understanding thinking and its development (Minick, 1989; Moll, 1990b; Vygotsky, 1978, 1987; Wertsch, 1985). Hence he viewed thinking not as a characteristic of the child only, but of the child-in-social-activities with others (Minick, 1985). In terms of classroom learning, Vygotsky specifically emphasized the relation between thinking and what we would call the social organization of instruction (Moll, 1990b). He wrote about the "unique form of cooperation between the child and the adult that is the central element of the educational process" and how by this interactional process "knowledge is transferred to the child in a definite system" (Vygotsky, 1987, p. 169). It is these systemic properties of instruction that Vygotsky thought provided a special socialization of children's thinking.

In particular, Vygotsky concentrated on the manipulation of language as an important characteristic of formal schooling. He thought that formal instruction in writing and grammar, by refocusing attention from the content of communication to the means of communication, provided the foundations for the development of conscious awareness and voluntary control of important aspects of speech and language (Minick, 1987). He believed that schooled discourse represented a qualitatively different form of communication from everyday discourse because words act not only as means of communication, as they would in everyday talk, but as the object of study. During classroom interactions the teacher directs the children's attention to word meanings and definitions and the systematic relation among them that constitutes an organized system of knowledge. Formal instruction, then, with its special organization and discourse, through its social and semiotic mediations, provides children with the resources to develop the capacity to consciously manipulate and voluntarily control crucial sociocultural symbolic systems.

The above theory suggests that it is incorrect to think of the zone as solely a characteristic of the child or of the teaching, but of the child engaged in collaborative activity within specific social (discourse) environments. From our perspective, the key is to understand the social transactions that make up classroom life. Within this analysis the focus of study is on the *sociocultural system* within which children learn, with the understanding that this system is mutually and actively created by teachers and students. What we propose is a "collective" zone of proximal development. As we illustrate with our case study, it is this interdependence of adults and children, and how they use social and cultural resources, that is central to a Vygotskian analysis of instruction.

Understanding Classrooms as Sociocultural Systems

This case study presents data collected during weekly classroom observations over two academic school years in a bilingual third-grade classroom.[3] It is a special classroom that provides rich data for a Vygotskian interpretation. The teacher describes herself as a "whole-language" teacher. Central to this approach is a view of literacy as the understanding and communication of meaning (e.g., Goodman & Goodman, 1990). Both comprehension and expression are built and developed collaboratively by students and teachers through functional, relevant, meaningful language use. Therefore a major instructional goal of the teacher is to make the classroom a highly literate environment in which many language experiences can take place and different types of "literacies" can be used, understood, and learned by the students. This approach rejects the typical reduction of reading and writing into skill sequences transmitted in isolation or in a successive, stage-like manner (including such practices as having children sit quietly, follow mundane directions, only read assigned texts, fill out work sheets, and take tests.) Rather, it emphasizes the creation of authentic social contexts in which children use, try out, and manipulate language as they make sense and create meaning. The role of the teacher is to mediate these social contexts, in a Vygotskian sense, so that through their own efforts children assume full control of diverse purposes and uses of oral and written language.

These classrooms, then, allow insights into the social processes of literacy development that are unavailable in more typical settings. It is this process of social mediation that we want to highlight here: not the creation of individual zones of proximal development but of collective, interrelated zones of proximal development as part of a transactive teaching system. The knowledge about subject matter is learned through different types of social relationships facilitated by the teacher. This process is mediated in the sense that the teacher controls it strategically to engage students in different aspects of reading and writing. It is also mediated in the sense that the teacher creates future contexts in which children can consciously apply in new ways what they are learning.

Furthermore, this classroom is a bilingual one, using English and Spanish. The teacher's goal is to create conditions for learning the second language that are "additive," that is, perceived by all as a positive addition to a first language, with a strong emphasis on communication for academic purposes. In particular, there is an attempt to integrate written language in either the students' first or second language as part of every academic activity, where books are read in both languages and the students are free to write in their language of choice. For example, it is common for a student to read a book in English and write a summary in Spanish, or vice versa.

When presenting the case study we first describe a "typical day" to give the reader a good sense of the classroom's daily routine, the social system that is in place. Included is a description of a thematic unit centered on Native Americans that the teacher and students jointly develop. This unit illustrates well how the teacher creates diverse circumstances for the children to use and apply their considerable intellectual and linguistic resources. We see these theme units as dynamic contexts within which the children learn by manipulating knowledge and provide the teacher and themselves with many opportunities to evaluate how well they are using reading and writing as tools for analysis and for thinking. In our terms, these units are made up of connected zones of proximal development within which the children constantly redefine themselves as learners.

Typical Day: Creating a Literate Community

The classroom community includes 27 children (12 boys and 15 girls) who come from either the neighborhood or "barrio" surrounding the school (16 children) or who travel from other neighborhoods in the city (11 children) as part of a magnet desegregation program.[4] As is common in bilingual classrooms, there is considerable diversity in the children's language and literacy abilities. Fifteen of the children are monolingual English speakers and readers. Of these children, two (Sarah and Brooke) are rapidly learning to speak, read, and write Spanish. Elizabeth is the only English-dominant bilingual speaker, and she reads in both languages. Nine children are bilingual. Of the nine, Veronica, Susana, and Lupita are reading and writing in both languages; Francisco, Raymundo, and Roberto read both but are clearly Spanish dominant; and Rosario, David, and Ana are Spanish-only readers. Jaime is a Spanish-dominant speaker who came into the classroom in the fall speaking only Spanish and by the end of the year spoke and read some English as well. Acuzena is a monolingual Spanish speaker. She arrived in the United States from Mexico in the spring and reads only Spanish.

Each day for this classroom begins in the patio area of the school, where children, staff, and faculty meet to share announcements, sing, and recite the Pledge of Allegiance. After this morning ritual, the children enter the classroom, noisily put away their things, greet each other in English and Spanish, and move to the group meeting area in the center of the room. The teacher finds a chair, and the group quiets for announcements, calendar and weather information, and a discussion of the schedule for the day. She reads aloud to the children in either English or Spanish at least once each day.

After the opening story, the class moves into math centers. Little direction is necessary to get the children and adults moving around the classroom, gathering materials, and settling into four math groups located at various places in the classroom. This classroom is a functionally organized setting. There are several large tables in the room that, along with the ample amount of carpeted floor area, provide work space for the children and adults. Cubicles and cupboards are used by the children as storage space for their personal belongings, but the school supplies (pencils, paper, crayons, and the like) are shared by the classroom community. They are all within easy access of the children and are clearly labeled in both languages. A piano, loft, and the teacher's hidden desk allow children places to hide away to work, read, and visit.

Following math centers, the children usually go outside for recess, although some students request permission to stay inside to continue writing projects, illustrate books, catch up on assignments, and work on their second language. Roberto and Rafael ask to work on a collaborative book; Brooke asks to practice reading in Spanish; and Shelley finishes a filmstrip project. These children work independently, and the teacher uses this time to prepare for upcoming activities, plan with the student teacher, or interact with children inside or outside on the playground.

The children reconvene at the meeting area before they move into a language arts block that consists of a period of sustained silent reading (which the teacher calls DEAR: Drop Everything And Read), literature study groups, and writing workshop. The children are continuing studies of several authors. While the teacher and the student teacher meet with two of the literature groups, the other children either meet in their own author-centered literature groups independently or do DEAR.

DEAR in this classroom means an extended period of time (at least 15 to 30 minutes) spent reading any material of choice. The children and adults all read, and the reading materials are extensive and varied in type, topic, and language. The teacher frequently selects a piece of adolescent literature to read for her graduate children's literature courses. Newspapers are available and are usually the choice of the student teacher and the teacher assistant. They share articles with each other, chatting as they would over the breakfast table at home. Children read magazines, chapter books (books long enough to be segmented into chapters with few if any illustrations), books authored and published by students and the whole class, picture books, comic books, and nonfiction books. Children settle in comfortably with friends or alone during DEAR, finding niches under the loft or piano or lying on the floor. The DEAR period is not entirely silent, although it is subdued. Sometimes music plays in the background, and children enthusiastically share information and illustrations as they read.

The children and adults must use print to complete activities and "live" successfully in this highly literate classroom environment. The daily schedule is revised each morning and referred to by all participants throughout the day, for instance. Evidence of group learning, as recorded on charts and other public documents, includes the following: webs representing brainstorming sessions,[5] data collected during math and science experimentation, and ongoing records of thematically organized activities. They include lists of questions children generate at the outset of each new theme. Reading and writing are not only subjects in this classroom but essential aspects of the classroom's intellectual and functional daily life.

The teacher uses literature study groups to provide social reading experiences that complement the personal reading experience provided by DEAR. These study groups enable the children to share their reactions, analyses, and questions about children's trade books with their peers and teachers. The materials for literature study groups vary greatly and provide a wealth of opportunity for choice for the readers, as well as a wide assortment of literary examples. During an author's study group, the teacher supplied over 50 different books in text sets according to author, for example. The children read silently, individually or with a friend, before their groups meet for discussion. In addition to reading a variety of literature during literature study groups, the children learn biographical information about authors and illustrators, compare pieces of writing, extend their reading into writing and illustrations through literature logs and other writing projects, analyze plots, characters, settings, and other literary elements, and create story maps, among other activities. Literature groups are organized according to the interests and choices of the children, in contrast to traditional "reading groups," which are organized homogeneously by reading "ability." The groups allow children opportunities to study and enjoy literature with readers of all abilities, as well as readers of two languages, and provide them with frequent opportunities to mediate each other's learning through shared literacy experiences.

The following examples, taken from the transcripts of literature groups about popular children's authors William Steig and Byrd Baylor, reveal the nature of interactions that characterize this component of the curriculum. The teacher (T) opens the first session of the Steig group by eliciting the children's reactions to one of his books:

> **T:** *Sylvester and the Magic Pebble.* What did you guys think about this story?
>
> **Rita:** I think they cared a lot for him.
>
> **T:** What do you mean? You mean his parents?
>
> **Rita:** Yes.
>
> **T:** What made you think that when you read the story?
>
> **Rita:** Because they really worried about him.
>
> **T:** Who else wants to share something? I'd like to hear everybody's ideas. Then we can decide what we want to talk about. Sarah?
>
> **Sarah:** I think he got the idea of it when he was little, or maybe one of his friends got lost or something?
>
> **T:** What do you mean, he got the idea?
>
> **Sarah:** He got the idea for his parents to think that Sylvester got lost.
>
> **T:** You're talking about where William Steig might have gotten his ideas.
>
> **Sarah:** Yes.
>
> **T:** That maybe something like this happened to him or someone he knew. A lot of times authors get their ideas from real life things, don't they? Jon, what did you think about this story?
>
> **Jon:** It was like a moral story. It's like you can't wish for everything. But, in a sense, everything happened to him when he was panicking.
>
> **T:** When did you think he panicked?
>
> **Jon:** Well, when he saw the lion, he started to panic.
>
> **Richard:** And he turned himself into a rock.
>
> **Jon:** Yeah. He said, "I wish I were a rock."
>
> **T:** Right. And it happened, didn't it?
>
> **Richard:** It was stupid of him.
>
> **T:** So maybe he wasn't thinking far enough ahead? What would you have wished instead of a rock?
>
> **Richard:** A plane. A plane.
>
> **T:** An airplane? That would've been a good wish.
>
> **Sarah:** I would wish him to disappear.
>
> **T:** Wish the lion to disappear?
>
> **Jon:** I would wish the lion could turn into a tiny gnat and fly away.
>
> **Rita:** I wish he turned into a bird.

Note how the students contributed different levels of interpretation of the story in response to the teacher's open request. She summarizes the discussion thus far, saying, "Look at all the different kinds of things you had to say. Rita talked about the characters in the story and what they must have been feeling. Sarah took the author's point of view. And you saw it as a particular kind of story, Jon, as a moral story." The teacher asks the students to reflect on their reactions and justify them, and she is explicit about her goals. Note that she refers to the literature logs the students keep on the stories they have read.

T: What did you say in your log about the story when you wrote in your log yesterday?

Richard: That it was a good book.

T: Why would you say this was a good story?

Richard: I don't know.

T: I guess what I want is for kids to know why they think something is a good story.

As the discussion progresses the children use each other, their experiences, the text, and other stories they have read to mediate their understanding of the story. Throughout, the teacher participates in the discussion, revealing her thinking, contributing her observations along with the students, and elaborating on the children's comments.

As the talk continues, Sarah initiates a discussion to clarify her understanding of the text, and the group recalls the details of the plot to seek an answer. In the following segment of the transcript it is particularly interesting that after Sarah initiates an in-depth discussion she listens quietly to the group interpretation of the text. The teacher takes a notably quiet place in the lively discussion as well; in fact, twice her attempts to participate are interrupted by children. Eventually, Sarah verbalizes a conclusion to her own question.

Sarah: I was thinking, at the end, I always get mixed up, because when they have the rock on him, does Sylvester wish himself back, or do his parents?

Richard: Sylvester does!

Rita: No, they do!

Richard: Sylvester does! Sylvester does!

T: Can you find in the book where. . . .

Richard: It's right here, it's right here.

T: Wait a second. And Richard if you will. . . .

Richard: It says, " 'I wish I were myself again. I wish I were my real self again,' thought Sylvester."

Jon: Yes.

Rita: But his parents did that too.

Richard: But he said. . . .

Rita: They found the pebble and they. . . .

Richard: Put it on him.

T: Do you remember how the magic had to work?

Jon: It would have to be on Sylvester.

T: What was the only way the pebble worked?

Richard: If it was on the person.

T: If you had it in your hand, right?

Richard: Or on you.

T: So if he's a rock, he can't hold the pebble.

Jon: But he could support it.

Sarah: Yeah, he wished himself back.

As the discussion of the story continues, the children and the teacher explore several themes and interpretations that come about from a shared reading of the text. The discussion includes what the story might be like in another genre, such as a novel, how the action in the story alternates between panic and calm, and if the changing colors in the illustrations depict the changing seasons and why that would be important to the story. Near the end of the session, the teacher discusses with the students what they want to plan to do next. The teacher negotiates with the group, drawing on what has captivated them about the piece of literature. It is the teacher's way of facilitating the students' ownership of the discussion and purpose of the literature group.

Reading and writing merge during another author study about Byrd Baylor's work. After spending several days reading from a set of Baylor's books, Ilinca, Rita, and Mariah come together to discuss their impressions of the books, the commonalities across texts, and how they might share their reading with the rest of the class. Here again, the teacher mediates the children's understandings by using their ideas, questions, and interests to help them focus on meaningful discussions and presentations.

Ilinca: All the books are deserty. They all have to do with the desert—mostly the plants and animals.

Mariah: All the desert scenes look like they were painted with watercolors.

Rita: What I liked best was the lettering, the print. It was like in poetry. It doesn't have anything to do with poetry. Well, maybe a little. It sounded like poetry.

T: Poetry doesn't have to rhyme. It's more a way of expressing feelings and describing things. Do you think Byrd Baylor was expressing her feelings about the desert?

Rita: I can tell she's a gentle person. It sounds like she cares about the desert and doesn't want it destroyed.

Mariah: I read about Byrd Baylor in that newspaper article. She lives in the desert. Her house is kind of Indian style.

Ilinca: Maybe we could write about the desert, a plant, or animal and make it look like poetry like Byrd Baylor does. I like being in the desert. Could I write about being in the desert?

T: Yes, of course. That sounds like a wonderful way to share what you have learned with the rest of the class.

Mariah: And we could make pictures like the books too.

The group then spends time studying Peter Parnall's illustrations (in the Baylor books) more carefully, noticing how he uses simple lines and little color, and how only some parts of the plants and animals are detailed. They are not sure how to go about writing in a style similar to Byrd Baylor. The teacher suggests that first they simply write something about the desert that expresses their own feelings. She does the same, and then demonstrates breaking her prose into shortened segments to establish the rhythm that makes it more poetic. The children are pleased with the results. Here are some examples of the children's writing:

> I love
> to watch the hawk soar
> through the sky
> and the coyotes howl
> at night.
> The rabbits hop
> from cactus to cactus.
>
> > by Sarah

> The coyote
> eats by day and
> the coyote howls
> by night.
> The coyote
> goes out in the
> middle of the
> night to find
> his prey. At
> the time of
> dawn, he comes
> home, with good
> things to eat.
> The mother
> says (in coyote
> words) I was
> worried. —Don't
> worry, be happy.
> I thought
> you got
> caught. Who
> me? Never.
>
> > by Jon

As a participant in such literature groups, rather than solely the leader, the teacher strives to respond as a reader, to move beyond traditional comprehension questions, and to expand on teachable moments. Most remarkable is the teacher's trust of the children's questions and ideas. She clearly does not have a predetermined agenda for discussions and resulting projects but assists the children as a more experienced participating reader in the group to summarize their ideas, merge their questions, and conceptualize ways to present their learning to themselves and others. This important role of the teacher demonstrates her trust of children's transactions with the text and with each other, and her continuous sharing of control with them in curriculum development.

DEAR and literature studies transform into a writing workshop (WW) with a quiet direction or by turning off and on the lights. Materials and work partners change, and quiet talking about reading becomes active discussion about writing projects, illustration, and publication.[6] At the piano bench, Racheal and Lupita finish a conference with the student teacher about spelling and return to the publication process. Their story represents an interesting collaboration. Racheal, a monolingual English speaker, approached Lupita and invited her to join her in a project so that they could produce a bilingual book, Lupita being bilingual and biliterate. Their joint story concerns a young English-speaking girl who encounters a monolingual Spanish-speaking girl and the problems they face as they develop a relationship. In the course of their dialogue, Racheal says, "Lupita, you know what we should do?" and suggests a minor revision. "No, that won't sound good," counters Lupita. "Okay, you're right," Racheal adds, "I'm not good at the Spanish, Lupita." "You're not? Then just do the letters," comforts Lupita.

Jaime and Roberto are nestled under the loft. They are busy writing letters during WW time. The letters, written in Spanish, are headed across the room to David and Raymundo, who are scrunched under the study carrels. Jaime and Roberto are writing to them "because they don't want to be our friends, and we want them to," confides Roberto.

Meanwhile, Susana and the teacher are at the computer, putting a story on the word processor for final publication. Across the room a group of girls sit at a table covered with final projects deeply involved in an author's circle, reading their writing to one another, asking each other questions, and making revisions in their texts. Ana and the teacher assistant confer elsewhere about punctuation and spelling for a final draft. The room is busy with papers, pencils, markers, and crayons as children work at real authoring and illustrating.

The descriptions above only briefly touch on the variety of literacy events taking place simultaneously in this classroom. Many students have more than one project going on at one time, and their writing (in English, Spanish, or both) includes a variety of genres and styles. The teacher believes children are readers and writers, and she strives to support and enhance their continued development and success. As she states, she and her colleagues are "working hard to give the kids the knowledge that they can be learners." The students are trusted to select appropriate materials, writing topics, and language(s) for literacy activities. The teacher helps the children take risks with difficult materials and new genres and formats for reading and writing, with the aim of expanding their developing abilities. She describes the process of attending to traditional skills within a classroom emphasizing writing as a process:

> I keep almost everything that the kids write, so that I'm real aware of what things they are trying out when they are writing. If I see a lot of children exploring something, then I will do a short class lesson [about a skill]. We did that with quotation marks. There were a lot of kids trying to put conversations into their stories, but they don't use punctuation and they don't use speech carriers and you couldn't tell who was talking. So we spent a couple of days doing written conversations. The kids did them with each other in class, and they were also asked to do it with their parents at home. And then in the classroom we talked about how you put [the punctuation] in so you can tell who is talking. Then the kids went back and did that with their written conversations. I have seen that in their writing since then some of the kids are really starting to use the ideas we practiced. The speech carriers appeared right away, they were less sure what to do with the little marks, but some of the kids are using them now. And if I see them I say, "Oh, I see you are using quotation marks in your story." So most of the teaching about writing takes place along that line.

She continues by explaining how they use the children's reading to develop their writing:

> Also, we look as readers. We might look at how an author uses a particular stylistic kind of thing or how poets use things like alliteration and try out some more guided kinds of writing. We do some pattern kinds of writing sometimes when we're exploring things like that. And kids may or may not pick up things on their own when it comes to their writing, but I certainly see a lot of growth. And the spelling development is there, too, because I don't teach the spelling program either, and the kids are beginning to trust that they will learn to spell.

The children determine which language(s) they will use to read and write. The teacher ensures that the students develop strong literacy strategies in their first language, whether it be English or Spanish, as it serves as the basis for second language development. The children's desires to read and write in a second language are fostered, encouraged, and supported. Such efforts are facilitated by paired reading between students and between students and adults. Regardless of the language of choice, however, the emphasis of using literacy to make meaning remains the same.

A few minutes before noon, the children get ready for lunch. They put away writing materials and gather at the meeting area once again. The teacher takes a moment to comment on the morning's activities and set the stage for the afternoon. Frequently, the teacher's philosophy is shared during such moments, allowing the children open insight into her beliefs about learning. "Talking is probably the most important thing we do in here because you learn the most when you can talk while you work," the teacher tells the students.

Thematic Unit: Native Americans

When the children return from their lunch period, they become involved in work organized around thematic content. The theme under way is Native Americans. The teacher explains how much control the children have over the topics that form part of these theme studies:

> The theme cycles are pretty much controlled, the topics anyway, by the kids. Right away at the beginning of the year we go through a group brainstorm process where the kids will put out anything they are interested in studying, and we group things together. We put sharks and whales in the list together with someone [who] said ocean, so that related topics are chunked together. And then the kids are asked to vote for their ten most favorite, and those are the ones that we do as group theme cycles for the year. I put my things on the list, too.

Other topics chosen for intensive study during the year have been fairy tales, astronomy, ancient Egypt, and the ocean. As the teacher explains it, the theme studies involve both individual and collaborative projects among the students:

> [It] usually starts with some kind of a web, sometimes the kids would share what they already know, I usually ask them to generate lists of questions of what they want to know about and that helps arrange centers or activities, knowing what they're interested in, what their areas are. With the Native American unit we are doing right now, the kids wanted to do some independent research projects, but they also wanted to do centers. The reports they'll produce will probably be a page or a couple of pages, and we talked about binding them into a book for the library, because we found very little information in our school library to help us.

Based on the type of planning just described, the teacher collects wide and varied literacy materials to fill the classroom with information in both Spanish and English. Approximately 100 trade books, pieces of art, posters, and artifacts about Native Americans find their way into the classroom from the teachers, support staff, parents, and the children themselves.

The teacher makes use of the children's interests and ideas as she plans the learning experiences that will form part of the theme units. The themes involve large groups, small groups, and individual activities, and they integrate all subject areas. The organizational web (Fig. 1.1) illustrates the Native American theme as a whole.

Each theme culminates in some form of a product or demonstration of the group's learning. For example, the Native American theme produced a published class book that included all of the children as coauthors and a detailed bibliography. A theme about Egypt ended with an impressive transformation of the classroom into a museum, through which the students guided other classes. Yet another theme about the human body was presented in a class-published newspaper that was distributed to parents and

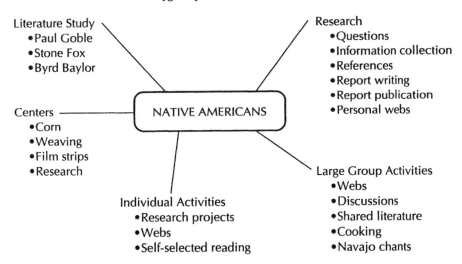

Figure 1.1 Organizational web: Native American theme.

children school-wide. These ideas evolve during the themes and are usually initiated by the children.

Four centers are included in the Native American theme study. At one side of the room, Angel, Roberto, Jaime, and Francisco are learning about corn. On their table is a basket containing blue and yellow corn chips to taste, a collection of trade books in English and Spanish about corn, a corn legend, and a colorful basket of squash and Indian corn. The teacher briefly joins the children to explain the procedure. When she leaves, the children taste the corn chips, read a book about corn, and write about each experience. The books are varied in style and language, and the children cheer when the teacher explains that she found a Spanish translation of one of the books for them (*Corn is Maize,* by Aliki).

Across the room, Rafael and Susana work with the teacher assistant on weaving. Each child has a forked branch that serves as the frame for the work. The teacher assistant helps the children select colors, measure the appropriate amount of yarn, and begin the weaving. Spanish dominates their casual and comfortable conversation as the children methodically weave colors of yarn around the natural looms. In the basket on their table are books about weaving and a diagram that labels the components of weaving in both languages, as well as the weaving materials.

In another center the children view a variety of film strips. The children are using this center as a resource for their ongoing research projects by viewing the films, including helpful information in their reports, and documenting them in their bibliographies.

The fourth center involves the children who are working on individual research projects. These children and the teacher are seated around two tables that are covered with bins of books categorized according to topic, 3×5 note cards, and children's work folders in manila envelopes.

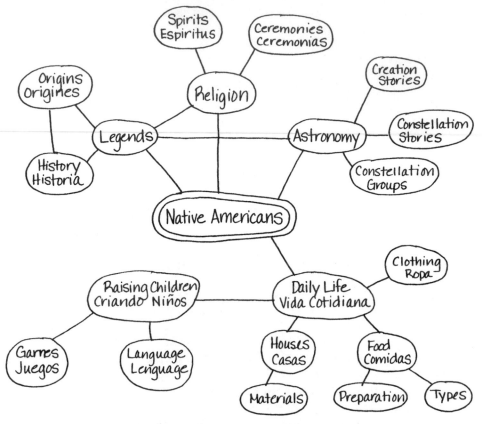

Figure 1.2. Class web: Native American theme.

Lupita, who is researching the Sioux, is reading a trade book in English called *Plains Indians,* concentrating on a section called "Games and Pastimes." As she reads, she records relevant information in Spanish on an index card. Her work provides a good example of the research process involved in this theme. The class as a large group began the theme by discussing and webbing the content they wanted to learn through their study. The result of their discussions is represented in Figure 1.2.

The students then create a web of information they want to know about their individual topics and write questions to guide their research. Examples of Lupita's questions are presented in Figure 1.3. The children may read and write in either language or a combination of the two, as Lupita's activities illustrate. As the children look for answers to their questions in resource materials, they record pertinent information on their cards, as shown in Figure 1.4.

Additionally, they record the books they use on a reference sheet that asks for information about the title, author, call number, and whether they will use the book for information or will not use the book. These sheets will

Lupita

Me gustaria, saber sobre
el tribu Siux.

¿En que teritorio vivian?

~~¿Porque no quirian a~~
~~la gente blanca?~~

¿Porque se pintaban
las caras y sus
caballos?

¿Que se, significaban
las plumas en sus
cabeza?

¿Porque sus jefes
tenian nombres
de animal?

¿Tenian una manera
especial de aser la
ropa?

Lupita

I would like to know about the Sioux tribe.
In what territory did they live?
Why did they not like white people?
Why did they paint their faces and their horses?
What was the meaning of the feathers in their heads?
Why did their chiefs have animal names?
Did they have a special way of making clothes?

Figure 1.3. Lupita's questions about Native Americans.

33

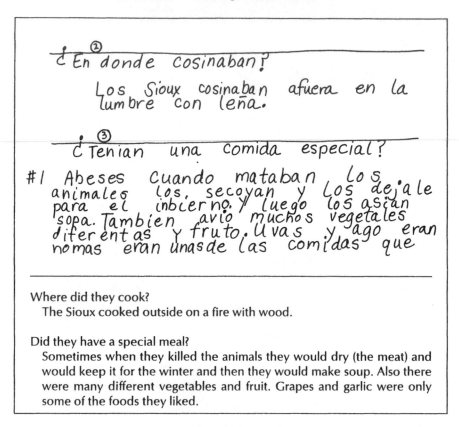

¿ En donde cosinaban?

Los Sioux cosinaban afuera en la lumbre con leña.

¿ Tenian una comida especial?

#1 Abeses Cuando mataban los animales los. secoyan y Los dej·a le para el inbcierno. Y luego los asian sopa. Tambien avio muchos vegetales diferentas y fruto. Uvas y ago eran nomas eran unasde las comidas que

---

Where did they cook?
   The Sioux cooked outside on a fire with wood.

Did they have a special meal?
   Sometimes when they killed the animals they would dry (the meat) and
   would keep it for the winter and then they would make soup. Also there
   were many different vegetables and fruit. Grapes and garlic were only
   some of the foods they liked.

Figure 1.4. Lupita's research cards.

become a bibliography when their upcoming reports are finished. Lupita's
partial bibliography is depicted in Figure 1.5.

Upon completion of the research, the children create a second individual
web summarizing the information they have obtained as a way to monitor
their own learning and write their reports. This entire process is graded by
the teacher according to the quality of the questions, the first web, the
resource list, the note keeping, the final report, the final web, and a compos-
ite overall grade. The children's final reports are bound in a published book
to donate to the school's library, where it will be catalogued and shelved for
the rest of the school to utilize as a reference document. Lupita's report is
shown in Figure 1.6.

Other children in the class follow a similar procedure. Consider Veronica, a Spanish-dominant bilingual child, who is studying the Yaqui Indians.
The teacher is sitting with her, reading to her from an adult level book written in English (*Southwestern Indian Tribes* by Tom Bahti). After she reads
a passage, the teacher translates the ideas into Spanish and discusses them
with Veronica in terms of her research questions. The teacher is absorbed in
the process herself; she is a co-researcher with Veronica, eager to learn and
discuss new knowledge with her student. Veronica incorporates a second

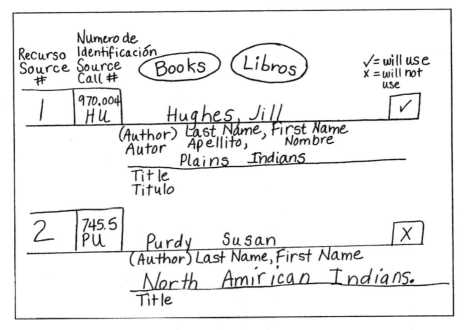

Figure 1.5. Lupita's bibliography.

source of information in her research project: She has interviewed a Yaqui teacher assistant in the school and kept a written record of her interview questions and the responses she elicited, which are incorporated into her final report; the interview is documented in her bibliography.

Richard and Evan are at the opposite end of the table studying the Anasazi. They are searching for information about weapons and how the Anasazi defended themselves. Richard finds a picture of an "atlatl," a missile launcher used for hunting, and they decide to use it for their answer. Each boy traces the illustration, cuts it out and tapes it to his index card. Evan finishes taping his and says, "This is cool," as he hurries over to Jason at another table to share what he has learned. Jason is discussing the Sioux and responds to Evan saying, "The Anasazi didn't trade with the white men. The Sioux just needed to buy iron for weapons, and they did the rest." Talk centered around the content of study is frequent and natural.

From the initial web, through the intermediate stages of planning, center activity, research work, and publication, the theme studies include authentic, captivating, integrated learning experiences, where the children use literacy to search for knowledge and to present their ideas to others in the classroom community and in the school.

Discussion

This classroom, organized into center activities, literacy events, and theme research projects, is structured so that children may work in various ways to

LOS INDIOS SIOUX

por María Guadalupe

Yo se llamo María Guadalupe y quise aprender del tribu Sioux porque casi no se mucho de ese tribu. Aprendí de los juegos que jugaban. También aprendí de los vegetales que comían y los nombres de los jefes.

Los Sioux vivían cerca del Trin River. Los Sioux no hacían muchas canastas.

A veces, cuando mataban los animales, los secaban y los dejeban para el invierno. Luego lo hacían sopa. También había muchos vegetales diferentes y frutz. Uvas y ajo eran unas de las cosidas que les gustaban. Los Sioux cocinaban afuera en la lumbre.

Estos son unos de los nombres de los jefes del tribu Sioux: Sitting Bull—jefe del tribu Sioux, Chief Ball—Hunkpapa Teton, Chief Red Horn Bull—Ogalala, and Rain-in-the-face.

También aprendí los juegos de los Sioux. Uno se llama "tiren lo del caballo" que jugaban antes de cazar o de peliar. Jugaban tirando a otros al suelo. También había otros juego que dos hombres tenían que poner un palo por un hoyo. El que ponía el palo por el hoyo primero ganaba.

THE SIOUX INDIANS

by Maria Guadalupe

My name is Maria Guadalupe and I wanted to learn about the Sioux Tribe because I hardly know anything about that tribe. I learned about the games they played. I also learned about the vegetables which they ate and the names of their chiefs.

The Sioux lived near the Trin river. The Sioux did not make many baskets.

Sometimes, when they killed animals, they dried them and left them for winter. Later they would make them into soup. Also there were many different vegetables and fruits. Grapes and garlic were some of the foods which they liked. The Sioux cooked outside on a fire.

These are some of the names of the chiefs of the Sioux tribe: Sitting Bull—chief of the Sioux tribe, Chief Ball—Hunkpapa Teton, Chief Red Horn Bull—Ogalala, and Rain-in-the-face.

I also learned the games of the Sioux. One was called "pull him off the horse" which they played before hunting or fighting. They played by throwing others to the floor. There was also another game in which two men had to place a stick in a hole. The one that put the stick in the hole first would win.

Figure 1.6. Lupita's final report.

accomplish their individual and group academic goals. There is no limit to what the children may learn about Native Americans or themes centered around other concepts. There is no ceiling on the possible level of intellectual work or the learning potential of the children. The teacher allows and encourages children to stretch their abilities and to take risks with new experiences, materials, and challenges. Simultaneously, the design of the curriculum and the participation of the teacher support the children and ensure success, acting as a safety net for those children who take risks, especially in their second language. Throughout, the children are perceived not only as active participants in their own learning but are encouraged to be responsible for their own academic development and behavior; and they are actively involved in diverse classroom activities. The classroom is socially and culturally organized to support and advance those goals.

The curriculum indicates a value placed on the children's learning *processes* as well as on completing products. With the Native American theme, the children not only learn information about their theme of study, but they learn the valid procedures of research. These third grade children are responsible for conceiving their own questions, guiding their own learning with biliterate materials and experiences, and following a sophisticated research sequence. They are expected to display skills at using reference materials and to articulate their awareness of the reasons for keeping records of reference materials. The research process culminates in a report, wherein children learn to produce a piece of writing in a specific genre at the same time that they are providing the school library with real, researched, referenced information. The research process will be repeatedly initiated by the children as they explore other subject areas in the future.

Bilingualism in this classroom is both a goal and a powerful resource for learning; it is an integral part of their classroom community and a means for children to expand their literate and social experiences. In the study centers and groups, Spanish is used interchangeably with English, so the children learning English can both understand the content in their dominant language and expand their vocabulary and comprehension in their second language. Whenever appropriate information is recorded in either language, with decisions for language choice made by the children and the teacher. The teacher strives to provide the children with materials in English and Spanish because they expand the children's literate worlds and to use their bilingualism to create interesting, advanced conditions for literacy use and language learning. In general, however, the students' and teacher's bilingualism is used as a resource to expand opportunities to obtain, create, and communicate knowledge and to develop the social relationships so essential to this classroom's work.

The materials in the classroom form part of the collective zone, serving as cultural mediators, helping to extend the amount and type of learning possible for any child. Included in the materials for the Native American unit, for example, are a great number of books, such as information books, legends, cookbooks, music and art books, and many pieces of children's lit-

erature of various genres that deal with Native American topics. Many of
the books are at an adult level. The children read these books selectively and
glean information pertaining to their self-selected topics and specific questions. The books are sometimes difficult, but the teacher assumes that with
her assistance the students can read and use them. This point is illustrated
by the interaction between Veronica and the teacher, described above. The
teacher helped Veronica, a dominant Spanish speaker and reader, translate
and discuss a difficult text from English into Spanish, rather than assuming
that Veronica could not handle the information or that she needed an easier
task.

Although adult-directed lessons are relatively rare in this classroom,
there is definitely adult involvement in the children's work. The teacher's
guidance is purposely mediated, almost hidden, embedded in the activities.
It is clear that the teacher assumes a variety of roles during the course of a
day and even during one theme. These roles can be succinctly described as
follows:

1. As *guide and supporter,* the teacher is crucial for helping children
   take risks, focus their questions and ideas, and translate them into
   manageable activities, ensuring that each child finds academic
   success.
2. As *active participant in the learning,* the teacher can research theme
   topics along with the children, combining her own content questions
   with demonstrations of the research process.
3. As *evaluator* of the children's individual and collective development,
   the teacher uses anecdotal records, notations of children's individual
   interests, and reflections about transcripts from literature study
   groups, and demonstrates her knowledge about children and learning.
4. As *facilitator,* the teacher utilizes conscious planning of the environment, curriculum, and materials to provide functional and purposeful uses for language, literacy, and learning processes.

All of these teacher roles constitute mediation.

An essential factor contributing to the success of this classroom and its
value for interpreting Vygotskian theory is the reality that children have
considerable control over virtually all aspects of their own learning experience. They select groups, reading materials, writing topics, theme topics,
and language to use for each. They generate their research questions and
negotiate their learning tasks with their teacher. The teacher allows and promotes this sharing of power, based on her trust of them as learners. She
explains it as follows:

> It's taken a lot of trust to give control to the children, but I think that I've
> really been rewarded in the long run. The day may not run smoothly, and
> it may not look organized to people who are not knowledgeable about what
> is going on in the classroom; but I think the learning that is going on on the

children's behalf and on my own is much more genuine and meaningful when it is like that.

The teacher's trust in the children's abilities enables her to set high expectations for them; their trust in her allows them to take risks, experiment, and collaborate with her in learning. Learning in this classroom is not only an individual achievement but a joint accomplishment between adults and children.

Practice Informing Theory

We have depicted a classroom characterized by a complex but coordinated set of practices that form part of a third-grade curriculum. These practices capture some key elements of Vygotsky's concept of a zone of proximal development but, as we have tried to show, in a broader and much more socially distributed fashion. This classroom contains elements that may exceed Vygotsky's formulation or, at the very least, shed light on how narrowly we may have been interpreting and applying his ideas.

When examining the practices that constitute our case study it becomes evident that the usual definition of the zone of proximal development is pretty barren; it cannot help interpret what goes on in this diverse, yet systematic, classroom. Limitations are largely overcome when the concept is understood as part of a broader theoretical framework that takes the development of mind in social practice as its central problematic (Minick, 1989). It then becomes clear that the zone is itself a mediating concept, a "connecting" concept, as Bruner (1987) suggested, that helps integrate Vygotsky's more encompassing theoretical view (for more detailed discussions see Minick, 1989; Moll, 1990a; Valsiner, 1988).

One aspect of this broader view is particularly relevant to our case study: the centrality of the concept of mediation to Vygotsky's formulations, including not only social interactions but semiotic mediations. This semiotic emphasis brings with it a focus on meaning as central to human activity (e.g., Bakhurst, 1986) that is often ignored during discussions of the zone. The emphasis is usually on the transmission of skills from adult to child, as is the case with typical classrooms. Yet our case study suggests that a different, more transactional view of the zone is possible, one that focuses on the co-construction of meaning as facilitated by the various activities that make up classroom life.

Central to this formulation is the emphasis on the active child developing the cultural means to assist his or her own development. In our case study the children select topics for study at the beginning of the year, choose books to read and issues to analyze, specify research questions to address, use literacy in various ways as part of classroom activities, create texts for authentic purposes, and publicly display their learning, including the development of novel products, based on their real questions about the world.

The role of the adult is to provide mediated assistance, indirect help, that does not displace the direction and control children give to the tasks and activities. The goal of this mediated assistance is to make children consciously aware of how they are manipulating the literacy process, achieving new means, and applying their knowledge to expand their boundaries by creating or reorganizing future experiences or activities. Our case study suggests that an apt definition of the zone, at least as applied to classroom analysis, must include the active child appropriating and developing new mediational means for his or her own learning and development.

Finally, our case study highlights issues about social relationships and teaching that are not usually considered within Vygotskian formulations, especially as they relate to education. We have mentioned the importance of the sharing of control between teacher and students, the development of mutual trust, the importance of the authenticity of materials and tasks, the types of discourse that make up learning events, the use of bilingualism as a resource, and the teacher's and students' perception of their roles as learners. We consider these qualitative issues in educational practice. We studied them holistically, as separate issues and in relation to how they form the classroom's social and cultural system. Our methods included participant observations, interviews of teachers and students, collection of materials, and audiotape and videotape analyses. We find these methods indispensable if the units of study are active subjects within diverse and dynamic social environments. These methods are fully compatible with Vygotsky's developmental emphasis, his insistence on a historical method, and his focus on how humans use cultural resources as tools to transform the present into the future.

Notes

1. This case study formed part of a much broader study that included household observations and close collaboration with teachers for analyzing and developing classroom practices (e.g., Moll & Greenberg, 1990). Portions of this chapter were included in the project's reports to the funding agency, the Office of Bilingual Education and Minority Language Affairs, Department of Education. We appreciate their support.

2. For additional discussions of this key theoretical concept, see, e.g., del Río and Alvarez (1988); Minick (1985, 1987); Moll (1990a); Palacios (1987); Rivière (1984); Rogoff and Wertsch (1984); Tharp and Gallimore (1988); Valsiner (1988); Vygotsky (1978, 1987); Wertsch (1985).

3. Kathryn F. Whitmore conducted these observations. For purposes of this chapter we have collapsed several observations into a description of one representative day, concentrating primarily on language arts activities. We would like to thank the teacher for sharing with us her observations, transcripts of lessons, and the writing of the students. She actively collects data in her own classroom not only as part of her graduate studies but to understand better how she is teaching and how the children are learning. She has been our teacher as well.

4. Readers not familiar with the politics of race in the United States may not know this term. In brief, it is usually meant to depict a school located in a Black or Latino neighborhood that has been made attractive to Anglo-Saxon families because of a special characteristic, for example, an emphasis on teaching with computers. The hope is that these families will voluntarily send their children there to integrate what would otherwise be an ethnically or racially segregated school. Alternately, desegregation schools may be located in predominantly Anglo neighborhoods, and minority children are bussed into the school. All desegregation programs receive additional funding and programs, including such personnel as fine arts teachers, counselors, and librarians.

5. Many elementary classrooms use webs, which resemble spider webs in their final design, to record information and questions. Webbing is especially helpful as a visual tool for categorization and organization of ideas. An example of a content theme web in Figure 1.2.

6. Writing workshop is part of a process approach to writing that is becoming common in classrooms in the United States. It involves the following steps: topic selection, composition of a first (rough) draft, sharing the draft with friends and readers, revision of the draft, editing in a conference with the teacher or teacher assistant, illustration if appropriate, and final publication. Final products are usually shelved in the classroom library for open reading.

7. The translation of Lupita's writing is not a literal one. For example, it is difficult to capture invented spellings from one language to another. Consequently, the translation is void of miscues and invented spellings.

References

Anyon, J. (1980). Social class and the hidden curriculum of work. *Journal of Education, 162*(1), 67–92.

Bakhurst, D. J. (1986). Thought, speech and the genesis of meaning: on the 50th anniversary of Vygotsky's Myslenie i Rec' [Speech and Thinking]. *Studies in Soviet Thought, 31,* 102–29.

Bruner, J. (1987). Prologue to the English edition. In *L. S. Vygotsky. Collected Works* (Vol. 1, pp. 1–16) (R. Rieber & A. Carton, eds.; Minick, N., transl.). New York: Plenum.

del Río, P., & Alvarez, A. (1988). Aprendizaje y desarollo: La teoría de actividad y la zona de desarollo proximo [Learning and development: activity theory and the zone of proximal development]. In C. Coll (ed.). *Psicología de la educación [Psychology of education]* (pp. 1–34). Madrid: Alianza.

Goodlad, J. (1984). *A place called school.* New York: McGraw-Hill.

Goodman, Y., & Goodman, K. (1990). Vygotsky in a whole language perspective. In L. C. Moll (ed.). *Vygotsky and education* (pp. 223–50). Cambridge: Cambridge University Press.

Griffin, P., & Cole, M. (1984). Current activity for the future: the zo-ped. In B. Rogoff & J. Wertsch (eds.). *Children's learning in the "zone of proximal development"* (pp. 45–64). San Francisco: Jossey-Bass.

Minick, N. (1985). L. S. Vygotsky and Soviet activity theory: new perspectives on the relationship between mind and society. Unpublished doctoral dissertation, Northwestern University.

Minick, N. (1987). Implications of Vygotsky's theories for dynamic assessment. In
    C. S. Lidz (ed.). *Dynamic assessment* (pp. 116–40). New York: Guilford
    Press.
Minick, N. (1989). Mind and activity in Vygotsky's work: an expanded frame of ref-
    erence. *Cultural Dynamics, 2,* 162–87.
Moll, L. C. (ed.). (1990a). *Vygotsky and education.* Cambridge: Cambridge Univer-
    sity Press.
Moll, L. C. (1990b). Introduction. In L. C. Moll (ed.). *Vygotsky and education* (pp.
    1–30). Cambridge: Cambridge University Press.
Moll, L. C., & Greenberg, J. (1990). Creating zones of possibilities: combining social
    contexts for instruction. In L. C. Moll (ed.). *Vygotsky and education* (pp. 319–
    48). Cambridge: Cambridge University Press.
Oakes, J. (1986). Tracking, inequality, and the rhetoric of school reform: why schools
    don't change. *Journal of Education, 168,* 61–80.
Palacios, J. (1987). Reflexiones en torno a las implicaciones educativas de la obra de
    Vygotski [Reflections in terms of the educational implications of Vygotsky's
    work]. In M. Siguán (ed.). *Actualidad de Lev S. Vygotski [Actuality of Lev S.
    Vygotsky]* (pp. 176–88). Barcelona: Anthropos.
Rivière, A. (1984). La psicología de Vygotski [The psychology of Vygotsky.] *Infancia
    y Aprendizaje, 27–28*(3–4), 7–86.
Rogoff, B., & Wertsch, J. (eds.) (1984). *Children's learning in the "zone of proximal
    development"* (pp. 7–18). San Francisco: Jossey-Bass.
Tharp, R., & Gallimore, R. (1988). *Rousing minds to life: teaching, learning and
    schooling in social context.* Cambridge: Cambridge University Press.
Valsiner, J. (1988). *Developmental psychology in the Soviet Union.* Sussex, Great
    Britain: Harvester Press.
Vygotsky, L. S. (1978). *Mind in society.* Cambridge, MA: Harvard University Press.
Vygotsky, L. S. (1987). Thinking and speech. In *L. S. Vygotsky. Collected Works*
    (Vol. 1, pp. 39–285) (R. Rieber & A. Carton, eds.; Minick, N., transl.). New
    York: Plenum.
Wertsch, J. V. (1985). *Vygotsky and the social formation of mind.* Cambridge, MA:
    Harvard University Press.

2

First-Grade Dialogues for Knowledge Acquisition and Use

ANNEMARIE SULLIVAN PALINCSAR,
ANN L. BROWN, and JOSEPH C. CAMPIONE

Increased attention to the dialectical relation between the individual and the social aspects in the acquisition of knowledge has led to a burgeoning of interest regarding collaborative learning. Whether propelled by Piagetian theory regarding the role of cognitive conflict in the presence of differing perspectives or Vygotskian theory regarding the internalization of dialogues initially experienced in social contexts, there is interest in how increasingly divergent classrooms can become learning communities—communities in which each participant makes significant contributions to the emergent understandings of all members, despite having unequal knowledge concerning the topic under study.

In this chapter we consider the role that structured dialogues assume in fostering a learning community. Specifically, we describe the use of reciprocal teaching with first-grade students working toward an understanding of simple biological concepts related to the theme of animal survival. We present the outcomes of these dialogues and then discuss these outcomes in terms of the facilitative features of the instruction, including the form of discourse within which the children and teachers were operating and the role of the texts.

Reciprocal Teaching

Reciprocal teaching is an instructional procedure that features guided practice in the application of four concrete strategies for the purpose of understanding text. Students and teachers take turns leading discussions about shared text. These discussions are not, however, open-ended. The dialogue leader (adult or child) begins the discussion by *asking questions* about the content of the text. The group discusses these questions, raises additional questions, and, in the case of disagreement or misunderstanding, rereads the text. Whereas the questions are used to stimulate discussion, *summarizing* is used to identify the gist of what has been read and discussed and to prepare the group to proceed to the next portion of text. Once again, there is discussion for the purpose of achieving consensus regarding the summary. The third strategy, *clarification,* is used opportunistically for the purpose of restoring meaning when a concept, word, or phrase has been misunderstood or is unfamiliar to someone in the group. Finally, the discussion leader provides the opportunity for *predictions* regarding upcoming content. Group members generate their predictions based on their prior knowledge of the content of the text as well as clues provided in the text itself (e.g., embedded questions).

These strategies were selected for a number of reasons; they represent the kinds of strategic activity in which successful readers routinely engage when learning from text. They provide the occasion for making explicit and visible the mental processes useful for constructing meaning for text. Finally, these strategies support a discussion, providing an interactive and socially supportive context in which to learn about learning from text.

The role of the teacher in reciprocal teaching is to scaffold the involvement of the learners in the discussion by providing the explanation, modeling, support, and feedback that will—in time—enable full participation of the students in the dialogue. The supportive aspects of the instruction are removed as the students, as a group and as individuals, internalize or adopt the dialogue in which they have become full participants in a social context.

Vygotsky's perspective is essential to understanding cognition in social contexts. In Vygotsky's theory, development is the process of learning to use intellectual tools through social interactions with others who have greater expertise in the use of those intellectual tools.

> The greatest change in children's capacity to use language as a problem solving tool takes place somewhat later in development, when socialized speech (which has previously been used to address an adult) is turned inward. Instead of appealing to the adult, children appeal to themselves; language thus takes on an intrapersonal function in addition to its interpersonal use. [Vygotsky, 1978, p. 27]

Hence the most effective social interaction is one in which joint problem solving occurs, guided by an individual who is skilled in the use of these intellectual tools. However, there are additional conditions that must be in place to render the social interaction effective. One of these conditions is that the problem-solving activity occur within the participants' "zone of proximal development," a concept provided by Vygotsky to characterize a dynamic region of sensitivity to learning the skills of the culture. Vygotsky proposed that this region could best be understood by considering both the actual developmental level of the individual and the potential developmental level.

> The zone of proximal development is the distance between the actual developmental level as determined by independent problem solving and the level of potential development as determined through problem solving under

adult guidance, or in collaboration with more capable peers. [Vygotsky, 1978, p. 86]

Inasmuch as each member shares in the activity of constructing the meaning of the text to the extent that she or he is able, reciprocal teaching dialogues create a zone of proximal development (Brown & Palincsar, 1989). What enables all members to participate in the dialogue is the presence of others, particularly the teacher, who can scaffold the efforts of participants in the interaction by providing support that is both temporary and adjustable—and informed by the individual needs of the participants.

Scaffolding has typically been examined in mother–child interactions within the context of problem-solving activity (Wertsch, 1978; Wood & Middleton, 1975) and language acquisition (Cazden, 1979; Greenfield, 1984; McNamee, 1980; Scollon, 1976). Within reciprocal teaching dialogues we have observed that teachers scaffold the engagement of their students by: (1) linking students' previous contributions to new knowledge arising in the text; (2) requesting that students elaborate on their ideas; (3) restoring direction to the discussion; and (4) reworking students' contributions so they are integrated into the discussion (Palincsar, 1986).

Most research on reciprocal teaching has been conducted in the area of reading and listening comprehension instruction by general, remedial, and special educators. Generally, the instruction has been conducted in small groups (averaging six to eight). Students entering these studies scored approximately 30% correct on independent measures of text comprehension and participated in the intervention for a minimum of 25 instructional days. The criterion we applied to determine success was the attainment of an independent score of 75 to 80% correct on four of five consecutively administered measures of comprehension, assessing recall of text, ability to draw inferences, ability to state the gist of material read, and application of knowledge acquired from the text to a novel situation. Using this criterion, approximately 80% of both the primary and middle school students were judged successful. Furthermore, these gains were observed to be maintained for up to six months to a year following instruction (Brown & Palincsar, 1982; Palincsar & Brown, 1984, 1989).

For the typical reciprocal teaching research, the children have read an array of unrelated texts drawn largely from readers and trade magazines for children. This selection of text provided little opportunity for cumulative reference and the acquisition and use of knowledge over time. In the study discussed in this chapter, we sought to investigate how the dialogues could be used, not only for the purpose of teaching children how to learn from text but also how to acquire and achieve ownership of new knowledge. The dialogues were used to learn simple science concepts related to the following animal survival themes: protection against enemies, natural pest control, protection from elements, adaptation and extinction, camouflage, and mimicry. These themes were represented across the texts with which the groups were working. For example, the Protection Against Enemies theme was presented in separate passages about porcupines, diodins, turtles, and armadillos.

Lessons

The participants in these lessons were six first-grade teachers, each of whom worked with a group of six students, five of whom were identified as at risk for academic difficulty based on teacher opinion and standardized and informal measures of listening comprehension. For example, these children typically scored below the 35th percentile on a standardized test of listening comprehension (Stanford Early School Achievement Test). For each teacher, there was also a matched control group. The children in the control group listened to the same passages that were being used in the discussions with the experimental children but responded only to questions regarding these passages; they did not engage in discussions regarding their content.

The study began with the administration of pretest measures designed to assess both comprehension and the children's ability to recognize and use the principles that were to be presented in the instructional passages. The comprehension measure was administered by reading a passage to each child and, after the reading, asking the child to respond to a series of questions. The questions included measures of recall and inference, as well as one question designed to test the child's understanding of the theme of the passage. These comprehension measures were administered to the experimental and control children, not only on a pretest and posttest basis but also throughout the intervention, generally on the following schedule: After two days of dialogue on a theme, the children were administered an assessment passage that concerned yet another instantiation of the theme. Included in the assessments conducted during the intervention were questions designed to measure the child's ability to identify the analogy between the subject of the assessment passage and subjects that had been discussed in class during the dialogues. For example, the assessment passage used in conjunction with the intervention passages on the garden hunter and ladybugs (within the theme of Natural Pest Control) concerned the usefulness of the praying mantis. To assess the students' understanding of the gist of the passage, they were asked, "Why do farmers and gardners appreciate the praying mantis?" To assess their ability to relate the analogous information read in the assessment passage with that presented in the instructional passage the children were asked, "How is the praying mantis like the lacewing that you learned about in class?" Both the experimental and control children attained 47% correct scores on those comprehension assessments administered prior to the thematic dialogues. When examining those questions that assessed the ability to identify the theme of the passage, the experimental students were successful only 29.2% of the time during baseline. This figure compares with a mean of 27.2% for the control students.

To assess the children's ability to identify and use the analogy underlying the various topics and to determine how this ability changed over the course of the discussions, the children were presented a classification task in which they were asked to sort pictures that represented one of two themes (e.g., protection against enemies and adaptation/extinction). The children were asked to sort the pictures into two piles so that "the ones that go together are in the same pile" and to talk out loud as they thought about which pile into which they would put each picture. In addition, when the children were finished sorting, they were asked once again how they decided which pictures belonged together. This sorting task was repeated three times until each theme and its constituent subjects were sorted. At the time of pretesting, 43% of the sorting decisions made by the experimental children were based on the physical characteristics of the objects, whereas only 13% were made based on the thematic similarities. The decisions of the control children were also principally guided by physical characteristics (37% of the time) as they sorted by theme only 14% of the time (Clark, 1983).

After the administration of these pretests, both the experimental and control students participated in three lessons designed to introduce them to the concept "similar" at a concrete and an abstract level. The experimental groups then began their discussions. One passage was read to the children each day, for a total of 20 passages over 20 consecutive days of instruction. The basic format of reciprocal teaching dialogues was used; the children and teacher took turns leading the discussion in which they questioned one another about the content of a passage as it was read in segments. In addition, with each segment the group summarized the content, generated predictions about upcoming text, and worked to clarify ambiguous information.

The following transcript is provided to illustrate the general reciprocal teaching procedure. The children were reading about the snowshoe rabbit, and it was the sixteenth day of dialogue. The teacher had just read a segment of text describing the season in which baby rabbits are born and the ways in which the mother rabbit cares for her babies.

Kam (dialogue leader): When [were] the babies born?

Teacher: That's a good question to ask. Call on someone to answer that question.

Kam: Robby? Milly?

Milly: Summer.

Teacher: What would happen if the babies were born in the winter? Let's think.

Several children make a number of responses including: "The baby would be very cold." "They would need food." "They don't have no fur when they are just born."

Kam: I have another question. How does she get the babies safe?

Kris: She hides them.

Kam: That's right but something else. . . .

Teacher: There is something very unusual about how she hides them that surprised me. I didn't know this.

Travis: They are all in a different place.

Teacher: Why do you think she does this?

Milly: Probably because I heard another story and when they're babies they usually eat each other or fight with each other.

Teacher: That could be! And what about when that lynx comes?

Several children comment that that would be the end of all the babies.

Travis: If I was the mother I would hide mine, but I would keep them all together.

Kris: If the babies are hidden and the mom wants to go and look at them, how can she remember where they are?

Teacher: Good question. Because she does have to find them again. Why? What does she bring them?

Milly: She needs to bring food. She probably leaves a twig or something.

Teacher: Do you think she puts out a twig like we mark a trail?

Several children disagree and suggest that she uses her sense of smell. One child, recalling that the snowshoe rabbit is not all white in the winter suggests that the mother might be able to tell her babies apart by their coloring.

Teacher: So we agree that the mother rabbit uses her senses to find her babies after she hides them. Kam, can you summarize for us now?

Kam: The babies are born in the summer. . . .

Teacher: The mother. . . .

Kam: The mother hides the babies in different places.

Teacher: And she visits them. . . .

Kam: To bring them food.

Travis: She keeps them safe.

Teacher: Any predictions?

Milly: What she teaches her babies . . . like how to hop.

Kris: They know how to hop already.

Teacher: Well, let's read and see.

When presenting the first passage within each theme, the teacher was urged to first determine if the children would, in the course of their discussions, focus on the content that represented the theme of that passage. If the children failed to do so, the teachers were encouraged to make the theme of the passage explicit after it had been read completely. However, with subsequent passages related to the theme the teachers were asked to foster the children's recognition of the theme and analogous information across the texts read. The following dialogue segment illustrates how it occurred in one group reading the passage on polar bears from the theme Protection from Elements. This story is the fourth one the children have read on this theme; the previous ones were about Eskimoes, penguins, and the hippopotamus.

The children were discussing the first segment of the text, which had informed them where polar bears can be found. The text made no mention of the other subjects discussed on this theme, and the information that related to how the bear protects itself from the harsh cold had not yet been introduced. Nevertheless, the children recognized similarities between the information presented thus far and information acquired at earlier readings.

Missy (dialogue leader): Where do the polar bears live?

Teacher: That would be a good question to ask, wouldn't it?

Traver: They live in the snow.

Several children [*in unison*]: Caves.

Traver: They live in a kind of cave.

Rodney: They live in Alaska like the Eskimoes do.

Traver: And the penguins.

Teacher: Good for you, you have just pointed out something that is. . . .

Traver [*interrupting*]: They [the penguins] have an ice cave too.

Rodney [*interjecting an observation that leaps across themes*]: And the polar bear has fur, looks like quills [in reference to an earlier passage about porcupines] but it ain't quills.

Troy: [The fur] is a big glove like.

[*From here the children made predictions that the "glove" of the bear could be compared to the layers of clothing discussed when reading about Eskimoes.*]

The children's recognition and use of thematic information was manifested in a number of ways, including the fact that the children would generate questions asking how two things were alike, summaries that included information across texts, clarifications about the ways in which two subjects were different, and numerous predictions that were predicated on information read in previous texts. For example, in each of the six groups, having discussed the way in which the walkingstick insect protects itself from enemies by its appearance as well as its behavior (i.e., imitating a fallen twig or leaf), the children, recognizing that the pipefish was another creature that assumes the appearance and characteristics of the plant life within which it lives, predicted that the story would also identify the enemies of the pipefish. In addition, there were numerous occasions when the children simply spontaneously interjected their discoveries and speculations, often accompanied by little squeals of delight, as though they were "in on a secret."

Outcomes of the Lessons

To evaluate the outcomes of the lessons, we present the results of the comprehension measures administered during and after the intervention as well as the results of the classification posttest. Recall that the comprehension measures assessed children's understanding of passages that were thematically related but different from the passages about which the discussions were held. During baseline, both the experimental and control students averaged 47% correct on these assessments. The mean for the first ten days of instruction (which included discussions of three of the themes) was 49.9% for the experimental groups and 37.7% for the control groups. The mean for the second ten days of instruction was 70.0% correct for the experimental groups and 39.5% for the control groups.

With regard to their ability to identify the gist of the assessment passages after the first ten days of dialogues, the experimental children were correctly identifying the theme of the passage 45.5% of the time, whereas the control students were doing so only 14.9% of the time. Finally, the mean for the second half of the intervention for the experimental group was 63.9%, whereas for the control group it was 10.5%.

On those questions measuring the children's identification of the analogy between the assessment passage and an instructional passage used during the dialogues, for the first half of the instructional phase the experimental children achieved a mean score of 53.1%, whereas the control children achieved a mean of 27.0%. For the second half of instruction, the experimental children achieved a mean of 76.6%, whereas the control children earned a mean of 17.3%.

A second measure used to determine the children's ability to recognize and use the analogies inherent in both the instructional examples and novel examples was the classification task. The posttest classification task was administered by presenting pictures of the animals presented during the intervention, one at a time. The children were asked to recall information about each subject (e.g., "This is a porcupine. What do you remember about the porcupine?"). If the students mentioned the theme (i.e., porcupines have quills that protect it from its enemies), this response was acknowledged. If the child failed to mention the theme, the interviewer commented, "Another interesting fact about the porcupine is that it has spikes or quills all over its body to protect itself from its enemies." This procedure was repeated until piles were constituted for each of the themes, and the children made decisions about the pile in which each picture should be placed. Finally, the children were presented with new exemplars that they were once again asked to place in a pile while explaining their decision. For example, the yellow jacket was described as a black and yellow flying insect that lives in the United States and likes to eat hookworms, which are harmful insects that live on tobacco plants.

The results of the sorting tasks indicate that whereas the children in the control condition sorted principally by physical characteristics and used thematic information only 14% of the time, the children in the reciprocal teaching groups made 54% of their sorting decisions based on thematic similarities and only 29% were based on physical traits. In addition, when considering the sorting of novel subjects (i.e., animals that had not been presented in either the instructional or assessment passages), the experimental children used underlying principles that they speculated these animals shared (rather than physical features) 20% more than did the children in the control condition.

Analogy as a learning mechanism is a crucial factor in knowledge acquisition at all ages. Analogical thinking involves the transfer of knowledge from one situation to another via mapping the one-to-one correspondences between them. When noting commonalities, the learner goes beyond the surface features between problems and concentrates on the core similarities (Brown, 1989; Brown & Campione, 1981, 1984). It is worth noting that, although all of the children were exposed to the subjects covered in the texts, only those children engaged in discussions of the texts began to view the subjects as problem paths, facilitating transfer of knowledge from one situation to another. For the remaining children, it appears that the stories were viewed as unrelated. These first-grade, at-risk children did not discover the underlying principles; however, during the course of guided exploration of these principles in discussion, they achieved more creative and flexible use of their knowledge of these subjects and themes.

In summary, children in the reciprocal teaching discussion groups indicated changes in their ability to (1) understand text and identify the gist of the passages read, and (2) recognize and apply the analogical information in the texts.

Reflections on the Lessons and Their Outcomes

Earlier we proposed to discuss those processes that facilitated the collaboration of the teachers and students as they explored these biological themes. The literature is rich with references to the phenomenon whereby "the individual response emerges from the form of collective life" (Rogoff & Wertsch, 1984). This phenomenon has been identified in many ways. Bruner (1984), for example, referred to "the negotiation of shared meaning . . . the teacher interacting with the children . . . guiding them through successive zones of proximal development." Edwards and Mercer (1987) referred to "the 'hand-over' of control of learning from teacher to pupil." Harre (1987, p. 125) referred to "conversation in the Vygotsky space." What is not abundant in the literature is an accounting of how this process transpires.

In fact, the literature suggests that the "co-construction of knowledge" is one of the more controversial issues in this field of inquiry. Questions emerge in the order of: "Is it simply the teacher's knowledge that is being reproduced?" (Bloome, 1984). "Who's building whose building?" (Searle, 1984). How does one promote an "interaction between the teacher's meaning and those of his pupils?" (Barnes, 1982).

Underlying these questions is the practical as well as theoretically interesting issue of the "tension" between the child and the curriculum. How does one achieve compromise between allowing exploration and discovery and maintaining teacher control in pursuit of predetermined curriculum goals? (Dewey, 1902; Edwards & Mercer, 1987).

What we describe here are hypotheses and corroborating evidence regarding two features of the lessons that served to facilitate student–teacher collaboration in these dialogues: the form of the discourse and the nature of the texts.

Form of Discourse

The literature, particularly that generated by sociolinguists and others studying classroom interactions, offers many illustrations as to the manner in which true conversation among teachers and children is thwarted. The culprits include the asymmetry of power and knowledge between teacher and child (Bloome & Green, 1984), sociocultural differences among children and teachers (Heath, 1982; Michaels & Cook-Gumperz, 1979), and organizational constraints in classrooms (Mehan, 1979). These observations suggested that one important key to the successful use of discourse in classrooms is to determine ways in which children can *assume* a voice and teachers can *impart* a voice to children in these dialogues.

Our examination of the transcripts and interviews with the participating teachers suggest that the discourse structure in these lessons, defined principally by the use of the four strategies (predicting, questioning, summarizing, clarifying), as well as the turn-taking, served these purposes. The strategies provided an entrée for the students as they engaged in their roles as discussion leaders. In addition, they provided a mechanism whereby the students could collaborate. Finally, they provided a clear focus for both the teachers and the children in their shared discussions.

Indications of this conclusion include the fact that both teachers and children labeled the contributions they were about to make to the conversation. For example, on day 2 of instruction Ms. Johnson announced to the students: "All right. Listen as I make a summary." In that same lesson, a child in her group followed this pattern when he interrupted the question he was asking with the statement, "This is my question." In addition, teachers labeled children's contributions. For example, on day 3 a student asked the teacher, "What's a suit of armor?" The teacher's first response is, "Would you like to have that clarified?" In these first-grade groups, although the labeling of the strategies dropped out rather quickly (certainly by day 5 for most of the groups), the template provided by the strategies continued to be apparent but there was a shift in the flexibility with which the strategies were used; hence if one were to proceed through the transcripts, for the initial days of instruction questions were generally followed by summaries followed by clarifications and predictions. This order, in fact, reflects that by which the teachers introduced the use of the strategies.

Although it occurred at different points in time during the intervention, in each group there was a shift such that the use of strategies was driven by the content and the discourse itself. It is at this point that the students began to interject predictions as well as questions, even in the midst of the teachers' oral reading. This shift signaled the movement from ritualized to principled and active use of the strategies and the dialogue (Edwards & Mercer, 1987; Wertsch, 1980).

Interestingly, this shift was experienced by both the teachers and students. For example, teachers who initially read the segments of text with no pauses were observed to look up from the reading of the text at opportune times (e.g., when they read information that confirmed the group's predictions).

Flexible use of the strategies in the discourse was at least the case until things began to go "wrong." For example, on day 11 when a subset of Ms. Mackey's group began to take the discussion afield (as suggested by the tangential nature of the discussion and the fact that the discussion was now dominated by two children), Ms. Mackey interjected, "All right. I think that, boys and girls, you're just talking. We have to do four things. And we have to do them orderly." Indeed, there were times when the children, frustrated that the direction of the discourse was unclear, demanded, "What is it we're doing now? Is this our summary?"

The strategies then, provided a means for the children to "try out" their ideas; however, in addition, they represented language in the form of tools (Vygotsky, 1978) to be used, in a public manner, to solve the problems of understanding these texts and their inherent themes. How the teachers induced children to use these strategies as tools is equally important to understanding the outcomes of these discussions.

The first feature we discuss is the role of playfulness in drawing students into these discussions. Ms. Mackey's group was about to listen to a story about the porcupine. She began the dialogue:

> Mackey: "Our first story is called "The Porcupine." Now, we usually predict from the title, don't we? So, obviously the story is going to be about—what, Chris?"
>
> [*One of the lessons one learns early in discussions with first graders is that there is nothing that is "obvious."*]
>
> Chris: A porcupine has a friend that's a cactus, and he has a girlfriend that's another cactus.

This response led to an array of predictions from other members of the group that were largely fantasies. Across the teachers, we observed a considerable degree of tolerance for these flights of fancy. Discussions with the teachers suggested that such playfulness had an important role in enticing young children to become engaged in the text as well as with the strategies. How teachers responded to this playfulness differed. On some occasions teachers provided the children information, such as, "Oh, what if I told you this was a true story?" while on other occasions the teachers would simply read the text and allow the children to deduce that for themselves.

The second feature we wish to discuss is the support, or *scaffolding*, provided by the teacher to maintain the children's engagement in the dialogues. Griffin and Cole (1984) drew our attention to the fact that the support that adults provide in the zone of proximal development is not necessarily of amount but of kind. Indeed, our examinations of the transcripts revealed that successful teachers called on a broad array of conversational devices and opportunities to support these young children's discussions; even within one lesson, and certainly across lessons, teachers were observed to use cued elicitations, paraphrasing of children's contributions, choral responses, framing of the children's responses, selective use of praise, and silence. In the literature on classroom discourse, some of these devices assume a negative connotation. For example, cued elicitations and paraphrases are often associated with teacher control and masking rather than the bridging of student and teacher understanding (Edwards & Mercer, 1987). Our observations of students and teachers engaged in dialogues and evaluations of the outcomes of these dialogues suggest that each of these devices assumes value (both negative and positive) only when examined in their complete context as defined by the children, the history of the instruction, and the text—to identify but a few of these variables (Erickson, 1982).

Role of the Text

An important contrast between these lessons and earlier reciprocal teaching dialogues was the use of the thematically arranged texts. The fact that the children were working with shared texts that constituted a usable, coherent, connected body of knowledge and the fact that these texts became part of a common knowledge base further promoted a community of learners.

The thematic nature of the texts led to the following two occurrences in the dialogues: (1) the children focused on the analogy; and (2) they cross-referenced texts. For example, one group was discussing the snowshoe rabbit. They had learned that this rabbit changes color in the winter and were generating their predictions about the upcoming text when Traver suggested: "About, probably like . . . probably he might get extinct?" This is interesting because the snowshoe rabbit was presented in the context of camouflage, and yet Traver made the connection between camouflage as a means of preservation and the consequence of not having such a means—extinction.[1]

Interestingly, the children not only made references to texts within and across the themes but, additionally, made reference to texts they read in contexts other than the reciprocal teaching dialogues. For example, in the text concerning ladybugs the children read, "The following spring, the ladybugs come out of their deep sleep." During the accompanying discussion, the children compared the ladybug's hibernation with the hibernation of bears, referring to a story entitled, "Black Bear Babies," which was written in a narrative genre and to which they had listened approximately three months prior to this discussion. This point is particularly noteworthy, as we had no evidence of children incorporating previous texts in their discussions before we began this investigation. The extension of reciprocal teaching discussions to texts with recurrent themes gave rise to a shift from learning how to learn from text to learning how to use knowledge acquired from text.

Conclusion

Dewey (1902), a contemporary of Vygotsky, urged that if educators:

> Abandon the notion of subject-matter as something fixed and ready-made in itself, outside the child's experience; cease thinking of the child's experience as also something hard and fast; see it as something fluent, embryonic, vital; . . . [then we would] realize that the child and the curriculum are simply two limits which define a single process. . . . [He urged that] "Just as two points define a straight line, so the present standpoint of the child and the facts and truths of studies define instruction. [Instruction] is continuous reconstruction, moving from the child's present experience out into that represented by the organized bodies of truth that we call studies. [p. 11]

We have described the role that teacher–student dialogues play in reconstruction, facilitated by a specialized form of discourse, in hand with the use of usable, coherent, connected topics of discussion. The theoretical underpinnings of reciprocal teaching attribute learning to the process of internalizing cognitive activities that were originally experienced in a social context. The children use metacognitive strategies to generate their own questions about the text, to relate their own knowledge to the new knowledge posed in the text, to summarize what they have learned, and to identify what they found confusing in the text and how they might proceed to render the text more meaningful. The teacher proceeds, with deliberate intention, to enable the children to acquire knowledge about reading and themselves as readers that will be useful to them. Because of the diversity of experiences and knowledge the children bring to these texts, each participant can make a useful contribution to the emerging understanding of the content at hand. In such a context, classrooms of diverse learners become communities of knowledge users.

Note

1. There is an interesting aside to this anecdote—testimony to the fragile nature of children's understanding. At the end of this lesson, the teacher made use of Traver's mentioning the theme of extinction and asked the children, "Why do you suppose the snowshoe rabbits are not extinct? She immediately called on Traver, who answered, "Probably smart like a dog." However, a second child in the group interjected, "Because he can change colors and blend in."

References

Barnes, D. (1982). *Practical curriculum study*. London: Routledge & Kegan Paul.
Bloome, D. (1984). Building literacy and the classroom community. *Theory into Practice, 25*(2), 71–76.

Bloome, D., & Green, J. (1984). Directions in the sociolinguistic study of reading. In P. D. Pearson, R. Barr, M. Kamil, & P. Mosenthal (eds.). *Handbook of reading research.* New York: Longman.

Brown, A. L. (1989). Analogical learning and transfer: what develops? In S. Vosniadou & A. Ortony (eds.). *Similarity and analogical reasoning* (pp. 369–412). Cambridge, England: Cambridge University Press.

Brown, A. L., & Campione, J. C. (1981). Inducing flexible thinking: a problem of access. In M. Friedman, J. P. Das, & N. O'Connor (eds.), *Intelligence and learning* (pp. 515–30). New York: Plenum Press.

Brown, A. L., & Campione, J. C. (1984). Three faces of transfer: implications for early competence, individual differences, and instruction. In M. Lamb, A. Brown, & B. Rogoff (eds.). *Advances in developmental psychology* (Vol. 3, pp. 143–92). Hillsdale, NJ: Lawrence Erlbaum Associates.

Brown, A. L., & Palincsar, A. S. (1982). Inducing strategic learning from texts by means of informed, self-control training. *Topics in Learning and Learning Disabilities, 2*(1), 1–17.

Brown, A. L., & Palincsar, A. S. (1989). Guided, cooperative learning and individual knowledge acquisition. In L. Resnick (ed.). *Knowing, learning and instruction: essays in honor of Robert Glaser* (pp. 393–451). Hillsdale, NJ: Lawrence Erlbaum Associates.

Bruner, J. (1984). Vygotsky's zone of proximal development: the hidden agenda. In B. Rogoff & J. V. Wertsch (eds.). *Children's learning in the zone of proximal development* (pp. 93–97). San Francisco: Jossey-Bass.

Cazden, C. B. (1979). Peekaboo as an instructional model: discourse development at home and at school. In *Papers and reports on child development* (no. 17, pp. 1–19). Stanford, CA: Department of Linguistics, Stanford University.

Clark, E. V. (1983). Meanings and concepts. In P. H. Mussen (ed.). *Carmichael's manual of child psychology.* In J. H. Flavell & E. M. Markman (eds.). *Vol. 3. Cognitive development* (pp. 787–840). New York: Wiley.

Dewey, J. (1902). *The child and the curriculum.* Chicago: University of Chicago Press.

Edwards, D., & Mercer, N. (1987). *Common knowledge: the development of understanding in the classroom.* London: Methuen.

Erickson, F. (1982). Taught cognitive learning in its immediate environments: a neglected topic in the anthropology of education. *Anthropology and Education Quarterly, 13*(2), 149–80.

Greenfield, P. M. (1984). A theory of the teacher in the learning activities of everyday life. In B. Rogoff & J. Lave (eds.). *Everyday cognition: its development in social context* (pp. 117–38). Cambridge, MA: Harvard University Press.

Griffin, P., & Cole, M. (1984). Current activity for the future: the zo-ped. In B. Rogoff & J. V. Wertsch (eds.). *Children's learning in the zone of proximal development.* San Francisco: Jossey-Bass.

Harre, R. (1984). *Personal being.* Cambridge, MA: Harvard University Press.

Heath, S. B. (1982). Questioning at home and at school: a comparative study. In G. Spindler (ed.). *Doing the ethnography of schooling.* New York: Holt, Rinehart & Winston.

McNamee, G. D. (1980). The social origins of narrative skills. Unpublished doctoral dissertation, Northwestern University, Evanston, IL.

Mehan, H. (1979). *Learning Lessons.* Cambridge, MA: Harvard University Press.

Michaels, S., & Cook-Gumperz, J. (1979). A study of sharing time with first grade students: discourse narratives in the classroom. In *Proceedings of the 5th annual meetings of the Berkeley Linguistic Society.* Berkeley, CA.

Palincsar, A. S. (1986). The role of dialogue in scaffolded instruction. *Educational Psychologist, 21*(1,2), 71–98.

Palincsar, A. S., & Brown, A. L. (1984). Reciprocal teaching of comprehension fostering and comprehension monitoring. *Cognition and Instruction, 1*(2), 117–75.

Palincsar, A. S., & Brown, A. L. (1989). Classroom dialogues to promote self-regulated comprehension. In J. Brophy (ed.). *Advances in research on teaching* (Vol. 1, pp. 35–72). Greenwich, CT: JAI Press.

Rogoff, B., & Wertsch, J. V. (1984). *Children's learning in the zone of proximal development.* San Francisco: Jossey-Bass.

Scollon, R. (1976). *Conversations with a one-year-old.* Honolulu: University Press of Hawaii.

Searle, D. (1984). Scaffolding: who's building whose building? *Language Arts, 61*(5), 480–83.

Vygotsky, L. S. (1978). *Mind in society: the development of higher psychological processes* (M. Cole, V. John-Steiner, S. Scribner, & E. Souberman, eds.). Cambridge: Harvard University Press.

Wertsch, J. V. (1978). Adult–child interaction and the roots of metacognition. *Quarterly Newsletter of the Institute for Comparative Human Development, 1,* 15–18.

Wertsch, J. (1980). The significance of dialogue in Vygotsky's account of social, egocentric, and inner speech. *Contemporary Educational Psychology, 5,* 150–62.

Wood, D., & Middleton, D. (1975). A study of assisted problem-solving. *British Journal of Psychology, 66,* 181–91.

3

Dynamics of Discourse: Literacy and the Construction of Knowledge

GEN LING M. CHANG-WELLS and GORDON WELLS

Work in both child language and cognitive development concurs in seeing the child as a meaning maker (Bower, 1974; R. Brown, 1973; Bruner, 1983; Newson, 1978; Wells, 1985). The linguistic repertoire the child builds and the expanding mental model of the world that he or she inhabits are the results of the child's constructive effort, achieved through a progressive and cumulative process of hypothesis formation, testing, and modification. Moreover, what is true of learning during the preschool years seems to continue to be true of later learning, even during adulthood. Each new step in the constructive process results from a transaction in which what is already known is brought to bear on new information, creating new meaning and enhancing understanding and control.

It thus seems clear that there can be no such thing as "objective knowledge," in the sense of knowledge that is independent of particular individuals who know. Indeed, "knowledge" is not an entity at all, but a mental state—the state of understanding arrived at by learning, that is, through the various constructive processes involved in coming to know. To be sure, what a person knows can be represented in the form of linguistic propositions, and these propositions may be given general assent. However, it does not follow that the knowledge of which these propositions are formulations is identical from one knower to another because for each knower the propositions are embedded in a unique structure of personal knowing arrived at through a particular, socially situated learning biography (Rommetveit, 1985).

Not all knowledge is propositional, however. Much of what we know consists of routines, procedures, and strategies that we deploy to achieve larger goals of various kinds. Recalling the distinction made by Ryle (1949) between "knowing how to" and "knowing that," it seems that both the procedures and the activities to which they contribute are best described in terms of "knowing how to." So, for example, we talk both of knowing how to ride a bicycle or write a report and of knowing how to apply corrective feedback when steering or of how to justify beliefs and opinions. We refer to this type of knowledge as *procedural knowledge*.

In practice, however, most activities require a transaction between both types of knowledge, with the relative weight depending on the nature of the activity. When writing a report, for example, we need to know not only about the topic (*propositional knowledge*) but also how to select the salient points, provide supporting justification, and compose them into a rhetorically effective structure (procedural knowledge). Moreover, as with propositional knowledge, procedural knowledge has to be constructed through personal engagement in the activities in which such knowledge is enacted. On the other hand, unlike formal propositional knowledge, which tends to be tied to specific domains, the sorts of routines and strategies that constitute procedural knowledge, once acquired, may be applied *in principle* across a range of domains.

Research has drawn attention to another type of knowledge, *metacognition,* or knowledge about one's own mental processes and the control of these processes to achieve one's intended goals. As with the other forms of knowledge, metacognition is constructed by the individual. Instead of resulting from direct engagement in activities, however, it arises from reflection on how one engages in these activities and, in particular, on the procedures used.[1]

However, to argue that all types of knowledge are individually constructed is not to ignore the role of other people in the process. Studies of language acquisition clearly show the contribution of the child's parents and other caretakers in providing the evidence on which the child constructs his or her representation of the language system and in facilitating the acquisition process through the contingent responsiveness of their style of conversation with the child (Bruner, 1983; Wells, 1985). Similarly, the mother's manner of engaging with the child in a construction task was shown to be positively correlated with the child's success in learning to perform the task (Wood, Bruner, & Ross, 1976). However, in neither children's learning of language nor their learning through linguistic interaction do the parents of the more successful children attempt to assist them through direct instruction.

This follows from the view adopted here of coming to know, whether during the preschool years or the subsequent stage of formal education. Because knowledge has to be individually constructed, it cannot be transmitted from one individual to another simply by uttering the appropriate propositions, despite what many educational theorists seem to believe.[2] The interpretations that individual listeners place on what they hear or read depends on their existing understanding and on their interpretations of the total context in which the propositions are encountered. If learners are to come to know what their teachers know, therefore, more is required than the presentation of propositional knowledge through talk or text. As well as the presentation of the new information, there needs to be extended opportunity for discussion and problem-solving in the context of shared activities, in which meaning and action are collaboratively constructed and negotiated. In other words, education must be thought of in terms not of the transmission of knowledge but of transaction and transformation.

In arriving at this perspective, we, like others, have been strongly influenced by Vygotsky's ideas about the development of higher psychological functions and, in particular, by his concept of the "zone of proximal development" (Vygotsky, 1978). With his emphasis on the sociocultural origin of these psychological functions and through his theorizing of the means whereby the cultural becomes internalized to become the individual, Vygotsky has given us a framework within which to explore the conception of education as transaction. In the body of this chapter we intend to explore the implications of this framework further through the analysis of a number of episodes of classroom discourse.

Our aim in presenting and analyzing these data is to address two themes, both of which we believe are natural extensions of Vygotskian ideas about school learning. The first concerns the role of literacy in the sort of learning that Vygotsky considered to be characteristic of schooling. The second concerns factors that shape interaction in the zone of proximal development over and above the cognitive, for example, institutional factors such as role relationships and interpersonal factors such as individual differences in mental and affective representations.

School Learning and Literacy

Discussing the relation between learning and development, Vygotsky contrasted school learning with preschool learning as follows: "Learning as it occurs in the preschool years differs markedly from school learning, which is concerned with the assimilation of the fundamentals of scientific knowledge" (1978, p. 84). What he meant by "the fundamentals of scientific knowledge" was left unexplained, but from statements gleaned from elsewhere in his translated writings (Wertsch, 1985, Chap. 4), it seems that what he had in mind involves at least three dimensions of change in mental functioning that are associated with the processes of schooling in modern society.

The first dimension has to do with what he called the "intellectualization" of mental functions, that is, the process of bringing them under conscious and voluntary control. This process depends heavily on the mediational function of the symbolic-communicative systems of language, which enable the mental functions themselves to be made the object of attention and reflection. This dimension of change seems to have much in common with what was described above as the development of metacognitive knowledge and control.

The second dimension has to do with "decontextualization," the ability to detach a concept from the particular spatiotemporal contexts in which it was first encountered or, at a different level, to distinguish what is said in a text from what the text means in a particular context. This ability is crucial for exploitation of the symbolic property of linguistic signs when reasoning, as the oft-repeated account of the Central Asian peasants' difficulty with the syllogism concerning bears in Novaya Zemlya so clearly illustrates (Luria,

1976). Decontextualizing, along with drawing appropriate inferences from the set of propositions that make up a text, or recombining propositions in a different way in order to make a point in an effective rhetorical manner, is an instance of the sort of knowhow that was referred to earlier as procedural knowledge.

The third dimension of the change in mental functioning associated with schooling is a movement toward the integration and systematization of what is known within the formal frameworks provided by theoretical knowledge. To some extent it can be seen as an outcome of the first two types of change that have already been discussed. When what has been learned from experience can be symbolically represented and deliberately thought about, patterns and connections become apparent that are not noticed by an unreflective mind. However, more is required if thinking is to be described as theoretical. First, in addition to being able to represent his or her beliefs in the form of coherently related sets of propositions, the learner is also expected to be able to justify those beliefs. Second, he or she is expected to be able to formulate knowledge in a variety of spoken or written genres according to the task in hand. This involves being able to use, over and above the narrative, those genres that are associated with what Bruner (1986), by contrast, called the 'paradigmatic' or logicoscientific mode of thinking.

Unlike metacognitive and procedural knowledge, which potentially applies across domains, the extent to which propositional knowledge is formally organized in terms of explicit theories is uneven across substantive domains. In modern societies, formal or scientific ways of thinking exist side by side with less formal ways of thinking. When predicting the weather, for example, appeal is made to such saws as "evening red and morning gray, sets the traveler on his way," as well as to the short-term and long-term weather forecasts prepared by meteorologists. Similarly for individuals, knowledge in some areas of experience is formally organized in terms of coherent overarching theories, and in others it takes the form of *ad hoc* assemblages of information with no consistent organization. One of the main aims of schooling, we would argue, is by systematically engaging with specific substantive areas of experience to enable students to develop metacognitive and procedural knowledge, which can then be brought to bear in formalizing their propositional knowledge in yet other domains.

However, what is significant with respect to all of these dimensions of change in mental functioning is that they are dependent on literacy, when this is understood not simply as the encoding and decoding of written language or the use of written texts for functional purposes but as engaging with texts of all kinds in ways that exploit the symbolic representation of meaning as a means of empowering intrapersonal mental activity (Wells, 1987; 1990). It is precisely the development of the ability and disposition to engage in "literate thinking" (Langer, 1987) through the use of texts that is the school's major responsibility in literate societies. However, this responsibility is fulfilled, we argue, only when students are enabled and encouraged to engage with texts in an "epistemic" mode across a wide range of domains and for a variety of purposes, so that literate thinking becomes pervasive in their lives both inside and outside the classroom.[3]

Where students *are* encouraged to engage with texts epistemically, they discover three important functions that literacy serves, in addition to the transmission of information to facilitate social action. It enables:

1. Accumulation and organization of information in a systematic and formal manner
2. Fixing of meaning in a permanent, decontextualized form, which allows for comparative interpretation and revision
3. Objectification of the outcome of thinking, which facilitates reflection on the thinking processes involved

During the development of the intrapsychological functions of the individual, we suggest, these functions of literacy correspond, respectively, to the construction of domain-specific propositional knowledge, the acquisition of procedural knowledge for operating on texts as representations of propositional knowledge, and the emergence of metacognition, or what Vygotsky called the "intellectualization of mental functions." It seems, therefore, that it is the development of literate thinking in particular, rather than schooling in general, that makes possible the construction of scientific concepts and hence the evolution of higher mental processes.

From Interpersonal to Intrapersonal

It is in relation to the attempt to explain how this goal of school learning is achieved, however, that Vygotsky's thinking has been most productive, although it was in the context of studies of first-language development that its significance was perhaps first seen. Here the problem was to square the recognition that language is a cultural system that preexists the individual child's learning of it with the compelling evidence that the course this learning takes is determined as much by the self-directed constructive efforts of the learner as by the instruction provided by the members of the learner's community.

Although there had been little research on language acquisition at the time Vygotsky was writing, he prefigured the explanations that have been proposed in more recent years. In a brief comment on the early development of speech he introduced the concept of the zone of proximal development (ZPD), in which he stated that "learning and development are inter-related from the child's very first day of life"; he then went on to theorize how, through participation in collaborative activity with an adult or more able peer, children are able to "grow into the intellectual life of those around them" (1978, p. 88). When developing Vygotsky's ideas in recent years, child language researchers have made appeal to such notions as "the guided reinvention of language" (Lock, 1980), "the language acquisition support system" (Bruner, 1983), or, quite explicitly, learning in the ZPD (Wells, 1985). These same ideas, we believe, can also illuminate the ways in which classroom discourse—and, more particularly interactions between people about texts—provide opportunities for the internalization and subsequent utilization of literate modes of thinking and communicating.

A full understanding of *internalization*—the process whereby the individual, through participation in interpersonal interaction in which cultural ways of thinking are demonstrated in action, is able to appropriate them so they become transformed from being social phenomena to being part of his or her own intrapersonal mental functioning (Cole, 1985)—has yet to be achieved (Bereiter, 1985). Nevertheless, it is clear that the process (1) involves the construction rather than the copying of the function in question; (2) depends on the mastery of the appropriate cultural system of symbolic representation; and (3) takes place through social interaction (Wertsch, 1985). Not surprisingly such a specification, with some modifications, is not very different from one that might be given of what is involved in comprehending a speaker's or writer's message in any linguistic interaction.

During conversational interactions, speakers formulate linguistic representations of their meaning intentions with respect to the matter at hand. Listeners, similarly, use their understanding of the matter at hand, together with their construal of the situation in which they are jointly engaged and of the speaker's likely intentions in that situation, to construct a plausible interpretation of the meaning of the observable linguistic (and paralinguistic) signs. Both participants modify their representations in light of the feedback they receive on their own formulations from the contributions of the other participant(s). In this way, although the meanings intended by the speaker are not copied into the mind of the listener and vice versa in the next turn, the interpersonal interaction provides a forum in which the participants calibrate their representations of events and states of affairs against those of the other participants and realign and extend their existing mental models to assimilate or accommodate to new or alternative information.

The same interactions that allow calibration of substantive knowledge also provide enactments of the procedural knowledge that participants deploy when constructing and operating on that propositional knowledge. Thus it is in conversational meaning-making, with the support and scaffolding provided by an adult, that the learner, through engaging in the moves of discourse, is enabled to enact the mental procedures involved, even though he or she may not yet have a full understanding of the significance of the moves that are made. As Wertsch and Stone (1985, p. 166) put it:

> One of the correlates of the fact that interpsychological semiotic processes require the use of external sign forms is that it is possible to produce such forms without recognizing the full significance that is normally attached to them by others. As a result, it is possible for the child to produce seemingly appropriate communication behavior before recognizing all aspects of its significance as understood by more experienced members of the culture. One of the mechanisms that makes possible the cognitive development and

general acculturation of the child is the process of coming to recognize the significance of the external sign forms that he or she has already been using in social interaction. In more informal terms our claim is that children can say more than they realize and that it is through coming to understand what is meant by what is said that their cognitive skills develop.

This same process applies, we would argue, in at least some episodes of classroom discourse. As children talk with a more expert member of the literate community about texts, created either by themselves or others, they encounter, externalized in discourse, the knowledge that is called on in literate thinking about the topic of the text. This includes propositional knowledge about the topic and procedural knowledge about how to engage appropriately with the text; it may also involve metacognitive discussion about those procedures or about the nature and organization of their propositional knowledge on the topic. Moreover, because they are co-participants in the discourse, they are able to appropriate the ways of speaking and, by discovering their significance through using them appropriately in the context of joint activities, to construct for themselves the corresponding forms of knowledge on the intramental plane. It is thus through talk about texts that children construct and develop facility in the mental activities that are involved in the literate thinking that makes possible the construction of "scientific knowledge."

At the same time, classroom discourse is concerned with more than just the topics that make up the curriculum, viewed from a cognitive perspective. Each individual's understanding of a topic is rooted in his or her experience, which is steeped in personal and cultural values as well as being located in a particular historical and geographical space. In addition, classroom participants—teachers as well as students—bring with them assumptions and preconceptions about appropriate ways of acting and speaking, which may differ markedly from one individual to another. Furthermore, the way in which individuals engage with a topic on any particular occasion depends on their self-image as a learner and on his or her immediate feeling state, which may be affected by factors that have nothing to do with the task in hand. Thus it is not only ideational meanings that must be negotiated during discourse but also attitudes, feelings, values, and in some cases even the right or obligation to participate at all.

What it means, then, to engage in effective discourse in the student's zone of proximal development is more complex than was perhaps originally recognized. Our aim in presenting the following episodes, selected from observations in two classrooms during the course of a 3-year longitudinal study in four schools serving multilingual communities, is to try to understand something of this complexity.

Preparing for the Novel Presentations

The first set of episodes is taken from a project arising from the reading of novels in a grade six class. The students had been working in teacher-assigned groups on a novel appropriate to their reading level. After completing the reading, each group was given the same assignment: to make a presentation to the rest of the class that gave the other students an understanding of the novel. The original instruction was to use both written and oral modes; in practice, most groups chose to include a dramatization of part of the story, a collage of pictures with accompanying explanatory captions, and texts in various written genres, such as newspaper reports, a "Wanted" poster, a letter from one of the characters, and so on. During the presentation, there was also to be an opportunity for discussion between the presenting group and the rest of the class.

The episodes that follow have been selected from a video recording of a complete morning session spent preparing for their presentations. Just prior to the first episode, Helen Whaley, the teacher (T, in the dialogue below), has reviewed the four components with the entire class in the context of putting together their programs. "It is your right to prepare your program whatever way you so desire," she has reminded them, "So long as it achieves your purpose. What is the purpose of your program? That's what you have to keep in mind." By making it clear that the responsibility for planning the programs was the students'—as was the case in preparing the component parts—the teacher ensured that the students believed they had ownership of the finished product. This point was important for giving them the motivation to work at the demanding task of reviewing and revising their programs.[4]

T: Let's find out what things we need to check on to be sure you're ready for presentation. Danny?

D: How organized?

T: How—what things are we going to look at to see if they're organized? We are going to look at organization. Nadir?

N: Does it make sense?

T: If what makes sense?

N: The play

T: All right. So first of all you're going to check the play.

N: Then the written work

T: [*Writing on board*] Does it make sense?

[*The next few turns are spent in discussing the editing of the written texts.*]

T: Anything else we want to check for? Phoung?

P: If the pictures also what's er—*—

T: [*Writes*]

J: What you have to say is * *

T: Yes I'm glad you mentioned this because I'd almost forgotten it but I went back Friday night and I was reading some of those things.
 Make sure your text explains your picture.
 Remember, twenty-four of us have not read your text, so when I went back and took a look at one of the—the picture collages, and underneath it said "This is Judy Horton."

If I didn't know who Judy Horton was it tells me not much more than this is Santa Claus.

[In the next few turns the teacher expands on this example.]

T: But you see you haven't helped me as a reader. If you don't give me a little guidance and if I'm a skier I think skiing, so tell me a little bit about it.

This is important [*writes*]. "Text and picture—what kind of information are you really giving?"

I think everybody needs to take a look at that to make sure you are telling us something significant, not just putting a label on it like "This is a spoon" Huh?

Is there anything else you need to check in your organization? your play? your written work?

We are all assuming something here, I think. We're talking about the written work and we're talking about the play. But we—we've not attended to something that is essential if the play is going to happen and if the written work is going to be explained.

What supports all this?

Ss: We do.

T: YOU do. Right. So what d'you have to know about you as a group? Bev?

B: Who's doing what?

T: Right [*writes*]. "Do we know who's doing what? And do *they* know they're doing it?"

In a previous paper (Wells, Chang, & Maher, 1990), we distinguished three broad modes of interaction commonly observed in the classroom: presentation, collaborative talk, and interaction with self. A further distinction was made within collaborative talk: talk between peers of approximately equal expertise in the context of a task in which they are jointly engaged, and talk in which one of the participants (usually a teacher) draws on his or her greater expertise to provide tutorial support and guidance. This episode is clearly an example of collaborative talk, with the teacher acting in a tutorial role. Her aim is to help the class to decide on the criteria to be used by the groups in reviewing their presentations, the chief of which is: "Does it make sense?" In terms of the distinction made in the first section of this chapter, she is helping them to bring their procedural knowledge to bear when deciding whether their texts are both informative and internally consistent. At the same time, by soliciting and then herself offering explanations of the need to check their presentations in this way, she is inviting them to engage in a metacognitive activity. She wants them to understand the importance of taking account of the needs of the audience: "Make sure your text explains your picture. Remember 24 of us have not read your text"; "make sure you are telling us something significant."

Left to themselves, most of the students would probably neglect the audience's needs. Indeed, the teacher had noticed that some of the captions for their pictures were not particularly informative. Familiar with the story themselves, they had failed to see that what was clear to them would be uninterpretable by those who lacked their knowledge of the story. However, with the scaffolding provided by her questions and prompts, the students were able to construct a set of criteria to use for reviewing their material and, as we shall see in the following episodes, to apply these criteria to the texts that they had created.

The teacher also addressed another dimension of group work: the need for explicit agreement about the organization of the joint activity. This point and the need to find ways of resolving disagreement had been a secondary, but prevailing, concern throughout the project, and it runs, as a subtext, through each of the episodes that follow. In a class of young adolescents from varied cultural backgrounds, allegiances and antagonisms based on culture or gender can easily lead to disruption of a group's activities. As Tharp and Gallimore observed, cooperative group activity "will be influenced by the cultural repertoires of students more strongly than will any other setting" (1989, p. 184). These problems therefore need to be recognized and addressed. In the class discussion, the issue was raised as one of group members knowing "who's doing what," and the teacher, because of her professional interest in physical education, drew an analogy, as she frequently did, from the domain of team sports.

A short while later, the issue surfaces again when, having agreed to what has to be done, the class splits into groups to check on their presentations and prepare their programs. Within minutes, Danny approaches the teacher to ask for her help. His group, which includes Andrew, Govinda, Julie, Minh, Nadir, and Phuong, is having difficulty. They are, as he puts it, "in chaos." As they give their different versions of what has happened, the nature of the problem makes clear the importance of interpersonal collaboration as a factor that mediates both learning and task performance.

The immediate problem is that three picture collages had been produced within the group, and as they began to consider how to organize their presentation they had become concerned about the considerable amount of overlap in their contents. As they relate the sequence of events, it becomes clear that this situation had arisen because different subgroups had worked on the collages without consultation among them. Not surprisingly, the subgroups had tended to duplicate material.

The teacher tackles the problem by focusing on the collages, one at a time. They start by examining the one prepared by Julie. Julie prefers to work with one particular girlfriend or alone, and she has found it difficult to collaborate with the rest of the group. Her independence—admirable in some contexts—has generated some resentment among a few of the other students, which accounts for their proposal that it should be Julie's collage that is first subjected to scrutiny. As one of them says about it, "We don't know nothing." Not surprisingly, this puts Julie on the defensive. In the discussion that ensues, therefore, more is at stake for her than for the other students. Although less clearly represented in the transcript than the ideational content of the talk, this affective dimension is just as important as the ostensible topic in determining the course that the discussion takes.

The teacher chooses to address the interpersonal problem indirectly by inviting the group to look closely at the individual collages. In so doing, she avoids the emotionally charged issue of collaboration, or lack of it, and gets the group to attend to a more intellectual dimension of their task. What becomes apparent as they consider particular picture-caption items is the differences that exist between them in the mental representations they have formed of the characters and events in the novel on the basis of their individual reading. Moreover, because they have been engaged in parallel rather than joint activity in the preparation of the collages, there has been no occasion to compare their representations in collaborative talk and so to discover and reconcile differences in their interpretation of the text. Not surprisingly, therefore, the criteria used for selecting pictures they cut out of magazines have differed from one individual to another. For example, whereas the age of the character is the most important factor for one student, it is the hair color for another and the background against which the character appears for yet another.

Although it was Julie's unwillingness to work with boys and other interpersonal difficulties of this kind that originally led to the group splitting into subgroups, it is now the intellectual consequences of their failure to work together that have to be addressed. With the teacher to help the students face up to them, disagreements about the pictures selected become the basis for some valuable learning about the relation between particular details and the larger text to which they contribute, as is seen in the sequence of episodes that follows. What is here clearly illustrated is the way in which a particular strategy for evaluating the appropriateness of pictures in a collage is first introduced into the interindividual space of the joint activity by the teacher. Then, as further pictures are considered, the strategy is taken over by one, and then several, of the students so that by the end of the session most of the students are well on the way to being able to deploy this strategy on their own initiative.

During the first of these episodes, the teacher starts by asking Julie to explain her collage. After she has identified all the pictures, the teacher asks what sort of pictures Julie has chosen to make up her collage, thereby requiring the group to infer the selection criteria she had used. On inspection, they are discovered to be the characters and events significant to the development of the story. More discussion then follows, in which it is agreed that the pictures also contain equipment referred to in the story. It is in relation to one such piece of equipment that the following discussion occurs.

T: There's one question I have. What kind of skis are these?

J: I don't know [*softly*].

[*Children lean forward to look more closely. Several suggestions are made, all of them inaudible.*]

T: For use on what or in what conditions?

G: For—⟨ground-⟩

S: * mountains

P: Er— Downhill ski

Ss: Yes

T: Are they?

J: No I don't think so.

N: Slalom?

G: Cross-country?

M: No mountain skis . . . downhill.

[*Several speak at once.*]

T: OK I can see—how many of you people here have ever water-skied?

A: Those are water skis?

D: Those are water skis?

T: Those are water skis.

?: * * * *

Ss: Oh yeah.

T: If you've never water-skied you might not pick this up.

[*Several laugh.*]

T: But you were right when you said slalom but they're slalom water-skis. Er—they have a totally different—er—size and um [*Ss laughs*] and cr— binding. But because you have never water-skied you didn't pick that up.

I have here somewhere in our books a whole bunch of winter—skiing— er—magazines, where you can get pictures of winter skis.

J: I think we saw that book.

T: You probably saw it. I think this is a marvelous idea to have a ski pic- ture, but let's make sure we get skis for winter conditions.

Maybe I'm the only one who will notice the difference but since I noticed [*laughs*] let's see if we can fix that up.

This episode is a good example of joint meaning-making as they con- sider whether the overall requirement—to make sure that their material "makes sense"—has been met. Noticing an inconsistent detail (people do not use water skis to make an escape down a snowy mountain side), the teacher invites the group to join with her in articulating the mismatch between the information provided in the text and the information con- veyed by the selected picture. The understanding that is thereby jointly con- structed is the requirement for internal consistency between all the details that make up the "possible world" created by the novelist and now repre- sented by the students in their collages.

T: OK Let's have some explanation.

[*seeing hand up*] OK. Question.

D: It's supposed to be snowing.

T: Yes.

A: This is summer [*referring to the background in one of the pictures*].

D: . . . and it's summer.

T: OK. All right [*agreeing*].

J: <u>It's just maybe</u> * *

D: <u>They should be</u> wearing, well, warmer clothes.

J: Yeah ⟨but it's going to be summer⟩.

D: But they came * in the winter so—

T: <u>How—</u>

T: <u>How could we</u> - ..

P: <u>and came out as</u> * *

T: <u>—satisfy</u> the fact that the background looks like summer but we want
the back— background to look like winter? What can you do?

P: <u>Make snowflakes.</u>

G: * the background *

This first example was the result of Julie's ignorance about the appearance of different types of skis. However, once the students have been alerted to the importance of consistency of detail between novel and collage, they begin to find other discrepancies. Danny is the first. Looking at another of Julie's chosen pictures, he objects, "It's supposed to be snowing—and it's summer" (referring to the background in the picture), and the group goes on to discuss possible ways of overcoming this difficulty. "Excellent suggestion," comments the teacher, "then you get rid of the conflicting information."

In the next few minutes, other students find further discrepancies and, for each, suggestions are made for resolving the problem. From the discourse, it is clear that what had initially been an interpsychological procedure, directed by the teacher, has now been appropriated by several of the students, who are able to initiate further cycles—at least in the context of this rather competitive social setting.

From Julie's perspective, on the other hand, these episodes are much less satisfactory. First one, then another, of her chosen pictures is being criticized, and her attempts to justify her selections are given little attention. However, not all the comments are entirely negative. As the group is examining the picture to which Danny objected, Andrew makes a suggestion that is more sensitive to Julie's feelings. He proposes to "cut out the man—and get another background." This compromise recognizes the validity of the (unexpressed) criteria that Julie had used in selecting the type of man to be represented, while finding a way of making the picture as a whole match the winter setting of the novel. Julie willingly agrees to this suggestion.

A few minutes later, Phuong points to another picture she considers to be discrepant according to her personal criteria.

T: Yes, Phuong?

P: The dog isn't Arthur [= *the dog in the picture isn't appropriate*].

Ss: Yeah [*laughs*] * *

J: But it's hard to find a dog that's Arthur.

G: It doesn't matter. It's a dog

A: [*To P*] How do you know how it [*i.e., Arthur, the dog*] looks?

D: I know * *

P: From the book.

D: He's a husky.

P: Oh yeah.

A: Or Japanese Ikitza.

J: He looks like a timber wolf or—

T: [*laughs*] You've got a good point. Sometimes you'll get too precise then you'll—you'll cause yourself to come to a grinding stop because you may not find a picture of a husky with the exact coloring.

[*The next few turns are concerned with deciding how important accuracy is.*]

T: Do you think—You've really got a choice.
      If you can't find a picture of that kind of dog, then are you saying don't use any dog at all or use a dog and say this represents Arthur?

A: * choose a dog that represents Arthur

P: Don't use a dog.

G: Use a dog.

T: Is Arthur important to the story?

J, G, A, & M: [*in chorus*] Yes.

D & L: [*in chorus*] No.

J, G, A, & M: [*in chorus*] Yeah.

D: What did he do?

P: He ran away.

S: He got—he got—he came back with the people, remember?

G: Yeah. He—he helped them out of the tunnel. *

A & N: Yeah.

A: Remember when he was trapped in the tunnel * * *

[*Several speak at once.*]

A: * * out then he followed Arthur all the way round and ⟨dragged⟩ him out

G: Yeah.

N: Yeah.

[*Several speak at once in agreement.*]

T: I've got another question. How is it they got lost?

A: Arthur.

N: Arthur.

T: Is Arthur important?

A, N, & G: Yeah.

T: OK.

As can be seen, what was initially a teacher-directed strategy has now become a group strategy for reviewing the pictures as interpretations of elements in the novel. However, in this episode, as they consider the picture of Arthur, the teacher introduces another interpretive strategy. As well as asking whether the picture is accurate in relation to the novel, she suggests they also ask whether the element depicted is of critical importance to the story. To answer this question requires not only an understanding of the story but an ability to hold the whole story in mind in order to evaluate the relative significance of the various constitutive roles the characters play in shaping the narrative.

In arriving at the decision that the inclusion of a picture of Arthur is justified, they have considered a number of episodes in the story in which he has a significant role. Clearly, Arthur is important. But does the picture have to show a husky? Pragmatic considerations come to bear here. It has not proved possible to find a picture of a husky, but the picture Julie has selected is not too inappropriate. In any case, as Govinda points out, the rest of the class has not read the novel and so does not know what sort of dog was involved; moreover, in the play they have prepared, the type of dog is not specifically mentioned. Julie's picture can therefore remain.

Although it is not obvious in the transcript, paralinguistic behavior such as Julie's facial expression and the critical edge in Phuong's intonation, which are clearly evident on the videotape, serve to alert the teacher to the feelings that are being generated in Julie by peers, who tend to be too critical. Thus to offset what might be potentially negative consequences of some of the children's moves in the interaction, the teacher turns it from being an issue charged by emotions to one that is academic by posing the fundamental question: "Is Arthur important to the story?" More importantly, the function of her moves is to nudge the children into engaging in the mental operations necessary to access and identify requisite information from the mental representation they have of the novel as a whole. It also enables them to include in their consciousness a distillation of elements from experiences that are critical for a decision about the dog because they exemplify relations such as those of cause or consequence.

The episodes we have just examined all occurred in one phase of a larger project, the purpose of which, in the teacher's words, was "to show that you have understood what you have read by explaining the story" through different forms of re-presentation. In an obvious sense, this is a task that would fit almost any definition of literacy: It starts from reading a novel and leads to the production of further texts in a variety of genres.

However, we wish to suggest that because of the procedures required to carry out the task and because of the conscious understanding of these procedures that is explicitly promoted in the whole-class and group interactions, the activity is literate in a more profound sense. As a result of the requirement that each group "re-present" their understanding of the novel they have read in a number of different modes, the students are pushed to engage with all the texts involved in an epistemic mode, evaluating significance, checking for intertextual consistency of detail, and disembedding their understanding of the various parts of their presentation from the total story context in order to make their texts intelligible to an uninformed audience.

Yukon Project: Getting Started

In the previous section, we saw students working with relative success in collaborative groups on topics they had had a large part in choosing. However, the ability to choose a topic for investigation, as well as the strategies necessary for working collaboratively in a group, do not emerge spontaneously; they must be learned. How to get started on a collaborative project is the issue that is addressed in the following episodes, selected from observations made during the course of one unit of work in a grade three/four class in a school serving a multiethnic neighborhood.

For two weeks in February the complete program of the entire school was devoted to the theme of winter. Ann Maher, the grade three/four teacher, introduced the theme to her class with a reading of the ballad "The Cremation of Sam McGee" by Robert Service, which recounts the death due to extreme cold and subsequent unconventional cremation of Sam McGee, a gold prospector and miner from Tennessee. The class then spent two days in group work, designing and making displays to advertise the book. After a second reading of the ballad, the teacher asked the children to suggest ideas for topics arising from the poem that they would be interested in studying. A great variety of ideas was suggested, all of them focusing on the Yukon as a cold and wintry place. As the questions were proposed, the teacher wrote them on the blackboard; after 30 minutes or so she helped the class group them into a number of superordinate categories, such as climate, travel, and discovery.

As in the previous classroom, the teacher was concerned about providing a framework in which the projects could be carried out by the children. Therefore, the following morning, as they were reviewing the questions that had been suggested, she explained how the superordinate categories they had used to group them could be related to terms such as 'history', 'geography', and 'science', which label school subjects and are also used to organize the arrangement of books in the library. From the discussion that followed, it was clear that these terms were new to all but one or two of the children. However, by introducing them and helping the children to use them in relation to their own specific questions, she was, in the words of Wertsch and Stone (1985), enabling them gradually to come to understand "what is meant by what is said" and so to extend their repertoire of ways of making sense of the information they would meet in school.

Having introduced these new ideas, the teacher returned to the more practical matter of getting started on their particular projects. The emphasis, in her characterization of the task, was on "exploring" and "finding out."

At this stage, it was the development of strategies for embarking on an inquiry that was her first objective, as is illustrated in the first episode presented below. Once the children had made a choice, however, the substantive topics of their inquiries and appropriate methods for tackling them were given greater prominence, as is seen in later episodes.

The first episode occurred just after the morning recess, which followed the discussion referred to above. When the children returned, the teacher met with each of the still-forming groups to discuss their plans. The first group consisted of Brian and Kim, whom the teacher rightly judged to need considerable help in finding a topic.

T: Do you want to come here and think about what projects you're going to work on? But what—what really interests *you?*

Things about the animals? the people?

B: Yukon.

T: What about the Yukon in particular do you think you'd like to study? Have you thought about that? Mm?

B: * * I started that already. I started one or two questions.

T: Oh, you have some questions? Which—which ones are you really interested in answering? What are your questions?

B: My thing is on my desk.

T: Don't remember what they are?

D'you want to go and get them?

B: Yeah.

[*Brian goes to fetch his paper. While he is gone, she turns to Kim, who has been standing listening.*]

T: Kim? Have you started to think about what questions you'd like to have answered? [*Kim looks at her but does not answer.*]

Maybe you could start by looking over some other people's questions; that might give you an idea of something that you would like to find out. [*Turning to Brian, who has returned with his paper.*]

Mm! These are yours that you're interested in studying, are they? [*reads*] "Why did the people got the name of Yukon in Canada?"

It sounds like you're interested in studying what happened when the first people discovered or found the Yukon.

Is that what you're interested in? Why they named it that? Is that what interests you Brian? Uh-huh.

[*reads*] "Why do people live—" It looks like that question isn't finished. What else were you going to say?

B: They hunt.

T: That's a very interesting question. I'd be interested in that one too. Do we have any books or materials around here where you might start to look for some answers?

You don't know? Well, why don't you start to look through some and see if you can find any. If you have any more questions add them to your sheet. Do you know what to do now?

B: [*nods*]

T: Are you going to work on your own or with somebody else?

[*Brian looks at Kim.*]

T: So you might—you two might talk about it to see if you're both interested in—in studying about the history of the Yukon area? You're interested in maps, too, aren't you, Brian?

B: Yeah.

T: Yeah. I wonder if there's some way you could work on the map of the Yukon, too. Think that would fit into your question?

B: Yeah.

[*T turns to Kim, who asks about Tennessee.*]

T: Tennessee is in the—in the United States. If we get—um—he used to live in Tennessee way down south in the United States. If you get me the globe, I'll show you.

[*Brian and Kim go to fetch the globe.*]

Finding a question that is amenable to investigation is difficult for any researcher. Hence it is not surprising that these two boys, who have never been faced with such a challenge before and who are still learning English, the language of the classroom, find it daunting. Where do you find questions? How do you know whether you would be interested in working on a question once you have found it? As yet, they have no experience to help them answer these questions, so they are tongue-tied in the face of the teacher's helpfully intended questions. She, on the other hand, believes that most topics can prove interesting once one has made a commitment to becoming involved with them. At the same time, however, she knows that it is important to connect with existing interests, so she goes to considerable lengths to try to find out what they are. Brian, at least, offers her some clues in the questions he has written down. Kim, on the other hand, has no ideas as yet. To Kim she suggests the strategy of looking at the questions other people have provided. Knowing that Kim and Brian are friends, she also suggests Kim might work with Brian: "You two might talk about it."

Then she remembers an interest Brian had shown in maps. Perhaps it would be an entry point to finding a topic that would interest them. At this moment Kim fortuitously asks a question about Tennessee, the home of Sam McGee, and the teacher, seeing here a more specific topic with which to capture the boys' interest and attention, sends them off to fetch the globe while she spends a few minutes with another group.

When the teacher rejoins them, they have been exploring the globe for some minutes. With her help, they look first for Tennessee and then the Yukon, and they then discuss the distance between them. Looking farther afield, the boys notice with surprise how small England is. They go on to talk about countries represented on the globe while the teacher talks with another child. Finally, she turns back to Brian and Kim.

T: OK, I want to talk to you two. Now you've spent a lot of time looking at the globe, haven't you? You look both very interested in maps. I wonder

if you could try and draw a map as part of your project? Would that interest
you?

[*B and K look dubious.*]

T: You could do the * *

B: Too hard.

T: For you? Well how about—

B: Tracing.

T: Tracing? Pretty small; that's the only trouble, isn't it?

[*two inaudible utterances*]

T: Would you feel brave enough to try to draw one to make it larger? You
could just use a—a scrap of paper and try it out. Do a rough copy to see how
it works. You never know it might work * * * . Want to try a rough copy?

B: [*still somewhat reluctant*] ⟨I don't know⟩

T: Well, who's going to know if you don't know? How about you, Kim?
Do you want to try?

K: * * * *

T: It's a good idea to try it out. If you want to go to the cupboard and just
take a piece of—you know the big paper—the newsprint—just for a rough
copy. OK? And see how it works out. If you don't try it, you'll never know.

B: OK.

At one level, this episode is still concerned with finding a topic that might
interest the two boys. The teacher thinks that if they started to draw a map
they might become more involved with the information that the map represented or even with the whole issue of the ways in which information is
graphically represented in maps. At another level, the issue is one of developing interest, which is intrinsic to much of children's motivation to learn.
Brian and Kim's initial reactions to drawing a map are not enthusiastic: It's
"too hard." Tentatively, Brian suggests tracing instead, but, as the teacher
says, the map would be pretty small.

Brian's response clearly expresses resistance. One possible explanation is
that he is not sufficiently interested in drawing a map to wish to undertake
such a challenging task. He had, after all, proposed two questions of his own
and neither of them involved maps. An alternative explanation is that,
although he is genuinely interested in maps, the free-hand drawing the
teacher is suggesting seems to him to be beyond his capabilities.

The teacher, on the other hand, concerned to get the two boys started,
recognizes the affective dimension behind what appears to be an unwillingness to take a risk. The strategy she initially adopts is to emphasize that it's
only "a rough copy to see how it works." The implication is that if it does
not work they can throw it away. Still somewhat reluctantly, the two boys
allow themselves to be persuaded.

The problem the teacher diagnosed here is not an uncommon one.
Viewed from the teacher's perspective, fear of failure or of making mistakes
holds back many learners from committing themselves to tasks that appear
to them to be too challenging. Without that involvement, however, there is

no opportunity for learning. Hence they must be nudged into making a start on *something* if they are to derive any benefit from this unit of work. On the other hand, the boys did not have an identical agenda between them or with the teacher; it is not surprising, therefore, that there is reluctance on their part when they know they are being coerced into doing something together.

In many classrooms, the teacher would resolve the problem by simply telling them what to do. However, although this solution might overcome the immediate difficulty, it would not solve the underlying problem. Children can only become active inquirers in the classroom by being given the space to explore alternatives, whether they are suggested by the teacher or by themselves. Opportunities must also be provided to develop the interest and curiosity that are so important to energize learning. It was this knowledge that was behind the teacher's actions in making the link between Tennessee and the Yukon and in giving the boys some time to be by themselves so their curiosity might be whetted.

Throughout this project, through episodes of interaction such as those examined here, the teacher provided for Brian and Kim and for other children like them appropriate scaffolding within which they could learn to choose a question for study and learn to take a risk. To create this scaffolding involves a teacher attending to the relation between children's affects and the learning tasks they undertake. And this, in turn, requires teachers not only to be sensitive to the children's degree of involvement in interaction with them but also to engage in talk with them in ways that develop the children's involvement and affects.

The next episode involves another pair of boys, Sean and Jeffrey. They have already settled on their topic and are engaged in generating questions to guide their research. In contrast to the previous pair, it is clear that Sean does not lack confidence or decisiveness. On the contrary, he is quite sure about what he is doing. Jeffrey, too, in his own estimation is making good progress with his questions. However, having different ideas about what constitutes a good question, they are having difficulty working together. Their raised voices can be heard in the background, as they argue about what information to include in their project on wolves. The teacher goes to try to help them sort out their problem.

> T: You know, I've got a suggestion, boys. You're both doing the same topic.
> You might—you might find it easier to deal with if you both took your own piece of paper and did your reading and your writing, and when you've found out your answers then you talk about how you can work together for your good copy of your project.
> Would that—
> S: Yeah, but he's putting down answers that we all know already.
> T: That's all right.
> J: Maybe not [= *maybe not everybody knows*].
> T: Maybe not. That's true.

S: Well, I already know.

J: But I'm ⟨going to tell⟩.

T: [*To Sean*] Yeah, but just because you know—

J: So maybe people don't know. You know but maybe other people don't know.

T: Good point, Jeff, good point.

S: He said um—"Why do they go hunting?" and * * * those guys even know * * * for food.

J: Well maybe other people don't know [*truculently*].

T: Jeff, Jeff. Sounds to me like you have a different idea of what you write down on a project to Sean and that's all right. That's what makes it so interesting is the way different people answer the questions—even the questions they think about. I wouldn't be concerned about that.

Why—why don't you think about using a piece of paper of your own, for your rough copy anyway.

S: OK.

T: [*to Jeffrey*] Want to think about that?

The benefits of collaboration between peers for learning through inquiry have been argued by others than Vygotsky (e.g., Sharan & Sharan, 1976; Slavin, 1983), and they can be seen in the episodes from the novel study discussed above. However, as both theorists and practitioners are aware, these benefits do not follow automatically from providing opportunities for children to work in groups on topics of their own choosing. Children have to learn how to deal with differences of opinion at all levels, from deciding on the topic to be investigated to the distribution of responsibility for carrying out the various constituent tasks.

On the surface, the disagreement between Sean and Jeffrey appears to be about the sort of information that it will be appropriate to present to their classmates. Sean is taking his own level of knowledge about wolves as the criterion for deciding about what further questions should be posed, whereas Jeffrey recognizes that some members of their potential audience may be less well informed than they. Lurking underneath the surface, however, is a more threatening difference: the images the two boys have of themselves and of each other. Jeffrey feels that his ability is being questioned when Sean objects to his questions, and in his vigorous defense of possibly less knowledgeable peers it is not difficult to hear an assertion of his own worth.

The teacher is clearly sensitive to this affective dimension of the disagreement, and by emphasizing the positive value of alternative ways of thinking, she validates both Sean's and Jeffrey's ways of approaching their topic. A common perspective, if it is to be an effective basis for joint activity, cannot be imposed by one participant on the other but must be achieved through positive recognition of alternative points of view and their eventual synthesis or by the voluntary acceptance by one of the participants of the greater validity of the other's arguments. Recognizing that neither of these options has much chance of success at this moment, the teacher suggests a temporary strategy—that of working independently on their first drafts. This will allow each boy to follow his own chosen course while leaving open the possibility of collaborating later on the final outcome of their project.

The final episode we wish to consider comes from a later stage in this unit of work. We have chosen it because, in contrast to the previous episode, it illustrates how differences in level of ability within a group can be used to everyone's advantage. In its focus on the co-construction of an explanation, it also provides another example of apprenticeship in literate thinking through oral interaction. However, what makes this episode different from those considered so far is that the "text" under discussion here is an artifact that the child has constructed. Nevertheless, in important respects, we argue, this artifact functions in much the same manner as the collage texts in the grade six classroom discussed above to elicit an epistemic engagement.

Marilda is a grade four student, who is spending her second year at this grade level. Her topic is the weather and, in particular, the sun's effect in producing convection currents in the air to give rise to wind. As a result of reading a book of experiments to perform, Marilda has made a weather vane by stapling a rectangle of stiff paper, 3 inches by 2 inches, to one end of a drinking straw and fixing the straw to the eraser on the end of a pencil with a needle so the straw pivots around the needle. The straw itself rests on a wooden bead, which functions as a washer to ensure that the straw swings freely. With her friend Jacinta, she has taken her "windfinder," as she calls it, into the school yard to test it; in the classroom the two of them have also simulated the wind by blowing at the apparatus. At this point she takes the windfinder to show it to the teacher.

M: Miss * [*trying to attract T's attention for 10 seconds*] It's here, my windfinder.
T: OK, so here's your windfinder. That's a good name for it, isn't it?
[*Marilda blows windfinder.*]

T: Eric, have you seen this windfinder?
E: Yes, last year we were studying about it.
T: Uh-huh. [*to Marilda*] Can you explain—can you explain how it works?
S: [*who is passing*] Yes, I know how it works.
E: ***
T: Oh I—I—excuse me, Eric, I was really—I was really talking to Marilda. [*to Rosa*] Maybe you'd be interested in this. Do you want to come over here?
[*Several children have gathered around, including Jacinta.*]
M: When you—when the wind blows—it's trying to find the wind. When the wind blows this points to which direction it's coming from [*pointing to the pointer on her windfinder*].
J: Yeah, like— * [*takes the windfinder and blows at it, causing the pointer to point at herself. She has done this several times before with Marilda.*]
M: See, it points round to you.

T: Why's it pointing to you? [*Referring to Jacinta, but addressing the question to the whole group.*]

E: Cos she's the one who blew and if you keep um— [*Maggie tries blowing and Jacinta gives her instructions.*]

M: It stays in the same spot cos—cos the wind's—

T: Why?

J: Cos it needs a big surface to blow on, to push it.

T: Come on [*encouraging Marilda to continue*].

M: Cos the—cos the wind's blowing that direction and it—

C: No, why did it go?

M: It's not coming in a different way.

E: Because it doesn't have a piece of paper over here [*pointing to the pointer end*].

J: **

T: What would happen if you had a piece of paper over there?

M: It'd turn around?

J: Because it needs a big surface to blow on to push it.

T: So it's—

E: And that's a big surface.

T: So it's got something to do with the surface of the paper?

Ps: Yeah.

T: And the air?

E: Mm.

M: And the—this thing—maybe [*indicating the bead, which acts as a washer*]—

T: Oh and—

E: It's the needle.

J: ⟨No I think it's got to turn-⟩

E: It's the needle, it's the needle that—well not the needle but the—the straw. It's the straw has the hole.

M: This makes it—

E: The straw has the hole and the hole like causes it to—to make a wiggly turn.

T: Yes [*somewhat doubtfully*].

E: **

M: No, it's this that makes it—

T: Which? The bead?

M: Yeah.

T: The bead. You think the bead is very important?

M: Yeah.

T: Why? Why do you think that's important?

J: Let's try it without the bead.

M: Cos the—

T: That's a good idea. That—that would be a way of finding out if it's really important. First, why do you think the bead's important?

M: Well .. some machines they have a—

E: It's a nuisance.

M: —the little round things—

E: Yes, but some machines don't have them.

T: Ballbearings? You mean ballbearings?

M: Yeah, so maybe like it might make it—might help by spinning it, like spinning.

T: It's got something to do with the spinning and then making it easier to spin. I like your idea, Jacinta. That's a very interesting idea—taking the bead out.

I don't know whether Marilda would want to do that now or not.

J: Want to.

M: OK, I'll try it.

[*Marilda and Jacinta go away to try the experiment.*]

Unlike the other episodes we have considered, this one involves a temporary group. Marilda, delighted with her windfinder and intrigued by its operation, has brought it to share with her teacher, rather as a writer shares his or her first draft with a sympathetic reader. Looking at the construction, the teacher not only shares the student's pleasure but also expresses her genuine interest by asking her how it works. The other children who have gathered round soon join in the discussion.

To have to explain what one knows to another person is an excellent way of discovering just how well-founded that knowledge is. In order to present the matter clearly so another can understand it, one must identify the key elements and make the relations between them explicit. Sometimes this process leads to an increase in one's own understanding, as connections are consciously made and attended to that had previously been glossed over in one's own private thinking. Equally often one finds that there are parts that had seemed clear that are not well understood at all.

For Marilda, the request is timely. She has already made a number of observations that enable her to answer the teacher's question with a descriptive generalization: "When the wind blows, this [pointer] points to which way it's coming from," the accuracy of which is borne out when Jacinta acts as the wind. "See, it points round to you," says Marilda, with satisfaction. This exchange raises another, more difficult question: Why does the windfinder point to the person who is blowing? Juxtaposed in this way, these two utterances bring into sharp focus the distinction between (1) noticing and being able to tell how something works and (2) understanding and being able to explain the principles that underlie its operation. It is the latter that is critical in provoking the hypothesis generation, which is the central feature of this episode of collaborative talk.

During the next few minutes, the question is taken up by most of the children in the group, with Jacinta and Eric taking the lead. Their answers, although incomplete, show that these two children have recognized that the explanation is to be found in the unequal surface areas on either side of the pivot: "Cos it needs a big surface to blow on, to push it" (Jacinta) and "Because it doesn't have a piece of paper over here" (Eric), pointing to the end of the straw with no paper attached). Marilda's own contribution, split over several turns, remains close to the level of direct observation: "It stays in the same spot cos the wind's—cos the wind's blowing that direction and it—it's not coming in a different way." This explanation is certainly relevant to the solution.

The children are not merely competing to give the most acceptable answer, however, even though there is a considerable overlap in their speaking turns. They are clearly also listening to each other and building on each other's contributions, most obviously in Eric's addition to Jacinta's statement:

> **Jacinta:** Because it needs a big surface to blow on to push it.
>
> **Eric:** And that's a big surface [pointing to paper].

In addition, they are attempting to provide justifications for their suggested explanations.

Nor is it only those who seem closest to grasping the explanatory principle who are able to advance their own understanding by making connections in this way. Having had her attention directed to the structure of the weather vane by the other two children and by the teacher's summary, it is Marilda who introduces the possibility that the bead, too, has a facilitating function in enabling the straw to spin freely. Spurred on by each other, all three children have become involved in the inquiry and are attempting to extrapolate from their observations to possible principles of operation. Jacinta's suggestion that they should put Marilda's hypothesis to an empirical test is the obvious next step and the interaction ends with the two friends going off to carry out the experiment.

Compared with some of the earlier episodes, this one shows the children playing a more dominant role in the interaction, as they collaboratively build up a tentative explanation of how the windfinder works. This, however, does not mean the teacher's role is unimportant. On the contrary, we argue that it is her initiating request and her periodic summarizing of what has been said that helps the exploration to proceed in such a focused manner. This is not to suggest that the children might not have asked the questions of their own accord and perhaps come up with similar answers, but the fact that the discussion proceeds as fruitfully as it does owes much to her timely intervention.

Several features are worth a comment. The first is the natural way in which the teacher responds to Marilda's evident pride in her windfinder by drawing other children in to share her interest. In so doing, she creates a genuine audience to whom Marilda can be asked to explain how the windfinder works. Marilda is a child from a Portuguese-speaking family whose experience of school prior to this year had been notably lacking in occasions of success. In fact, her previous teacher had judged it necessary for her to repeat the grade four year. By giving her the chance to be the "expert," the teacher is helping her to develop confidence in herself as a learner, which is crucial if she is to participate actively in the learning opportunities provided. Second, we note the way in which the teacher enables her to receive assistance in performing the task of providing an explanation of how the windfinder works. Recognizing Marilda's limited ability to explain on her own, the teacher indirectly invites the other children to help. The result is both a more complete account of the principles involved in the operation of the windfinder and a collaborative enactment of what it is to give an explanation. From this, Marilda develops sufficient understanding to be able, herself, to suggest a detail that she thinks to be important and also to respond to the teacher's further question: "Why do you think the bead's important?" These two instances of the teacher's sensitive and strategic interaction clearly exemplify how she enables Marilda, with the help of her peers, to perform at a level of competence beyond what she can manage alone.

Finally, we must point up the relevance of this and the previous episodes for the development of literate thinking (Chang & Wells, 1988). Whether it be a simple artifact, as with Marilda's windfinder, or the questions that are to be used to structure an inquiry, or even the topic itself, the teacher treats the children's representations of meaning as texts that need to be engaged with epistemically as they set goals, decide what content to include, and explain and justify their beliefs and intentions. Reviewing these and other episodes with us, as we viewed the video recording together at the end of this unit of work, the teacher expressed her recognition of both the textlike nature of the children's "products" and the importance of collaborative talk about them as the means whereby they appropriate the literate procedures of text-supported thinking and doing, which mediate the "assimilation of the fundamentals of scientific knowledge."

Conclusion

In his development of the theory of learning in the zone of proximal development, Vygotsky did not have access to conversational data of the sort that can now be obtained through the use of audio and videotape recorders. Therefore, although conversational interaction played a central role in his theory, he was able to discuss it only in very general terms. With the aid of these technological devices, however, it is now possible to capture episodes of naturally occurring interaction in a form that allows repeated viewing or hearing of the original "raw" data. The effects of this essentially methodological revolution have been far-reaching, not least in the support they have given to theories of linguistic interaction that emphasize the constructive nature of the acts of listening and reading, as well as those of speaking and writing (de Beaugrande, 1980; Tierney & Pearson, 1984; Wells, 1976). They have also rendered apparent the centrality of the negotiation of meaning in the achievement of intersubjectivity, that is, the construction of "common knowledge" (Edwards & Mercer, 1987), on which the theory of learning through interaction depends (Rommetveit, 1985; Wells, 1981; Wells & Chang, 1989).

As a result of this technological development, a number of investigations have been conducted that draw on recordings of classroom interaction to study the ways in which the learning–teaching relation is enacted in a variety of classroom conditions (e.g., Cazden, 1976; Hammersley, 1977; Mehan, 1979; Michaels, 1986; Tizard & Hughes, 1984). Within this broad area, some researchers have approached the issue from a specifically Vygotskian perspective, studying, for example, the technique of "reciprocal teaching" (Palincsar, 1986; Palincsar et al., this volume), or peer–peer collaboration (Forman & Cazden, 1985). However, the study closest in theoretical perspective to the one from which the episodes presented in this chapter are drawn is the KEEP project (Tharp & Gallimore, 1988), from which we have adopted the term "instructional conversation" to describe the sort of collaborative tutorial talk that occurs in the ep. ᵈes we have presented.

One way in which we have attempted to extend Vygotskian thinking in this chapter, then, is by giving detailed attention to a number of episodes of instructional conversation, in which the teacher attempts to assist the performance of one or more students in the context of a joint activity. In most studies of teacher–student interaction to date, researchers have concentrated on episodes selected from classrooms in which student tasks are, in general, preplanned and initiated by the teacher within a fairly tightly organized schedule. In the classrooms studied here, by contrast, there is much more negotiation: Although the teacher sets the superordinate goals to be met in a unit of work extending over several weeks, the students have a much greater role in selecting and organizing the tasks to achieve them.

Of course, a great deal of the learning that occurs in these classrooms takes place as students work together (more or less) collaboratively, without the involvement of the teacher. We have documented elsewhere episodes of this sort of interaction that occur as students assist each other in the performance of a joint activity (Chang & Wells, 1990, Wells et al., 1990). However, in this chapter we have concentrated on episodes in which the teacher *is* present in order to study the nature of the teacher's interventions in learner-directed activities. In other words, this chapter has examined examples of "contingently responsive instruction," in contrast to examples of the sort of instructional conversation that occurs in teacher-directed activities, which most other researchers have studied. This point is particularly true of the episodes arising from the review of Julie's collage, the disagreement between Sean and Jeff, and Marilda's demonstration of her windfinder.

As we initially viewed and reviewed these episodes, what became apparent to us was the multifaceted nature of the assistance that was given, as the teacher responded to the demands of the task in which the children were engaged, the nature of the texts involved, and the characteristics of the individual children who made up the group. We also recognized that if we were to understand the nature of this assistance we could not afford to ignore the multidimensional nature of the interaction through which it was given. It is the discussion of the complex interplay of these elements during interaction that constitutes the second way in which we have attempted to extend Vygotsky's theory of learning and teaching.

Instructional conversation, in the activity contexts we have explored, is concerned not only with the academic and the intellectual. To attend only to these components is to miss the powerful role that affect plays in motivating and integrating learning and development. Most teachers are intuitively aware of this, as is apparent from observing their nonverbal and paralinguistic behavior. In fact, our observations show that the teachers personalize academic concerns by giving explicit attention to the affective state of the learner as, for example, when Brian's teacher communicated to him her personal knowledge that he was interested in maps. Such expressions of understanding of individual children's feelings and interests are an important component of contingent responsiveness because they play a key role in the establishment and maintenance of intersubjectivity. When studying teacher–student conversation, therefore, it is important to take account of moves that serve a phatic and personalizing function during interaction, as they provide evidence of the ways in which participants give, and respond to, affective cues during conversation. It can thus be seen that the affective dimension of classroom interaction deserves further investigation, both in terms of its influence on the way in which joint activities are played out and with respect to the role it plays in children's emotional and intellectual development.

Cultural heterogencity may also add to the complexity of interaction in many classrooms. For example, cultural variations among participants in their task representations, problem-solving strategies, and mental models may significantly influence the way in which group members interrelate during joint activity and hence determine what is available for each to learn. Sean and Jeff's wolf project and the grade six children preparing the program for their final presentations are cases in point. From these episodes we can see how the manner in which instructional conversation cues and mediates learning becomes even more complex when there is a difference of opinion among the participants as to whose understanding is used as the basis for deciding what counts as knowledge and what can be assumed to be known (Edwards & Mercer, 1987). It is within this gray area of what is known and not known, what is relevant and irrelevant information, and how they are signaled and marked by patterns of language use that cultural differences have their educational impact. Over time, the ways in which these differences are negotiated and validated affects what are accepted as the appropriate norms of interaction and interpretation in classrooms; these "norms," in turn, have consequences for the evolution of each student's socially organized forms of emotional and mental representations and functions.

Finally we have attempted to show how Vygotsky's rather programmatic characterization of school learning can be given greater substance through an exploration of the role of literacy in the construction of knowledge. Central to this enterprise is epistemic literacy and, in particular, the talk about text in which this mode of engagement is jointly enacted and the relevant psychological functions made available for internalization.

Throughout our data analyses, we have attempted to demonstrate that it is at points of negotiation of meaning in conversation that learning and development occur, as each learner's individual psychological processes mediate (and at the same time are mediated by) the constitutive intermental processes of the group. Furthermore, the group's constitutive processes are organic, as the locus of control shifts according to differential expertise as well as the ongoing change in participants' understanding as the conversation unfolds. In sum, we have treated complete, contextualized episodes of conversation as the minimal units for cultural-cognitive analysis as a contemporary methodology for understanding Vygotsky's ideas on consciousness (1934), the zone of proximal development (1978), and the cultural–historical nature of learning (1978).

It is our view that further exploration of text-based instructional conversations is the means by which we shall get closer to understanding Vygotsky's notion of "good learning." In pursuing this idea, we have searched our data for instances of learning that is in advance of development as it applies to higher mental functions and literacy development. In our work in the two classrooms, we observed that the development of the students' higher and more abstract mental processes—for example, those of reflection and meta-awareness—was integral to, and dependent on, the children's understanding of knowledge construction processes, which they had gained from prior engagement with the text-based activities of making a collage, a windfinder, and other artifacts arising from their study of the Yukon. Indeed, close analysis of the data makes it clear that both teachers exploited the learning gained from text production experiences to introduce and extend their students' development of mental functions, which are integral to learning about one's learning and actions. What is also noteworthy in these instances of conversation is the extension of the notion of props and scaffolds to include the textual products that are outcomes of interrelated learning activities. Scaffolding (Bruner, 1985) is not only provided by an adult or more competent peer but occurs in the triangulation of adult, child and child-produced texts, especially those texts that represent work in progress.

The arguments we have developed in this chapter are not only of theoretical and research interest, however. We believe that our suggestions as to what constitutes good learning in classrooms are of immediate relevance to teachers. Indeed, it is by closely examining the instructional conversations that we engage in about our students' texts that, as teachers and teacher educators, we can address and reimagine how to replace a transmission-oriented mode of imparting information and skills by an approach to learning and teaching that is dialectical, organic, and generative.

Notes

The research reported in this chapter was carried out as part of the project "Language and Learning: Effecting Change through Collaborative Research in Multilingual Schools," under grants received from the Ontario Ministry of Education, the Toronto Board of Education, and the Ontario Institute for Studies in Education. However, the views expressed here are those of the authors and not necessarily those of the funding agencies. We should like to thank Helen Whaley and Ann Maher for collaborating with us in the classroom inquiries on which this chapter is based.

1. Distinctions of the kind made here between different types of knowledge are controversial. Moreover, the boundaries between them are not as sharp as might appear from this brief exposition. Nevertheless, we believe that there is considerable support for distinctions of this kind in the literature. What we have called propositional knowledge is also widely referred to by such terms as declarative or factual knowledge, or simply as the knowledge base (Brown, 1975). What we have called procedural knowledge, that is, the procedures and strategies that are brought to bear when performing an activity, have received considerable attention in relation to comprehension (Brown & Day, 1983), writing (Bereiter & Scardamalia, 1987, Flower & Hayes, 1981), and remembering (Butterfield & Belmont, 1977). As has been pointed out in a number of reviews, metacognition is a term with several, overlapping applications (Brown et al., 1983; Schoenfeld, 1992). We have used it here to refer to both the information that thinkers have about their own cognitive processes and the executive control they exert over these processes.

2. Heap (1985), for example, characterized this conception of education, which he attributed to the English ethnography of education tradition, as follows: "The corpus of knowledge for each lesson is conceived as the curriculum. It is formulated as existing in a preconstituted form, prior and external to the running of the lesson. Instruction is conceived as the transmission by the teacher of this corpus to students. The corpus is fully under the control of the teacher. This control is exercised by the teacher, usually through the asking of questions. These questions are rarely requests for information, and are more akin to 'testing'" (p. 246).

3. This conception of literacy as a repertoire of modes of engaging with texts in ways appropriate to the type of text involved and one's purpose in using them has been developed at greater length elsewhere (Wells, 1987; 1990). What distinguishes the epistemic mode from the others is that in this mode, instead of treating the text as something given, the reader or writer approaches it as a tentative and provisional attempt to capture current understanding in an external form so that both text and understanding may be interrogated, extended and revised.

4. In this and the following transcripts, . = 1 second of pause; ⟨ ⟩ enclose segments where the transcription is uncertain; * = a word that was inaudible; underlining indicates segments that were spoken simultaneously; CAPS mark words spoken with emphatic stress.

References

Bereiter, C. (1985). Toward a solution of the learning paradox. *Review of Educational Research, 55,* 201–226.

Bereiter, C., & Scardamalia, M. (1987). *The psychology of written composition.* Hillsdale, NJ: Lawrence Erlbaum Associates.

Bower, T. (1974). *Development in Infancy.* San Francisco: W. H. Freeman.

Brown, A. L. (1975). The development of memory: knowing, knowing about knowing, and knowing how to know. In H. W. Reese (ed.). *Advances in child development and behavior* (vol. 10). Orlando, FL: Academic Press.

Brown, A. L., & Day, J. D. (1983) Macrorules for summarizing texts; the development of expertise. *Journal of Verbal Learning and Verbal Behavior, 22,* 1–14.

Brown, A. L., Bransford, J. D., Ferrara, R. A., & Campione, J. C. (1983). Learning, remembering, and understanding. In P. H. Mussen (ed.). *Handbook of child psychology* (*vol. 3.*). In J. H. Flavell & M. Markman (eds.). *Cognitive development.* New York: Wiley.

Brown, R. (1973). *A first language.* Cambridge, MA: Harvard University Press.

Bruner, J. S. (1983). *Child's talk: learning to use language.* New York: Norton.

Bruner, J. S. (1985). Vygotsky: a historical and conceptual perspective. In J. V. Wertsch (ed.). *Culture, communication and cognition: Vygotskian perspectives.* Cambridge: Cambridge University Press.

Bruner, J. S. (1986). *Actual minds, possible worlds.* Cambridge, MA: Harvard University Press.

Butterfield, E. C., & Belmont, J. M. (1977). Assessing and improving the executive cognitive functions of mentally retarded people. In I. Bialer & M. Sternlicht (eds.). *Psychological issues in mentally retarded people.* Chicago: Aldine.

Cazden, C. B. (1976). How knowledge about language helps the classroom teacher—or does it: a personal account. *Urban Review, 9,* 74–90.

Chang, G. L., & Wells, G. (1988). The literate potential of collaborative talk. In M. MacLure, T. Phillips, & A. Wilkinson (eds.). *Oracy matters.* Milton Keynes, England: Open University Press.

Chang, G. L., and Wells, G. (1990). Concepts of literacy and children's potential as learners. In S. P. Norris and L. M. Phillips (eds.). *Foundations of literacy policy in Canada.* Calgary, Alberta: Detselig Enterprises.

Cole, M. (1985). The zone of proximal development: where culture and cognition create each other. In J. V. Wertsch (ed.). *Culture, communication, and cognition: Vygotskian perspectives.* Cambridge: Cambridge University Press.

De Beaugrande, R. (1980). *Text, discourse, and process: toward a multidisciplinary science of texts.* Norwood, NJ: Ablex.

Edwards, D., & Mercer, N. (1987). *Common knowledge: the development of understanding in the classroom.* London: Methuen.

Flower, L., & Hayes, J. (1981). A cognitive process theory of writing. *College Composition and Communication, 32* (4), 365–387.

Forman, E. A., & Cazden, C. B. (1985). Exploring Vygotskian perspectives in education: the cognitive value of peer interaction. In J. V. Wertsch (ed.). *Culture, communication, and cognition: Vygotskian perspectives.* Cambridge: Cambridge University Press.

Hammersley, M. (1977). School learning: the cultural resources required by pupils to answer a teacher's question. In P. Woods & M. Hammersley (eds.). *School experience: explorations in the sociology of education.* London: Croom Helm.

Heap, J. (1985). Discourse in the production of classroom knowledge: reading lessons. *Curriculum Inquiry, 15,* 245–279.

Langer, J. A. (1987). A sociocognitive perspective on literacy. In J. A. Langer (ed.).

Language, literacy and culture: issues of society and schooling. Norwood, NJ: Ablex.

Lock, A. (1980). *The guided reinvention of language.* London: Academic Press.

Luria, A. R. (1976). *Cognitive development: its cultural and social foundations.* Cambridge, MA: Harvard University Press.

Mehan, H. (1979). *Learning lessons.* Cambridge, MA: Harvard University Press.

Michaels, S. (1986). Narrative presentations: an oral preparation for literacy with first graders. In J. Cook-Gumperz (ed.). *The social construction of literacy.* Cambridge: Cambridge University Press.

Newson, J. (1978). Dialogue and development. In A. Lock (ed.). *Action, gesture and symbol: the emergence of language.* Orlando, FL: Academic Press.

Palincsar, A. (1986). The role of dialogue in providing scaffolded instruction. *Educational Psychologist, 21,* 73–98.

Rommetveit, R. (1985). Language acquisition as increasing linguistic structuring of experience and symbolic behavior control. In J. V. Wertsch (ed.). *Culture, communication, and cognition: Vygotskian perspectives.* Cambridge: Cambridge University Press.

Ryle, G. (1949). *The concept of mind.* Harmondsworth, Middlesex: Penguin Books.

Schoenfeld, A. H. (1992). Learning to think mathematically: problem solving, metacognition, and sense-making in mathematics. In D. Grouws (ed.). *Handbook for research on mathematics teaching and learning.* New York: Macmillan.

Sharan, S., & Sharan, Y. (1976) *Small group teaching.* Englewood Cliffs, NJ: Educational Technology Publications.

Slavin, R. E. (1983). *Cooperative learning.* New York: Longman.

Tharp, R. G., & Gallimore, R. (1988). *Rousing minds to life.* New York: Cambridge University Press.

Tierney, R. J., & Pearson, P. D. (1984). Toward a composing model of reading. In J. Jensen (ed.). *Composing and comprehending.* Urbana, IL: National Conference on Research in English and the ERIC Clearinghouse on Reading and Communication Skills.

Tizard, B., & Hughes, M. (1984). *Young children learning: talking and thinking at home and at school.* London: Fontana.

Vygotsky, L. S. (1934). *Myshlenie i rech'.* Moscow: Sotsekriz. (Translated as *Thought and language* Cambridge: MIT Press, 1962.)

Vygotsky, L. S. (1978). *Mind in society: the development of higher psychological processes.* Cambridge, MA: Harvard University Press.

Wells, G. (1976). Comprehension: what it means to understand. *English in Education, 10* (2), 24–37.

Wells, G. (1981). *Learning through interaction.* Cambridge: Cambridge University Press.

Wells, G. (1985). *Language development in the pre-school years.* Cambridge: Cambridge University Press.

Wells, G. (1987). Apprenticeship in literacy. *Interchange, 18* (1/2): 109–123.

Wells, G. (1990). Talk about text: where literacy is learned and taught. *Curriculum Inquiry, 20* (4), 369–405.

Wells, G., & Chang, G. L. (1989). Intersubjectivity in the construction of knowledge. Presented at the Biennial Conference of the Society for Research in Child Development, Kansas City, MO, April 1989.

Wells, G., Chang, G. L., & Maher, A. (1990). Creating classroom communities of literate thinkers. In S. Sharan (ed.). *Cooperative learning: theory and research.* New York: Praeger.

Wertsch, J. V. (1985). *Vygotsky and the social formation of mind.* Cambridge, MA: Harvard University Press.

Wertsch, J. V., & Stone, C. A. (1985). The concept of internalization in Vygotsky's account of the genesis of higher mental functions. In J. V. Wertsch (ed.). *Culture, communication, and cognition: Vygotskian perspectives.* Cambridge: Cambridge University Press.

Wood, D. J., Bruner, J. S., & Ross, G. (1976). The role of tutoring in problem solving. *Journal of Child Psychology and Psychiatry, 17* (2), 89–100.

4

Discourse, Mathematical Thinking, and Classroom Practice

PAUL COBB, TERRY WOOD, and ERNA YACKEL

Aspects of an ongoing research and development project in elementary school mathematics that has as an overriding goal the development of a framework within which to coordinate sociological and psychological analyses of classroom life are discussed in this chapter. We must state at the outset that neither the theoretical nor the pragmatic aspects of our work were initially derived from neo-Vygotskian theory. Informed by an almost exclusively cognitive constructivist perspective, we initially intended to analyze individual children's learning as they participated in classroom mathematical activity. Our interest in symbolic interactionism and ethnomethodology developed in concert with our growing awareness of the insufficiency of this initial theoretical orientation. It subsequently became apparent that the way in which we were attempting to make sense of classroom life was, in many respects, compatible with certain of Vygotsky's theoretical notions, particularly his work in what Minick (1987) has identified as the last of the three phases of his intellectual development (i.e., 1933–1934). We use sample episodes repeatedly in the main body of this chapter to illustrate our current view of classroom life and to highlight similarities and differences with Vygotskian theory. First, however, we give a brief overview of the project.

Overview

The initial pragmatic goal of the project was to develop instructional settings in second-grade mathematics' classrooms that are compatible with implications of the constructivist theory of knowledge (von Glasersfeld, 1984). To this end, we conducted a year-long teaching experiment in one second-grade classroom. All instruction was conducted by the classroom teacher, who was a member of the project staff. She taught mathematics four days each week and joined us for project meetings one day a week. During these meetings we reflected on the events of the previous week and discussed instructional issues pertinent to subsequent lessons. In doing so, we and the teacher became a small pedagogical community that engaged in joint pedagogical problem solving.

Given the diversity of our backgrounds, we contributed to this joint activity in different ways. For example, the researchers were familiar with the models of young children's conceptual development in arithmetic (Cobb & Wheatley, 1988; Steffe, Cobb, & von Glasersfeld, 1988; Steffe, von Glasersfeld, Richards, & Cobb, 1983) that were used to guide the development of instructional activities. In particular, we drew on the models to anticipate (1) what might be personally problematic for children at various conceptual levels when they interpreted possible instructional activities and (2) what mathematical constructions they might make as they attempted to resolve their problems. It should be noted that this view of learning as active construction to resolve experientially based problems was applied to all areas of second-grade mathematics including arithmetical computation. The teacher, for her part, drew on both her general practical wisdom and her knowledge of the students to make a variety of suggestions. For example, it was at her insistence that the teaching experiment was extended from the initially proposed four months to the entire school year. She had the final say in discussions on how the classroom would be organized for instruction and on how the instructional activities would be used in her classroom. In addition, she made suggestions about the types of instructional activities that might be appropriate for her students and decided the format of student activity sheets.

The general instructional strategy for all areas of second-grade mathematics, including arithmetical computation, was small-group work followed by a teacher-orchestrated whole-class discussion of the children's problems, interpretations, and solutions. A description of a "typical lesson" can be found in Cobb, Yackel, and Wood (1989) and a discussion of the rationale for and examples of small group interactions in Yackel, Cobb, and Wood (1991). Data collected during the teaching experiment included video-recordings of every mathematics lesson for the entire school year; video-recorded individual interviews conducted with the students at the beginning, middle, and end of the school year; copies of all the children's written work; field notes; and open-ended audio-taped interviews conducted with the teacher.

The emphasis on mathematical communication in both small-group and whole-class settings reflected our developing view that mathematics is a social activity—a community project (Bauersfeld, 1980; Confrey, 1987; De Millo, Lipton, & Perlis, 1986; Steffe, 1987)—as well as an individual constructive activity. The role we initially attributed to social interaction was that of a catalyst for autonomous individual cognitive development. For example, we argued that opportunities to construct mathematical knowledge arose from attempts to resolve conflicting points of view (Perret-Clermont, 1980), attempts to reconstruct and verbalize an interpretation or solution (Levina, 1981), attempts to distance the self from ongoing activity in order to understand an alternative interpretation or solution (Sigel, 1981), and, more generally, attempts to mutually construct a consensual domain for mathematical activity and discourse with others (Barnes & Todd, 1977). We subsequently accepted arguments that mathematical activity can be viewed as intrinsically social in that what counts as a problem and as a resolution has normative aspects (Bauersfeld, 1988; Lave, 1988a,b; Solomon, 1989; Voigt, 1989; Walkerdine, 1988).

In addition to the importance attributed to social interactions and communication, other contrasts with traditional mathematics instruction included the complete absence of grading and of individual pencil-and-paper seat work. However, perhaps the most radical departure from traditional practice was the rejection of the assumption that all the students should make certain predetermined mathematical constructions when they completed and discussed their solutions to particular instructional activities. Voigt's (1985) microanalysis of classroom mathematical discourse illustrates that dialogues typically degenerate into social guessing games when teachers attempt to steer or funnel students to a procedure or answer they have in mind all along. During the course of such dialogues, students learn highly contextual strategies that enable them to act in accord with the teacher's expectations. As a consequence, the construction of mathematical knowledge becomes an incidental by-product of the interaction. Dialogues in which the teacher acts as the sole validator of knowledge with respect to predetermined standards can be contrasted with those in which the teacher and students together constitute a community of validators. In the latter case, the teacher's role is to initiate and guide a genuine mathematical dialogue between the students. The teacher makes it possible for students to say how they actually interpreted and solved tasks and influences the course of the dialogue by capitalizing on students' contributions (Wood, Cobb, & Yackel, 1990). In the case of computation procedures, for example, the teacher did not attempt to steer students to the standard addition and subtraction algorithms. Instead, she framed the children's interpretations, solutions, and, implicitly, their understandings of place value numeration as topics of discussion. In addition, she reformulated their explanations and justifications in terms that were more compatible with the mathematical practices of society at large and yet were accepted by the children as descriptions of what they had actually done. Thus rather than funneling the children's contributions, the teacher took her lead from their contributions and encouraged them to build on each others' explanations as she guided conversations about mathematics. As a consequence, the mathematical meanings and practices institutionalized in the classroom were not immutably decided in advance by the teacher but, instead, emerged during the course of conversations characterized by what Rommetveit (1986) called a genuine commitment to communicate.

During the year following the classroom teaching experiment, 17 other second-grade teachers were inducted into the project and used the instructional activities as the basis for their mathematics instruction. Results of a quantitative evaluation indicated that the performance of project students was significantly superior to that of their nonproject peers on a scale designed to assess students' conceptual understanding of arithmetic, the difference being approximately one standard deviation (Cobb et al., 1991). In addition, project students were significantly more likely to believe that one succeeds in mathematics by attempting to make sense of things and significantly less likely to believe that success stems from conforming to the teachers' or other children's solution methods, from attempting to be superior to classmates, or from being lucky, neat, or quiet (Nicholls, Cobb, Wood, Yackel, & Patashnick, 1990; Nicholls, Cobb, Yackel, Wood, & Wheatley, 1990).

Frequent observations of the project classrooms, initially weekly and then once every two weeks throughout the school year, indicated that they could typically be characterized as places where mathematical meanings were explicitly negotiated. In general, they bore a much closer resemblance to the first project classroom than to traditional classrooms. These observations are consistent with the finding that the pedagogical beliefs of the project teachers at the end of the school year were significantly more compatible with socioconstructivism than those of their nonproject colleagues, the difference being approximately two standard deviations. Discussions of the teacher development aspect of the project and of the teachers' learning during the course of interactions with their students can be found in Cobb, Wood, and Yackel (1990), Cobb, Yackel, and Wood (1988), and Wood et al. (1990). For the purposes at hand, it suffices to note that both we and the teachers had to cope with a variety of institutional constraints that tended to foster the reproduction of traditional instructional practices. It is here that the influence of the broader sociopolitical activity system on our attempts to initiate and guide educational changes at the classroom level become apparent. For example, the teachers had to address all of their school district's objectives for second-grade mathematics regardless of whether they could be justified in terms of our understanding the processes by which young children construct mathematical knowledge. Furthermore, the students were required to take a state-mandated accountability test of so-called basic skills. Students who failed this test had to attend summer school for remediation and, if necessary, repeat second grade. Both we and the teachers were aware that administrators and members of the community at large would tend to judge the educational value of the project almost exclusively in terms of these test scores (see Tharp, Chapter 11, this volume). It was for this reason that we developed quantitative assessment instruments compatible with our educational goals and values. We must stress that this quantitative aspect of the project did not contribute to the improvement of either teacher induction activities or classroom instructional practices. Nonetheless, it was invaluable in that it allowed us to participate in the debate at the broader sociopolitical level and to argue that the state-mandated test addressed a narrow range of educational goals that were open to question. In addition, we were able to demonstrate that, despite the absence of drill and formal instruction in the standard computational algorithms, the performance of project and nonproject students did not differ significantly on the computational subtest of the state accountability test and that project students were significantly superior on the concepts and applications subtest. As a consequence, school district administrators permitted teachers to continue to participate in the project and allowed other teachers to join the project.

Sociopolitical Setting of Educational Change

Thus far we have emphasized how our participation in the broader social action system influenced project activities. We did in fact initially assume that we could accommodate to the institutional constraints unproblematically and exclusively focus on changes in educational practices at the classroom level. In other words, we believed that the flexibility of the broader system was such that we could pursue our educational goals and values without finding ourselves in situations of conflict. This initial belief proved to be unfounded in that we and the teachers became embroiled in an ongoing confrontation with certain school board members (Dillon, 1990). This conflict was at least temporarily resolved after a two-year period when the school board voted unanimously to support the project at second grade and to allow it to be extended to the third grade level. As we reflect on these experiences, we came to realize that our attempts to initiate and guide changes at the classroom level precipitated changes in the broader sociopolitical setting. For example, some of the administrators and school board members modified their views about what is important and should be valued in children's mathematics education. In addition, changes in the teachers' practices, beliefs, and values were not restricted to specific issues concerning the learning and teaching of second-grade mathematics. It also appears that they modified their perceptions of their own and others' roles in the school and in the school district as they participated in this confrontation and attempted to explain and justify their classroom practices. Given our initial assumptions, it should be clear that the teachers' developing professionalism was an unanticipated consequence of their participation in the project.

Although admittedly anecdotal, these reflections on our own and the teachers' actions suggest that classroom practice and the social action system at the school district and wider community level are dialectically or reflexively related (cf. Lave, 1988a). In particular, changes in one precipitate changes in the other; and, more generally, neither exists without the other. In making these comments, we find ourselves in agreement with a basic tenet of Leont'ev's activity theory as interpreted by Minick (1989a): that an individual's psychological development is profoundly influenced by his or her participation in particular forms of social practice. We do, however, reject any analysis that takes a particular social practice such as schooling or the mathematics education of young children as pregiven. Thus although we see great value in the work of Solomon (1989) and Walkerdine (1988), we question their metaphor of either students or teachers being *embedded* or *included* in a social practice. Such metaphors tend to reify social practices, whereas we believe that they do not exist apart from and are interactively constituted by the actions of actively interpreting individuals (Bausersfeld, 1980; Blumer, 1969; Voigt, 1985). By making this point, we are attempting to avoid any tendency that subordinates the individual to the social and loses sight of the reflexive relation between the two. In the case of our project, for example, changes in the teachers' conceptions of mathematics teaching and learning derived from their activity while interacting with us and with their students led to changes in the broader social action system in which they participated. This proposed interdependence between psychological development and the social context in which it occurs is consistent with Vygotsky's (1934/1984) notion of the social situation of development and, more generally, with a hermeneutic conception of the relation between activity and context (e.g., Bateson, 1973; Cazden, 1986; Gadamer, 1986; Winograd & Flores, 1986). In particular, as Vygotsky argued, psychological development depends on the social situation in which the individual acts; and conversely, the social situation of development is itself a function of the child's development (Minick, 1989b). As we turn to consider what happened in the classroom of our study, we attempt to illustrate that the reflexive relation between the individual and the social holds for students' mathematical development as well as for teachers' pedagogical development. All sample episodes included in the discussion are taken from the initial year-long teaching experiment data.

Renegotiating Classroom Social Norms

Our initial observations in the classroom at the beginning of the teaching experiment had some rhyme and reason to them in that we were familiar with the culture of the school as a consequence of our own experiences as both students and teachers. At the same time, we were immediately struck by the complexity of classroom life as we strove to find some way of organizing the flood of immediacies that threatened to swamp us when we interpreted classroom events in terms of our own common sense, experience-near concepts (Geertz, 1983). As a first step toward making sense of the particulars of classroom life, we found it useful to distinguish between two intertwined levels of conversation in both whole-class and small-group settings. At one level the teacher and students did and talked about mathematics, and at the other level they talked about talking about mathematics.

Whole-Class Discussions

The distinction between the two levels of classroom activity first became apparent when we viewed recordings of whole-class discussions conducted for the first lessons in the school year. The teacher's expectation that the children should verbalize how they interpreted and attempted to solve instructional activities ran counter to prior experiences of class discussions in school (Wood et al., 1990). During first grade, dialogues had been initiated with the intention of steering the children toward an officially sanctioned solution method. As a consequence, class discussions were, for the children, situations in which they took it for granted that they were to infer what the teacher had in mind rather than to articulate their own understandings. Furthermore, they assumed that the teacher would publicly evaluate the correctness or incorrectness of their responses. Hence there was a potential conflict between the teacher's (T) and children's expectations for each others' activity. Against this background, consider the following episode that occurred during the first day of school. The discussion centered on the word problem, "How many runners altogether? There are six runners on each team. There are two teams in the race."

> T: Jack, what answer-solution did you come up with?
>
> Jack: Fourteen.
>
> T: Fourteen. How did you get that answer?

The teacher called on Jack with the expectation that he would explain how he had interpreted and solved the problem. However, Jack interpreted the teacher's question as a request for an answer and presumably expected the teacher to evaluate his reply. Instead, she accepted his answer without evaluation and restated her initial question. At this point in the episode, the teacher's and Jack's expectations for each other's activity were in conflict. The teacher was not merely attempting to elicit an account of Jack's solution but was also negotiating with him on how to engage in mathematical discourse. By restating her question, she indicated that Jack had not acted in accord with her expectations. The correctness of his answer was irrelevant at this point in the conversation; it was the act of merely giving an answer that was inappropriate. The episode continued.

> Jack: Because 6 plus 6 is 12. Two runners on two teams . . . *(Jack stops talking, puts his hands to the side of his face and looks down at the floor. Then he looks at the teacher and then at his partner, Ann. He turns and faces the front of the room with his back to the teacher and mumbles inaudibly.)*
>
> T: Would you say that again? I didn't quite get the whole thing. You had—Say it again please.
>
> Jack *(softly, still facing the front of the room)*: It's six runners on each team.
>
> T: Right.
>
> Jack *(turns to look at the teacher)*: I made a mistake. It's wrong. It should be twelve. *(He turns and faces the front of the room.)*

The teacher continued to negotiate explicitly how to engage in mathematical discussions with Jack. However, Jack interpreted the situation as warranting acute embarrassment as soon as he realized his answer was incorrect. In effect, he acted as though the teacher had publicly evaluated his answer. This further conflict between expectations confounded the teacher's intention that the children should publicly express their thinking and, more generally, engage in mathematical practice characterized by conjecture, argument, and justification. Richards (1991) has called practice that has these characteristics "inquiry math" to distinguish it from the typical stultifying discourse of "school math." It is our contention that these two forms of classroom mathematical practice constitute two qualitatively distinct activities in Leont'ev's (1981) sense of the term. This claim is corroborated by the observation that changes in classroom mathematics practices precipitated changes in the wider sociopolitical activity system. In light of this contention, it should be apparent that we view the process of renegotiating classroom social norms as one in which the teacher and students together interactively constitute the classroom mathematical activity system that constrains their individual mathematical actions.

In the portion of the sample episode considered thus far, Jack and the teacher had been talking about mathematics—the themes were Jack's answer and his solution. At this point in the episode, the teacher initiated a new conversation in which she and the children talked about talking about mathematics. The issue of how to interpret situations in which a mistake has been made then became a topic of conversation (Feldman, 1987).

> **T** *(softly)*: Oh, okay. Is it okay to make a mistake?
> **Andrew:** Yes.
> **T:** Is it okay to make a mistake, Jack?
> **Jack:** Yes.
> **T:** You bet it is. As long as you're in my class it is okay to make a mistake. Because I make them all the time, and we learn from our mistakes—a lot. Jack already figured out, "Ooops, I didn't have the right answer the first time" *(Jack turns and looks at the teacher and smiles)*, but he kept working at it and he got it.

This interaction fits the elicitation–reply–evaluation pattern of traditional classroom discourse (Mehan, 1979), the evaluative statement being, "You bet it is." This pattern was characteristic when the teacher and students talked about talking about mathematics. The teacher typically initiated dialogues at this level by asking known-information questions such as, "Is it okay to make a mistake?" and had in mind a particular way in which she wanted the children to interpret the situation under discussion. In contrast, her initial elicitation when they talked about mathematics—"Jack. What answer-solution did you come up with?"—was an information-seeking question. She did not know how Jack had solved the task and genuinely wanted to find out.

More generally, interaction patterns and the teacher's and students' roles differed at the two levels of discourse. The teacher attempted to involve the students in the process of negotiating mathematical meanings when she and the children performed and talked about mathematics. In our terms, she was in effect initiating the children into a novel interpretive stance to mathematics—that of inquiry mathematics as a form of social practice that was qualitatively distinct from traditional school mathematics. The manner in which she initiated and guided the renegotiation of social norms during the course of conversations at this level was implicit and subtle, as exemplified by the restatement of her initial question. When these subtle attempts failed, she framed situations in which her own and the children's expectations for each other were in conflict as paradigm cases and made them explicit topics of conversation, as was illustrated in the sample episode. In the process, the dialogue shifted to talking about talking about mathematics. At this level, the teacher was much more directive. It follows from Batson's (1973) analysis of context and from Leont'ev's (1981) distinction between activity and action that these two levels of conversation are logically distinct though interdependent. Consequently, it makes sense to say that the teacher overtly exercised her institutionalized authority to make possible the development of a classroom mathematics tradition in which the children could say what they really thought mathematically.

It should be clear from the sample episode that the teacher did not plan the renegotiation of classroom norms in advance. She did not have an explicit list of topics for renegotiation; and indeed no such list could ever be complete (Mehan & Wood, 1975). Instead, these topics emerged as the teacher and children talked about and did mathematics in the whole-class setting, and as such they were interactional accomplishments. The manner in which the teacher capitalized on unanticipated events by framing them as paradigmatic situations in which to discuss explicitly her expectations and the children's obligations constituted a crucial aspect of her expertise in the classroom. The teacher's initiation of these shifts in the level of dialogue did not appear to be and were not reported by her as conscious decisions. Rather, they seemed to evidence her situated knowledge-in-action (Lave, 1988a; Schon, 1983)—her resonance with the interactionally constituted situation in which she was a participant. Thus in line with Vygotsky's latter work and with activity theory, it appears that explicit renegotiations of social norms were not consciously induced by thought but, instead, originated in joint activity as the teacher and students did and talked about mathematics (Minick, 1989a, p. 123). It was by initiating shifts from one level of discourse to the other that the teacher initiated and guided the explicit negotiation of both mathematical meanings and classroom social norms with her students.

In general, the relation between the two levels of conversation was dialectical or reflexive. Topics discussed when talking about talking about mathematics emerged when the teacher and children did and talked about mathematics. Conversely, the explicit renegotiation of the social norms that regulated classroom life influenced both subsequent mathematical activity and discussions in which the teacher and children talked about mathematics. We represent this relation as follows:

Talking about talking about mathematics

Talking about and doing mathematics

As has been noted, these interdependent levels correspond to those of establishing the classroom mathematics tradition or the classroom activity system and of individually and collectively constructing mathematical ways of knowing within the constraints of the evolving classroom tradition. The reflexive relation we propose between the levels is consistent with Vygotsky's (1934/1984) discussion of the social situation of development. One can in fact interpret the process of renegotiating classroom social norms as one in which the students participated in the interactive constitution of the social situation in which their mathematical development occurred.

Despite these obvious consistencies between our analyses and both Vygotsky's latter work and his activity theory, it should be acknowledged that Soviet theoreticians have, for the most part, focused on the influence of social practices on individual thought and development (Wertsch, 1985). Although they acknowledged that these practices evolve historically, there is nonetheless a tendency to reify them when conducting psychological analyses. For example, Vygotsky's (1934/1987) analysis of the dependence of scientific concepts on school instruction takes as a given a classroom scientific practice akin to what we have called the school mathematics tradition. Thus he emphasized the importance of formal definitions and of the teacher's explicit explanations. As becomes increasingly apparent in the remainder of this chapter, we too believe that students' psychological development is profoundly influenced by the social practices in which they participate. However, we wish to avoid the reification of these practices and, instead, prefer to emphasize that a practice such as inquiry mathematics is interactively constituted in the classroom and does not exist apart from the activities of the individuals who participate in its constitution (Maturana, 1980). As a consequence, the classroom mathematics tradition both constrains the teacher's and students' development and evolves together with their individual psychological development. It is in redressing the balance and considering the influence of individual development on social practices that we find great value in symbolic interactionist theory in general (e.g., Blumer, 1969; Mead, 1934) and in its application to mathematics education in particular (e.g., Bauersfeld, 1980, 1988; Krummheuer, 1983; Voigt, 1985, 1989).

Returning now to consider further the process by which social norms were renegotiated in the second-grade classroom, we thus far have considered only situations where occasions to talk about talking about mathematics emerged during the course of whole-class discussions. The teacher also initiated renegotiations by framing events she had observed when the children worked in groups as topics of whole-class conversation. Two topics that emerged during the course of group interactions were those of cooperating and of each child thinking things through for himself or herself (Yackel et al., 1991). The following episode occurred during a whole-class discussion when the teacher asked Brenda and her partner Dan to report an incident she had previously observed.

T: Dan.

Dan: They [another pair] were bothering us.

Brenda: They were telling us the answers.

T: Oh. You know when people give you the answers, boys and girls, does that really help you understand what you're doing? You don't know how you got it, you might as well just not waste your pencil.

The teacher consciously decided to call on Brenda and Dan in order to make the obligation that the children should figure things out for themselves and develop their own mathematical understandings, an explicit topic of conversation. The teacher's second statement served to legitimize Brenda and Dan's indignation and to provide a rationale for their complaint. Later in the episode, she asked the following.

T: How did you handle the situation?

Brenda: We just said we didn't want the answers. . . . We were on the same question, and they were telling us the answer. We didn't pay any attention, because we wanted to figure it out for ourselves.

T: Good! Good for you. I'm proud of you. It's easy to take someone else's answer, isn't it, than think about it yourself?

Students: Yeah.

T: Sure it is. I could just fill these all in *(points to the problems)* and say these are the answers kids. But would you learn anything?

Brenda *(interrupts):* We have to think for ourselves. We can't have other people think for us. . . . They might be wrong.

T: That's right.

It can be seen that, as in the previous episode, the teacher had in mind how the children ought to interpret the situation. She was, in effect, asking known-answer questions as she discussed the obligations she expected the children to fulfill as they did and talked about mathematics.

The topics of cooperating and understanding were eventually institutionalized by the classroom community to the extent that conversations about them could be initiated without drawing on paradigm cases. For example, the following discussion occurred early in January before the children began to work in groups. The children had just returned from two weeks of vacation.

T: When you're working together, what are you going to have to be doing with your partner?

Lois: Solve the answer.

T: Find the solution. And what else is your responsibility to you and your partner? To each other? Let's hear from Craig.

Craig: Share.

T: Share and what else. Ron?

Ron: Cooperating.

T: Cooperating, good! What's another thing you need to do, Rick?

Rick: Make sure you agree on what the answer is.

T: Make sure you—for instance, Rick and Chris. Chris says, "This is the answer?" and it may be right and it may be wrong but he—what's his responsibility to Rick?

Karen: He's supposed to tell Rick how he got that.

T: Exactly. So if I call on you two, what if Rick says to me, "Well, Chris did that answer?"

Lois: You're not going to "buy" that.

T: That's right. I'm going to say, "It's your responsibility to find out how you two came up with that answer, and it's also Chris's responsibility to be sure that Rick kind of understands how they got that answer."

Once again, the teacher was relatively directive as she articulated her expectations and discussed the children's obligations and responsibilities with them. This episode also illustrates that the teacher and children had together developed a language with which to talk about talking about mathematics during the first half of the school year. As we have seen, this way of speaking grew out of their joint activity as they discussed paradigmatic cases that arose while doing or talking about mathematics. Certain aspects of inquiry mathematics, such as explaining, justifying, and collaborating, had become objects of reflection in a consensual domain constructed mutually by the teacher and students. As such, these aspects of mathematical activity were interactively constituted as taken-to-be-shared objects of experience during the course of inquiry mathematics activity and took their meaning from this social practice. In making this point, we are in effect illustrating Leont'ev's (1978) notion of "predmet." As Minick (1987) noted, Leont'ev's theoretical work can be viewed as an attempt to extend the consideration of social phenomena beyond face-to-face interaction and to develop a framework that relates the world of taken-to-be-shared objects with systems of individual and social activity. To this end, he coined the term "predmet" to denote the characteristics of a taken-to-be-shared object as they arise during the course of the social activity in which the object is incorporated. He further stressed that a taken-to-be-shared object is defined by its characteristics or properties, and consequently new objects develop and emerge during the course of activity. Thus from his perspective the object world cannot be defined independently of activity. Our contention that aspects of mathematical activity in the second-grade classroom emerged as taken-to-be-shared objects is highly compatible with Leont'ev's arguments; these abstract objects can be viewed as predmets. We also note our contention is consistent with Lampert's (1990) claim that the meanings of terms such as "understand," "explain," and "justify" are relative to the classroom mathematics culture. A relatively detailed analysis of the relation between the differing meanings of these terms and classroom mathematics practices is described by Cobb, Yackel, and Wood (in press).

Small-Group Interactions

It was during the whole-class discussions that the teacher initiated and guided the explicit renegotiation of social norms with all the children. In effect, the classroom community mutually constructed or constituted an evolving communal story about mathematics during the course of these discussions. These whole-class negotiations influenced the children's activity as they worked in small groups. We have seen, for example, that cooperating and thinking things through emerged as topics during whole-class conversations. In addition, we can interpret the teacher's interactions with the children during small-group work as attempts to initiate the renegotiation of social norms and thus acculturate them into inquiry mathematics. Once again, the two levels of discourse are apparent.

As a consequence of explicit discussions of issues such as cooperating and thinking for themselves, the children came to realize that they were expected to fulfill these obligations in the unique setting of their ongoing small-group interactions (Yackel et al., 1991). This task was problematic for many children in that they had not previously experienced situations in which they were explicitly expected to collaborate to learn in school. Participation in inquiry mathematics in which individuals coordinate their mathematical activities and engage in mathematical discourse was beyond the realm of their prior experiences. In a very real sense, the teacher had to guide the children's developing abilities to engage in genuine mathematical communication as they worked together (Wood & Yackel, 1990).

The following episode occurred as Karen and Craig were completing the tasks $47 + 19 = \_\_$, $48 + 18 = \_\_$, and $49 + 17 = \_\_$. The teacher approached the children as they completed the task $47 + 19 = \_\_$, for which Karen had arrived at the answer 66. The teacher listened to Karen's explanation and then read the next problem.

> T: Okay. Now this is 48 plus 18 equals. Okay, let's take a look here.
>
> **Karen** [*holding up her thumb, starting to count*]: Forty-eight, forty. . . . That's just the same.

As Karen excitedly pointed to "$47 + 19 = 66$" on the activity sheet, the teacher looked at Craig and waited for him to respond, but he continued to write his answer to the previous task on the sheet. She then took his turn in the dialogue and asked Karen, "What is just the same?" Because she did so, Karen was obliged to explain her solution and continue the dialogue.

> **Karen:** If you take 1 from the 19 and put it with the 7 (*she hesitates and looks at teacher, while Craig leans forward to look closely at the problem*), and [it] makes 48 and that makes this just the same [as 48 plus 18].
>
> T: Do you see that Craig? Do you see what she is trying to say?

By making this elicitation, the teacher attempted to involve Craig in the dialogue. These attempts, however, were initially unsuccessful. To this point, they had talked about mathematics, the topic being Karen's solution. The teacher then initiated a conversation in which Craig's nonparticipation was framed as a paradigm case and became an explicit topic of discussion. During the course of talking about talking about mathematics, the teacher discussed with Craig her expectation that when Karen gives a solution to a

problem, he is obliged to listen and to try and understand the explanation.
The teacher then initiated a return to talking about mathematics.

> **T:** Look at the next problem, 48 plus 18 equals. She said it is the same number.
>
> **Karen:** Ya, because you take 1 from the 19 and add it to the 47 and that makes . . . *(hesitates).*
>
> **T:** Forty-eight.
>
> **Karen:** Forty-eight and 18 . . .
>
> **Craig** *(interrupts)*: Oh! I know what she's trying to say. Take 1 from here and add it here.
>
> **T:** Right!

The teacher's initial statement was interpreted by both Karen and Craig as
an elicitation for Craig to attempt to understand Karen's solution. Her final
comment, "Right," seemed to evaluate the appropriateness of both their
interaction and Craig's interpretation of Karen's explanation.

> **Craig:** It's got to be the same answer, or you can add it here and add to here *(points from "47" to "48" and from "18" to "19").*
>
> **Karen:** No take one from . . . *(she points to "19")* and add it here *(points to "47").*
>
> **T:** Exactly.

The teacher's first evaluation, "Right," did not serve as an elicitation but was
merely inserted in Karen and Craig's discussion. Her final evaluation,
"Exactly," indicated that Craig understood Karen's explanation and that
the children had arrived at a consensus. As such, this evaluation served to
close the episode initiated by her comment, "She said it is the same number." Having guided the children's participation in a mathematical dialogue, she implicitly communicated to them that such dialogues close with
a consensus.

In this episode, Karen and Craig collaborated to learn with the teacher's
initiation and guidance. The teacher, in effect, helped Karen and Craig
understand the meaning of such terms as "cooperate" in their concrete situation by making it possible for each child to experience active involvement
with the other in a collaborative dialogue about mathematics. It is, of course,
possible to analyze this interaction in terms of the teacher scaffolding the
children's activity. However, such an analysis would tend to lose sight of
the influence of the classroom mathematics tradition and downplay both the
children's interpretive activity and their active contributions to the interaction. It is for this reason that we prefer to emphasize that the teacher and
children together constitute a novel form of joint mathematical activity
while simultaneously acknowledging the institutionalized power imbalance
between the teacher and children. In general, the children became increasingly competent as they collaborated in small groups with the teacher's guidance (Wood & Yackel, 1990), thereby changing the social situation of their

development. Following Vygotsky (1933/1976), one can in fact argue that the children created a zone of proximal development for themselves when they participated in collaborative small-group activity in that they could, at times, engage in more advanced mathematical activity than they could had they worked alone (Yackel et al., 1991). Such a view emphasizes that children's social realities are relative to their levels of development and stands in stark contrast to characterization of development as the transfer or transmission of culturally developed modes of thinking from those who know to those who do not.

Classroom Community

We see a strong analogy between the activity of the second-grade classroom community and that of a scientific research community (Cobb, Yackel, & Wood, 1992). The teacher's initiation and guidance of the classroom community's transition from the social practice of school mathematics to that of inquiry mathematics brings to mind Kuhn's (1970) discussion of a scientific revolution. The notion of the classroom community's evolving mathematics tradition is compatible with the view that what counts as science and as rationality cannot be specified in terms of a historical criterion (Barnes, 1982; Bernstein, 1983; Rorty, 1980). Instead, scientific knowledge and the encompassing research tradition are continually reconstructed together, with each informing the other. These two processes are analogous to the two levels of discourse we have discussed. At one level, the topics of discourse were mathematical, and at the other level they were the social norms that regulate the activity of doing and talking about mathematics.

The fundamental difference between a community of mature scientists and a classroom community is, in Leont'ev's (1978) terms, that mathematical activity in school and mathematical or scientific activity in a research community are informed by different motives. It is in fact for this reason that we have cautioned against the currently fashionable idea that students in school can be adequately conceptualized as apprentice mathematicians (Cobb et al., in press). In our view, there are necessarily important differences between the classroom inquiry mathematics tradition and what we call the research mathematics tradition, and that these differences reflect differences in the functions of schools and research communities in society. Nonetheless, the analogy between the classroom and a scientific community is of value in that it highlights the complexity of teaching. In particular, the teacher with whom we worked skillfully initiated and guided the analogue of a scientific revolution in her classroom. It does not, however, cast her in the role of a social engineer. She did not engineer the classroom social setting for the children on her own; instead, the inquiry mathematics tradition was constructed mutually by the teacher and students. It was an interactional accomplishment whose constitution was initiated and guided by the teacher (Bauersfeld, 1988).

Social Norms and Individual Beliefs

Thus far we have focused on social norms and the classroom mathematics tradition but have said little about individual children's beliefs. In doing so, we have viewed classroom life primarily from an anthropological rather than a cognitive perspective (Cobb, 1989, 1990). Following Comaroff (1982) and Lave (1988a,b), we take the relation between the communal tradition or culture and individual experience of, and action in, the lived-in world to be dialectical. It can be represented as:

Cognitive   Anthropological

We can illustrate this relation by considering classroom social norms and what we take to be their cognitive correlates, the teacher's and children's individual beliefs about their own and other's roles and the general nature of mathematical activity (Cobb et al., 1989). For the discussion of social norms, we have focused on regularities in classroom social interactions that, from the observer's perspective, constitute the grammar of classroom life. In doing so, we have tacitly assumed that these regularities are manifestations of *shared* knowledge (Gergen, 1985). For example, the manner in which the children routinely interpreted situations in which someone told them an answer can be taken as indicating that they share a belief in the value of developing their own mathematical understanding. However, when we view interactions from the cognitive perspective and focus on individual children's interpretations of their own and others' activity, it becomes apparent that there were differences in their individual beliefs. It is evidenced by both classroom observations and the children's responses to a beliefs questionnaire. From this perspective, the most that can be said when interactions precede smoothly is that the teacher's and children's beliefs *fit* in that each acted in accordance with the others' expectations (Bauersfeld, 1988; Voigt, 1985, 1989; von Glasersfeld, 1984). Situations in which social norms were renegotiated occurred when there was a lack of fit—when either the teacher's or a child's expectations were not fulfilled. In the language of anthropology, renegotiations occurred when there was a perceived breach of a social norm (Much & Shweder, 1978). It was by capitalizing on such breaches and making them topics of conversation that the teacher and, to an increasing extent, the children initiated and guided the renegotiation of social norms and thus influenced others' beliefs. These beliefs in turn constituted the cognitive bases of their individual interpretations of situations that arose during the course of social interactions. We represent the relation between beliefs and social norms as follows:

Individual beliefs   Social norms

This relation can be summarized by saying that individual interpretations that fit together constitute the social norms that constrain the individual interpretations that generate them. This situation, we believe, is an instantiation of the general relation between communal culture or social practice and individual experience. Such a view is, as we have seen, compatible with Vygotsky's analysis of the social situation of development.

A further compatibility with Vygotsky's work becomes apparent once we note that the teacher's and students' beliefs constituted the cognitive bases for their interpretations of classroom events, and these interpretations were in turn the bases for their emotional acts (Harre, 1986). Hence it follows that their emotional acts were intimately related to their cognitive appraisals of situations and, as a consequence, had a normative, social aspect. As an illustration, consider again the episode in which Jack became embarrassed when he realized that he had made a mistake in public. His emotional act would have been appropriate in the setting of the school mathematics tradition in that students are typically expected to produce correct answers and are held accountable if they do not (Lave, 1988b; Tharp, Chapter 11, this volume). When the teacher made this incident a topic of conversation, she in effect told Jack and the other children that an interpretation of mistakes as warranting embarrassment was inappropriate in her classroom and, by doing so, initiated and guided the development of an inquiry mathematics tradition. The teacher also capitalized on the children's emotional acts on numerous other occasions to initiate an explicit renegotiation of classroom social norms. We have argued elsewhere that these interactions call into question analyses that distinguish cognitive and affective activity, and they illustrate that affects, interests, and goals are normative in the same sense as are beliefs (Cobb et al., 1989). To say that the teacher attempted to teach the children how they ought to feel emotionally in certain situations is, from our perspective, synonymous with saying that she attempted to teach them how they ought to interpret those situations cognitively. Such a contention is, of course, consistent with Vygotsky's attempts to develop a unified view of mind and to relate it to the social activities in which the thinking, feeling individual participates (Forman & McPhail, Chapter 9, this volume).

The three dialectical relations we have discussed thus far can themselves be related to each other, as shown in Figure 4.1. We have also used the figure to introduce a relation between individual mathematical knowledge and communal mathematical practices. This relation is the focus of discussion in the next section when we consider the process by which the teacher and students negotiated mathematical meanings as they talked about and did mathematics.

Negotiating Mathematical Meanings

A scientific research tradition constitutes the taken-for-granted background against which a community of scientists engages in empirical and theoretical work. Similarly, the evolving classroom mathematics tradition constituted the background against which the teacher and second graders did and talked about mathematics. As we have seen, this background came to the fore when

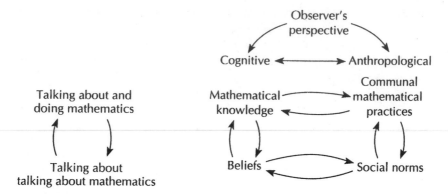

Figure 4.1. Partial relations between observer's perspective and levels of discourse.

either the teacher or a child perceived that a social norm had been breached (Garfinkel, 1967). Against the background of the social norms discussed previously, consider the following routine episode that occurred in February. The teacher and children were discussing solutions to a task that involved adding three twelves.

> **T:** Jason and Brenda, how did you do it?
>
> **Jason:** I added up—Well if—one plus one plus one. Well, one plus two, one more equals three.
>
> **T:** Uh, huh.
>
> **Jason:** Two plus two equals four and two more equals six. Takes it up to 36.
>
> **T:** How about you, Brenda?

In contrast to the episode that occurred on the first day of the school year, Jason took it for granted that he was obliged to explain his solution process, not merely give an answer. We can also note that the teacher did not evaluate Jason's explanation. The teacher's elicitation was an information-seeking question, and a reply that provided the information reflexively completed the interaction (Mehan, 1979). As Sacks, Schegloff, and Jefferson (1974) noted, interactions with this two-part sequential structure are characteristic of polite everyday conversation. In contrast, typical school interactions initiated by known-information questions have a three-part sequential structure of elicitation–reply–evaluation. In general, the structure of conversations in which the teacher and children talked about mathematics differed markedly from both typical school mathematics interactions and their conversations when they talked about talking about mathematics. This difference is the product of prior negotiations of social norms and as such instantiates the more general point that the nature of face-to-face interactions are influenced by the social practice that the participants constitute during the course of their interactions.

The episode continued:

Brenda: Well, I got 33. I just counted . . . first I counted by two's.

T: All right.

In contrast to the typical discourse of school mathematics, Brenda's incorrect answer passed without comment. The teacher's comment "All right" seemed, in this context, to mean something like, "You counted by two's, I understand what you are doing." It therefore indicated that Brenda's reply to the information-seeking question was appropriate; she was acting in accord with the teacher's expectations.

Brenda: Two, four, six.

T: Two, four, six.

Brenda: And then ones, and I came up with 36.

T: Alright. So what they did. They split up their twelves into tens and twos. They added up their twos and added up their tens and then they combined that number. I'll bet that's what a lot of you did.

The interactional sequence was reflexively closed when the teacher indicated that she understood Brenda's explanation by commenting "All right" for a second time. She then explained one aspect of her interpretation of the children's solution to the class. In doing so, the teacher spoke of what *they* did, as though attributing her explanation to both children's solutions. Based on our observations of the teacher's interactions with the two children both before and after this episode and on the teacher's comments in project meetings, we believe that she was in fact referring only to Brenda's solution. The teacher indicated by both word and deed throughout the year that she realized that Jason's conception of ten was relatively immature and that the ones of which he spoke were literally ones, not tens, for him. The manner in which he added by columns was his version of the standard addition algorithm taught in first grade. He added three ones and then three twos and finally juxtaposed the resulting numerals, "3" and "6", to arrive at his answer of 36. In short, his solution reflected an understanding of the conventional notational system but not the underlying place value concepts. From the teacher's perspective, nothing in Jason's solution was relevant to her purpose of acculturating the children to the place value conceptualization of numbers as practiced in the wider community. For this reason, Jason's solution passed without comment, and the teacher immediately asked Brenda for her explanation.

Our observations of the teacher's interactions with Brenda throughout the school year and her comments to us indicated that she knew that Brenda's conception of ten was relatively sophisticated. As a consequence, although Brenda said "And then ones," the teacher believed that her solution did not merely reflect conformity to the conventional notational system but reflected an understanding of place value numeration. The teacher capitalized on this inferred aspect of Brenda's solution to explicate it for the rest of the class, a process that Newman, Griffin, and Cole (1989), following Leont'ev (1981), called "appropriation." In doing so, the teacher spoke of splitting and combining numbers, implicitly indicating that in inquiry mathematics one acts on numbers as mathematical objects. This approach contrasts with the traditional characterization of mathematics as a collection of rules for manipulating elements of conventional notation systems that do not necessarily signify anything. More generally, the teacher and children in project classrooms interactively constitute a taken-to-be-shared mathematical reality composed of experientially real mathematical objects, whereas those in traditional classrooms typically construct taken-to-be-shared procedural instructions (Cobb et al., in press). Much and Shweder's (1978) identification of five qualitatively distinct types of norm is relevant in this regard in that it appears that mathematics as a normative activity is constituted as truths in project classrooms and as instructions in traditional classrooms. There are therefore differences in the quality of the entities that emerge as teachers and students do and talk about mathematics in the two instructional settings. We noted an instantiation of Leont'ev's (1978) notion of predmet when we discussed the process of renegotiating classroom social norms. Recall that the term refers to a taken-to-be-shared object and its characteristics as they emerge during the course of social activity. We see here a further instantiation of this notion at the level of doing and talking about mathematics in that qualitative differences in the emerging mathematical entities reflected and were reflected in qualitative differences in classroom mathematics traditions. Once again, we stress that the students were not simply embedded in differing mathematical activity systems. Rather, they participated in the constitution differing systems (i.e., differing classroom mathematics traditions) and thus in the constitution of the social situations of their development. Furthermore, they contributed to the continual regeneration and evolution of their classroom mathematics traditions as they interactively constituted qualitively different entities while doing and talking about mathematics. By characterizing the situation in this way, we once again question the tendency to reify social activity systems and instead emphasize the reflexive relation between the individual and the social.

Returning now to the sample episode, we observe that the way in which the teacher phrased her explication of Brenda's solution indicates that she had developed a routine that enabled her to cope with a potential conflict between two purposes she sought to achieve. On the one hand, she wanted the children to collaborate when they worked in pairs and, whenever possible, to arrive at mutually acceptable solutions. On the other hand, she wanted to highlight aspects of solutions that were significant from her perspective as an acculturated member of wider society. She would have undermined the first of these purposes if she had overtly singled out Brenda's solution for comment. Instead she resolved the tension by the simple expediency of talking about "what they did," thereby creating the illusion that it was a joint production while simultaneously discussing what she considered to be an important aspect of Brenda's solution. By doing so, she subtly legitimized the mathematical practice of splitting a number such as twelve into ten and two. Her attempts to facilitate the institutionalization of this intellectual practice by the classroom community proved successful as the school year progressed (Cobb et al., 1989).

The sample episode we chose is routine and proceeded smoothly. The teacher did not have to initiate the renegotiation of social norms and did not have to cope with either an overt conflict between mathematical solutions or an unexpected mathematical conjecture. The very "ordinariness" of the sample episode serves to illustrate the routine complexity of the teacher's activity as she initiated and guided the negotiation of mathematical meanings. She routinely supported the children's attempts to describe their mathematical thinking by interjecting comments ("Uh, huh," "All right," "2, 4, 6, . . ."), attempted to understand how they interpreted and solved tasks, and highlighted what she took to be significant aspects of their solutions. In doing so, she routinely drew on her understanding of individual children's mathematical knowledge as she attempted to initiate them into mathematical practices that were compatible with those of the wider community.

We have noted contrasts in the discourse structure and in both the teacher's and students' activity when the classroom community negotiated social norms and when it negotiated mathematical meanings. The teacher and students mutually constructed differing obligations for their own activity and differing expectations for other's activity in the two situations. For example, the children expected the teacher to ask information-seeking questions when they talked about and did mathematics. The teacher for her part expected the children to say how they had interpreted and solved mathematical problems. For the children to fulfill this obligation, the teacher was herself obliged to respect their explanations and to guide mathematical dialogues in ways that were not construed by the children as explicit evaluations of their contributions. Thus the teacher had to fit her activity to that of the children as well as vice versa. Such observations again emphasize the children's active contributions to the interactions in which they participated, a point that tends to be overlooked if one focuses on the teacher and regards her as scaffolding children to higher levels of performance. This said, we would not want to dismiss the power imbalance as the teacher attempted to initiate her students into the mathematical practices of wider society.

Despite the commonalities we have discussed, conversations in which the teacher and the children talked about mathematics did differ from polite everyday discourse as one would expect given the function of the school as a social institution. This point is illustrated in the sample episode by the manner in which the teacher regulated the children's turn-taking. To be sure, the children frequently did take the initiative. For example, the teacher closed the sample episode in which Brenda and Jason explained their solutions but Brenda had more to say. Brenda continued by explaining that the solution to the task under discussion—adding three twelves—could be used to solve the next task, adding four twelves: "One other thing. This one can help you get this one." But such initiatives had to be implicitly sanctioned by the teacher if they were to be incorporated into the ongoing discussion. The teacher's regulation of the children's turn-taking and the manner in which she highlighted certain interpretations and solutions but not others indicates that there are commonalities as well as differences between school mathematics and inquiry mathematics, at least as manifested in the classroom we observed. The comparisons and contrasts of inquiry mathematics with both school mathematics and polite everyday conversation suggest that it is a unique form of social practice worthy of intensive study in its own right.

As a final point, note that we characterized one goal of mathematics instruction as the initiation of students into the mathematical practices of the wider society. This characterization implies a certain view of mathematical knowledge. We previously spoke of social norms as the anthropological correlates of individual children's beliefs. Similarly, we can speak of the mathematical practices institutionalized in the classroom as the anthropological correlates of individual children's mathematical ways of knowing. In this view, mathematics does not consist of timeless, ahistorical facts, rules, or structures but is continually negotiated and institutionalized by a community of knowers. This view is consistent with recent developments in the philosophy of mathematics (Lakatos, 1976; Tymoczko, 1986), with the findings of historical analysis that mathematical practices evolve (Bloor, 1983; Grabiner, 1986; Kitcher, 1983), and with the empirical finding that mathematical practices differ across communities (Carraher, Carraher, & Schliemann, 1985; D'Ambrosio, 1985; Saxe, 1988, 1989). In this view, mathematical activity in the classroom occurs against a background of mathematical practices that have been institutionalized by the classroom community and are taken as self-evident by its members. Thus the background for mathematical activity and dialogue is constituted by the results of prior negotiations of mathematical meanings as well as by current social norms. During the sample episode, for example, we described the task under discussion as adding three twelves. In fact, the task was posed in a balance format. The children were given a drawing of a pan-balance with three boxes each labeled "12" on one pan and one unlabeled box on the other pan. The interpretation of this diagram as requiring the addition of three twelves to "make it balance" had been so institutionalized by the classroom community that the children did not have to explain or justify why they were adding three twelves. The teacher and children took it for granted that others interpreted the drawing in the same way they did; it was part of the interactively constituted background against which they talked about mathematics.

As a further example, within the wider community we take it for granted that whole numbers are composed of units of ten and one. As members of this community, we have jointly institutionalized this intellectual practice as a mathematical truth (Wittgenstein, 1964). This process had not occurred in the second grade classroom. It was for this reason that the teacher thought it necessary to explain that "they split up their twelves into tens and twos." From the anthropological perspective, we can characterize her comment as serving to initiate and guide the institutionalization of this practice so the classroom community would eventually make it a mathematical truth.

From the cognitive perspective, she was facilitating individual children's construction of mathematical knowledge. As we have noted, this practice was progressively institutionalized. Anthropologically, the conceptualization of numbers as composed of units of ten and one became increasingly shared. During the course of this process, the children participated in the evolution of their social situation of development in that they could now act in a taken-to-be-shared reality in which the composition of number as tens and ones was beyond justification. However, it should be noted that when we interviewed the children individually at the end of the school year, it was apparent that this mathematical practice had a variety of qualitatively distinct meanings for them. From the cognitive perspective, their conceptions of place value numeration were not shared but, instead, fit sufficiently for them to talk about mathematics without becoming aware of discrepancies in their mathematical interpretations. In short, they individually constructed conceptualizations that were adequate for the purpose of coordinating their mathematical activity with that of others as they completed tasks and engaged in collaborative mathematical activity.

The relation between individual children's mathematical knowledge and the mathematical practices institutionalized by the classroom community is an instantiation of that between the cognitive and anthropological perspectives:

Individual   Communal
mathematical knowledge   mathematical practices

This relation can be summarized by saying that individual mathematical activities that fit together constitute the institutionalized mathematical practices that constrain the individual mathematical activities that generate them. This conception of the relation between individual and cultural phenomena emphasizes the central role that collaborative activity plays in inquiry mathematics. As Bruner (1986, p. 123) put it:

> [I]t follows from this view of culture as a forum that induction into the culture through education, if it is to prepare the young for life as lived, should also partake of the spirit of a forum, of negotiation, of the recreating of meaning. But this conclusion runs counter to traditions of pedagogy that derive from another time, another interpretation of culture, another conception of authority—one that looked at the process of education as a *transmission* of knowledge and values *by* those who knew more *to* those who knew less and knew it less expertly.

Conclusion

The relations between individual mathematical knowledge and individual beliefs, and between institutionalized mathematical practices and social norms, as shown in Figure 4.1 are analogous to that between a scientific community's creation of scientific knowledge and a scientific research tradition. This scheme is the current result of our attempts to make sense of life in one classroom. We acknowledge that it is limited in that it ignores the linkages with the broader sociopolitical setting and, more generally, with the function of the school as a societal institution. Nonetheless, we have found it useful in our attempt to cope with the complexity of classroom life.

With regard to research, the American tradition, at least in mathematics education, has historically focused on individual students' mathematical cognitions. This tradition has now been widened to include consideration of students' beliefs. However, with rare exceptions (e.g., Lampert, 1990; Schoenfeld, 1987) mathematics educators have yet to take an anthropological stance toward classroom life (Eisenhart, 1988). The fundamental lesson we have learned during the course of our project is that it is essential to adopt this perspective even if one's primary concern is to understand individual students' construction of mathematical knowledge. Students' mathematical learning is influenced by both the mathematical practices and the social norms negotiated and institutionalized by the classroom community. In Vygotsky's terms, these practices and norms constitute the immediate social situation of development. In concert with his contention that this situation can be defined only relative to children's current level of psychological development, we have repeatedly emphasized that the second graders in the project classroom actively participated in the interactive constitution of mathematical practices and social norms. In addition, we have attempted to illustrate that the nature of the teacher's and children's face-to-face interactions were constrained by the classroom mathematics tradition viewed as an evolving social practice. The reflexivity between this practice and their concrete interactions becomes apparent when one notes that the classroom mathematics tradition was constituted during the course of the teacher's and students' ongoing interactions. The value of an analysis that gives heed to classroom mathematics tradition also became apparent when we noted the relevance of Leont'ev's concept of predmet. In particular, we argued that qualitative differences in the objects of mathematical activity constituted in project and nonproject classrooms should be understood with respect to differences between the school mathematics and inquiry mathematics traditions. As a final point, we noted in passing the compatibility between our analysis of the process of renegotiating social norms and Vygotsky's attempts to develop a unified theory of mind in social practice.

In closing, we observe that the scheme represented in Figure 4.1 also gives some sense of the multifaceted nature of teaching. During the course of her practice, the teacher with whom we worked coordinated the activities of facilitating individual children's construction of mathematical knowledge, influencing their beliefs and initiating and guiding the negotiation of both communal mathematical practices and social norms. Frequently, her acts served multiple functions as she interacted with students. Not surprisingly, these various activities were often in conflict. Lampert (1985) succinctly captured a tension with which teachers must cope when she said that teaching "is an argument between opposing tendencies within oneself in which neither side can come out the winner. From this perspective, my job [as a mathematics teacher] would involve the tension between . . . pushing students to achieve and providing a comfortable learning environment, between covering the curriculum and attending to individual understanding" (p. 183). This conflict, in concrete form, is the tension between the cognitive and anthropological perspectives as it is realized in the lives of teachers.

Note

The project discussed in this chapter is supported by the National Science Foundation under grant MDR-885-0560 and by the Spencer Foundation. All opinions expressed are, of course, solely those of the authors.
Several notions central to this chapter were elaborated during the course of discussions with Heinrich Bauersfeld, Gotz Krummheuer, and Jorg Voigt at the University of Bielefeld, Germany.

References

Barnes, B. (1982). *T. S. Kuhn and social science.* New York: Columbia University Press.

Barnes, D., & Todd, F. (1977). *Communicating and learning in small groups* London: Routledge & Kegan Paul.

Bateson, G. (1973). *Steps to an ecology of mind.* London: Paladin.

Bauersfeld, H. (1980). Hidden dimensions in the so-called reality of a mathematics classroom. *Educational Studies in Mathematics, 11,* 23–41.

Bauersfeld, H. (1988). Interaction, construction, and knowledge: alternative perspectives for mathematics education. In T. Cooney & D. Grouws (eds.). *Effective mathematics teaching* (pp. 27–46). Reston, VA: National Council of Teachers of Mathematics and Lawrence Erlbaum.

Bernstein, R. J. (1983). *Beyond objectivism and relativism: science, hermeneutics, and praxis.* Philadelphia: University of Pennsylvania Press.

Bloor, D. (1983). *Wittgenstein: a social theory of knowledge.* New York: Columbia University Press.

Blumer, H. (1969). *Symbolic interactionism: perspectives and method.* Englewood Cliffs, NJ: Prentice Hall.

Bruner, J. S. (1986). *Actual minds, possible worlds.* Cambridge, MA: Harvard University Press.

Carraher, T. N., Carraher, D. W., & Schliemann, A. D. (1985). Mathematics in the streets and in schools. *British Journal of Developmental Psychology, 3,* 21–29.

Cazden, C. B. (1986). Classroom discourse. In M. C. Wittrock (ed.). *The handbook of research on teaching* (3rd ed.). New York: Macmillan.

Cobb, P. (1989). Experiential, cognitive, and anthropological perspectives in mathematics education. *For the Learning of Mathematics, 9* (2), 32–42.

Cobb, P. (1990). Multiple perspectives. In L. P. Steffe & T. Wood (eds.). *Transform-*

ing children's mathematics education: international perspectives (pp. 200–215). Hillsdale, NJ: Lawrence Erlbaum.

Cobb, P., & Wheatley, G. (1988). Children's initial understandings of ten. *Focus on Learning Problems in Mathematics, 10* (3), 1–28.

Cobb, P., Wood, T., & Yackel, E. (1990). Classrooms as learning environments for teachers and researchers. In R. B. Davis, C. A. Maher, & N. Noddings (eds.). *Constructivist views on teaching and learning mathematics. Journal for Research in Mathematics Education No. 4* (pp. 125–46). Reston, VA: National Council of Teachers of Mathematics.

Cobb, P., Yackel, E., & Wood, T. (1992). A constructivist alternative to the representational view of mind in mathematics education. *Journal for Research in Mathematics Education, 23,* 2–33.

Cobb, P., Wood, T., Yackel, E., Nicholls, J., Wheatley, G., Trigatti, B., & Perlwitz, M. (1991). Assessment of a problem-centered second grade mathematics project. *Journal for Research in Mathematics Education, 22,* 3–29.

Cobb, P., Yackel, E., & Wood, T. (1988). Curriculum and teacher development: psychological and anthropological perspectives. In E. Fennema, T. P. Carpenter, & S. J. Lamon (eds.). *Integrating research on teaching and learning mathematics* (pp. 92–131). Madison: Wisconsin Center for Educational Research, University of Wisconsin–Madison.

Cobb, P., Yackel, E., & Wood, T. (1989). Young children's emotional acts while doing mathematical problem solving. In D. B. McLeod & V. M. Adams (eds.). *Affect and mathematical problem solving: a new perspective* (pp. 117–148). New York: Springer-Verlag.

Cobb, P., Yackel, E., & Wood, T. (in press). Characteristics of classroom mathematics traditions: an interactional analysis. In C. Maher & R. Davis (eds.). *Relating schools to reality in mathematics learning.* Englewood Cliffs, NJ: Prentice Hall.

Comaroff, J. L. (1982). Dialectical systems, history and anthropology: units of study and questions of theory. *Journal of South African Studies, 8* (2), 143–172.

Confrey, J. (1987, July). *The current state of constructivist thought in mathematics education.* Paper presented at the annual meeting of the International Group for the Psychology of Mathematics Education, Montreal.

D'Ambrosio, U. (1985). Ethnomathematics and its place in the history and pedagogy of mathematics. *For the Learning of Mathematics, 5* (1), 44–48.

De Millo, R., Lipton, R., & Perlis, A. (1986). Social processes and proofs of theorems and programs. In T. Tymoczko (ed.). *New directions in the philosophy of mathematics* (pp. 267–285). Boston: Birkhauser.

Dillon, D. (1990, April). *The wider social context of innovation in mathematics education.* Paper presented at the annual meeting of the American Educational Research Association, Boston.

Eisenhart, M. A. (1988). The ethnographic research tradition and mathematics education research. *Journal for Research in Mathematics Education, 19,* 99–114.

Feldman, C. F. (1987). Thought from language: the linguistic construction of cognitive representations. In J. Bruner & H. Haste (eds.). *Making sense: the child's construction of the world* (pp. 131–162). London: Methuen.

Gadamer, H. G. (1986). *Truth and method.* New York: Crossroad.

Garfinkel, H. (1967). *Studies in ethnomethodology.* Englewood Cliffs, NJ: Prentice Hall.

Geertz, C. (1983). *Local knowledge.* New York: Basic Books.

Gergen, K. J. (1985). The social constructionist movement in modern psychology. *American Psychologist, 40,* 266–275.

Grabiner, J. V. (1986). Is mathematical truth time-dependent? In T. Tymoczko (ed.). *New directions in the philosophy of mathematics* (pp. 201–213). Boston: Birkhauser.

Harre, R. (ed.) (1986). *The social construction of emotions.* Oxford: Blackwell.

Kitcher, P. (1983). *The nature of mathematical knowledge.* Oxford: Oxford University Press.

Krummheuer, G. (1983). Das Arbeitsinterim im Mathematikunterricht. In H. Bauersfeld (ed.). *Lernen and Lehren von Mathematik* (pp. 57–106). Cologne: Aulis.

Kuhn, T. S. (1970). *The structure of scientific revolutions* (2nd ed.). Chicago: University of Chicago Press.

Lakatos, I. (1976). *Proofs and refutations.* Cambridge: Cambridge University Press.

Lampert, M. L. (1985). How do teachers manage to teach? Perspectives on the problems of practice. *Harvard Educational Review, 55,* 178–194.

Lampert, M. (1990). When the problem is not the question and the solution is not the answer: mathematical knowing and teaching. *American Educational Research Journal, 27,* 29–63.

Lave, J. (1988a). *Cognition in practice: mind, mathematics and culture in everyday life.* Cambridge: Cambridge University Press.

Lave, J. (1988b, April). *Word problems: a microcosm of theories of learning* Paper presented at the annual meeting of the American Educational Research Association, New Orleans.

Leont'ev, A. N. (1978). *Activity, consciousness, and personality.* Englewood Cliffs, NJ: Prentice Hall.

Leont'ev, A. N. (1981). Chelouek i Kul'trua [Man and culture]. In *Problemy razvitiia psikhiki* [Problems of the development of mind] (4th ed., pp. 410–435). Moscow: Moskovskogo Universiteta.

Levina, R. E. (1981). L. S. Vygotsky's ideas about the planning function of speech in children. In J. V. Wertsch (ed.). *The concept of activity in Soviet psychology* (pp. 279–299). Armonk, NY: M. E. Sharpe.

Maturana (1980). Man and society. In F. Benseler, P. M. Hejl, & W. K. Kock (eds.). *Autopoiesis, communication, and society* (pp. 11–32). Frankfurt, Germany: Campus Verlag.

Mead, G. H. (1934). *Mind, self, and society.* Chicago: University of Chicago Press.

Mehan, H. (1979). *Learning lessons.* Cambridge, MA: Harvard University Press.

Mehan, H., & Wood, T. (1975). *The reality of ethnomethodology.* New York: John Wiley.

Minick, N. (1987). The development of Vygotsky's thought: an introduction. In R. W. Rieber & A. S. Carton (eds.). *The collected works of L. S. Vygotsky. Vol. 1. Problems of general psychology* (pp. 17–38). New York: Plenum.

Minick, N. (1989a). *L. S. Vygotsky and Soviet activity theory: perspectives on the relationship between mind and society.* Literacies Institute, Special Monograph Series No. 1. Newton, MA: Educational Development Center.

Minick, N. (1989b). Mind and activity in Vygotsky's work: an expanded frame of reference. *Cultural Dynamics, 2,* 162–187.

Much, N. C., & Shweder, R. A. (1978). Speaking of rules: the analysis of culture in breach. *New Directions for Child Development, 2,* 19–39.

Newman, D., Griffin, P., & Cole, M. (1989). *The construction zone: working for cognitive change in school.* Cambridge: Cambridge University Press.

Nicholls, J., Cobb, P., Wood, T., Yackel, E., & Patashnick, M. (1990). Dimensions of success in mathematics: individual and classroom differences. *Journal for Research in Mathematics Education, 21,* 109–122.

Nicholls, J., Cobb, P., Yackel, E., Wood, T., & Wheatley, G. (1990). Assessing young children's mathematical learning. In G. Kulm (ed.). *Assessing higher order thinking in mathematics* (pp. 137–154). Washington, DC: American Association for the Advancement of Science.

Perret-Clermont, A. N. (1980). *Social interaction and cognitive development in children.* Orlando, FL: Academic Press.

Richards, J. (1991). Mathematical discussions. In E. von Glasersfeld (ed.). *Constructivism in mathematics education* (pp. 13–52). Dordrecht, Netherlands: Kluwer.

Rommetveit, R. (1986). Language acquisition as increasing linguistic structuring of experience and symbolic behavior control. In J. V. Wertsch (ed.). *Culture communication and cognition* (pp. 183–205). Cambridge: Cambridge University Press.

Rorty, R. (1980). Pragmatism, relativism, and irrationalism. *Proceedings and Addresses of the American Philosophical Association, 53,* 719–738.

Sacks, H., Schegloff, E., & Jefferson, G. (1974). A simplest systematics for the analysis of turn taking in conversation. *Language, 50,* 696–735.

Saxe, G. B. (1988, January). *The interplay between children's learning in formal and informal social contexts.* Paper presented at the conference on the Scientific Practice of Science Education, Berkeley, California.

Saxe, G. B. (1989). Selling candy: a study of cognition in context. *Quarterly Newsletter of the Laboratory of Comparative Human Cognition, 11* (1&2), 19–22.

Schoenfeld, A. H. (1987). What's all the fuss about metacognition? In A. H. Schoenfeld (ed.). *Cognitive science and mathematics education* (pp. 189–216). Hillsdale, NJ: Lawrence Erlbaum.

Schon, D. A. (1983). *The reflective practitioner.* New York: Basic Books.

Sigel, I. E. (1981). Social experience in the development of representational thought: distancing theory. In I. E. Sigel, D. M. Brodzinsky, & R. M. Golinkoff (eds.). *New directions in Piagetian theory and practice* (pp. 203–217). Hillsdale, NJ: Lawrence Erlbaum.

Solomon, Y. (1989). *The practice of mathematics.* London: Routledge.

Steffe, L. P. (1987, April). *Principles of mathematical curriculum design in early childhood teacher education.* Paper presented at the annual meeting of the American Educational Research Association, Washington, D.C.

Steffe, L. P., Cobb, P., & von Glasersfeld, E. (1988). *Construction of arithmetical meanings and strategies.* New York: Springer-Verlag.

Steffe, L. P., von Glasersfeld, E., Richards, J., & Cobb, P. (1983). *Children's counting types: philosophy, theory, and application.* New York: Praeger Scientific.

Tymoczko, T. (1986). Introduction. In T. Tymoczko (ed.). *New directions in the philosophy of mathematics* (pp. xiii–xvii). Boston: Birkhauser.

Voigt, J. (1985). Patterns and routines in classroom interaction. *Recherches en Didactique des Mathematiques, 6,* 69–118.

Voigt, J. (1989). The social constitution of the mathematics province—a microethnographical study in classroom interaction. *Quarterly Newsletter of the Laboratory of Comparative Human Cognition, 11* (1&2), 27–34.

Voigt, J. (1989). Social functions of routines and consequence for subject matter learning. *International Journal of Educational Research, 13,* 647–656.

Von Glasersfeld, E. (1984). An introduction to radical constructivism. In P. Watzlawick (ed.). *The invented reality* (pp. 17–40). New York: Norton.

Vygotsky, L. S. (1933/1976). Play and its role in the mental development of the child. In J. S. Bruner, A. Jolly, & K. Sylva (eds.). *Play: its role in development and evolution* (pp. 537–554). New York: Penguin Books.

Vygotsky, L. S. (1934/1984). Voprocy detskoi vozrastnoi psikhologii [Problems of child age psychology]. In D. B. El'konin (ed.). *L. S. Vygotskii, Sobranie sochinenie: detskaia psikhologiia [L. S. Vygotsky, collected works. Vol. 4. Child psychology]* (Vol. 4, pp. 244–385). Moscow: Pedagogika.

Vygotsky, L. S. (1934/1987). Thinking and speech. In R. W. Rieber & A. S. Carton (eds.). *The collected works of L. S. Vygotsky. Vol. 1. Problems of general psychology.* New York: Plenum.

Walkerdine, V. (1988). *The mastery of reason: cognitive development and the production of rationality.* London: Routledge.

Wertsch, J. V. (1985). *Vygotsky and the social formation of mind.* Cambridge, MA: Harvard University Press.

Winograd, T., & Flores, F. (1986). *Understanding computers and cognition: a new foundation for design.* Norwood, NJ: Ablex.

Wittgenstein, L. (1964). *Remarks on the foundations of mathematics.* Oxford: Blackwell.

Wood, T., Cobb, P., & Yackel, E. (1990). The contextual nature of teaching: mathematics and reading instruction in one second-grade classroom. *Elementary School Journal, 90,* 497–514.

Wood, T., & Yackel, E. (1990). Teacher's role in the development of collaborative dialogue within small group interactions. In L. P. Steffe & T. Wood (eds.). *Transforming children's mathematics education: international perspectives* (pp. 244–252). Hillsdale, NJ: Lawrence Erlbaum.

Yackel, E., Cobb, P., & Wood, T. (1991). Small group interactions as a source of learning opportunities in second grade mathematics. *Journal for Research in Mathematics Education, 22,* 390–408.

5

Creating and Reconstituting Contexts for Educational Interactions, Including a Computer Program

PEG GRIFFIN, ALEXANDRA BELYAEVA,
GALINA SOLDATOVA, and the VELIKHOV-HAMBURG
COLLECTIVE

> The sense of a word . . . is the sum of all the psychological events aroused in our consciousness by the word. It is a dynamic, fluid, complex whole, which has several zones of unequal stability. Meaning is only one of the zones of sense, the most stable and precise zone. A word acquires its sense from the context in which it appears; in different contexts it changes its sense. [Vygotsky, 1986, pp. 244–45]

We take Vygotsky's description of sense as a suggestion, perhaps an invitation, to study context carefully. Vygotsky argued for the importance to educators of the relation between the contexts in which children participate and the concepts they acquire (Vygotsky, 1986, pp. 190–209). The other members of his troika during the early part of this century, Luria and Leont'ev, produced works rich in descriptions of context in which the practical activities of the researcher and the subjects and pragmatic realities from the wider world intermingle with basic theory: Luria's "romantic science" (1979) and Leont'ev's "leading activities" (1981) can hardly be considered without evoking images of Zasetsky and World War II (Luria, 1972) or the day-to-day jokes and bickering as families and peer groups shop, play, and face homework assignments (Leont'ev, 1981, Section 3). Vygotskians of the next generation (e.g., Davidov, 1988a,b,c; El'konin, 1975; Meshcheryakov, 1979) have concentrated on contexts within which children grow and develop through play and learning activities, necessarily including detailed descriptions of specific content domains, concrete cultural artifacts (e.g., materials and equipment), and the sociohistorical situation. In a framework that emphasizes sociogenesis (the origin of an individual's psychological functions in the social, cultural, and historical world), it is not surprising that Vygotsky, his colleagues, and his followers called on contextual variations as they studied human development and remediation. This framework has influenced our work, leading us to examine more closely the state of research involving contexts and to become involved in the specific details of constructing contexts, including the cultural artifact (educational software) that is prominent in contexts where children use computers.

One might gather from the Vygotskian quotation above that research could be designed to hold a word or concept constant while varying the context or vice versa, and the interest in the issue would be exhausted. Contemporary studies in a variety of disciplines, however, force us to recognize that a context is also dynamic, fluid, and complex, not established beforehand like the "backdrop" prepared for a stage play; a context emerges, being "constituted" in large measure by words used by context participants and their other actions. *How to Do Things with Words* (1962) by the philosopher J. L. Austin has become a key text concerning the constitutive power of words; the conversational analysis of sociologists (e.g., Sacks, Schegloff, & Jefferson, 1974) has stimulated study of the dynamics involved, focusing especially on the reflexive relations between structures and participants who work together as contexts are constructed. Although much is still being debated about how to understand meaning, sense, words, participants, contexts, and the relations holding among them, one thing is clear: It is reasonable to accept that words and contexts are mutually constituting; although problematic, attention to the details of context construction can be productive.

This chapter is derived in particular from our experience in two countries with The Pond program (Kosel & Fish, 1984), but in the following sections we draw on and describe theoretical constructs from sociohistorical psychology, from philosophy, and from conversational analysis. After a discussion of context, alternate views of the functioning of educational computer programs in them, and the relation between some theoretical constructs and software options, we describe The Pond and its tasks. Then six specific aspects of the program in use are discussed in detail to illustrate our main point: Educational software can participate in a polilogue (a conversation with many participants), such that it plays a role in constituting an educational context. Authoring components and option keys in educational software can be used to arrange for collaborative communication between the "programmers' voice" and the people in specific local learning activities. Our conclusion points toward the associated contexts that must be dealt with in order to influence local educational polilogues where we try to "make sense" with children.

Context

A context description, simply put, is an attempt to say "what is going on here" (Erickson & Schultz, 1977). For several years we have been a part of a group of researchers undertaking joint activity using new communication technologies. [See Volume 11, No. 3, *The Quarterly Newsletter of the Laboratory of Comparative Human Cognition,* especially Belyaeva and Cole (1989) therein, for a more complete description.] As part of this work, constituting it and being constituted by it, we engage in subprojects related to computer use by children of midelementary school age in the United States and Russia. In summer camps and after-school clubs, we work with a mixed group of children (urban and rural, socially privileged and not, good and poor school performers) and adults (researchers from a variety of disciplines, teachers, business people, college students, and paraprofessionals). The children's computer use varies widely (e.g., word processing, database programs, programming languages, simulations, more traditional educational software, and games). Electronic mail and computer conferences are the mainstay of child and adult work, allowing communications that are speedy and informal.

The subproject involving The Pond has had three phases to date. In the first phase (Griffin, Belyaeva, & Soldatova, 1992), we examined communication in the zones of proximal development (Vygotsky, 1978, Ch. 6)— henceforth called Zo-peds—that occurred under different conditions of use of the program. We studied various groups of users (child acting alone, cooperative peer, competitive peer, and expert/novice) and other teaching/learning strategies (passive teacher, fantasy figure teacher communicating via computer, construction of three- and two-dimensional models, order of presentation of examples) in order to characterize the kinds of communicative acts, learning activities, and auxiliary means (Vygotsky, 1978, Ch. 4) that could take advantage of the program's potential to promote children's concept development.

This chapter is about the second phase, software critique and revision, which has resulted in a new version of the software (Kosel & Fish, 1989). The third phase involves using the revised program in a variety of circumstances. It is a part of our continuing work in both countries as part of after-school clubs and in more constrained settings (e.g., Lemons, 1990; Lemons & Samoilenko, 1990).

Adequate Description of Context

On other occasions or when written by a different member of our group, the description of the context of our work varies from the above; different aspects of the project are seen as necessary or possible to include, as relevant or irrelevant. Descriptions of context, too, are sensitive to the contexts with which they are mutually constitutive. Given this variability, a problem arises about evaluating the adequacy of the treatment of context. Although we can learn a great deal from studies that have developed since the 1920s when Vygotsky wrote, we still encounter difficulties accepting Vygotsky's invitation to attend to context. As Vygotsky described the relation between "sense," meaning, and context, he claimed, "The dictionary meaning of a word is no more than a stone in the edifice of sense, no more than a potentiality . . ." (1986, p. 245). Contemporary work identifies some other "stones" the edifice[1] would need and the context must provide, for example, the semantic significance of grammatical constructions, the media and mediation, communicative acts, social roles and classes, cultural (and ethnic) conventions and artifacts, institutional constraints, past history, and negotiated goals imaging the future. However, there is no accepted consensus about what to focus on for a sufficient study of context.

Different strategies have emerged in studies that both elucidate and make powerful use of the notion "context." Concentration on specific domains of application (e.g., health care, education, child development) is one strategy for successful work with context (e.g., Labov & Fanschel, 1977; McDermott, 1976; Mehan, 1979; Ochs, 1988; Scheflen, 1974). Another strategy is exhibited in the work of linguists and translators: What is needed to interpret the communication determines the aspects of context that require attention. For example, Leont'ev wrote, "The game 'Chelyuskinites,' for instance, can be found at quite different stages of development, but how different its sense is for the child!" (1981, p. 390). The translator added a note about polar explorations during the 1930s, an icebreaker, the passengers, an accident, and an airlift rescue, emphasizing the fame of and admiration for this episode in Russia. What the description of context should include was determined intuitively and post hoc. When relied on in a linguistic study (e.g., Sadock, 1974), this strategy can be criticized as leading to a treatment of context as static—as simply a backdrop, a residual category.

Another strategy for describing contexts is to define the parameters that must be addressed to determine constituent elements a priori. Anthropologist Dell Hymes (1972) produced such a framework for the ethnography of speaking; more recently, Barwise and Perry (1983) developed a system for situational semantics. These efforts are criticized as overly simple (omitting some necessary aspects) or reductionist (deemphasizing the dynamic, emergent nature of context in favor of aspects that are more compatible with the formal mechanisms).

Other studies concentrate on the general but concrete properties of the beginnings and endings of contexts that provide ways to identify specific instances even without operational definitions based on constituent parts (see especially the studies of boundaries and transitions within and between contexts, e.g., Cahir, 1978; Goodwin, 1986; Schegloff, 1968; Schegloff & Sacks, 1973). The general issue of how a scientific study of contexts can proceed has also been addressed. Erickson and Schultz (1977) concentrated on the need for analysts to take the perspective of the participants as they act and react to make up the context; Goodwin and Goodwin (in press) can be read as an update of this strategy, emphasizing the problem of multiple coexisting contexts.

The strategy we use is to create contexts and to act within them. In addition to the aspects of the context that we are able to articulate and reflect on because of the literature available, our everyday activities (preparing for and actually negotiating "what is going on here" with the other participants) help to call to our attention the aspects of context that are important to our work.

(Re)constituting Contexts and Formative Experiments

Two lines of research underlie our decision to create contexts, taking a detour into special settings, rather than to undertake "naturalistic observations" of existing situations where computers are used for education. First, Vygotskian research has always relied on such context creation in the use of the Zo-ped. Current scholars in this tradition, (e.g., Davidov, 1988b, p. 13; El'konin, 1975, especially p. 50) point out problems that arise when ordinary school situations are relied on for data. They argue that research that fails to create new artifacts and situations for learning reveals less about, for instance, child development or the influence of education on development, than it reveals about the particular, current forms and content of schooling on which a society has agreed. Although the children and teachers constitute the context observed by a researcher, the equally constitutive power of the societal status quo biases what the researcher can see about children, teachers, educational practices, tools, and materials. Pessimistic findings from data gathered under current pedagogical conditions can severely underestimate the power of instructional theory and practices to influence development and may fail to provide an impetus or ideas for designing better education.

A second line of research reinforces this concern for our particular topic. There have been studies of computers introduced into U.S. classrooms (e.g., Mehan, Moll, & Riel, 1983; Michaels, 1985) demonstrating that the use of this new artifact in the educational setting is strongly influenced by preexisting pedagogical practices and larger societal issues (e.g., gender, ethnic, and socioeconomic bias). Naturalistic observation, then, reveals much about the existing social ordering in the classroom and how it recapitulates the larger societal ordering (see Cole, Griffin, & LCHC, 1987, for a review) but may well limit our view as we try to determine how computers might be used to promote development not "expected" under current societal conditions. Mehan et al. (1983, p. 226) argued against assuming that "the status quo is the appropriate context for computer use," and asked, "Why should we expect that the same practices that have produced wide-spread academic failure will create propitious environments for computer use?"

As we go beyond observation and create contexts to study computers in education, we can be seen as generalizing on Vygotsky's argument (1978, p. 85–89) about the need for Zo-peds. Vygotsky advised us to assess and teach children based on what they can do in collaboration, rather than on what they can accomplish in isolation; otherwise, our study lags behind the children's development, so we characterize the history of a child, failing to capture the ongoing process or to promote future development. Vygotsky (1978, p. 87) described the Zo-ped as a "tool through which the . . . course of development can be understood." The Zo-ped tool was used for studying the individual's internal development; our created contexts can be seen as a tool to study the development of educational contexts and computer programs used in them.

This tool fits into a class known as formative experiments,[2] not well known in the United States. Davidov (1988b, p. 53) described them in this way:

> The formative experiment may, in our view, be called an experiment in
> Ngenesis-modeling. . . . This method rests upon the construction and re-con-

struction of new curricula for upbringing and teaching and of modes whereby those curricula may be actualized.

In effect, a formative experiment is a Zo-ped that treats not just the children as developing entities but also the researchers, teachers, and materials.[3] Commentaries about Vygotskian research in the United States have focused on the freedom to act and to change constraints by the experimenter (or more competent other), but there has been little focus on the equally important notion of goal/task formation. The question of interest is not *if* a certain type of subject performs correctly on a criterion task under certain conditions but, rather, *how* the participants, including the experimenter, accomplish *what* task, using cultural artifacts. The task and goal are purposefully vague; they are underspecified initially from the perspectives of both subject and experimenter. A formative experiment specifies task and goal as the participants experience "drafts" of it being constructed, deconstructed, and reconstructed. The coordinations and discoordinations of the participants in the experiment make public "what is going on here"—what the task is. In this way of working, goal formation and context creation are a part of the material taken as data, not given a priori.[4]

The "final draft" in a formative experiment appears only when there is a return to the situations of the status quo, to an examination of how the new goals, tasks, and materials are negotiated in the contexts the researchers purposefully failed to observe "naturalistically." The focus in this chapter is on two important elements of a formative experiment: (1) the people, including programmers, who constitute the context as they engage in social interaction (the interpsychological plane) through which subsequent versions of the goal and task can emerge and where coordinations and discoordinations can be observed for analysis; and (2) a genetic analysis of the content domain, organizing the current cultural store of information and artifacts in the domain to stand as a first "draft" of the goals and task involved.

Social Interactions When Computers Are in the Context

Existing evidence suggests that a one-child one-computer situation is often undesirable (see Cole et al., 1987 for a review). During the first phase of our work with The Pond (Griffin et al., 1992) we arranged contrasting contexts and described the advantages that accrue as children work with peers and teachers, rather than in isolation. Although it might be claimed that rigor and clarity recommend studying simple systems, such as one child with one computer, studies in the Vygotskian framework recommend otherwise. Luria demonstrated (1932, pp. 14–24) that otherwise "hidden" aspects of dynamic processes can be made noticeable only by the coordinations and discoordinations that surface in a method that combines systems, rather than attempting to reduce the situations found in the real world. If the isolated child with computer (or just some idealized ergonomic or perceptual features of the machine or program alone) is focused on out of contexts of use, the analyst's vision is blurred; such reductionism is the least informative for research on cognitive change: All the other participants in the polilogue are hidden and their contributions abbreviated or frozen; they are present but look like noise to the scientist who can neither investigate nor control for them.

In contrast to viewing the computer as a dialogic partner with a single child, we have previously (e.g., Griffin & Cole, 1987) viewed and used the computer as a "medium" that facilitates geographically widespread communication and that has properties different from those of other media (e.g., face-to-face oral language or written language and graphics not involving computers). Another sense of the computer-as-medium derives from face-to-face contexts where certain computer software appears to redefine and enhance communication between adults and children (LCHC, 1982). Other subprojects in our current joint work emphasize the computer as "tool" (Vygotsky, 1978, Ch. 1; Leont'ev, 1981, p. 217) as teachers, researchers, and children make conscious and flexible use of the "computer-as-medium" to negotiate solutions to problems (e.g., idea generation, expression, comprehension, or sociocultural relations among participants).

Our Context for This Phase of the Project Revisited

At first, we viewed The Pond as a tool for teachers and children as they were engaged in educational polilogues to build the contexts we were studying. Educational software such as The Pond program can be used to present a token of a task and then to record, evaluate, and reward a response. Although apparently accomplished by the computer on which the software is running, these "actions" are initiated and controlled by the people in the context; the software is static, with a small range of stereotyped responses to keypresses made by teachers and children. Because the people in the context have the dynamic characteristics (wide range of unpredictable initiations and responses) that are crucial for negotiations of "what is going on here" (for constituting the context), we had not expected the computer program to act as an independent contributor to the context. We began to encounter occasions, however, where the software was "blamed" for interrupting the work of the children and teachers, for contradicting ideas the participants were trying to develop.[5] There was nothing "wrong" with the computer or the program; it was performing the small range of responses to keypresses adequately. The screen displays, however, were relevant to far more than the immediate keypress.

Part of our contexts had been "prefabricated" by the programmers of the software; their contributions about what could and should be done in the educational context were revealed in the screen displays. The programmers had to be treated as "hidden" members of the communicative interactions, with distant but powerful "voices." We then created a new context so we could involve the programmers overtly and more closely in our work. This new context involved a series of face-to-face meetings in San Diego and Moscow, interspersed with computer-mediated conference communication. Through this context we used our developing experience with children and The Pond to examine how the distant voice of the programmers could become more cooperative and productive.

Theoretical Constructs and Software Opportunities

The "programmers' voice" frozen into the program but helping to constitute the contexts of its use can be seen as equivalent to presuppositions in discourse. In ordinary language philosophy, presuppositions are said to be "nontruth functional." This point is best illustrated by "conversational traps" such as the following: Certain questions can be answered with "yes" or "no"; however, if they contain a presupposition, either denial or agreement traps the answerer into agreeing with the truth of the presupposition. To wit, "Have you stopped drinking too much?" Whether answered with "yes" or "no" suggests that the answerer has previously drunk too much. Presupposing, rather than overtly asserting, something can be powerful. Many of our notes about the "turns" The Pond contributed to our contexts were complaints about "traps" occasioned by presuppositions from the programmers' voice.

With conversations, one can call a halt to the operation of a presupposition, make an overt expression of it, and deal with it explicitly. Participants can take conversational turns and collaborate with each other to establish what is to be meant. In some computer programs, "option keys" can be pressed in the midst of an activity in order to force the overt expression of underlying material and sometimes to change it. In many cases, however, there is little chance for users of computer programs to take a turn that denies presuppositions. Below we discuss specific presuppositions about educational activity and the participants in them, and we describe our efforts to make The Pond software a more cooperative "interactant" in face-to-face contexts with children by using option keys to make some information overt or by providing a "pre" to the activity in an authoring component.

The term "authoring" is used in computer circles to indicate that a program allows a user to collaborate with the program designers in order to tailor aspects of the program to make it suitable for use in a particular context. In our terms, authoring allows us to interact with the presuppositions in the "programmers' voice," exercising some choice over the computer program's contributions to the educational context. The effects of authoring are almost paradoxical: The program becomes more directly tied to a particular concrete circumstance, yet the program can rise to the demands of many concrete circumstances.

Authoring can be seen as analogous to the structures called "pre's" by conversational analysts. A clear, but impolite, example of a pre occurs when someone takes a turn to ask "What are you cooking?" instead of immediately providing the "answer" turn to an invitation to dinner. It is obvious that a pre comes before something else that is expected (here a turn that accepts or declines the invitation), but it is important to note that they "prepare" for future parts of the interaction, governing not only the speaker's turns but even those of others. These pre turns "migrate," so that some invitations include reference to the kind of information that a pre might otherwise be used to seek, e.g., "I found some salmon at the market this morning. Can you come over to dinner?" There can be a pre for a whole conversation as well, for example, "I have some bad news," or "Can I ask you a question?" (Schegloff, 1980). In a computer program, authoring is usually accommodated by adding a component or module to be used before the "real" program is run. Authors (users with information about how to access the authoring component, often by pressing a particular key at the opening screen) are presented with a menu that allows them to adjust the way the program will operate when it is used later; elements may be added or subtracted, or alternatives may be chosen.

The Pond

There were three initial advantages of The Pond for our work: The general domain addressed, mathematics, was of special interest to the project[6]; it relies less on English language ability than other programs, important for international work; it runs on low-power computers that could be freely used in then existing political and economic circumstances (the Apple II series in the United States and the Pravetz from Bulgaria in Russia).

What Is The Pond?

At one level of description, The Pond is about the recognition of a pattern and the representation of it with symbols for the numbers 1 through 5 and arrows for four directions (up, down, right, and left). A written description of a computer program is unsatisfying; Vygotsky might have said it is difficult to convey the "sense" we have of it generated by our experiences in many contexts. Accepting our limits, we here provide a description of the basic scenario, the primary screen display, the moves available to the users, and options in the program.

Scenario

In a pond dotted with lily pads, there is a frog that hops from lily pad to lily pad when directions are entered from the keyboard. If the frog is directed to jump where there is no lily pad, it balks at hopping onto grass or it falls into the pond with a splash, then clambers back onto a lily pad. One lily pad is the "starting point" where the frog sits at the beginning; another lily pad, marked by a unique color and design, is the "ending point." If the frog reaches the "ending point," it winks an eye and celebrates, saying "Whoo-

Используйте ↑, ↓, ←, →
для движения лягушки

Нажмите ↵ если решение готово

Figure 5.1. Basic screen display (from Russian *Prud*, otherwise similar to English *Pond*).

pie!" in one part of the program and "You made it!" in another. The users can encounter many pond problems, differing in the layout of the lily pads and on the starting point of the frog, some with more complicated patterns than others, and some with "distractor lily pads" on which the frog does not need to hop to get to the end.

Screen Display

Most of the time a portion of a pond shows on the top three-quarters of the screen. There is a grass border and room for about five lily pads down and six across; the frog sits at the starting point in one of the corners. At first, the bottom of the screen has instructions: "Press ↑ ↓ ← → to move your frog. Press RETURN when you know the pattern." (See Figure 5.1 for a sketch of virtually the same screen but in the revised version that allows the use of Russian.) As the frog hops, the screen is redrawn, revealing further portions of the pond and producing an effect like a camera "panning" across the pond.

Users' Moves

Users can move the frog one hop at a time by pressing an arrow key (or the keys I, K, J, and L) in the "exploratory" mode. However, the frog balks at hopping onto the ending point lily pad. If the users press the RETURN key, they begin the "formula entry" mode. The first portion of The Pond with the frog at the "starting point" is shown; underneath is the space for the users to enter a formula made of a series of "steps" (units made of a directional arrow and a number). The screen prompt reads "ENTER your first move. ↑ ↓ ← →." The users press a key to move a box on the screen over one of the arrow drawings, pressing RETURN when the desired arrow is boxed. Then the prompt changes: "How many? Pattern: → 1 2 3 4 5." The users now move a box to choose a number (e.g., 3). The prompt changes to "How many? Pattern: →3," showing the first "step" chosen; thereafter the formula-so-far is always available on the screen. After the RETURN is pressed, a prompt appears for another step: "ENTER your next move. Pattern: →3 ↑ ↓ ← → GO! Erase." The users can continue to enter "steps" composed of arrow–number pairs or to "erase" steps previously entered. If the users move the box to "go," the "execution" mode begins. The frog enacts the series of hops described by the formula. If the formula is incorrect, the frog either splashes into the water or balks at hopping onto the grass border and returns to the starting point; if the formula is a correct one, the frog makes it to the "ending point" lily pad, where it winks and celebrates.

For most Pond problems, there is not room on the formula line to type in all of the steps in the pattern; the box on the screen automatically moves to "GO" after six steps have been entered. Furthermore, it is *never* necessary to use more than six steps. The longest formula needed in the program is "four steps," for example, "right 2, down 3, right 3, up 1." The formula *repeats:* The frog follows each step until the last and then executes the first step again and each of the others until it lands at the "ending point" and stops, even if it has not executed a full "step" or a full iteration of the formula.

Options

Two option keys can be used in the "exploratory" mode. The "9" key adds highlighting that "flashes" on and off, indicating the correct path for the frog, helpful for the ponds that have distractor lily pads. The "0" key changes the screen display completely to show all the lily pads in the Pond in miniature on one screen, omitting the color and detailed depiction of the frog, land, and water. This diagram is helpful for problems that have long chains of hops in a step and more than two steps in the formula, as a complete iteration of such formulas cannot be seen on one screen in the larger depiction. Both the "9" and the "0" keys are disabled during the formula entry mode.

When a problem has been completed, a choice appears: "Do you want the same problem? YES NO." If the users decline, the screen offers the opportunity to work with a different Pond problem but one that has the same name as the problem just finished. If the users choose not to work with such a Pond problem, they are presented with a screen that includes a menu of different names of Ponds. This menu and prompts for using it are also available at the beginning of the program, even before the users have worked out one basic scenario. The names indicate different *kinds* of Ponds: Each Pond problem can be categorized according to the number of "steps" (two, three, or four) required for the formula and by whether the Pond includes some distractors. The menu, shown in Figure 5.2, overtly labels the "steps" distinction but covertly indicates the Ponds with distractor pads by offering them as the even-numbered choices. Users who choose "Billy Bob's Ponds," the two-step Ponds with distractors, may get a Pond that requires the formula "down 3, right 4" even though the display includes some other lily pads that are not part of the pattern. There are many possible two-step Ponds with distractors that could be presented to the users; the one that appears is random.

When the program is first booted on the computer, right after the title screen, there is another menu for a choice between "practice" and "game." The above description applies to both parts. However, in the "game," the users must start on the beginning problem type and are automatically promoted to the next higher numbered type if they are successful with three problems of a current type. Success is mediated by a point system: users start with 35 points and lose them as they "explore" with hops, option keys, or "go" to execute incorrect formulas. Along the way, the players are notified of how many points remain. If they run out of points before they have a correct solution for a Pond, the game is over; if they are promoted to a Pond of a new type, they are awarded 35 more points to "spend." If the players complete the three "Twister Ponds," a rainbow and celebration appear on the screen.

In the "game" part of the program, there is a choice available that does not occur in the "practice" part. The program first asks, "How many players are there? 1 2." The two-player choice brings up another screen, asking for each player's name. The names are used to cue turn-taking between the players. One player is presented with one Pond of the current type and keeps his or her turn until the points run out or the problem is solved; then the same kind of turn is given to the second player. The players' points are accumulated separately.

Two-step patterns
    1. Farmer Jane's Ponds
    2. Billy Bob's Ponds
Three-step patterns
    3. Puzzle Ponds
    4. Lost Ponds
Four-step patterns
    5. Maze Ponds
    6. Twister Ponds

Press the → or ← to move the box to your number.
Press Return
        1   2   3   4   5   6

Figure 5.2. Menu of the original version of The Pond.

Tasks Involved in The Pond

Solving a Pond problem requires *representing* the frog's hops with a series of direction–number pairs that can be communicated via keypresses in order to have the frog move from the "starting point" to the "ending point." For the two-step Ponds, users can figure out what to represent by noting directional changes and counting the hops until the next change; for example, users who say, "Right, 1, 2. Up, 1, 2, 3, 4. Right, 1, 2. Up 1, 2, 3, 4" can represent the chant with the formula "→2 ↑4 →2 ↑4." For two-step Ponds, the relations among counting hops, representing them, and solving the problem is immediate.

In most respects, four-step Ponds are like the two-step ones; the interesting exception is that the *repeating* formula must be taken into account. Those solving two-step Ponds can ignore that their representation is a formula that repeats; they can attempt to represent the whole pattern; and even though there is not enough room on the formula line, the solution can be successful. The program "takes over" after the users have entered six steps of a formula, moving the cursor box to GO and releasing the frog to execute the formula. Entering four or six steps instead of a repeating formula of two steps has the desired effect. Although the users might not notice it, the program repeats their noneconomical formula that has within it two or three iterations of the economical two-step formula. For the four-step Ponds, attempts to represent the whole pattern often result in noticeable failure. For example, if the users accurately represent "as much as there is room for" of a four-step Pond by using the pattern "→2 ↑1 →3 ↓4 →2↑1," the automatic move to GO shows the frog splashing into the water on the 16th hop, the second iteration of the second step in the six-step formula entered. The four-step formula rather than the six-step one proves to be a more complete representation of the whole pattern, once the repeating nature of the program is taken into account. The relation between counting hops and representing them is still immediate, but the notion "repeat" mediates the understanding of the number of steps needed to represent the whole pattern.

With three-step Ponds, another problem is encountered: Users must *reanalyze* the information they obtain from counting the hops between lily pads. At first glance, these ponds seem to have a two-step repeating pattern, except for the first chain of hops in the design. To represent a pattern that accommodates the first chain, the users must reanalyze their "first glance"; what you immediately see and count is *not* what you need to get. There must be mediation to transform the mathematical objects—the numbers and the formula as a whole. There are two types of three-step Ponds that require reanalysis.

Many three-step Ponds involve a formula in which the first and last steps have the same direction. For these Ponds, there is no bi-unique relation between direction change and the beginning of a new step in the formula; two steps can occur in a chain of hops going in the same direction. Figure 5.3 (similar to the view produced by the "0" option in the program) shows

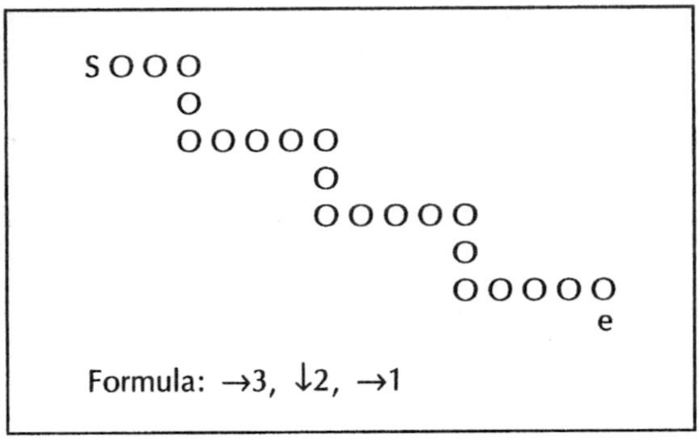

```
S O O O
    O
    O O O O O
        O
        O O O O O
            O
            O O O O O
                e
```

Formula: →3, ↓2, →1

Figure 5.3. Diagrammatic view of a Pond with reanalysis.

pond of this type. A "→4 ↓2" formula would work, except for the first chain of hops on the top line. (Recall that the last step executed need not be complete, so the one hop down in the last column is not a problem.) A four-, five-, or six-step formula fails shortly after the formula starts to repeat. In order to accommodate the top line of hops, the third chain of hops must be reanalyzed; "→4" can be decomposed into "→3" and "→1." The first chain of hops as well as the rest of the pattern can be accommodated with the formula with "→3, ↓2, →1," and the *repeating* operation of the formula composes again the "4" that appears to be needed.

Figure 5.4 depicts the other kind of reanalysis found in three-step Ponds. In these cases the first and third steps have opposite directions, and the frog backtracks. Direct progress toward the "ending point" lily pad must be replaced by an indirect approach; inefficiency at the level of the hops is required for an efficient formula. The problem in Figure 5.4 looks at first glance like a Pond with some distractor lily pads; if the first column could be ignored, a "→5, ↓2" formula would work. The first chain of four hops must

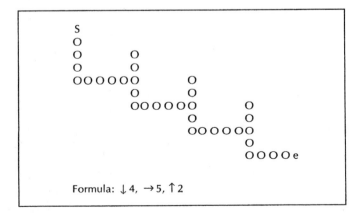

Formula: ↓4, →5, ↑2

Figure 5.4. Diagrammatic view of a Pond with reanalysis and backtracking.

be taken into account, but "↓4 →5 ↓2" results in failure when the program's repeating operation applies it again. The hops that appear to be the first and second ones in the repeating short "↓2" chain can be reanalyzed as the third and fourth hops in a longer chain ("↓4") if an "↑2" step precedes it. With the formula "↓4 →5 ↑2" the third step leaves the frog where it can succeed as the program begins the next iteration of the formula with the "↓4" needed to handle the first chain; the frog backtracks down the two hops it just went up, and repeats the first step, "↓4."[7]

Vygotskian View of the Tasks

Pond problems that make reanalysis necessary are particularly interesting in the light of neo-Vygotskian formative experiments concerned with "learning activity." Over the past 25 years, El'konin, Davidov, and their students and colleagues have amalgamated Vygotsky's (1986, pp. 146–209) early interest in the special characteristics of concepts that develop primarily in educational contexts and Leont'ev's related activity theory (1981, p. 391). Recognizing that there is no strict dichotomy, Vygotsky contrasted the development of concepts in the concrete situations faced in everyday life contexts (his term was "spontaneous concepts") with the developmental history of concepts met in the context of lessons and "mediated" by cultural tools such as experimental procedures and models or diagrams (his term was "scientific concepts"). As Vygotsky had called for (1986, p. 208) in his critique of a "stage theory" of development, Leont'ev studied more details of more contexts, the "life-span" of development, noting that, depending on particular sociohistorical circumstances and a person's age, some kinds of context are experienced frequently and are the settings in which his or her "developmental leaps" can be observed or elicited; Leont'ev called these contexts "leading activities," which could account for the changes in motivational, methodological, and domain specific structures that are addressed by "stage" theories of development. Markova (1979) discussed the "life-span" of activities (from birth to more than 60 years) and defined the "learning activities" she worked on with Davidov and El'konin in further developments of the theory: Learning activities are those that are organized by adults and are aimed at the children's acquisition of knowledge, that is, "the acquisition of socially elaborated methods of analyzing and transforming various objects (linguistic, mathematic, etc.)" (Markova, 1979, p. 24).

Ponds with three-step solutions require analysis and transformation of the number of hops that are seen and counted; in Figure 5.3 what can be counted as 4 becomes a 1 and a 3; in Figure 5.4, the 2 becomes a part of 4. Furthermore, ponds with three-step solutions require that the formula emerge as an object of analysis and transformation. A formula for two- and four-step Ponds can be seen as several mechanically combined "isolated, independent elements" (Vygotsky 1986, p. 211): Elements of direction and number are combined into a larger element called a *step;* the steps are combined in the still larger element called the *formula;* and iterations of the formula are repeated in the largest element called the *pattern*. For three-step Ponds, the formula is not just a collection of elements of smaller scope and a constituent of an element with a larger scope; it is "a unit" for analysis (Vygotsky, 1986, p. 211), which pulls together all the parts and reveals interdependencies. While working with a three-step formula, the problem-solvers "reach down" to the lowest level constituents, determining, for example, that the direction "right" must be stated twice and the number 4 must be decomposed (Fig. 5.3) or that an "up" must be added and a 4 must be recomposed (Fig. 5.4). At the same time, the problem-solvers must work with the steps in the formula as interdependent, not just adjacent, noting, for example, the complementarity of adjusting the first and third steps in Figure 5.3 and the generation of the third step to accommodate the first step in Figure 5.4. Finally, problem-solvers have occasion to "reach up" to repetition, as they depend on the "next iteration" of their formula unit to make sense of the third steps they composed, which steps would otherwise be "too short" or "unnecessary."

Cataloguing the mathematical objects that might be evoked in educational contexts with The Pond is insufficient: Attention must be paid to the kinds of problem that should be used as a starting place in the activity in order to promote notice and discussion of these objects. The "genetically primary example" is a central aspect of formative experiments on learning activity: it is the "genetic foundation . . . for the later exposition of concrete phenomena in all their variety and diversity" (Markova, 1979, p. 63). The generalization that is sought in a learning activity is not just a collection, a grouping of things that are alike on some basis. Rather, it is a "substantive abstraction [that] reflects a genetically primary relationship that forms a functional foundation of the system of knowledge of any particular field" (Markova, 1979, p. 64). To promote the formation of substantive abstractions, the concrete task provided for the children and teacher to work with must be carefully chosen: "The specific nature of the learning task consists in the fact that through resolving it the children master a general mode for the resolution of all the particular tasks of a given type" (Davidov, 1988c, p. 39).

If a lesson starts in the wrong place, with examples that are not genetically primary to the domain, an "epigenetic byway" may be encountered: A child may solve what looks like a component part of a task or an easier version of the task only to find that such an experience leads to nothing helpful about the problems that manifest the full complexity of the domain. (See Griffin and Cole, 1987, pp. 206–9, where this issue is discussed in terms of the larger issue of complete curricula.) Evidence from the first and third phases of our work with Pond suggests that the two-step Ponds can function as epigenetic byways. We found that many children (ages 7 to 11 years) who had progressed to the point where they were regularly succeeding with two-step Ponds could not easily transfer this skill to three-step Pond problems; some found it difficult (even impossible) to use peer or adult support for success with three-step Ponds (Griffin et al., 1992; Lemons, 1990). In contrast, the transition to four-step Ponds was not noticeably difficult for the children in our contexts. The following genetic analysis of the problems can account for this outcome.[8]

What renders two-step Ponds inappropriate for use as genetically primary examples is that they can be solved without attention[9] to repetition or reanalysis, the fundamental substantive aspects of the domain. In contrast, three-step Ponds motivate the use of a repetitive formula. If the users try to represent the whole of a Pond (e.g., for Figure 5.3: "$\rightarrow 3 \downarrow 2 \rightarrow 4 \downarrow 2 \rightarrow 4 \downarrow 2 \rightarrow 4 \downarrow 2$" etc.) the program automatically moves to GO after six steps have been entered. The repetition in the program causes "trouble" by executing step 1 again despite the user's intentions, and the frog splashes into the water (for Figure 5.3, as step 2 begins the second time). The automatic six-step limit that made it easy to avoid repetition in the case of two-step Ponds causes trouble that makes it necessary to deal with the repeating nature of the formulas for both three- and four-step Ponds.

The second problem with two-step formulas as genetically primary examples is that they do not require reanalysis. The three-step problems are characterized by having the same or exactly opposite directions for the first and last steps. The logical opportunities to provide such cases with patterns that have two-step formulas are limited,[10] and none is supplied on the program diskettes. Although reanalysis would be possible in these few two-step cases, there is no motivation for using one rather than the other of the formulas that would result, so long as the numbers used and the number of steps used are within the constraints of the program. In contrast, the three-step cases cannot be solved without reanalysis; that is, the reanalysis is motivated. (See Leont'ev, 1981, pp. 210 ff., regarding motivation in activity systems and Davidov, 1988a, regarding motivation in learning activity.) A few four-step Ponds appearing on the program's diskette require reanalysis.

Our conclusion is that the three-step Ponds are the genetically primary examples in the domain of work with the Pond program. With a three-step Pond as the genetically primary example in the context, the "trouble" caused by repetition and reanalysis affords a chance for teachers and children to have the kinds of rich educational discussions involving the interesting aspects of the task that provide the foundation for them to rise to the concrete diversity found in two- and four-step Ponds.

Critique and Revisions

Our stance here is not to argue that a neo-Vygotskian analysis is necessary and sufficient for developing software; there are no demonstrations that other analyses or interpretations are in error or less powerful. In this section, we demonstrate (1) the possibility of relying on Vygotskian notions for comfortable and useful work concerning software for use with children, and (2) the desirability of such as a part of creating contexts for studying children, in both meanings of that ambiguous construction—children who are studying an academic domain and adults who are attempting to understand their activity.

As Fish and Kosel worked to produce the original version of The Pond, other theories and experiences informed their work. The cases below illustrate what we might call "clashes" between the theoretical attitude toward the object we were taking and the programmers' theories, expressed practically in the software design and emerging in our contexts as we used the software. The first three were successfully resolved by adding components to the software so different outlooks could coexist comfortably; the last three cases did not lead to such solutions.

Menu and Genetically Primary Example

The discoordination between the menu of the original Pond program and our discussion (just above) of the Pond tasks provide a clear-cut example. The numbering and the paratactics (sequencing) of the menu (Fig. 3.2) express a presupposition that the two-step ponds are the ones with which to start.[11] We wanted to deny this presupposition and use three-step Ponds as a genetically primary example for our contexts.

The authoring component, programmed into the revised versions of the software, allows a "pre" conversation to influence the expressions in the menu about proper sequencing of the problem types. Typing ⟨control–T⟩ as soon as the program is booted provides the collaborating author with a chance to design the menu that is presented to the next users of the diskette. As time and development go on in the local contexts, the author can reenter the authoring component and collaborate to design a different set or sequence of Pond types to be presented to subsequent users of the disk. The author may prepare a menu that makes use of a genetically primary example (presenting at first only three-step Ponds and later the full range in any order) or a menu that presupposes an easier to more difficult progression from representation of hops, to engagement with the repeating formula, to reanalysis (switching the order of three- and four-step Ponds). Other analyses of the situation can also be accommodated: An author can choose a set of Ponds that single out the "distractor" Ponds or choose to hide "clues" in the menu that reveal whether there are distractor lily pads and how many steps are involved in the named type. The authoring component does not replace one presupposition about the scope and sequence of the domain with another; rather, it allows negotiation between the "programmers' voice" and the voice of those responsible for the local educational context in which the software is used.

Dividing the Labor to Communicate the Task

A computer program can also clash with the norms for interpersonal relations and desirable educational practices in local contexts of use. In The Pond, the "game" part invites the user to involve another person, but the "practice" part does not; when more than one user is involved, individual competition, adjudicated by points, is promoted. It constitutes a suggestion that learning or practicing are solo activities, up to the individual, and that only when one is ready to play and compete does another person enter into the activity. Given our Vygotskian conviction that learning is a social process, we saw such a suggestion as a problem and made adjustments in contexts with children, that is, asking two children to play as one player in the "game," involving multiple users in the "practice," or using "practice" as an end in itself and ignoring the "game" (Griffin et al., 1992). However, such adjustments serve to emphasize that the social situation presupposed by the program contrasted with our norms. Because the software company had also developed strong interests in cooperative learning environments (Solutions, 1988), we worked together to have the "programmer's voice" presuppose more social learning.

With pairs or groups of users at the keyboard, different kinds of "turn taking" practices can be invented or arranged as a means for promoting various divisions of labor. Turn changes in the "game" part of Pond are explicitly programmed to occur at the completion of each Pond problem. The content of each player's turn is independent of and more or less the same as that of the other player, with emphasis on the "fair" chance of each player to perform more or less proficiently. It is a classic competitive situation.

When dyads or groups are working cooperatively, a person can take on a "specialist role" that contributes to the whole in combination with the "specialist roles" of others. Necessary acts are divided up; the task is united as the various users accomplish a part of the whole. The content of the participants' turns is not similar; rather, it is complementary and sequentially interdependent. Each person's turn is affected by more or less proficiency on the part of other users or by colleagues who have different ideas of what the task is. Users of the original Pond program can negotiate a variety of turn-taking routines, each associated with different divisions of labor (e.g., between "explorers" and "formula enterers," between steps within the formula entry phase, between direction and number specialists within the steps).[12] As the children cooperate by taking turns *within* a problem and *switching roles between* problems, the talk that coordinates them socially and practically involves interesting cognitive aspects of the task on which they are cooperating. There is a practical and immediate motivation for users to pay attention to what others are doing, make suggestions, ask questions, communicate their ideas about what should be done to accomplish the task, and indeed debate their notions of what the task is.

One interesting cooperative division of labor required new programming because it relies on a transformation in the ordering of the actions involved in formula entry. Instead of interspersing the acts that represent direction and number as the original program requires, the direction pattern can be viewed and represented as a whole, followed by the number pattern as a whole (or vice versa). In our revised version of the program, one user can specialize in the direction part of the formula, entering all the directions during one turn. Then, after the turn change, another user provides numbers to be used with each direction. This division of labor allows adults and children to create different contexts in which to entertain a different "sense" of the mathematical objects involved in Pond problems. First, for those experienced with other divisions of labor for the Pond tasks, it presents a transformation of (at least) the sequential organization of the operatory aspects (Rubtsov, 1987), affording the opportunity for discussion of the alternatives and the underlying properties of the domain that unites them. Second, even for novices, the overt orientation to the "whole formula" as a unit of analysis can be discussed as the users make it appear on the screen in two "drafts"— once with only directions and later with direction-number pairs. Finally, and particularly with mixed expert-novice groups, because the "direction specialist" implicitly also chooses how many steps will be used, the first turn taken can provoke discussions about (1) how one "recognizes" the number of steps needed, and (2) differing opinions about the number of steps needed that display knowledge (or ignorance) of the requirement to reanalyze three-step Ponds.

There are four diskettes provided in the revised version of the program; choosing among them constitutes an "authoring" act. One aspect of the choice is relevant here (the other applies in the section just below). Two of the diskettes can be used by those who choose to omit the competitive "game" and include the new component, which arranges turn-taking to allow cooperation between "direction specialists" and "number specialists."

Language and Culture Differences

As with any program, Pond poses some "start up" problems for users (following screen directions, finding keys, becoming familiar with variations for different parts of the program) that are magnified for those with little or no computer or keyboard experience, and, of course, for the researchers and children who speak Russian and ordinarily use the Cyrillic alphabet. Compared to many other programs, The Pond minimizes these problems because it makes use of so few keys, includes so many screen prompts, makes it easy to "erase," and uses symbols in place of many English words.

There is a familiar tenor, a warm tone, in the program's contributions to the verbal interactions that presupposes that the users are mainstream American English-speakers: The names given to the Ponds (Fig. 5.2) are like those found in books and board games in nurseries and early primary grades in the United States. Success is greeted with "whoopie," an expression rich in connotations for Americans. For researchers immersed in the work of Vygotsky and his students, it is easy to see that children and adults appropriate the presuppositions of shared language and culture, thereby forming a foundation for developing questions as well as answers relevant to the task (Vygotsky, 1986, Ch. 6, Sec. 4). It is equally easy to note that users who do not share the language and cultural presuppositions miss the tone (or need to focus on it so much that it assumes a different importance).

Our contexts of use in Russia included materials and activities to deal with this problem, but a change in the program design was needed to allow choices that would reflect the diversity of language, alphabet, and culture that users of The Pond bring to the situation of use. The new version of The Pond includes two diskettes whose opening screen identifies the program as *Prud* (literal translation of Pond) but in the Cyrillic alphabet (see also Fig. 5.1, above). The frog celebrates in the Russian version with *Kva Kva,* similar to the English "ribbit." In both languages, the names of the Ponds on the menu have been changed, omitting references to outside entities that might be more familiar to some children than others (e.g., instead of "Farmer Jane's Ponds," the two-step pattern without distractors are named "Tadpole Ponds"). Both diskettes in each language have the new authoring component to tailor the problem set presented on the menu; and one diskette for each language includes the new cooperative, noncompetitive division of labor and excludes the competitive game.

Advancing Technology

It is clear that beyond our project other languages and cultures must be considered, not just for other countries but also for the diversity in both the United States and Russia. Are we then to be faced with a tall stack of diskettes for every program we use in educational contexts? The need for four diskettes in our revised version is related to the limitations of the computer facilities common to educational settings; the Apple II and Pravetz computers have limited RAM and slow processors. However, if even these machines are connected in a local area network (LAN), the choice among diskettes can also be computerized as an authoring option with the alternative versions stored on a LAN's main "file server."

The next three cases describe critiques about the original program that were not used in the revised program. They have the same character as the above—looking toward more collaboration with programmers and allowing for diversity to fit varying local educational contexts. The more extensive revisions called for in the sections below are feasible only if LAN technology becomes more readily available in educational settings or if the computers commonly used in schools are those that have more capacity and faster processors.

Language Form Choice

Program designers make choices about the specific language forms used to "interface" with the user groups. This general characteristic of language use (multiplicity of forms for the same function) has been studied a great deal. How speakers or writers phrase things they want or need to say indicates different presuppositions and invites different responses. An example of such linguistic choice occurs in The Pond program where a problem can be "recycled" (i.e., used again); the choice of whether to do it is given to the users with an invitation on the screen: "Do you want the same problem? Y N" Even as we write, we can hear former 8-year-old participants in our Zo-peds saying, "Bo-o-ori-i-ing," or "Why?" as they choose N ("no"). Adults in the face-to-face context have to be nimble to "defer" the answer to the invitation and to insert information and motivation for a positive response if such is in their educational plan. Other language forms could appear on the screen to phrase this choice (similar to the conversational device of aug-menting an invitation to dinner with information about what is being served).

Try to do this problem faster.   Y   N
Try to do this problem exactly the same again.   Y   N
Can you do this problem with a different formula?   Y   N
Will you switch turns and use this same problem?   Y   N
Do you want to teach this problem to someone?   Y   N
Do you want to challenge others to do this problem?   Y   N
Do you want some friends to try this problem?   Y   N

These language forms can function just as well to prompt the users to choose between the same alternatives, but they also carry suggestions about "why" the same problem might be done in terms of educational practices or social relations. The first form supports a situation of use that values practice toward automaticity, and the second promotes exact repetition. The third form suggests a value placed on alternative analyses or creative diversity. The fourth works for a context where reciprocity of actions are a valued part of learning events or where there are efforts to foster more (or more inde-pendent) actions by particular group members. The last items indicate par-ticular social relations that can hold in a context: student/teacher, compet-itors, friends.

Authoring in a computer program can involve more than just "multiple choices" from a menu. There can also be "fill in the blank" portions that allow a teacher or researcher to compose an expression, thereby controlling what it conveys to users who "interface" with it. The forms can be chosen to cohere with the particular socioeducational situation of use so that the program's contributions to the context presuppose locally suitable values and norms.

Graphics and Changing Contexts

The animated frog is most winsome, but sometimes when it is told to "go" it hops "too slowly" for the good of the local context. In fact, of course, it always hops at the same rate; but for some users sometimes it is too slow. A Vygotskian view does not need to resort to a "personality" deficit analysis; it is not (or at least not only) that such users are "hyperactive" and cannot inhibit distraction. The problem is a function of more than an individual; it is related to specifics of the changing context. When the slow progress of the frog co-occurs with a context boundary, it is not regarded as problematic;

but it can be a remarkable problem when it occurs in the midst of a context, interrupting the ongoing rhythm of the interaction, "winding down" (Mehan, 1979), and threatening to preempt the continuation of the interaction by inviting a "closing" (Schegloff & Sacks, 1973). Although the fine tuning of contributions to oral conversations that differentiate continuations from interruptions and the like has been examined (e.g., Goodwin, 1986), there has been little notice of these aspects of contexts involving interactive computer programs (but see Griffin & Cole, 1987, p. 221).

When novices or experts are constituting the context, the slow speed co-occurs with possible context boundaries and elicits little notice or complaint. Novice groups treat each problem as a separate segment, a token of a type, mostly because the program designers use the same scenario and include several tokens on the same diskette. The unity among the problems is imposed by a force external to the current group of users—a "given," frozen, presupposition not treated as negotiable or available for reflection in the ongoing communicative activity. The hopping frog serves as a monitor for their previous acts—Did they press the right keys, choose the right directions and numbers—within the current specific problem. They can accept the context boundary invited by the slow frog; their interest in whether or when another problem is presented is not governed by their apprehension of a unity among problems but by matters such as how much time is left, how cute the frog is, how nice it is to be with the other participants in the group. For experts, each and *any* Pond problem can stand as an exemplar complete unto itself of the whole issue, similar to an abstract of an article. The slow frog provides an appropriate context boundary, closing one demonstration of the experts' mastery. Whether they begin another context depends on the other demands and opportunities (e.g., showing off or being graded) in the face-to-face context.[13]

The slow frog is noticeable when the users are making a transition from the specific to the general, that is, when the discussion references not just the particular aspects of the specific Pond and formula present on the screen but also substantive abstractions about Pond problems previously met and solution strategies that should "always work." (see Davidov, 1988a,b,c, for a general discussion; and Griffin et al., 1992, for application related to The Pond.) In these situations, the scope or frame of the participants' activity is shifting; there is concern about how the current problem is related to once and future Ponds, to the nature of Ponds. The end of a specific problem with the slow frog is not a context boundary for these users. When the frog "goes," it is the computer's *turn* in a longer interactional sequence: The users have proposed a formula related as much to "any" Pond as to the specific one. The response should "back-channel" the specific assessment, supporting the users' focus on the general and provoking continuation of the longer sequence (cf. Goodwin's 1986 treatment of continuations in oral language). The computer's turn is obligatory but should be conventional, abbreviated, economical, and speedy, the way routines are issued in conversations (compare "How're you?" "Fine, you?"). Instead, it slows down, suggesting a boundary that these transitional user groups did not anticipate; it *elaborates* the response, suggesting that the topic is "the specific Pond," not the general issues with which the transitional group had begun to deal. From the point of view of the more competent members in a Zo-Ped with users in transition, the program's response to an unsuccessful formula (when the frog quickly splashes into the water) is more cooperative and productive, as the group can quickly continue to discuss the nature of the problem in the face of the errors, having avoided the invitation to "close," to change contexts.

Ideally, the computer's turn should collaborate as the transitional user groups are generalizing and reaching for the underlying abstractions that apply to a large number of specific problems. A *diagrammatic* depiction of the execution of the formula would not only avoid an invitation to premature closure of the context and focus on specific Ponds; it would also bring an intellectual tool into the context, one that users can generate themselves on other occasions. In the Vygotskian framework, "abbreviated" representations such as diagrams play an important role in problem-solving and development (Davidov, 1988a,b,c; Markova, 1979; Vygotsky, 1978, 1986; with respect to The Pond, Griffin et al., 1992). As a tool, the diagram can "migrate" (King, 1988, Ch. 4) to different parts of the context, for: (1) organizing notes while collecting the data about new specific ponds; (2) entertaining alternatives while uncovering a formula; and (3) recalling, comparing, and contrasting different tokens of Ponds previously encountered.

The revision we propose for this problem and the ones in the next case involve an option key rather than an authoring component. In these cases collaboration with the "programmers' voice" within the situation of use with the children is desirable for two reasons: (1) The need for an option changes quickly, even within one session of use of the software; (2) the complaints about the slowness of the frog are often uttered by the children just before it occurs, suggesting their readiness to assume control over it. *Option keys* (e.g., 0 and 9 in the original version of The Pond) are like requests for a contribution by one member of a conversational group; for example, "Tell me what happened, Barney, but, please, make it short." During the exploration phase of the program, the 0 option key shows a diagrammatic representation of the whole Pond. This diagram, with a moving cursor to represent the hopping frog, could be an option invoked as GO is chosen, taking care of situations where the frog should be more speedy (as the elaborate screens need not be redrawn). An option key to toggle on or off the abbreviated version of the execution sequence promotes collaboration between the local group of users and the "programmers' voice," so the software can respond to the changing character of developing students; otherwise the software functioning independently can hinder the educational polilogues involving users in transition.

Seeing Information and Making Sense of Meaning

Many users count the lily pads and come up with numbers that are just one too large. The hops, which should be counted, can be seen clearly on the screen when the frog is moving. When the users are entering the number of hops in the formula, however, the frog is not moving; the hops are then represented only as spacing between the much more salient lily pads. This problem persists or recurs for some users. In Vygotskian terms, the "sense" these users have of the arrow–number symbol is not coordinated with the "meaning" of them on which the program relies; the solution implied in this way of stating the problem is to enrich the contexts that generate sense. In the exploratory part of The Pond, the users press an arrow key to see the frog hop one lily pad at a time; pressing the right arrow key five times in this part of the program is functionally equivalent to using the "→ 5" step in the formula entry mode. If, in the exploratory part, the users could press an arrow key and then enter a number, there would be an occasion for the group of users to discuss the "meaning" of the arrow–number symbol, the way it relates to hops in contrast to lily pads.

Another problem involves observations of how coordination with the "meaning" of repeat in the program allows experts to "see" more than is actually depicted. Before any hint of it appears on the screen, some users act as if they see the pattern segmented in ways that represent iterations of a formula, not just the smaller segments cued by direction changes for all to see. Experts, however, have trouble communicating this private vision to other users who are not yet expert enough. If during both the exploratory and formula entry parts of the program the users could choose to see the diagrammatic representation with iteration segments marked or separated spatially, the expert–novice communication could rely on the "programmers' voice" as a welcome collaborator.

Both of these problems could be solved by adding new option key components to the program. The users in situ could choose to toggle on the extra alternatives that programmers can offer to stimulate and refine the contributions of other members to the educational polilogue.

Conclusions

Programmers from a successful software company and researchers interested in communication in a Vygotskian framework worked together to develop a revised Pond program that incorporates three revisions:

1. The presuppositions in the users' menu about scope and sequence for the domain are negotiable in the new authoring component.
2. The suggestion that only competition is social has been countered with the explicit cooperative learning "practice" component.
3. Language and cultural presuppositions that are familiar for members of two societies are accommodated by new diskettes, allowing a choice between a Russian *Prud* or an English Pond.

Technical limits prevented programmed solutions in three other areas:

1. presuppositions about the motivation for an activity that are embodied in the language forms used to interface with the users;

2. support for contexts where generalizations are being sought by avoiding suggestions for premature closure and providing a diagrammatic depiction; and
3. assistance for communication of the "private visions" of more proficient users who appear to "see" hop sequences and iterations not currently marked on the screen display.

Disruptions and disappointments in contexts where the software was used led us to recognize that the "programmers' voice" joins with the other voices to constitute educational contexts. If all had gone smoothly, we would have continued to view computer programs as media and tools; but we uncovered a new view when the "programmer's voice" conflicted with other voices. Its presuppositions revealed hidden alternate notions about educational contexts—the program's contributions to the discourse should not be viewed as sabotaging our context-creation efforts but, rather, as competing with it. The solutions devised were a kind of peaceful "coexistence"—allowing for diversity and control in the local educational context with authoring components and option keys. Two more questions arise: Does this work apply to other educational software? Can it be useful in actual educational contexts?

Educational Software

There are two parts to the issue of educational software: designing software and making use of it in educational research. We do not claim that the list above is a sufficient guide for creating or revising educational software, but we do claim that it is necessary for program designers to pay attention to: (1) authoring components and options keys as parts of educational software; (2) alternative analyses of subject matter; (3) the diversity among children and educational practices and the processes of children's growth; and (4) the power of the presuppositions in the programmer's voice.

Our approach developed a context where researchers and members of a software publishing company grappled to make the "programmer's voice" a cooperative contribution in diverse local educational polilogues; but the context also has an impact on researchers' approach to problems involving computer use. Before entering this new context, we bypassed many aspects of the "nuts and bolts" reality of the new technology with which we were working, concentrating instead on ways to augment the "given" program in face-to-face contexts. We had relied on many artifacts and plans to support interactions with children involving The Pond program (Griffin et al., 1992), including materials for drawing and building three-dimensional models of the problems; directions for alternate tasks, some using the same software; methods to "save" particular Pond problems to be used later or to be sent to a collaborator over a computer network; "scripts" suggesting talk, props, word processors, and other computer programs to be used in activities with the children.[14] Our colleagues from the software company showed interest in our solutions; indeed, the company packages much of its software (including The Pond) in a notebook with similar suggestions and materials.

However, as "more proficient others" in a Zo-ped context should, they gave us the opportunity to go beyond thinking of the programs we worked with as "given." As they led us to consider concrete details of educational software design and practical realities about current and future technology in educational contexts, we reflected on other prior experiences and developed new questions. For example, we had seen LANs in Moscow that mix more and less powerful computers, but we had seen them primarily as a way to be economical and reduce the need for expensive disk drives. We had noted some interesting educational applications (Rubtsov, Kriski, & Lesko, 1987) with connected computers, but we had not before appreciated the class of opportunities and questions that LAN technology and more sophisticated processors offer to educational research, particularly with regard to studies of learning and development in cooperative contexts. Although specific concrete work must be undertaken, there is good potential for combining analyses of communicative contexts and genetic analyses of particular domains for developing instruments for research and practice of value to education.

Extended Contexts

We have relied on what software companies have to offer; but, as much, we have relied on our communication with each other to anticipate problems and be prepared to solve them, including the development of noncomputer auxiliary means to which we referred above. The Velikhov-Hamburg project, the larger context for this work, gives our small group access to communication via computer with a wide variety of partners who have different ways to notice problems and devise solutions. Can this process be available to participants in other educational contexts?

Recognizing the need for support for specific software extends the context to *local education* agencies. There are structures in place in the United States for practicing teachers and child-care workers to collaborate with others. Professional associations and computer networks of computer-using educators are developing quickly and spreading widely. In one state an on-line database includes descriptions of software, opinions about it, and activities and materials that have been developed to make good use of it; practicing educators are expected to add to the database as well as read it (Finzer, Holmberg, Rozura, Sohn, Wong, & LHS, 1986). There are difficulties to be faced in contexts that include local education agencies, so educators can have the opportunity in time and equipment and the motivation to collaborate with each other on a regular and productive basis (e.g., McNamee, Lipschultz, & Stutzman, 1990, who described the initiation of community child-care center workers into the computer-mediated collaborations in our project.)

The context must also be extended to *teacher education* institutions. For noncomputer solutions, authoring components, and option keys to be functional in educational polilogues, educators need opportunities to consider the ways computers can participate in educational contexts. Authoring choices and options could even serve as a part of a context for studying the variations that exist among educational theories and practices as well as among and within populations of children. Courses focusing on educational philosophy or teacher–student interaction may be more appropriate for such preparation than separate courses dealing with computer use.

In this phase of our work with The Pond, it might be said that we missed the "bull's-eye" context for education: Face-to-face interactions with children were referred to only fleetingly. We have concentrated here on another context; it cannot be related to the contexts with children as larger or smaller or before or after but as coexisting and mutually interdependent. The problem of locating the necessary and sufficient constituents of a context is not just the puzzle for scholars that we described above; it is a practical problem derived from the essentially dynamic nature of contexts. As members of a context go about conducting overt business as well as constituting the context, there are opportunities and necessities for them to recognize the impact of "hidden members" that appear to be intruders from overarching, coexisting, prior, or expected contexts. Thus do contexts grow, as our senses grow within them.

Notes

The Velikhov-Hamburg (also known as Velham or Vega) collective officially began in October 1986 with participants from the Soviet Union and the United States, coordinated by Alexandra Belyaeva and Michael Cole. Since then the Soviet Union has been dissolved. The project continued as a joint project with Russia because the work has always taken place at research laboratories, schools, and children's centers located in Russia, although researchers in the project, originally affiliated with Soviet national institutions, come from other parts of the Commonwealth of Independent States (Georgia, Ukraine, Armenia, Kazakhstan). Most likely, some of those who have made up Velham at different times would not agree with some of the contents of this chapter. The roster of Velham members most associated with this particular sub-project, in addition to the three authors, are Alfred Alamazyan, Gail Arita, Bertram Bruce, Valerie Crawford, Michael Cole, Judy Diamondstone, Derek Edwards, Lusia Gaidar, Miroslav Koshelyuk, Melissa Lemons, Vladas Leonas, Sarah Michaels, Leonid Milgram, Richard Ricard, Valerij Rudenko, Vladimir Rubtsov, and Martha tum Suden. Special thanks for cooperating in this phase of the work go to Marge Kosel and Michael Fish of Sunburst Communications, Incorporated, as well as to the institutions that have supported the effort, The Carnegie Corporation of New York and The International Fund of Moscow.

The material herein is based on a paper presented at the American Educational Research Association 1989 Annual Meeting in San Francisco, March 28, in Part 2 of the Division C Symposium: Extending Vygotskian Theory.

1. Contemporary scholars known as "postmodernists" or "deconstructionists" would debate the analogy to an "edifice," arguing against an analyst having any

recourse to a relatively permanent structure. Although we cannot debate this point fully here, we refer the reader to Luria (1979) for discussion of how the study of permanent structures need not be "acontextual" or "nonemergent."

2. The term bears little if any relation to "formative evaluation," a description of ways to collect and analyze data about particular treatment programs in U.S. educational research.

3. See Davidov (1988a,b,c) for a precis of the curricula in Russian language, mathematics, and fine arts. Our work with one computer program can be criticized for failing to focus on the whole curriculum area. We justify on two grounds the limits of our work: (1) The larger sociopolitical context demands that we look for small "chunks" of activity that can be recontextualized in diverse circumstances in order to undertake joint international work because of massive differences in the educational systems and the great diversity of cultural practices and values within each country. (2) A computer program may be used for different activities in different curricula, i.e., that it may be an arena for practicing different skills and for promoting discourse about different concepts. In fact, some members of our group were initially interested in The Pond in relation to the learning of computer programming, whereas others were more interested in mathematics.

4. See Newman, Griffin, and Cole (1989, pp. 54–75) for an account of some of these mechanisms.

5. There are two sources for the records documenting this point: (1) Computer-mediated conference notes during the implementation of work with children (from June 1987 to November 1988) include detailed field notes and more casual complaints and queries about use of the software. They indicate aspects of the program with which we were not content, mentioning occasions when the program interfered with the work of the children, the teachers, and other researchers. (2) In September 1987 and July 1988, internal project presentations and reports of attempts to analyze and code tape and field note records of the interactions with the children include references to the difficulty of allowing for the program's varying contribution to the educational polilogue.

6. At the start of our work, the public climate was such that care had to be taken to demonstrate that: (1) collaborative work between the two countries could address problems inside each country that had been widely perceived and reported on; and (2), even though the collaborative work involved the education of young children in the two countries, it did not mean that the political and cultural values and practices of either country would be imposed on the other. A widely perceived problem in the United States was the inadequacy of mathematics education, and the public in the Soviet Union was aware of the difficulty of introducing computers effectively into institutions for primary education. Furthermore, domains such as mathematics and the natural sciences were less likely to engender fears of cultural domination than were domains from the social or behavioral sciences or the humanities.

7. In some cases the number to be reanalyzed is larger than the largest number (5) available for input in the formula; this point has proved to be of great help to teachers (adult or peer) who are trying to introduce reanalysis to a novice player.

8. We are here ignoring the role of problems with distractors in the genetic analysis. Our experience suggests that they pose little problem and offer no particular help for learning about representation, repetition, or reanalysis.

9. There is some screen activity that affords notice of the repeating nature of the execution of the formula: The formula typed in stays on the screen during its execution, and a box highlights the step that is being executed. So, if users enter six steps, the box moves back to the first step after the sixth is executed, allowing one to notice

the repetitive nature. However nothing in the program motivates the use of economical repeating formulas for two-step Ponds.

10. There are two possible two-step Ponds for the type of reanalysis represented by Figure 5.3, where the first and the last steps must be in the same direction. The pattern for these Ponds would be straight lines—vertical or horizontal. A Pond that was just a long line could be reanalyzed; for example, a "right 3, right 2" formula could be reanalyzed as "right 2, right 3" or "right 1, right 4," etc. The second type of reanalysis, represented in Figure 5.4, requires that the first and last steps be of opposite directions, so that the frog backtracks; a few limited two-step cases can be produced within the constraints of the program. They would also be straight lines; for example, given a chain of four hops down, the formula "down 4, up 2" could work, even though in practice the execution would stop when the "ending point" was reached at the end of the "down 4" step.

11. Even nongenetic task analyses cannot applaud the original menu sequence as a matter of going from easier to harder, gradually adding more difficult elements of the task. The two- and four-step Ponds can be seen as related along an easier–harder dimension; the patterns to recognize and represent become longer, and most four-step Ponds enable the users to add an element: attention to repetition. However, the easier-to-harder progression is broken by the three-step Ponds, which require reanalysis, making them more difficult than all but a few of the four-step Ponds rarely encountered by users.

12. In our contexts, where handwritten notes and models are used as auxiliary means, the turn-taking could involve the use of these artifacts as well.

13. Sometimes the formulas of experts are wrong, and there can be new information given by the slow frog splashing into the water; but experts treat their errors as "slips," as a mistyping, a miscounting, or a misperception, not as a misunderstanding about the particular problem or the general class of them. The new formula is entered speedily, accompanied by as much declaration of certainty as was the first. The "higher order" formula can organize the "lower order" counting, keypress, and vision skills; and it can provide a monitor for such skills during the execution phase (Vygotsky, 1978, Chs. 3 and 4). For novice groups, these "lower order skills" display no such organization; each in turn assumes a major role in the interaction and is laboriously monitored as it is being done.

14. For example, faced with the problem (described above) of children counting lily pads instead of hops (having a "sense" discoordinated with the meaning the program relied on), we used role-playing to enrich the contexts that could generate a different sense. The solution turns the table on the notion "computer simulation." We simulate the computer program's scenario. That is, we arrange some "props," (e.g., chairs) to represent the lily pads of the current Pond problem showing on the computer screen, assign someone the "role" of frog, and have others act as a "Greek chorus" chanting the count as the acting frog hops from chair to chair. As we "simulate" the computer program, there is ample opportunity to discuss (and make salient) the difference between counting hops and counting pads. These contexts can externalize the discoordination an individual is experiencing and provide occasions for reflection and social negotiation toward coordination.

References

Austin, J. L. (1962). *How to do things with words.* New York: Oxford University Press.

Barwise, J., & Perry, J. (1983). *Situations and attitudes*. Cambridge, MA: MIT Press.

Belyaeva, A. V., & Cole, M. (1989) Computer-mediated joint activity in the service of human development: an overview. *The Quarterly Newsletter of the Laboratory of Comparative Human Cognition, 11* (3), 45–57.

Cahir, S. (1978). *Transitions: activity within and between activity*. Unpublished PhD dissertation, Georgetown University.

Cole, M., Griffin, P., & LCHC (1987). *Contextual factors in education: improving science and mathematics education for minorities and women*. Madison: National Research Council, Wisconsin Center for Education.

Davidov, V. V. (1988a). Problems of developmental teaching: the experience of theoretical and experimental psychological research. Part 1. *Soviet Education, 30* (8).

Davidov, V. V. (1988b). Problems of developmental teaching: the experience of theoretical and experimental psychological research. Part 2. *Soviet Education, 30* (9).

Davidov, V. V. (1988c). Problems of developmental teaching: the experience of theoretical and experimental psychological research. Part 3. *Soviet Education, 30* (10).

El'konin, D. B. (1975). Primary schoolchildren's intellectual capabilities and the content of instruction. In L. Steffe (ed.). *Soviet studies in the psychology of learning and teaching mathematics. Children's capacity for learning mathematics* (pp. 13–54). Chicago: School Mathematics Study Group, Stanford University & Survey of Recent East European Mathematical Literature, University of Chicago.

Erickson, F., & Schultz, J. (1977). When is a context? *ICHD Newsletter, 1* (2), 5–10.

Finzer, W., Holmberg, M., Rozura, S., Sohn, A., Wong, A., & Lawrence Hall of Science at the University of California, Berkeley. (1986). *Technology in the curriculum: the data relator handbook*. Sacramento: California State Department of Education.

Goodwin, C. (1986). Between and within: alternative sequential treatments of continuers and assessments. *Human Studies, 9,* 205–17.

Goodwin, C., & Goodwin, M. H. (in press). Context, activity, and participation. In P. Auer & A. di Luzio (eds.). *The contextualization of language*. Amsterdam: Benjamins.

Griffin, P., & Cole, M. (1987). New technologies, basic skills, and the underside of education: what's to be done? In J. Langer (ed.). *Language, literacy, and culture: issues of society and schooling*. Norwood, NJ: Ablex.

Griffin, P., Belyaeva, A., & Soldatova, G. (1992). Socio-historical concepts applied to observations of computer use, *European Journal of Psychology of Education, 7*(4), 269–86.

Hymes, D. H. (1972). Models of the interaction of language and social life. In J. J. Gumperz & D. Hymes (eds.). *Directions in sociolinguistics.* (pp. 35–71). New York: Holt, Rinehart, & Winston.

King, C. A. (1988). *Social facilitation of reading comprehension*. Unpublished PhD dissertation, University of California at San Diego.

Kosel, M., & Fish, M. (1984). *The Pond*. Pleasantville, NY: Sunburst Communications.

Kosel, M., & Fish, M. (1989). *Prud and The Pond: Velikhov-Hamburg project version*. Pleasantville, NY: Sunburst Communications.

Laboratory of Comparative Human Cognition (1982). A model system for the study of learning difficulties. *Quarterly Newsletter of the Laboratory of Comparative Human Cognition, 4* (3), 39–66.

Labov, W., & Fanschel, D. (1977). *Therapeutic discourse: psychotherapy as conversation.* Orlando, FL: Academic Press.

Lemons, M. P. (1990). Evaluation of a jointly created educational computer game. Presented to the Psychology Department, University of California at San Diego.

Lemons, M. P., & Samoilenko, E. (1990). Organizing and executing a cross-national evaluation of a jointly created educational game. Presented at The Second International Congress for Research on Activity Theory.

Leontiev, A. N. (1981). *Problems of the development of mind.* Moscow: Progress Publishers.

Luria, A. R. (1932). *The nature of human conflict.* New York: Liveright.

Luria, A. R. (1972). *The man with a shattered world.* New York: Basic Books.

Luria, A. R. (1979). *The making of mind.* Cambridge, MA: Harvard University Press.

Markova, A. K. (1979). *The teaching and mastery of language.* White Plains, NY: M. E. Sharpe.

McDermott, R. (1976). *Kids make sense.* Unpublished PhD dissertation, Stanford University.

McNamee, G. D., Lipschultz, D., & Stutzman, C. (1990). Supporting inner city teachers' and children's entry into telecommunications. Presented at The Second International Congress for Research on Activity Theory.

Mehan, H. (1979). *Learning lessons.* Cambridge, MA: Harvard University Press.

Mehan, H., Moll, L. C., & Riel, M. M. (1983). *A quasi-experiment in guided change.* Report No. G-83-0027. Washington, DC: National Institute of Education.

Meshcheryakov, A. (1979). *Awakening to life.* Moscow: Progress Publishers.

Michaels, S. (1985). Classroom processes and the learning of text-editing commands. *Quarterly Newsletter of the Laboratory of Comparative Human Cognition, 7* 3, 69–79.

Newman, D., Griffin, P., & Cole, M. (1989). *The construction zone: working for cognitive change in school.* Cambridge: Cambridge University Press.

Ochs, E. (1988). *Culture and language development: language acquisition and language socialization in a Samoan village.* Cambridge: Cambridge University Press.

Rubtsov, V. V. (1987). The functions of the machines in the learning activity: logical and psychological aspects of computer based instruction. In *Second international conference on children in the information age: opportunities for creativity, innovation and new activities* (pp. 202–14). Sofia: Bulgarian Medical Academy.

Rubtsov, V. V., Kriski, A. P., & Lesko, V. A. (1987). *Kinematika-1.* Moscow: Computer Laboratory, Academy of Pedagogical Sciences.

Sacks, H., Schegloff, E., & Jefferson, G. (1974). A simplest systematics for the organization of turn-taking for conversation. *Language, 50,* 696–735.

Sadock, J. (1974). *Towards a linguistic theory of speech acts.* Orlando, FL: Academic Press.

Scheflen, A. E. (1974). *How behavior means.* New York: Jason Aronson.

Schegloff, E. (1968). Sequencing in conversational openings. *American Anthropologist, 70,* 1075–95.

Schegloff, E. (1980). Preliminaries to preliminaries: "can I ask you a question?" *Sociological Inquiry, 50* (3 & 4), 104–52.

Schegloff, E., & Sachs, H. (1973). Opening up closings. *Semiotica, 8,* 289–327.

Solutions (Vol. 3, No. 1) (1988). Pleasantville, NY: Sunburst Communications.

Vygotsky, L. S. (1986). *Thought and language.* Cambridge, MA: MIT Press.

Vygotsky, L. S. (1978). *Mind in society: the development of higher psychological processes.* Cambridge, MA: Harvard University Press.

COMMENTARY

Time to Merge Vygotskian and Constructivist Conceptions of Knowledge Acquisition

GIYOO HATANO

The five chapters in this section made an agreeable impression on me, a sympathetic outsider of the North American Vygotskian school. All are based on the authors' long-standing research on knowledge acquisition in the classroom, and they propose some extension or revision of the Vygotskian conception of learning by instruction. More precisely, their proposed extension has been motivated by the need to understand and develop further their target instructional practice. As Moll and his associates (this volume) put it, "practice can exceed as well as inform and elaborate" theoretical notions.

There are several commonalities across the chapters. In short, each chapter is oriented in its own way to a more dynamic (re)interpretation of the Vygotskian conception and suggests a less didactic approach to instruction. Considering that Vygotskians have emphasized almost exclusively the teacher's responsibility for organizing learning for students' acquisition of effective strategies and scientifically correct concepts, and thus supported current forms of instruction heavily controlled by the teacher, these suggested extensions and revisions are especially welcome.

This commentary indicates, first, my subjective appraisal of the current Vygotskian conception of knowledge acquisition and tries to locate needed extensions as the background for reviewing the chapters. Then I examine how much these needed extensions have been achieved by the chapters. Finally, I discuss a few problems still to be solved within the Vygotskian framework.

Needed Extensions and Revisions

Previous Contexts for Interpreting Vygotskian Theories

As the editors of this volume point out in the Preface, many ideas of Vygotsky seem to have been interpreted in a rather narrow fashion. This point is particularly true for his conception of learning or knowledge acquisition and teaching. As a consequence, as Moll et al. aptly put it, the emphasis of Vygotskian approaches to instruction is "usually on the transmission of skills from adult to child, as is the case with traditional classrooms." Though there have been a few notable exceptions (e.g., Newman, Griffin, & Cole, 1989), Vygotskians have failed to propose alternative ideas to conventional educational practice, which relies heavily on direct teaching of solution routines for test-like problems. Innovations such as converting the conventional classroom into a place for collective search for understanding have seldom been proposed by Vygotskians, though the theory certainly allows for them.

The Vygotskian conception has not been as fertile in educational reform as it could be, partly because it has been interpreted in terms of the empiricism that has dominated American education and educational research. According to the empiricist's view, the core of educational process is the transmission of ready-made knowledge from outside to the individual mind, which is like a blank slate. The Vygotskian conception interpreted within this framework is compatible with conventional didactic teaching, including "rote, drill and practice instruction," which is the reality for disadvantaged children (Moll et al., this volume).

How Vygotskian theory was introduced to educational researchers has also influenced its interpretation by the educational community. That is, the Vygotskian conception was often contrasted to the Piagetian one, which had been attractive to some innovative educators. From the Vygotskian perspective, the Piagetian conception of knowledge acquisition has a number of serious deficiencies and thus was judged unable to serve as a sound basis for educational reform unless properly supplemented. Among others, Piagetians were criticized for emphasizing individual construction of knowledge without paying attention to: (1) the role of more capable members in the society (and their knowledge); (2) cultural artifacts that mediate interactions between individuals and their physical environments; and (3) larger sociohistorical contexts of learning-teaching processes. Therefore Vygotskians have been busy criticizing Piagetians' "romantic child-centered constructivism" without clearly differentiating their conception from transmissionism (Hatano & Newman, 1985).

As a result of these contextual variables, the so-called Vygotskian conception of knowledge acquisition by instruction has been established. In a somewhat caricatured form, it can be expressed as follows.

1. Knowledge to be acquired by the learner (a less mature member of the society) is possessed by the teacher (a more mature member) usually in the form of a set of skills or strategies for solving the target problems; the teacher is assigned by the society the job of transmitting the knowledge.

2. The learner is brought into the instructional situation to solve a few samples of the target problems together with the teacher; the teacher communicates the knowledge in a verbally coded form (as a set of commands or condition–action pairs) and demonstrates how to solve the problems by using this coded form of knowledge.

3. The teacher asks the learner to take over the solution steps she or he can, with other steps being executed by the teacher; the supporting

role of the teacher becomes less and less important as the learner acquires the knowledge.
4. When the learner becomes able to solve the problems without help from the teacher, it is considered that the knowledge has been transmitted successfully.

Needless to say, the above "Vygotskian" conception is only one possible interpretation of Vygotsky's emphasis on the social origin of individual cognition in general and his notion of "the zone of proximal development" in particular—one that approximates cultural transmission. We might explore other possible interpretations. Moreover, although the so-called conception does not make any explicit commitments as to the nature of the learner or of the social interactions that enhance knowledge acquisition, it is often accompanied by a set of hidden empiricist assumptions: (1) the learner is rather passive in nature; (2) he or she does not (have to) understand the meaning of the skills taught or construct knowledge that goes beyond them; (3) only the interaction with the teacher, who is always more capable than the learner, facilitates the acquisition; and (4) the teacher is the only source of information and evaluation.

These hidden assumptions do not seem plausible in the light of an accumulated body of evidence in educational research as well as in cognitive science. Findings in these areas strongly suggest that humans are generally active and competent in their everyday life and can benefit from a variety of interactions with other people and natural and artificial environments. Therefore some revisions are needed, even within the "transmission of skills" framework. This point leads us to a *moderate extension* of the Vygotskian conception of learning by instruction.

A more ambitious attempt is to expand the above conception to include the acquisition of conceptual knowledge, which enables learners to use the acquired skills flexibly and to invent new skills—in other words, to include the process of learners becoming "adaptive experts" (Hatano & Inagaki, 1986). This practice is almost equivalent to a reinterpretation of Vygotsky's theory as exemplifying "realistic constructivism" (Hatano & Newman, 1985), that is, an idea that knowledge is constructed by learners themselves under a variety of sociocultural constraints, which encourages educators to search for alternatives to didactic teaching. This attempt can legitimately be called a *radical extension* of the Vygotskian conception.

Toward Radical Extensions

Presenting in detail a "radically extended" Vygotskian conception of knowledge acquisition is beyond the scope of this short commentary. However, it is possible to discuss what assumptions about the nature of the learner and of supportive environments should replace the above hidden empiricistic assumptions. I suggest that the following four points, roughly corresponding to the four points outlined above, constitute the core of the assumptions for a constructivist Vygotskian conception. These *revising (innovating) assumptions* are generally accepted by the contemporary psychological literature, if not firmly supported by direct evidence.

1. *Learners are active.* It is part of the *zeitgeist* of contemporary cognitive psychology that humans are active agents of information processing and action. Humans often explore tasks beyond the demands or requirements of problem solving, and environments that do not permit active exploration are viewed as unpleasant.

It has also been found in developmental and educational studies that humans, from infancy to old age, enjoy taking initiatives and choosing from among alternatives. They not only explore objects but interact with other persons spontaneously. They tend to be lively and do well when they are allowed to do so.

2. *Learners almost always seek and often achieve understanding.* That people try to find meaning and understanding is a corollary of assumption 1. Our conversation is nearly impossible if participants do not try to interpret given utterances or are satisfied with an interpretation at a shallow level. It is well known from experimental studies that people generate an enriched representation of the presented information and try to interpret a given set of information coherently.

People not only try, but also often succeed, in achieving understanding. In other words, they are competent as well as active. This competence is frequently supported by their prior knowledge because it enables them to process new relevant information effectively. Understanding new information requires some relevant prior knowledge. It is well documented that, prior to instruction, students have acquired a body of fairly rich informal knowledge about a specific topic.

It is possible that learners construct, based on their understanding, knowledge that is in a sense beyond the information given by the teacher or even beyond what the teacher knows. Their invented knowledge is not always correct scientifically but is often plausible.

3. *Learners' construction of knowledge is facilitated by horizontal as well as vertical interactions.* Contributions of horizontal interaction to knowledge acquisition can be substantial, as during peer interaction. In addition to empirical data demonstrating the latter's facilitative effects on learning (e.g., Doise & Mugny, 1984), there are a couple of logical reasons why it is so. First, speaking generally, the less mature member in a vertical interaction is not highly motivated to construct knowledge, because she or he knows that the other member possesses that knowledge. In contrast, during horizontal interaction, members' motivation to disclose their ideas tends to be natural and strong because no authoritative right answers are expected to come immediately (Inagaki, 1981).

Second, the more mature member's knowledge cannot necessarily be verbalized in a communicable form (Schön, 1983); and even when it is, some part may be ignored by the less mature. Therefore we cannot always count on the vertical tutorial interaction. On the other hand, a student can often pick out a useful piece of information from other students who are not generally more capable (Hatano & Inagaki, 1991). Moreover, some members can be more capable than others at some moment during horizontal interaction.

4. *Availability of multiple sources of information enhances knowledge construction.* As understanding is to find coherence among pieces of information, and the construction of conceptual knowledge is often based on understanding, availability of multiple sources of information is expected to enhance the construction. It is especially beneficial for learners to have external sources of information other than the teacher because too much reliance on the authorized answer given by the teacher reduces students' motivation to understand and construct knowledge of their own. Among others, confirmation or disconfirmation of predictions by direct observation or consulting a reference book serves to enhance learning.

These revising assumptions can serve to constrain what the constructivist Vygotskian conception is like. They can also provide us with perspectives for reviewing proposed extensions, as can be seen in the next section.

How Successfully Have These Chapters Extended the Conception?

The five chapters are divided into three groups mainly for convenience of discussion: those proposing moderate extensions (Palincsar et al. and Chang and Wells), radical extensions (Cobb et al. and Moll et al.), and the presentation of analyses of artifacts (Griffin et al.). The grouping or labels attached to the groups should not be taken too seriously because a number of similarity metrics can be applied to the chapters.

Moderate Extensions

Although both Palincsar et al. and Chang and Wells proposed some extensions of the Vygotskian conception of knowledge acquisition, these proposals are moderate, not radical: Both groups of authors are concerned primarily with students' acquisition of strategies under the teacher's guidance and thus stay within the orthodox Vygotskian framework. Palincsar et al. discuss the possibility of creating "communities in which each participant makes significant contributions to the emergent understandings of all members" and thus suggests their willingness to support radical extensions of the Vygotskian conception, but this proposition is not elaborated any further in the chapter.

What Palincsar et al. did was to apply reciprocal teaching to first-graders' lessons on animal survival. A teacher and six children, many of whom were at risk for listening comprehension difficulty, took turns leading the discussion, in which they asked questions about the content of a passage from a text, summarized what had been read, clarified the meaning of expressions in it, and predicted what would follow.

In the process of reciprocal teaching, students were expected to internalize these strategies, which good comprehenders tend to use, as well as to acquire simple biological concepts. The authors claimed that "the most effective social interaction is one in which joint problem solving occurs, guided by an individual who is more skilled" in the use of such intellectual tools as the above strategies. The teacher's role was to ensure that the problem-solving activity would occur within the participants' zones of proximal development, by "providing support that is both temporary and adjustable."

The results indicated that reciprocal teaching in 20 lessons dramatically improved the children's ability to understand text and apply analogically the biological concepts in the text. This finding deserves mention because only a few prior studies in the Vygotskian tradition have yielded such strong and clear effects of social interaction (see also Palincsar & Brown, 1984).

However, reciprocal teaching as formulated by Palincsar et al. does not go far beyond "the transmission of skills from adult to child," though I have never observed myself its process. It should be examined why students acquire these strategies, that is, their motivational basis of the acquisition. If the strategies are acquired because of the teacher's authority or the strategies' usefulness when taking tests, not because they serve to enhance understanding (or search for meaning), reciprocal teaching cannot be taken as being based on the constructivist view and poses no real challenge to the so-called Vygotskian conception.

Chang and Wells also emphasize the role of the teacher in joint activities for developing students' procedural and metacognitive knowledge, though their position seems closer to those proposing radical extensions. Although they admit that "a great deal of the learning . . . takes place as students work together (more or less) collaboratively, without the involvement of the teacher" their chapter is mostly concerned with the teacher's intervention in learner-directed activities in two classrooms. The teachers assigned students an active role in selecting and organizing tasks, though all of them were to achieve the superordinate goals the teachers had established.

According to Chang and Wells, both children and adults are meaning makers; that is, they try to make sense of new information and thus are involved in the process of hypothesis formation, testing, and modification. Children, however, do not possess a rich repertory of strategies (e.g., how to start a project, how to deal with differences of opinion). Teachers certainly know these strategies but presenting them in a propositionally coded form is not enough for students to acquire them. There must be "extended opportunity for discussion and problem solving in the context of shared activities, in which meaning and action are collaboratively constructed and negotiated." Learning occurs at points of negotiation of meaning in conversation.

Thus although Chang and Wells' major concern is the transmission of strategies from the teacher to students, their assumptions about the learner and social interaction have aptly been updated in the constructivist direction. Moreover, instruction organized by Chang and Wells, different from reciprocal teaching, had a clear goal set for students' activities and teachers' interventions, that is, to make the presentation informative and enjoyable to the audience. Therefore the chapter can be taken as an appeal for creating a "functional learning environment" (Newman, 1985).

Chang and Wells pay due attention to the affective aspects of conversation. Their protocols clearly reveal that interactions are far from "purely cognitive." Children seemed to try to be academic winners, save face, avoid being looked down upon, and so on, especially during interactions with peers. In this sense, a school class is certainly different from a mother–child dyad in terms of its structural and motivational complexities.

Radical Extensions

Proposed extensions by Cobb et al. and Moll et al. are so radical that some readers may doubt that the authors are still Vygotskians. Cobb et al. demonstrate how researchers could become Vygotskians without giving up being constructivists. Through a long-term observational study of the "inquiry mathematics" classes of second-graders, the authors have come to realize that, in order to understand the process of students' construction of mathematical knowledge some Vygotskian ideas must be incorporated.

Among others, they have accepted a Vygotskian idea that doing mathematics is a social activity as well as an individual construction activity because what counts as a problem or as a solution has normative aspects. In other words, social norms of the classroom constrain students' mathematical actions and constructions. Therefore the teacher has an important role to play in establishing classroom norms that encourage active construction of mathematical knowledge. According to Cobb et al., this job can be achieved by "talking about talking about mathematics." Interestingly, the teacher's reactions tended to be direct and imposing at this metacognitive level. He or she may have grasped intuitively that students' cognitive activities can develop without frequent teacher intervention after the students have acquired the metacognitive beliefs necessary for monitoring their activities.

Another Vygotsky-inspired idea Cobb and his associates incorporated is that instructional processes are institutionally constrained. For example, what occurs in the mathematics class is strongly influenced by the role our society assigns to schooling or mathematics, though, as the authors emphasize, innovative mathematics instruction may alter some institutional constraints.

However, the authors' approaches to instruction as well as theoretical interpretations are still constructivist. They view learning as "active construction to resolve experientially based problems." This view is in contrast to the conventional characterization of learning as the transfer or transmission of culturally developed modes or products of thinking from those who know to those who do not. More specifically, their instructional procedure was "small group work followed by a teacher-orchestrated whole class discussion of the children's problems, interpretations, and solutions." and thus involved numerous horizontal interactions. The teacher took her lead from the students' contributions and encouraged them to build on each other's explanations as she guided conversations about mathematics. There was no grading and no individual pencil-and-paper seat work.

More importantly, the students were not expected to make certain predetermined mathematical constructions because it might force the students to learn how to act in accord with the teacher's expectation only. Cobb et al. take it as the goal of mathematics instruction for students to articulate their own understandings. The authors also indicate that the teacher did not act as the sole validator of knowledge in her classroom.

Students are described as active and spontaneous learners also by Moll et al. The third-grade bilingual classroom they studied from the Vygotskian point of view seems close to Cobb et al.'s inquiry mathematics classes that got started with the Piaget-inspired constructivist framework and incorporated a few Vygotskian ideas later.

Moll et al. explicitly point out the necessity of interpreting Vygotsky's notion of zone of proximal development in a more dynamic and encompassing way than is conventionally understood. Providing assisted performance for a task that is a bit difficult for students to solve by themselves and evaluating their independent performance later do not guarantee good instruction. Assistance may just be awful: Rote, drill and practice instruction is often offered to the less privileged population in our modern society.

Based on Vygotsky's own writings as well as their classroom observations, Moll et al. claim that the unique form of cooperation between the child and the adult that is central in the educational process is mutually and actively created by the teacher and students. Thus they admit that students' initiative, interaction with peers, and adult guidance are all indispensable. They also claim that children's search for meaning and significance, which plays a prominent role in Vygotsky's general theorizing, should be incorporated as a critical component in creating the zone of proximal development. Their protocols suggest that joint activities can "help children express and obtain meaning in ways that will enable them to make knowledge of their own."

In their classroom, students were allowed to choose topics that interested them. They could even generate their research questions and negotiate their learning tasks with their teacher. Thus in this classroom, individual students' initiative and the teacher's guidance coexisted. Learning was not an individual achievement but a joint accomplishment between adults and children. In other words, the teacher provided a safety net for children who would engage in diverse classroom activities.

Books and other materials are considered important resources for learning by Moll et al. By pointing out that these artifacts constitute part of the collective zone, the authors endorse a view that having multiple sources of information is desirable.

It will be interesting to examine similarities and differences among Cobb et al., Moll et al., and Itakura's (1962) hypothesis–experiment–instruction (HEI), which also capitalizes on students' dialogical (polilogical) interaction guided by the teacher. The following procedure is usually adopted in this Japanese science-education method: (1) Pupils are presented with a question with three or four alternative answers. (2) They are asked to choose one by themselves. (3) Pupils' responses, counted by a show of hands, are tabulated on the blackboard. (4) They are encouraged to explain and discuss their choices with one another. (5) They are asked to choose an alternative once again. They may change their choices. (6) Pupils are allowed to test their predictions by observing an experiment or reading a given passage.

The teacher in HEI, after presenting the problem, is a chairperson or moderator who tries to stay as neutral as possible during students' discussion. Thus although the teacher has control over the kinds of activities in which students are engaged, none of the members in the discussion group is taken as more capable by status than any other. In step 4, above, students often engage in lively discussions in a large group ($n = 40$ to 45). Several students may express their opinions often, but most of them tend to participate vicariously in the discussion, nodding or shaking their heads, or making brief remarks. There is empirical confirmation in step 6 that demonstrates clearly which answer alternative is correct. Itakura claims that students' predictions must be tested by observation or consultation independent from the teacher. Teachers in HEI seem to intervene directly least often but organize students' activities by providing the appropriate artifacts, that is, a well thought out series of problems.

Students in HEI are not explicitly asked to achieve understanding as a final task outcome. They are encouraged only to discuss which alternative is correct, and enduring comprehension activity is initiated primarily by their being presented a problem, the answer alternatives of which include plausible yet erroneous ideas. However, a few experimental studies (reviewed by Hatano & Inagaki, 1987) have revealed that Itakura's procedure enhances students' understanding of the scientific concepts and rules involved as well as their interest in confirming their predictions. It has also been suggested that students acquire metacognitive beliefs that evaluate understanding more highly than giving the correct answer through repeated participation in HEI.

Analyses of Artifacts

Griffin et al. deal with an apparently different topic, that is, critique and revisions of an educational software program, though it is part of a larger study on how computers might be used to promote development through a series of formative experiments. We generally assume that a context is constituted, not given beforehand, by participants' words and actions. Because software is static, it does not seem to contribute greatly to the constitution of context. However, as the authors put it, it embodies its programmer's "voice." In a sense, the programmer is a hidden member of the communicative interactions in which teachers and students are involved when they use the software. In fact, the authors have observed occasions where the software was "blamed" for not allowing smooth interactions.

Software involves programmers' tacit assumptions that, like "presuppositions" during discourse, are powerful in controlling other participants' behavior. However, because of their having options, negotiation between the programmer's voice and the voices of the other participants is possible to some extent. The authors report several interesting cases in which they succeeded in modifying the target software so it allowed more flexible negotiations, as well as unsuccessful cases where the software could not be changed because of technological limitations.

The authors' findings have important general implications for education as well as for educational research. Although artifacts are static products of human behavior, they function as if they had intentions, for example, creating contexts for activity and constraining live participants' actions and constructions. This point is also emphasized by Chang and Wells and Moll et al. Moreover, artifacts represent some people's voices, usually voices of people who have power. In other words, unless live participants consciously and intentionally try to avoid it, their educational activities are controlled to some extent by those who have power to produce and provide relevant artifacts. Textbooks and tests, among others, must be such artifacts (Apple, 1986). It is an important challenge for educational researchers to find ways to make these artifacts less directive.

Future of the Vygotskian Conception of Knowledge Acquisition

Summarizing Achieved Extensions

How can we summarize the findings and interpretations of the above five sets of Vygotskian studies? How much of the needed extensions and revisions have been achieved by them? Let me present a summary in terms of the four revising assumptions listed in the first section.

First, the active nature of learners is now taken for granted by most, if not all, of the authors. That students seek and often achieve understanding has also been accepted. Thus Revising Assumptions 1 and 2 seem to have replaced the empiricistic ones. These revising assumptions being accepted, the Vygotskians in this section are clearly different from empiricists, and some of them belong to the constructivist camp: Knowledge, at least in part, is constructed by individual students. It has also been made clear that the teacher's guidance affects students' knowledge acquisition in varied ways. The teacher not only transmits strategies through joint problem solving; through conversation, the teacher expands and elaborates "spontaneous" ideas by students and develops their metacognitive beliefs so the construction of relevant knowledge can be enhanced.

Second, all the authors have well recognized that peer interactions, especially when monitored by the teacher, can contribute to knowledge construction. Revising Assumption 3 has thus been accepted. A student may try to build his or her understanding on an idea presented by another through dialogue; and two or more students may try to negotiate and co-construct integrated ideas in joint activities. Although the teacher's feedback plays an important role, he or she is not the sole evaluator. The presence of peers is never considered to be a distraction from learning. Even heterogeneity of students' ideas and backgrounds is evaluated positively. When one of the editors of this volume wrote a chapter focusing on peer interaction some 5 years ago (Forman & Cazden, 1985), its theme was considered outside the Vygotskian mainstream. Now, however, it is legitimate to address peer interaction so long as the need for adult guidance is not ignored.

Third, it is unanimously agreed that, in addition to the teacher, other artifacts, embodying the voices of people who made them, can help students construct relevant and plausible knowledge. Among others, textbooks, other books, and software are important. They not only provide information but create a collective zone of proximal development. Revising Assumption 4 has firmly occupied its place.

In sum, as stated at the beginning of the commentary, there is a recognizable tendency across the five chapters to move away from transmissionism and toward constructivism at the theoretical level and to encourage students' active participation in joint activities more than passive attentiveness to what is presented verbally or demonstrated by the teacher at the level of instructional practice. Can we conclude that the Vygotskian conception of knowledge acquisition is being extended successfully? Generally speaking, does this tendency to extend and revise itself indicate a "healthy" state of Vygotskian theory?

My answers are affirmative to both questions, because I believe, in a Lakatosian manner, that (1) extending or revising its assumptions in the light of research findings and practical serviceability is needed for the Vygotskian research program to continue "progressing"; and (2) Vygotskian key notions constituting the "hard core" of the program can be kept intact, even when its peripheral, empirically falsifiable assumptions are updated. Some Vygotskian purists may be fearful of their losing theoretical identity if the active and competent nature of individual learners is emphasized, but this fear has no rational ground. As Chang and Wells correctly point out, to argue that knowledge is individually constructed is not to ignore the role of other people in the process of construction. Similarly, emphasizing the role played by interactions with peers and artifacts in students' construction of knowledge does not mean that guidance by the teacher is not critical.

I also believe that if we want to establish a generally acceptable conception or theory of knowledge acquisition there should be much more dialogue (or polilogue) among theories or research programs. This practice may lead us to attempt to strengthen one theory by incorporating insights from another, which is sometimes considered "problematic" (See Introduction of the October 1988 issue of *The Quarterly Newsletter of the Laboratory of Comparative Human Cognition*). In fact, Vygotskian theory has provided insights to supporters of other theories, among others, Piagetian theory (e.g., Brown, 1988; Cobb et al., this volume) and the cognitive science of instruction (e.g., Brown, Collins, & Duguid, 1989). Some Vygotskians want to provide insights to the "nativist/modularist" theory (e.g., Di Bello & Orlich, 1987). There is no reason why Vygotskians cannot incorporate insights from other schools. Even when attempted extensions and revisions are based on such insights (e.g., from information-processing psychology or genetic epistemology), it may not be problematic if those insights are harmoniously integrated into the whole of Vygotskian theory.

Problems Yet To Be Solved

Although I am willing to give my assent to many of the revisions and extensions by the five chapters, I am not fully satisfied with the resultant Vygotskian conception of knowledge acquisition. As the conception shifts from transmissionism to constructivism, two problems appear, or at least become more serious; and solution of them is urgently needed to make the conception more or less complete.

One problem is how to explain the sociogenesis of individual cognition from the constructivist view. The so-called Vygotskian conception, though too narrow in its scope, once offered a good explanation as to where students' skills come from and how they are "transmitted." In contrast, what a constructivist can offer now is too global and unspecified. In her attempt to offer a constructivist explanation for sociogenesis, Resnick (1987, p. 47) argued that "the environment and the culture provide the 'material' upon which constructive mental processes will work." This argument can be a good starting point for further discussion, if we can specify in more detail the nature of "material" and how it is worked on by an active mind.

Putting together the interpretations offered in these chapters, I would like to propose, though tentatively, the following four specifications regarding the nature of "the material provided by the environment and culture" or "sociocultural constraints."

1. Knowledge is often constructed when the learner interacts with the teacher (or a more capable member), peers, or artifacts embodying voices of others, creating jointly with them the context for interaction.
2. Through interaction something collective is produced; in other words, something is shared among its participants. This "something" can be a cooperative system for solving problems, discussed and negotiated meanings or understandings, common sense and social

norms defining situations and regulating behaviors, and so on. This process involves socioemotional components as well.

3. The learner incorporates (or assimilates, using Piagetian terminology) this "something" for generating, elaborating, and revising his or her knowledge.

4. The above (smaller) system of face-to-face interaction is embedded in a larger system, such as an institution or a community. The larger system may officially set a limit on the kinds of interactions that can occur within the smaller system. The larger system also influences interaction in the smaller system and thus the learner's construction of knowledge indirectly through a mediating individual (who is both a participant in the interaction within the smaller system and a member of the larger system) and an artifact.

The other problem is how to characterize spontaneous or everyday concepts (or conceptions) and scientific concepts, as well as the relations between the two. A solution of this problem is urgently needed because everyday concepts serve as the basis for interaction, negotiation, and sharing; and scientific concepts represent the best possible products of such joint activities. Better characterization of these beginning- and end-states of change induced by instruction would enhance our understanding of the process of socioculturally constrained construction of knowledge (Glaser & Bassok, 1989). Vygotsky's discussion of these types of concepts has often been ignored in Vygotskian instructional research because the so-called Vygotskian conception enabled them to start with the knowledge possessed by a more mature member, neglecting what the less mature member has already acquired.

An adequate solution of this problem probably requires Vygotskians to incorporate notions such as innate constraints and modularity. Harris (1990) suggested that there are certain widespread, accurate schemas in each discipline of everyday science, whereas other insights are much less accessible. The Vygotskian notion of sociogenesis does not mean that humans can acquire any piece of knowledge if they are socially supported. However, how and how much the process of social construction of knowledge is constrained by innate and early cognitive competence in each domain requires special consideration.

References

Apple, M. W. (1986). *Teachers and texts.* London: Routledge & Kegan Paul.

Brown, J. S., Collins, A., & Duguid, P. (1989). Situated cognition and the culture of learning. *Educational Researcher, 18,* 32–42.

Brown, T. (1988). Why Vygotsky? The role of social interaction in constructing knowledge. *Quarterly Newsletter of the Laboratory of Comparative Human Cognition, 10,* 111–117.

Di Bello, L., & Orlich, F. (1987). How Vygotsky's notion of "scientific concept" may inform contemporary studies of theory development. *Quarterly Newsletter of the Laboratory of Comparative Human Cognition, 9,* 96–99.

Doise, W., & Mugny, G. (1984). *The social development of the intellect.* Oxford: Pergamon Press.

Forman, E. A., & Cazden, C. B. (1985). Exploring Vygotskian perspectives in education: the cognitive value of peer interaction. In J. V. Wertsch (Ed.), *Culture, communication, and cognition: Vygotskian perspectives* (pp. 323–347). Cambridge: Cambridge University Press.

Glaser, R., & Bassok, M. (1989). Learning theory and the study of instruction. *Annual Review of Psychology, 40,* 631–666.

Harris, P. L. (1990). The nature of everyday science: a commentary. *British Journal of Developmental Psychology, 8,* 299–303.

Hatano, G., & Inagaki, K. (1986). Two courses of expertise. In H. Stevenson, H. Azuma, & K. Hakuta (Eds.), *Child development and education in Japan* (pp. 262–272). New York: W. H. Freeman.

Hatano, G., & Inagaki, K. (1987). A theory of motivation for comprehension and its application to mathematics instruction. In T. A. Romberg & D. M. Stewart (Eds.), *The monitoring of school mathematics: background papers: Vol. 2. Implications from psychology; outcomes of instruction.* Program Report 87-2. Madison: Wisconsin Center for Education Research.

Hatano, G., & Inagaki, K. (1991). Sharing cognition through collective comprehension activity. In L. B. Resnick, J. M. Levine, & S. D. Teasley (Eds.), *Perspectives on socially shared cognition.* (pp. 331–348). Washington, DC: APA.

Hatano, G., and Newman, D. (1985). Reply and response. *Quarterly Newsletter of the Laboratory of Comparative Human Cognition, 7,* 95–99.

Inagaki, K. (1981). Facilitation of knowledge integration through classroom discussion. *Quarterly Newsletter of the Laboratory of Comparative Human Cognition, 3,* 26–28.

Itakura, K. (1962). Instruction and learning of concept "force" in static based on Kasetsu-Jikken-Jigyo (hypothesis-experiment-instruction): a new method of science teaching. *Bulletin of National Institute for Educational Research, 52* [in Japanese].

Newman, D. (1985). Functional environments for microcomputers in education. *Quarterly Newsletter of the Laboratory of Comparative Human Cognition, 7,* 51–57.

Newman, D., Griffin, P., & Cole, M. (1989). *The construction zone: working for cognitive change in school.* Cambridge: Cambridge University Press.

Palincsar, A. S., & Brown, A. L. (1984). Reciprocal teaching of comprehension fostering and comprehension monitoring. *Cognition and Instruction, 1,* 117–175.

Resnick, L. B. (1987). Constructing knowledge in school. In L. S. Liben (Ed.), *Development and learning: conflict or congruence?* (pp. 19–50). Hillsdale, NJ: Lawrence Erlbaum Associates.

Schön, D. A. (1983). *The reflective practitioner.* New York: Basic Books.

II

INTERPERSONAL RELATIONS IN FORMAL AND INFORMAL EDUCATION

6

What Is Missing in the Metaphor of Scaffolding?

C. ADDISON STONE

The Scaffolding Metaphor

In 1976, Wood, Bruner, and Ross (1976) introduced the term *scaffolding* in the context of an analysis of adult–child interaction. They used the term as a metaphor for the process by which an adult assists a child to carry out a task beyond the child's capability as an individual agent. They described scaffolding as consisting of the adult's "'controlling' those elements of the task that are initially beyond the learner's capacity, thus permitting him to concentrate upon and complete only those elements that are within his range of competence." They argued, furthermore, that "the process can potentially achieve much more for the learner than an assisted completion of the task," and that it could result in "development of task competence by the learner at a pace that would far outstrip his unassisted efforts."

Wood and associates (1976) offered an analysis of the critical features of the scaffolding provided by the adult during an interactive problem-solving session. They noted first that the adult works with implicit theories of the task components, the necessary steps to solution, and the child's capabilities. The support provided by the adult was seen as serving several key functions: recruitment of the child's interest, reduction in degrees of freedom, maintaining goal orientation, highlighting critical task features, controlling frustration, and demonstrating idealized solution paths. In effective instances of scaffolding, they argued, the end result is greater individual mastery of the target task. The mechanism assumed to lead to this success was summarized in a companion paper by Wood and Middleton (1975, p. 190).

> The instruction serves to mark or highlight . . . task appropriate actions, providing [the child] with feedback which, though consistent with his actions, might not be inferred by him alone in the face of the many other competitors for relevance and attention which confront him. As he enacts and perfects such isolated task constituents, uncertainty about what to do and what to anticipate as a consequence of his actions diminishes, at least with regard to a subset of the task. This further frees the child to consider the wider or related task constraints and operations. At best, this process continues until he becomes acquainted with and skilled in all aspects of task activity to the point where he can initiate and control his own behaviour in the absence of an instructor.

In this early analysis of scaffolding, then, emphasis was placed on the adult's role as a support for the child for accomplishing the goal via task analysis and practice with subcomponents. The result was seen as independent functioning on the part of the child.

Limitations of the Metaphor

The initial discussions of scaffolding were focused on identifying and describing instances of such interactions and on documenting their effectiveness in instilling new capabilities in the child. At the time, little attention was paid to the mechanism by which this transfer of responsibility from the adult to the child was accomplished.[1] In contrast, more recent discussions of the concept of scaffolding have included a greater emphasis on mechanisms of transfer (variously termed transfer of control, internalization, and appropriation).[2] Much of this work has been influenced directly by the work of Vygotsky.

Although Wood and his colleagues did not draw explicitly on Vygotsky's work when formulating their ideas concerning scaffolding, there are clear parallels to Vygotsky's concept of the "zone of proximal development" (ZPD) (Vygotsky, 1978; 1987). These parallels have not gone unnoticed (e.g., Rogoff & Wertsch, 1984), even by the original authors themselves (Bruner, 1986; Wood, 1988). As is now well known, Vygotsky defined the ZPD as the distance between a child's "actual developmental level as determined by independent problem solving" and his or her "potential development as determined through problem solving under adult guidance or in collaboration with more capable peers" (Vygotsky, 1978, p. 86). In this context, the concept of scaffolding can be seen to represent both a means by which a child's "zone width" (or potential for new learning) can be assessed and as a means of observing the process by which the child is helped to capitalize on this potential. Indeed for many the term scaffolding has come to be synonymous with the process of adult–child interaction within the ZPD.

A persisting limitation of the metaphor of scaffolding relates to the specification of the communicative mechanisms involved in the adult–child interaction constituting the scaffolding process. These mechanisms are crucial to Vygotsky's theoretical framework; however, his own discussion of them was sketchy. Luckily, some efforts have been made by current writers to explore the potential of Vygotsky's original line of thinking. The work of Wertsch (1985) is particularly important in this regard. The purpose of the present chapter is to highlight some of the specific communicative mechanisms involved in the scaffolding process and, more generally, to explore certain implications of extending a Vygotskian-inspired analysis of scaffolding. These implications include the argument that the effectiveness of interactions (and therefore the potential for new learning) within the ZPD varies as a function of the interpersonal relationship between the participants.

Scaffolding as Semiotic Interaction

When analyzing the learning that takes place in the ZPD, Vygotsky (1987) argued generally that the mechanism involves the transfer of task responsibility from the social (intermental) level to the individual (intramental) level. In essence, the child's task approach comes to be mediated by the verbal and nonverbal directives provided by the adult during the interaction. This process is not, however, a simple matter of the child's literally "internalizing" the interchange between himself and the adult, as has been implied by some authors. Indeed, it is not even clear what such a process of literal internalization would look like. Instead, Vygotsky appeared to have in mind a much more subtle semiotic process, one that might be called "appropriation of meaning," or "semiotic uptake" (Wertsch & Stone, 1985).

To appreciate the spirit and implications of Vygotsky's analysis of internalization, it is useful to build on concepts from the field of linguistics. Such an approach was clearly consistent with Vygotsky's own agenda, as is evident in his discussions of sense versus meaning in the acquisition of word meaning, and of abbreviation in inner speech (Vygotsky, 1987). Extensions of Vygotsky's initial work in this area have begun (Bruner, 1986; Stone & Wertsch, 1984; Wertsch, 1985; Wertsch & Stone, 1985).

One such concept that seems to have some promise as a means of making sense of certain communicative dynamics within the ZPD is that of "prolepsis" (Stone, 1985; Stone & Wertsch, 1984). Although the term prolepsis itself dates from ancient rhetorical scholarship, it was reintroduced into modern psycholinguistics by Rommetveit (1974, 1979). The term refers to a communicative move in which the speaker presupposes some as yet unprovided information. Rommetveit argued that the use of such presuppositions creates a challenge for the listener, a challenge that forces the listener to construct a set of assumptions in order to make sense of the utterance. When the communication is successful, this set of assumptions recreates the speaker's presuppositions. Thus the listener is led to create for himself the speaker's perspective on the topic at issue.

A simple example of prolepsis is contained in the following dialogue between a tourist and a guard in an art museum.

> **Tourist:** Where is the Impressionist collection?
>
> **Guard:** [*Pointing to a display case in the distance*] Down the hallway just beyond the kitchenware.
>
> **Tourist:** I beg your pardon.
>
> **Guard:** Just beyond the Oriental pottery.

In this interchange, the guard makes his opinion about Oriental pottery clear, but he does not do so explicitly. Instead, he presents his perspective by forcing his listener to infer it. The initial referring expression, "the kitchenware," is presumed by the tourist to be a response to his question, but its exact relevance is unclear—hence the request for clarification. The subsequent clarification by the guard then allows the tourist to create the equation between Oriental pottery and kitchenware that the guard has intended to convey. The important point here is that the guard has conveyed information to the tourist by forcing him to seek a meaning for his utterance.

Although many instances of prolepsis during adult–child interactions would not be so provocative as the museum example, the effect of such interactions on the child's understanding of the adult's perspective on the situation at hand may be just as powerful. Indeed, the notion of prolepsis can be readily applied to the interchanges that occur during the adult–child interactions characteristic of scaffolding. During a prototypical interaction (Palincsar, 1986; Palincsar & Brown, 1984; Rogoff & Gauvain, 1986; Wertsch, 1979; Wood & Middleton, 1975) the adult might begin with a general question such as, "What piece goes next"? Then, as necessary, the adult would follow that question with more directed verbal or nonverbal directives that, in effect, provide the meaning presupposed by the initial, general directive. In this way the child comes to understand what was presupposed by the initial directive and is led to construct the adult's understanding of the task goal and of the appropriate means for achieving the goal.

An example of prolepsis in adult–child interaction may be of use. The example below is taken from a study of mother–child interaction (Rogoff & Gauvain, 1986) in which mothers were asked to assist their preschool children in placing pictures of everyday objects into groups in preparation for a memory test.

Mother: [*Picks up the picture of a bucket and holds it in front of the child.*] What's that?

Child: It's a bucket and it helps you carry things and. . . .

Mother: Yeah, and *it helps you clean.* [*Looks at child.*]

Child: [*Nods and pauses*]

Mother: [*While adjusting the broom in the box for cleaning materials*] OK, what else, do you see something else that helps you clean?

Child: [*Watches his mother's hand on the bucket card, then points to the bucket and then to the broom.*]

Mother: [*Nods*] The broom. So it should be put in here. [*Holds the bucket in the cleaning box.*]

Child: [*Takes the bucket from his mother's hand and places it in the correct box.*]

In this excerpt the mother is trying to help her child understand that a bucket goes with the partially assembled pile of other "cleaning materials." That is, the mother is trying to help the child see the value of using similarities in function as an organizing device. However, the approach is not one of explicit provision of a rule.

The mother's utterance "and it helps you clean" is proleptic in the same sense as the first example. That is, it assumes an understanding on the part of the child of the significance of functional information in this task. The child does not act on her hint for placing the picture, however, so the mother proceeds to help the child see the connection between the information about the object's function that she provided earlier and the correct placement of the broom. In this way, the child is led to place the picture correctly.

More importantly, for our purposes, it can be argued that the child has begun to appreciate the significance in the context of this task of information about an object's function. This goal has been accomplished by juxtaposing an underspecified (i.e., richly presupposing) utterance with its subsequent specification. The mother's initial utterance assumes a perspective on the task and an appropriate solution strategy that must be later spelled out for the child. The child, in turn, by making a connection between his mother's earlier proleptic remark and the task approach that it presupposed, is exposed to a new perspective on how to "play the game," which constitutes a heuristic for improving memory. Eventually, through repetitions of similar interchanges, there would be a transfer of responsibility for the memory strategy, a transfer motivated by the proleptic challenges. In the present case, the mother did not adopt this ploy intentionally (though she could have), but that fact does not diminish its potential utility.

The notion of prolepsis is similar in many respects to Grice's (1989)[3] now familiar concept of conversational implicature.[4] When introducing this concept, Grice attempted to point to a special class of implications conveyed during speaking. This class consisted of those implications that were conveyed *contextually* rather than logically. The key construct introduced by Grice in this context was termed the *cooperative principle*. Most simply, this principle holds that a speaker, when speaking on a given occasion, should make the contribution appropriate to the context, *and* that a listener should assume that it has indeed taken place. To specify what would count as "appropriate," Grice introduced a set of "conversational maxims," which hold that an utterance should be relevant, true, clear, and only as informative as is required. Grice's insight was to point out that, on the assumption that the maxims are generally obeyed, apparent violations of the maxims serve to convey additional meaning—meaning that is nowhere evident in the actual words uttered.

Grice gave a number of examples of implicatures[5] that illustrate the functioning of the various maxims. For example, note the following exchange (Grice, 1989, p. 32).

> **Speaker A:** Smith doesn't seem to have a girlfriend these days.
>
> **Speaker B:** He has been paying a lot of visits to New York lately.

In this example, Grice saw the maxim of Relevance at work. At first glance, this maxim appears to have been violated by B. It is actually not the case; and by assuming that B must be saying something that is relevant to the conversation, A is led to infer that B believes that Smith may indeed have a girlfriend in New York. Note that B's words themselves do not in any way imply this situation. It is his utterance *in context,* together with the maxim of Relevance, that invites the intended inference.

The following example illustrates that implicatures can also be created by intentional violations of the maxims (Grice, 1989, p. 37).

> Miss X produced a series of sounds that corresponded closely with the score of "Home Sweet Home."

In this case, the speaker has intentionally violated the maxim of Quantity. That is, he could have said simply:

> Miss X sang "Home Sweet Home."

It is by virtue of recognizing this intentional violation that we are led to infer something about the speaker's opinion of Miss X's performance.

Examples of prolepsis such as those presented earlier can be seen as special cases of conversational implicature. In the case of the museum guard, for example, his intended meaning goes forward only if the visitor assumes that his remark about kitchenware is relevant to the conversation. It differs from Grice's examples of implicature in one crucial respect: The shared context at that point in the conversation is not yet sufficient to allow the implicature to go through. Further specification is necessary, and the listener is motivated to seek it. Here is the element of anticipation characteristic of prolepsis. Thus prolepsis can be seen as a special type of conversational implicature in which the necessary context is specified *after* the utterance rather than before it. What is useful about the notion of prolepsis is its highlighting of the creative or transformative effect of such discourse turns via the communicative tension introduced by the speaker.

A related analysis of the construction of meaning during social interactions can be found in the work of Sperber and Wilson (1982). These authors built an analysis of comprehension around a modified notion of Grice's maxim of Relevance. What is unique about their contribution is its emphasis on the need to consider the "cognitive load" involved in such conversational inferences. In their view, during a conversation the listener is continually striving to impose interpretations on the speaker's utterances that make them maximally relevant to the linguistic and extralinguistic context. In so doing, the listener is led to construct aspects of the context presupposed by the speaker. In their words, "determination of the context is not a prerequisite to the comprehension process, but a part of it" (Sperber & Wilson, 1982, p. 76). They stressed, however, that this process is costly in terms of mental effort. One might add that it hinges on an optimal match between the current context assumed by the listener and that presupposed by the speaker (and necessary for correct interpretation of the utterance). If too much "common ground" is incorrectly presupposed, the message does not go through. If too little is presupposed, mutual trust might not be maintained (Rommetveit, 1979).

In any specific communicative exchange involving constructive comprehension processes such as those sketched by Rommetveit, Grice, and Sperber and Wilson, the result for the listener is a new perspective on the immediate context, or, a new "situation definition." This situation definition is, of course, not necessarily more sophisticated or more functional. It is merely more consistent with that presupposed by the speaker. However, when this process takes place between an adult, or "expert," and a novice, the result may have both of these characteristics.

In his discussion of prolepsis, Rommetveit (1974, 1979) added one additional element important to the general analysis of conversational inference. He argued not only that the process of prolepsis involves the construction of new understandings of a speaker's intended meaning but also that in situations characterized by what he termed "mutual trust" the process may increase the likelihood that the listener will adopt the speaker's perspective as his own. That is, prolepsis may be a powerful motivator of transformations in situation definition. Rommetveit (1979, p. 167) made this point clearly in the context of a discussion of prolepsis in fiction.

> [A]ssumed shared presuppositions may . . . also be conducive to intimacy and even lead to an expansion of the dialogically established HERE-AND-NOW. Such a process of prolepsis . . . is often encountered in fiction when the reader feels (correctly) that he has comprehended something in addition to what he actually has read. What from a strictly "objective" or "public" point of view appear as unwarranted presuppositions on the part of the creative writer may then more appropriately be conceived of as self-fulfilling assumptions by which the reader is made an insider of a tacitly expanded and enriched HERE-AND-NOW. He is made an insider—not merely informed about it—precisely because that expanded social reality is taken for granted rather than explicitly spelled out.

Rommetveit's argument suggests that the process of creating presuppositions pulls the listener into a new perspective on the situation at hand, one that the listener may adopt as his own. Rommetveit referred to this process as the construction of a greater "intersubjectivity." He argued that the chances of advancing intersubjectivity are far less in situations in which prolepsis is not so centrally involved. Such situations might include instruction that relies on explanation or step-by-step demonstration, although it should be stressed that the distinction between such situations and instructional interactions rich in prolepsis is one of degree rather than kind (see below). Indeed, theorists such as Rommetveit and Sperber and Wilson would undoubtedly argue that context creation is an inevitable component of all comprehension.

The potential value of exploring the semiotic dimensions of the interactions involved in scaffolding has been stressed by several authors. For example, the importance of a process similar to prolepsis has also been stressed by Rogoff (1986, pp. 32–33).

> In order to communicate successfully, the adult and child must find a common ground of knowledge and skills. Otherwise the two people would be unable to share a common reference point, and understanding would not occur. This effort toward understanding . . . draws the child into a model of the problem that is more mature yet understandable through links with what the child already knows.

Palincsar (1986) also stressed the importance of dialogue during scaffolding, drawing on examples from her own interactional studies of the fostering of reading comprehension via "reciprocal teaching." She argued that dialogue is the means by which support is provided and adjusted, and that it serves the function of "facilitating the collaboration necessary between the novice and the expert for the novice to acquire the cognitive strategy or strategies" (p. 95).

Another discussion of scaffolding provided additional proposals regarding the semiotic mechanisms involved. In the context of a general discussion of the relations between the individual and culture, Bruner (1986) took up once again the topic of scaffolding, this time from a more semiotic perspective. His analysis of the dynamics within the scaffolding situation is similar in several ways to the position being developed here. In particular, he drew on work in literary analysis and pragmatics to explore what he called the "constitutive" power of language. For example, he drew from the work of Grice to discuss the role of implicatures. In addition, however, he pointed to the creative value of other discourse devices such as certain classes of words that can serve to "trigger" presuppositions. For example, in the sentence, "John realized he was broke," the verb *realized* (a "factive verb") triggers the proposition that, "John was broke." It is important to note that such devices expand the domain of focus on semiotic mechanisms beyond that discussed above. Presuppositional triggers are unlike conversational implicatures or prolepsis in that their force is carried by the actual words rather than by the utterance in context. Thus they represent an additional class of context-creating devices.

Clearly, the semiotics of scaffolding are complex, and much work remains to be done to flesh out the picture of the communicative mechanisms embodied in successful scaffolding. Conversational implicature in general and prolepsis in particular are only two of many such mechanisms at work during adult–child interactions. As Bruner (1986) proposed, presuppositional triggers may also play an important role. What other semiotic mechanisms play a role in learning during scaffolded instruction? Here much work remains to be done. Several scholars have begun to consider the utility of Bakhtin's (1981) notion of "voice" in an account of interactions within the ZPD (Cazden, this volume; Wertsch, 1985, 1991). This work has the promise of extending the semiotic analysis of scaffolding into the sociolinguistic domain.

Although the discussion to this point has focused largely on the linguistic dynamics involved in effective scaffolding, the semiotic devices involved are clearly not just verbal. Nonverbal communicative devices (including gestures, eye gazes, and pauses) have long been implicated by others as crucial components of the scaffolding process (Rogoff, 1990; Wertsch, McNamee, McLane, & Budwig, 1980; Wood et al., 1976). The undeniable role of such factors poses a challenge: How can we move beyond the assumption that the "dialogue" constituting scaffolding is verbal to develop an integrative framework capable of incorporating a broader notion of semiotic interactions in scaffolding situations?

A useful first step for such an enterprise is implicit in comments provided by Grice (1989). Although most discussions of his framework (and indeed, the bulk of his own discussion) are focused on implicatures created via speech situations, Grice did not limit his description of the "cooperative principle" and its effects to the verbal domain. He noted, for example, that "talking [is] a special case, or variety of purposive, indeed rational behavior," and that there are "analogues [to the maxims] in the sphere of transactions that are not talk exchanges" (Grice, 1989, p. 28). Thus the construct of implicature can (and should) be broadened to encompass nonverbal interactions as well.

A similar point can be made with respect to prolepsis. The process of modeling a behavioral heuristic for accomplishing a goal can be seen as involving prolepsis, for example. From this perspective, the set of modeled behaviors constituting the heuristic is analogous to the initial proleptic utterance in a verbal exchange. Similarly, the highlighting of the (heretofore unanticipated) goal fulfillment corresponds to the resolution of the initial tension provided by the subsequent discourse. Working out an account of the dynamics involved in such nonverbal proleptic challenges may provide a means of understanding the powerful instances of children's learning via observations noted by several cross-cultural researchers interested in scaffolding (John-Steiner, 1984; Rogoff, 1990; Tharp & Gallimore, 1988).

Another issue for the future development of our understanding of the semiotics of scaffolding relates to the role of individual and developmental differences in effective scaffolding. The notions of implicature and prolepsis assume a complex interpretive interchange between individuals. What learner characteristics mediate the effectiveness of such interchanges? What significance should be attributed, for example, to linguistic facility? Contrary to much current opinion, Vygotsky placed considerable emphasis on the role of the child's developmental status and cognitive integrity in the dynamics of the ZPD. Vygotsky's concern with this issue was more evident in his writings on exceptional children (Vygotsky, in press) and in his late writings on developmental stages, in which he was trying to counter his colleagues' zeal for a model of total social determinism (Minick, 1989, personal communication; Vygotsky, 1984).

One class of developmental factors that must be considered when developing a picture of the semiotic dynamics within the ZPD is the child's growing mastery of the comprehension and use of various linguistic devices. For example, there is some evidence from developmental psycholinguistics of age-related sensitivity to the meanings implicit in verbs encoding the speaker's stance with respect to the message being conveyed (e.g., *may* and *could*). Clearly, the child's mastery of such forms is intimately related to the success of conversational inferences.

Although the discussion so far serves to highlight the need to refine and elaborate our understanding of the mechanisms of effective scaffolding, hopefully it serves also to indicate the potential utility of a semiotic perspective on such interactions. Much of the "work" of scaffolding is accomplished via the close communicative exchanges characteristic of these interactions. The following discussion explores the interpersonal aspects of these exchanges involved in scaffolding.

Interpersonal Dimensions of Scaffolding

If, as argued above, successful scaffolding involves the construction of shared situation definitions and if such construction involves a process of inference and trust, to use Rommetveit's (1979) terms, we must recognize that these interactions are not occurring between faceless functionaries. For the complex process of inferencing required in implicature and prolepsis to go forward, the individuals involved must share some minimal set of presuppositions about the situation at hand, and the two participants must respect each others' perspectives. The actors are engaged in an interpretive exchange, and the nature of the inferences involved in constructing a shared situation definition is a function of the past, present, and anticipated future interactions between the participants. This sequence, in turn, determines the range of perceived "fair" inferences and the context to be incorporated as ground for the inferences.

When developing a systematic perspective on the social dimension of the semiotics of scaffolding, at least two aspects of social interactions must be distinguished. The first relates to the situationally defined qualities of an interaction, and the second relates to a more enduring dimension of repeated interactions.

In his discussion of social relations, Hinde (1979) defined a relationship as "an intermittent interaction between two people" characterized by (1) interchanges over an extended period of time; (2) some degree of "mutuality" ("the behavior of each takes some account of the behavior of the other"); (3) a continuity between successive interactions; and (4) affective/ cognitive as well as behavioral components. In this definition, Hinde has clearly chosen to emphasize the cumulative and enduring qualities of the social interactions constituting a relationship.

Although it is useful for highlighting certain crucial attributes of social relationships, Hinde's definition deemphasized the importance of what Rommetveit (1974, 1979) called the "here-and-now." In this context it is important to remember that the social interactions involved in scaffolding (as in any social interchange) are goal-embedded. Thus the enduring "inertia" of a relationship captured by Hinde's definition is always filtered through the current goal structure of the situation.

These two aspects of a relationship—the current and the enduring—are closely related, both developmentally and situationally. In their sociological treatise on human behavior, Berger and Luckmann (1967) provided a symbolic interactional perspective on the developmental links between these two aspects of interpersonal behavior. Similar to Rommetveit, their view stressed initially the creative subjective force of what they call "face-to-face" interactions in the "here-and-now." However, they also provided a theoretical framework for appreciating the dynamics involved in the "institutionalization" of relatively stable social roles out of face-to-face interactions. Thus they saw social interactions as involving a complex interplay of context-determined and situationally general social forces.

Using this perspective, the social relationships within a scaffolding situation can be seen as involving both a subjective relation defined by the current activity (the "here-and-now") and symbolic qualities of social interchange crystallized out of past interactions. This complex interpersonal context acts as a filter through which an individual's learning opportunities via scaffolding must be viewed.

The interpersonal dimension of scaffolding is receiving increasing attention from scholars. Forman (1989; Forman & Cazden, 1985; Forman & McPhail, this volume), for example, has argued that there is a close correspondence between the initial and evolving nature of the interpersonal relationship between the participants in a peer dyad and the degree of cognitive progress made by a dyad across a series of joint problem-solving sessions. Rogoff (1990), in her analysis of past findings regarding social interactional influences on children's learning, has identified the factors of the relative "status" (authority) and "expertise" of the participants as important determinants of the differential effectiveness of scaffolding across various studies of adult–child and child–child interactions.

The dimensions of authority and expertise highlighted by Rogoff are important components of the critical interpersonal factors that mediate the success of scaffolding. However, additional factors must also be considered. One likely candidate in this regard is that of the affective dynamics of the relationship, that is, in Rommetveit's terms, the degree of mutual trust. This issue is taken up from a psychoanalytic perspective by Litowitz (this volume), who emphasizes the issues of resistance and identification on the part of the child. A similar argument, based on a different set of premises, was presented by Verdonik and associates (Verdonik, Flapan, Schmit, & Weinstock, 1988) with respect to "power plays" between parents and children as a factor in the child's demonstration of competencies. Disagreements regarding who is defining and directing the activity would clearly influence the direction and success of scaffolding.

Another factor that should prove useful in determining the interpersonal dynamics of the ZPD is the symbolic status of the to-be-learned activity in the learner's world. Goodnow (1990), for example, stressed the need to consider the relation of a skill to its explicit or implicit value in a given culture on the one hand and to the individual's social identity within the culture on the other. The important point here is that there are symbolic values attached to ways of seeing and doing that, in turn, influence the participants' interactions in scaffolding situations. From the perspective presented here, this influence is mediated in part via its effect on the participants' provision and uptake of appropriate semiotic challenges. If adults place little value on a particular child's learning of some skill, their interchange in the context of that activity is unlikely to provide the finely tuned directives necessary to encourage the child's inferences. Similarly, if children (or adult learners) place little value on the activity at issue, they are not motivated to engage in inferential interactions.

Although this discussion has, of necessity, only skimmed the surface of the relevant issues, it does serve to highlight the key role of interpersonal dynamics in scaffolding. Surely, one virtue of a semiotic perspective is its clear implication of the importance of these dynamics when mediating the impact of potential scaffolding experiences. Our challenge for the future is the development of a theoretical framework that captures the essential features of this process.

Expanded Metaphor

It is obvious that we have come a long way from the initial picture of scaffolding. The early discussions of scaffolding were focused primarily on describing a process of assisting the child in identifying, sequencing, and practicing subgoals for eventual guided assembly. We have moved away from this view of asymmetrical structuring of the passive child through a process of breaking down the task. We see now that scaffolding is a much more subtle phenomenon, one that involves a complex set of social and semiotic dynamics.

Currently, what we have is a picture of a fluid interpersonal process in which the participants' communicative exchanges serve to build a continually evolving mutual perspective on how to conceive the situation at hand. In the above discussion, two aspects of this process in particular have been emphasized. The first is the class of semiotic devices, such as implicature and prolepsis, that serve to encourage an interlocutor to construct and share the speaker's perspective. The second is the mediating influence of interpersonal relations and the social symbol value attached to situations and behaviors in this process of meaning construction. Both of these aspects are crucial components of a comprehensive understanding of the scaffolding process. It is my assumption that attempts to address these and other issues related to the semiotic dimension of scaffolding will prove fruitful conceptually and empirically. Hopefully, such an approach will help us to appreciate the implications of issues that Vygotsky only sketched for us.

Notes

An earlier version of this chapter was presented as part of a symposium titled Extending Vygotskian Theory at the annual meeting of the American Educational Research Association, San Francisco, April 1989. I would like to thank Joanne Carlisle and Ellice Forman for their comments on an earlier /draft.

1. The authors did note that the mechanism must rest on the child's ability to *recognize* the correct problem solution when it is achieved, even if he could not have produced it himself (Wood et al., 1976).

2. Another shift evident in discussions of scaffolding is a move from an emphasis on asymmetrical relations in which the adult is directing the child to an emphasis on mutuality. This trend is evident in terms used to refer to the scaffolding process: guided participation (Rogoff, 1990), instructional conversation (Tharp & Gallimore, 1988), and guided cooperative learning (Brown & Palincsar, 1989). This issue is discussed later in the chapter.

3. Grice's lectures on conversational implicature were originally delivered in 1967, but they were not published in complete form until 1989.

4. There is still debate among linguists about the exact "boundaries" of Grice's notion of conversational implicature. Thus, for example, whereas Grice distinguished conversational implicature from the more common pragmatic concept of presupposition (Levinson, 1983), Green (1989) has argued that implicature can actually account for presupposition (as well as other notions, such as reference and discourse cohesion).

5. The term "implicature" is used here as a shorthand for "conversational implicature." Actually, Grice distinguished conversational implicature (or, more exactly, "particularized" conversational implicature) from other, more conventional forms of implicature that share the general attribute of being less dependent on the utterance context and more tied to the actual words uttered.

References

Bakhtin, M. M. (1981). *The dialogic imagination*. Austin: University of Texas Press.
Berger, P. L., & Luckmann, T. (1967). *The social construction of reality: a treatise in the sociology of knowledge*. New York: Doubleday Anchor Books.
Brown, A. L., & Palincsar, A. S. (1989). Guided cooperative learning and individual knowledge acquisition. In L. B. Resnick (ed.). *Knowing, learning, and instruction*. Hillsdale, NJ: Lawrence Erlbaum Associates.
Bruner, J. (1986). *Actual minds, possible worlds*. Cambridge, MA: Harvard University Press.
Forman, E. A. (1989). The role of peer interaction in the social construction of mathematical knowledge. *International Journal of Educational Research, 13*, 55–69.
Forman, E. A., & Cazden, C. (1985). Exploring Vygotskian perspectives in education: the cognitive value of peer interaction. In J. V. Wertsch (ed.). *Culture, communication, and cognition: Vygotskian perspectives* (pp. 323–47). Cambridge: Cambridge University Press.
Goodnow, J. J. (1990). The socialization of cognition. In J. W. Stigler, R. A. Schweder, & G. Herdt (eds.). *Cultural psychology: essays on comparative human development* (pp. 259–86). New York: Cambridge University Press.
Green, G. (1989). *Pragmatics and natural language understanding*. Hillsdale, NJ: Lawrence Erlbaum Associates.
Grice, H. P. (1989). *Studies in the ways of words*. Cambridge, MA: Harvard University Press.
Hinde, R. A. (1979). *Towards understanding relationships*. London: Academic Press.

John-Steiner, V. (1984). Learning styles among Pueblo children. *Quarterly Newsletter of the Laboratory of Comparative Human Cognition, 6,* 57–62.

Levinson, S. C. (1983). *Pragmatics.* Cambridge: Cambridge University Press.

Minick, N. (1989). Mind and activity in Vygotsky's work: an expanded frame of reference. *Cultural Dynamics, 2,* 162–87.

Palincsar, A. S. (1986). The role of dialogue in providing scaffolded instruction. *Educational Psychologist, 21,* 73–98.

Palincsar, A. S., & Brown, A. L. (1984). Reciprocal teaching of comprehension-fostering and comprehension-monitoring activities. *Cognition and Instruction, 1,* 117–75.

Rogoff, B. (1986). Adult assistance of children's learning. In T. E. Raphael (ed.). *The contexts of school-based literacy.* New York: Random House, 1986.

Rogoff, B. (1990). *Apprenticeship in thinking: cognitive development in social context.* New York: Oxford University Press.

Rogoff, B., & Gauvain, M. (1986). Analysis of functional patterns in mother-child instructional interaction. In J. Valsiner (ed.). *The role of the individual subject in scientific psychology.* New York: Plenum.

Rogoff, B., & Wertsch, J. V. (1984). *Children's learning in the "zone of proximal development."* San Francisco: Jossey-Bass.

Rommetveit, R. (1974). *On message structure: a framework for the study of language and communication.* New York: Wiley.

Rommetveit, R. (1979). On codes and dynamic residuals in human communication. In R. Rommetveit & R. M. Blakar (eds.). *Studies of language, thought, and verbal communication* (pp. 163–75). Orlando, FL: Academic Press.

Sperber, D., & Wilson, D. (1982). Mutual knowledge and relevance in theories of comprehension. In N. V. Smith (ed.). *Mutual knowledge* (pp. 61–85). Orlando, FL: Academic Press.

Stone, C. A. (1985). Vygotsky's developmental model and the concept of proleptic instruction: some implications for theory and practice in the field of learning disabilities. *Research Communications in Psychology, Psychiatry, and Behavior, 10,* 129–52.

Stone, C. A., & Wertsch, J. V. (1984). A social interactional analysis of learning disabilities remediation. *Journal of Learning Disabilities, 17,* 194–99.

Tharp, R. G., & Gallimore, R. (1988). *Rousing minds to life: teaching, learning, and schooling in social context.* New York: Cambridge University Press.

Verdonik, F., Flapan, V., Schmit, C., & Weinstock, K. (1988). The role of power relationships in children's cognition: its significance for research on cognitive development. *Quarterly Newsletter of the Laboratory of Comparative Human Cognition, 10,* 80–84.

Vygotsky, L. S. (1978). *Mind in society.* Cambridge, MA: Harvard University Press.

Vygotsky, L. S. (1984). [*The collected works. Vol. 4. Child psychology*]. Moscow: Pedagogika (originally published in 1934).

Vygotsky, L. S. (1987). *Thinking and speech.* In R. W. Rieber & A. S. Carton (eds.). *The collected works of L. S. Vygotsky. Vol. 1. Problems of general psychology.* (N. Minick, translator). New York: Plenum (originally published in 1934).

Vygotsky, L. S. (in press). Problems of abnormal psychology and learning disabilities. In R. W. Rieber & A. S. Carton (eds.). *The collected works of L. S. Vygotsky. Vol. 2.* (J. Knox, trans.). New York: Plenum (originally published in 1925/1934).

Wertsch, J. V. (1979). From social interaction to higher psychological processes: a clarification and application of Vygotsky's theory. *Human Development, 22,* 1–22.

Wertsch, J. V. (1985). *Vygotsky and the social formation of mind.* Cambridge, MA: Harvard University Press.

Wertsch, J. V. (1991). *Voices of the mind.* Cambridge, MA: Harvard University Press.

Wertsch, J. V., & Stone, C. A. (1985). The concept of internalization in Vygotsky's account of the genesis of higher mental functions. In J. V. Wertsch (ed.). *Culture, communication, and cognition: Vygotskian perspectives* (pp. 162–79). New York: Cambridge University Press.

Wertsch, J. V., McNamee, G. D., McLane, J. G., & Budwig, N. A. (1980). The adult-child dyad as a problem-solving system. *Child Development, 51,* 1215–21.

Wood, D. (1988). *How children think and learn.* Oxford: Basil Blackwell.

Wood, D., & Middleton, D. (1975). A study of assisted problem solving. *British Journal of Psychology, 66,* 181–91.

Wood, D., Bruner, J. S., & Ross, G. (1976). The role of tutoring in problem solving. *Journal of Child Psychology and Psychiatry, 17,* 89–100.

7

Deconstruction in the Zone of Proximal Development

BONNIE E. LITOWITZ

Our views of how children develop and learn have undergone many changes. Of these changes, the one most associated with the name of Lev Semenovitch Vygotsky is that of the social construction of the individual. Vygotsky argued that development is social because it involves more than the endowment of the child and more than the child can effect on her own. Development requires another person and is thus literally social. The child's progress toward adulthood is effected through means that are shared by the collective group. Thus development is social in both aspects basic to its definition: involving another person and involving society as a whole.

Vygotsky's view of development arrived in an English-speaking world dominated by child-centered developmental theories, as expounded by Piaget, Chomsky, and Freud. In that context he offered a corrective reevaluation of the adult's role (Litowitz, 1989). Articulated in Vygotsky's own work and then by others drawing on his work, a "Vygotskian perspective" on development and learning has emerged. Neither on his own nor programmed by the adult, but working *with* the adult at a level beyond his individual capacities, the child gradually takes over the adult's functions. Activities engaged in by child and adult are shared by means of signs, such as gestures or speech, which provide the instruments for change within the child. Shared sign systems as used in specific activities are, then, both the material and the tools that constitute the socially constructed individual.

This chapter explores a question that Vygotsky recognized but did not answer: What motivates the child and the adult to perform as Vygotsky, and others following him, have proposed? I suggest that a narrow focus on what the child can do with or without an adult excludes the equally important question of how the child comes to be a person like the adult; to see speech only as a means to accomplish ends in activities obscures the role of speech in establishing a sense of self. Furthermore, I suggest that mastering activities and establishing a sense of oneself are not two distinct lines of development but are, rather, entwined in complex ways—that one cannot "study" one without the other.

Basic Concepts

Vygotsky claimed that "every function in the child's cultural development appears twice, on two levels: first on the social and later on the psychological level—first *between* people as an *interpsychological* category and then inside the child as an *intrapsychological* category" (Vygotsky, 1978, p. 128). The process by which *inter-* becomes *intra-* he called "internalization" or "interiorization." A description of the learning process that emphasizes the external and social becoming internal to the individual can equally be applied to behavioral conditioning or learning by imitation of a model. What distinguishes Vygotsky's perspective, however, is his exposition of the interaction between teacher and learner, specifically in his hypothesis of a third, relational element—the zone of proximal development—and what takes place there.

Vygotsky called the difference between what the child can do on her own and that which she can do in collaboration with a more knowledgeable other the *zone of proximal development*. The zone defines a space or range where learning takes place, and internalization describes the process of learning that takes place in that space. Examples of this process in the zone begin with two persons, one of whom is more knowledgeable than the other, usually a mother and a child but also a teacher and a student or an expert and a novice. These two persons working as a dyad approach a task or problem whose steps or solution are organized (sometimes called "scaffolded") by the more knowledgeable partner. The novice is propelled through the steps in such a way that he can ultimately take over the whole sequence, thereby demonstrating that what was performed externally by two persons has become internalized within one individual.

Careful study has shown that there are in fact several steps involved in this transfer of cultural knowledge. At first the novice is carried in the task: given just one part to carry out, guided with questions, directed through gesture or word, and so forth. Gradually, however, more and more of the steps are turned over to the novice until the novice shares the same organizational plan as the once-more-knowledgeable partner (Bruner, 1978). In the end, then, the members of the dyad who started out unequal become equal participants. The nonknower becomes, like the knower, able to take over responsibility for solving problems and completing tasks. Thus there are three distinguishing characteristics to this process: (1) cultural knowledge is transferred not from one person (adult) to another (child) but from two persons (the dyad) to one (the child); (2) the transmission is accomplished through semiotic means; and (3) the nonknower demonstrates equality in the dyad by becoming equally responsible for solving problems and accomplishing tasks.

Several authors have noted that progress from being carried in a task to becoming a full participant is capped by taking responsibility for the task. For example:

Getting dressed was relatively low for the younger children and high for the older. It may be that, although both groups of children had had considerable experience with this routine, the 4-year-olds were *only beginning to take responsibility* for it themselves and thus to have to predict its details. To the extent that a person must plan ahead, the script must become much more reliably established and automatic. The younger children presumably had not yet reached this point. [Nelson & Gruendel, 1986, p. 36; emphasis added]

Kaye also noted that taking responsibility is a gradual process.

While the infant *takes on a slowly increasing share of the responsibility for the interaction,* other parts of his role are performed for him, or the parents merely pretend he is performing them. In effect, then, he never really achieves autonomy until he has become a member of the system taking over functions that had been performed by the parent. [Kaye, 1982, p. 226; emphasis added]

Bruner described this gradual process in great detail beginning with the early appearance of reciprocity in interactions between caretaker and child who enter into formats or routines "contain[ing] demarcated *roles* that eventually become *reversible.*" (Bruner, 1983, pp. 27, 120; emphasis added).

Thus the progression from novice to knower involves more than a mere transfer of cultural knowledge; there is a shift in one's role vis-a-vis another person with respect to this knowledge. The shift from the reciprocity of equal partnership to the reversibility of equal responsibility has not been sufficiently clarified in the literature; I return to it below, suggesting that it can provide important insights regarding the social construction of the individual.

Underlying Assumptions

Underlying Vygotsky's scenario of sociocultural learning are two assumptions about the motivations of teacher and learner in dyadic interactions. First, the more knowledgeable member of the dyad (teacher/adult) is always performing two functions: solving the specific problem and teaching the novice how to solve the problem. Does it mean that there is an innate pedagogical impulse in us?[1] Second, the learner (novice/child) wants gradually to take on more and more of the adult's role in structuring tasks rather than just being carried or directed by another. Does it mean that children (novices) have an innate need to master problems and perform tasks in just the ways more knowledgeable others do? I do not mean to suggest that these motivations are in any way consciously held by the dyadic members, although that may be the case for teachers. Nor do I mean to suggest that these are unconscious motivations of which I am aware whereas the dyadic participants are not. These are, rather, simply assumptions that follow from Vygotsky's position, especially in the absence of alternate explanations.

Although not articulated, these assumptions clearly emerge in descriptions of both successful and failed learning in the zone. One finds in the Vygotsky-influenced literature many descriptions of perfectly orchestrated dyads, moving smoothly through the stages of adult-teaching and child-learning with few obstacles. The positive intent of both participants is rarely questioned; similarly, the smooth efficiency is rarely doubted.[2] When, as often happens, learning does not take place, we are left with two possible causes: Either the adult did not create the right scaffold, or the child was not able or did not choose to use the scaffolding provided. Such a child may be seen as deviant or even deficient in her ability to learn, requiring special structuring of tasks by an expert (e.g., a "special" educator).

Goodnow (1990, p. 279), however, raised a third possibility:

> My disappointment with the picture usually presented is that once again the world is benign and relatively neutral. To be more specific, the standard picture is one of willing teachers on the one hand and eager learners on the other. Where are the parents who do not see their role as one of imparting information and encouraging understanding? Where are the children who do not wish to learn or perform in the first place, or who regard as useless what the teaching adult is presenting?

Conjuring up parents who will not teach and children who will not learn confronts the "voluntarism" of the standard scenario (Henriques, Hollway, Urwin, Venn, & Walkerdine, 1984). Why would members of the dyad choose to deny their respective innate needs to teach and learn?

Goodnow offered one explanation, illustrated by an autobiographical example: her own inability to learn how to type. Proficiency in such a skill, she noted, would have identified her with a group of "girls who were expected not to do well academically" (Goodnow, 1990, p. 282). She explained that "areas of knowledge and skill are differentially linked to one's social *identity,* and that the linkings can help account for both acceptance and *resistance* to learning" (p. 282; emphasis added). In other words, the cause of her inability was neither poor teaching methods nor lack of ability on her part to use those methods nor even obstinate refusal. It was, rather, a question of "desire" (as we see below).

Goodnow's example points out two concepts missing from discussions of the zone of proximal development and a learning theory based on the process of internalization: identification and resistance. It is these concepts that are involved in the move from reciprocity to responsibility (mentioned above) and that can offer an alternative explanation of motivation for learning in the zone. Briefly, what motivates the child to master tasks is not the mastery itself but the desire to be the adult or to be the one the adult wants him to be. Such desires constitute identification with another person as described originally by Freud (1917, 1923) and elaborated more recently by Lacan (1977), Henriques et al. (1984), and others.

Identification and Resistance

Identification is a complex term that has many uses. Within the field of psychoanalysis, identification is most usually defined as the "psychological process whereby the subject assimilates an aspect, property or attribute of the other and is transformed, wholly or partially, after the model the other provides. *It is by means of a series of identifications that the personality is constituted and specified*" (Laplanche & Pontalis, 1973, p. 205; emphasis added). Thus identification is both a process of making oneself similar to others through various means (e.g., incorporation, projection, introjection) and the product or result of that process.[3] One forms identities by identifying with another person (e.g., a part or a trait) or by identifying another person with oneself. In a further twist on this process, Lacan (1977) has claimed that the earliest identifications, being based on images, create particular distortions that he described as the "imaginary register." He elaborated how one can identify not only with the other but also with what the other wants or desires; one may even seek to *be* the desire of the other. (The ambiguity of the original French—*désir de l'Autre*—covers numerous possibilities.)

In contrast, Erikson (1963) took the psychoanalytic concept of identity in the direction of membership in sociocultural groups, and it is from such a sociological perspective that Goodnow (1990, pp. 282–283) drew her conclusion:

> A link to social identity seems essential also in any Vygotskian account of negotiations toward a transfer of skill or a shared definition of a task. The negotiations one is willing to work on are likely to be those with people one perceives as similar, wishes to be like, or wishes to impress.

Presumably Vygotsky would concur, as he concluded *Thought and Language* (1986, p. 253) with the following challenge:

> To understand another's speech, it is not sufficient to understand his words—we must understand his thought. But even that is not enough—we must also know its motivation. No psychological analysis of an utterance is complete until that plane is reached.

To examine how the concept of identification might inform that plane of psychological analysis, we must return to internalization, using Vygotsky's own preferred example of semiotic mediation: speech.

In his writings about social, egocentric, and inner speech, Vygotsky exemplified how the transfer of cultural knowledge takes place through the process of internalization. The language of another becomes our own when we speak to ourselves as others first spoke to us. Thus as the child internalizes the language of the other that structures a task, she becomes the one who speaks in that manner. Speech is the mechanism by means of which roles become reversible (nonknower becomes knower). Yet it would be a mistake to see this construction of the individual through internalization only as a shift in sociocultural knowledge as content. Vygotsky warned that speech as internalized social mediation changes more than content; it creates new processes and forms of thinking and, indeed, of all higher mental functioning (e.g., perception, memory). With the addition of identification to psychological analysis we can add that not just cognitive structure is altered; psychosocial structure, or *lichnost* (personality), becomes altered as well. We may say that, as our inner speech is the internalized speech of others, our self is constituted by the internalized others who speak. Our selves are created out of these identifications with others, with social groups, and their desires. Their desires become ours; and we become their desires.[4] Whether we agree or refuse to teach or learn has its source at this level of psychological analysis.

If we accept that individuals are constituted in this way, we cannot assume a uniform internalized voice or only one way to transfer a skill. In an example of apprenticeship in skill-learning, illustrating the zone of proximal development, Kaye (1982, pp. 55–56) observed:

> The parental role . . . is [to] pose manageable subtasks one step at a time, and gradually pull that support away from [children] as their competence grows. . . . When my father taught me to swim he backed away as I paddled toward him. I can remember crying that it was unfair—but 25 years later I did the same thing to my son.

Although Kaye offered this anecdote as an example of an innate pedagogical impulse, an identification with his own father and thus with how fathers behave is an alternate interpretation. I would argue that it is a preferable interpretation because there are so many counterexamples. What can we say about the father who pushes his son off into deep water with: "Swim! Your cousin Helene is a year younger than you and she already knows how to swim!" Was this father's goal to teach or to compete with his brother through their respective children? Yet children do learn via the sink or swim method, and often in order to outperform a cousin or sibling. There is undoubtedly a wide variety of preferred methods through which sociocultural knowledge is transferred, depending on the targeted skill as well as intercultural, intracultural, and personal styles (Wertsch, Minick, & Arns, 1984). Nor is speech a uniform mechanism of internalization.

Bakhtin noted that "the ideological becoming of a human being . . . is the process of selectively assimilating the words of others" (1981, p. 341). He alerted us to the fact that speech is heteroglossic or polyphonic; that is, speech is dialogic within itself (1973, 1981). We are born into a language and internalize speech that has a history; it has its sources in many voices from many dialogues, making our speech in turn equally multiple. Contradictions and conflicts arise among these internalized voices, not just intersociologically and ideologically but also interpersonally. Speaking of the "intense interaction and struggle" within each utterance, Bakhtin stated: "The utterance so conceived is a considerably more complex and dynamic organism than it appears when construed simply as a thing that articulates the intention of the person uttering it, which is to see the utterance as a direct, single-voiced vehicle for expression" (1981, p. 354). Thus the dialogic

view makes every speech act not only indirect but contradictory and conflictual.

Because these multiple voices that embody roles and desires are the
sources of our subjectivity, we are fractured and split intrasubjectively,
unable to speak with one voice (Lacan, 1977). In Goodnow's example
above, the speech that structures learning how to type and the speech of the
person who knows how to type, i.e., the one you will become if you internalize that knowledge, may contradict one another—and these contradictions do not yield easily to sublation! Out of such struggles in identification
is resistance born.

Revisiting the Zone

The zone of proximal development addresses how the child can alter his
behavior by adopting my behavior to become more like me. As noted above
and by others (Nelson, 1986, p. 237), its use can come perilously close to a
description of learning as a neobehavioristic shaping of behavior. It is especially true when the adult's role is described as a series of carefully arranged
steps and teaching skills (e.g., "raise the ante," "communicative ratchet,"
"extension") and when the child's contribution as *tabula rasa* is to absorb
the language and structure from the adult input.

I have noted elsewhere (Litowitz, 1988) that the zone of proximal development is an adultocentric view of the child's behavior. As Goodnow
observed: "It is too exclusively concerned with what is being done by the
dispensers of knowledge" (1990, p. 280). The child's perspective, I have suggested, can be captured by another spatial metaphor: Winnicott's (1971)
"potential space." The potential space is the "area" that is neither what the
child nor the mother knows. It is the range of the child's grandiosity and
omnipotence. In that space the child sees herself as more capable than she
really is. Like Vygotsky and the zone of proximal development, Winnicott
connected the potential space to play, the use of symbols, and creativity.
Unlike Vygotsky, Winnicott noted its connection to fantasy and illusion.
One could say that a child performing in the zone of proximal development
with an adult believes himself to be accomplishing the task and that the
adult's organization of the task (what Winnicott called the "holding environment") permits that illusion or fantasy.

A child psychoanalyst once asked me how psycholinguists explain why
young children continue speaking when so much of what they produce is
phonologically, grammatically, and semantically in error: Do they not hear
that they are wrong a lot of the time, and do they not get discouraged? One
answer is that the force of the innate preprogram of a universal grammar
(LAD) prevails and needs only minimal practice. Another is that errors are
patterned and show rule acquisition; the child as little linguist must feel as

positive about acquiring those rules as linguists are about positing them. Still another answer is that, by speaking, children feel like adults and hear themselves as more competent speakers. Children may tolerate their lack of structural competence so long as pragmatically they are using language as adults do and thus using language to be adults. In fact, children do not feel incompetent unless adults interfere with their grandiose fantasy of enhanced performance.

Do adults create the potential for that illusion through a pedagogical impulse or because they also have a fantasy? I think the latter: They believe that the child can be/is becoming just like them. Thus identification (i.e., the process of "making similar" or "being like" [L. *idem:* "same"]) goes in both directions, from child to adult as well as from adult to child.

The role of parental fantasies is seldom noted in the literature on psychology or education (but see Kaye, 1982, pp. 189, 203). The use of fantasy in creating goals for activities is inexplicably underappreciated in Vygotsky's theory of learning, considering that Marx claimed (in *Capital*) that the difference between the most talented bees and even inept architects is one of imagination and fantasy. So we might say that mothers are as grandiose and omnipotent in their expectations for their children as children are for themselves. One could go even further to state that fantasy must be better understood if the concept of a dyad is ever to transcend the personhood boundaries of its two participants. That is, only a distortion of reality (i.e., a fantasy) allows one to treat another person as performing a function for oneself or as performing a function of which she is incapable (Kohut, 1971).

Some theorists have called attention to the child's contribution to the learning process by suggesting that the child may bring a different definition of the task to the dyadic process (e.g., Rogoff & Wertsch, 1984). It is important, they remind us, for adults to understand where the child is coming from so that they can more finely attune their assistance in the zone of proximal development, making the interiorization process easier for the child and avoiding resistances or obstacles to a smooth transition of knowledge (*inter—intra*). However, redefinition of the task to include the learner's perspective focuses attention on sociocultural knowledge as content. As we have seen, reexamining what we are asking the learner to do must also include whom we are asking the learner to become.[5] The zone of proximal development describes more than the transmission of cultural knowledge; dyadic roles and dialogic positions relative to that knowledge also become internalized.

Resistance as Identification: Some Examples

Although learners may resist teaching because of contrasting definitions of the task or even conflicting identifications, sometimes resistance is an early or primitive form of identification. That is, the very process that motivates internalization of knowledge may manifest resistance to cooperation in the smooth functioning of that process.

In a study of interactions between mothers and their preschool children, dyads were asked to engage in any free-play activity of their choice. Despite her child's objections, one mother insisted on reading a story with her child (perhaps to impress the videotapers). This mother tried several ways to engage her child in book-reading as an activity: "We do this all the time"; "you know you love to read books." But the child always refused: saying "no," turning away, refusing to sit still, grabbing the book from her mother. The mother tried to establish a routine in which the child would be forced to participate: "Oh, look, a little dog. What's he doing?" Refusing even to be carried in the activity, the child gave only absurd answers; reducing the task beyond even picture description, the mother asked how many eyes the dog has, to which the child responded, "five!" Such rejections of activities can signal early attempts to perform the adult's functions of choosing and structuring activities.

In another example, a 3+-year-old child with Down syndrome who is mainstreamed in a 2+-year-old nursery school class had learned over the course of the year how to participate with the other children in group action-songs at rugtime. Checking the teacher's and other children's actions, he would follow the record's instructions to touch the floor and point to the door, touch your head and point to something red, and so forth. Wanting to enhance his performance (perhaps for the university team videotaping in the classroom), a teacher took over his actions by holding his hands and dancing with him, twirling him to the music. He collapsed on the floor, totally dependent, and she had to take over all direction of his actions, even holding him upright. His drop in performance from equal participation to being literally carried in the task was in response to the teacher's refusal to relinquish functions to him.

Just as we used social-egocentric-inner speech to exemplify the process of internalization, so we can use the acquisition of negation to illustrate resistance and identification. Pea (1980) documented that the earliest expressions of negation by the child are refusal and rejection. (Self-prohibitive use of "no" is also relatively early, that is, using negation to oneself as others had used it previously to regulate one's behavior.) These first forms of negation are tied to interpersonal relationships (Spitz, 1957). In contrast, commenting on the nonexistence or disappearance of things or persons and especially denying the truth of a proposition (denial) are later acquisitions. The early forms of negation (refusal/rejection) serve to separate self from other in a primitive way: I am not you; I reject you; I refuse to participate. In contrast, denial places negation within a proposition that must be spoken by someone taking up a position *within* a dialogue and is therefore negation within participation: I am like you; I am participating, *but* I disagree with what you assert.

Becoming Responsible: Examples

Just as the refusal to participate in scaffolded activities may be an early stage in the identification-with-the-adult process, taking responsibility for an activity is an acceptance of identification that would permit the child to alter it by denial. In the following example, this exchange transpires midway in a study on the transfer from mother to 2;4- to 2;9-year-old child of a novel script involving a circus game (Lucariello, Kyratzis, & Engel, 1986, p. 158). Transmission of scriptal knowledge was to be accomplished by repeated joint action with the circus toys, noting at different points how the child (**C**) was internalizing the mother's (**M**) sequence of events, uses of objects, and roles of persons such as ringmaster, lion tamer, and so forth.

> **C**: [*Scoops the lions up off the floor and throws them into cage*] They not going to do tricks today.
>
> **M**: No tricks today! Oh, the children are going to be so disappointed!
>
> **C**: [*Scoops lions out of cage and puts them into ring*] The which lion's performing.
>
> **M**: What kind of tricks will they do?
>
> **C**: No lion man! [*Picks up tamer and puts it into ring with lions*]
>
> **C**: [*Cracks the tamer's whip against floor of ring*]
>
> **M**: What do the lions do?
>
> **C**: He doesn't want to do the hoops today. [*Throws the lions back in the cage*] He's going sleep; he's resting.
>
> **C**: No one's performing today.

In this case the child demonstrates the internalization of event knowledge by staying within the framed activity, but he negates the mother's acts for framed objects, thereby taking over her role as the one who decides what happens and how objects will be used.[6] Clearly, this child is not just learning script structure any more than children are *just* learning the forms and rules of negation in English.

I have made a similar point about the acquisition of pronouns (Litowitz & Litowitz, 1983). The child's progress from personal name or "me" to "I" for self-reference signals a critical shift from the child as object for another to his position as subject. "I" is both an index for each individual speaker and the shifting sign for every speaker; it is therefore the ideal semiotic marker for a new level of social relations, e.g., Lacan's (1977) "symbolic register." Children are not simply learning the forms of expression and rules of use for the pronominal system in English; they are learning how to participate reciprocally and then reversibly in discourses with others—to take up discursive positions relative to other persons with respect to what is being talked about or performed. Pronoun acquisition concretely reflects Vygotsky's maxim that "all development consists in the fact that the development of a function goes from *me* to *I*" (1989, p. 64). Being able to establish oneself as an equal "I" is to accept a shift from reciprocity to reversibility, an important step toward responsibility.

In the following examples, the 3+-year-old child from an earlier example takes responsibility for his actions and even takes on some of his teacher's functions. Following the exchange above when he collapsed with overassistance, he joined in a game where all sit in a circle with their feet in the center. The teacher acts frightened, exclaiming: "Oh dear, there's a boa constrictor!" She instructs the children to act frightened, whereupon this little boy adds, "We'd better hide!" heightening the atmosphere of mock terror that sets the scene for the actions to follow (Oh no, he's up to my toes; oh gee, he's up to my knees; oh my, he's up to my thighs . . . oh heck, he's up to my neck). In another game, all the children pretend to lie sleeping on the floor while the teacher steals into the rug area as a monster and scares them. After several repetitions, this little boy, pointing to himself, goes outside the rug area to become the teacher-as-monster. Thus he takes over her role in the game, going from reciprocity (the scared one to her scarer) to reversibility (the scarer to her scared one) in their roles.[7]

Conclusion

The desire to move beyond participation to responsibility is in itself an act of resistance, a resistance to being dependent and controlled by another. The motivation cannot be mastery of the other's skill but to be the other *by means of* mastery of the skill. Language plays a crucial role, not just as a social sign system (e.g., shared referent labels and denotative meanings) or as the means to do things (e.g., organize activities, regulate others and oneself), but as a means to be a human subject—that subject lying hidden in the syntax of *cogito ergo sum* who has been lost to linguistics and objectified as "experimental subject" in psychology. Only by reinstating subjectivity and its desires into our studies can we fully understand learning as an interactive process in the zone of proximal development. We then come to see how gradual, complex, and conflictual is the task of socially constructing an individual.

Notes

An earlier version of this material appeared in 1990 in *The Quarterly Newsletter of the Laboratory of Comparative Human Cognition 12*(4), 135–141.

1. "We see this [kind of behavior] in any adult, even in children. . . . It is a basic birthright of the human species . . . [with] adaptive value, . . . directly related neither to the individual's survival nor to reproduction. Instead, its raison d'etre is education, bringing up the young" (Kaye, 1982, p. 68).

2. The smoothness may have its roots in Hegelian dialectics, albeit reinterpreted

by Marx, in which conflict and contradiction are canceled out and overcome (*aufhebung*), always in a positive and progressive direction. The negation of negation in the dialectical process, however, ignores the fact that there are different kinds of negation (Pea, 1980; Wilden, 1984).

3. Identification has also been used in its general sense as the process in classification or categorization (*x'* is recognized as a member of the *X* class) or as in mathematics ($x = x$), for example, in Freud's (1900) discussion of dreams. Psychoanalysis also uses the term "internalization" to describe other-functions and relationships from which structures of the self and ego are constituted, e.g., Kohut's (1971) "transmuting internalizations." [For reviews on identification in psychoanalysis see Etchegoyen (1985) and Kanzer (1985).]

4. Kaye (1982, p. 237) quoted Delgado: "We cannot be free from parents, teachers, and society because they are the extracerebral sources of our minds."

5. One encounters here the same positivist emphasis as in discussions of language functions or pragmatics. Following Austin (1962), developmentalists have addressed learning what one can *do* by means of language, neglecting how that process creates who one can *be* through speech.

6. Certainly, issues of power and control are at work here but not in any simplistic sense (Henriques et al., 1984; Verdonik, Flapan, Schmit, & Weinstock 1988).

7. The anlagen of turn-taking in reciprocal games such as peek-a-boo are obvious (Bruner, 1983). Here I wish to stress that step beyond, which is responsibility.

References

Austin, J. (1962). *How to do things with words.* New York: Oxford University Press.

Bakhtin, M. (1973). *Problems of Dostoevsky's poetics.* Ann Arbor MI: Ardis.

Bakhtin, M. (1981). *The dialogic imagination: four essays by M. M. Bakhtin* (M. Holquist, ed.). Austin: University of Texas Press.

Bruner, J. (1978). The role of dialogue in language acquisition. In A. Sinclair, R.J. Jarvella, & W. J. M. Levelt (eds.). *The child's conception of language* (pp. 241–56). New York: Springer-Verlag.

Bruner, J. (1983). *Child's talk: learning to use language.* New York: Norton.

Erikson, E. (1963). *Childhood and society* (2nd ed.). New York: Norton.

Etchegoyen, R. (1985). Identification and its vicissitudes. *International Journal of Psycho-analysis, 66*(1), 3–18.

Freud, S. (1900). *The interpretation of dreams* (Standard Edition 4 & 5). London: Hogarth Press.

Freud, S. (1917). *Mourning and melancholia* (Standard Edition 14, p. 239). London: Hogarth Press.

Freud, S. (1923). The ego and the id (Standard Edition 19, p. 3). London: Hogarth Press.

Goodnow, J. (1990). The socialization of cognition: what's involved? In J. W. Stigler, R. A. Shweder, & G. H. Herdt (eds.). *Cultural psychology: essays on comparative human development* (pp. 259–286). New York: Cambridge University Press.

Henriques, J., Hollway, W., Urwin, C., Venn, C., & Walkerdine, V. (1984). *Changing the subject: psychology, social regulation and subjectivity.* New York: Methuen.

Kanzer, M. (1985). Identification and its vicissitudes. *International Journal of Psycho-analysis, 66*(1), 19–30.

Kaye, K. (1982). *The mental and social life of babies.* Chicago: University of Chicago Press.

Kohut, H. (1971). *The analysis of the self.* New York: I.U.P.

Lacan, J. (1977). *Écrits: a selection.* New York: Norton.

Laplanche, J., & Pontalis, J-B. (1973). *The language of psychoanalysis* (D. Nicholson-Smith, trans.). New York: Norton.

Litowitz, B. (1988). Early writing as transitional phenomena. In P. C. Horton, H. Gewirtz, & K. J. Kreutter (eds.). *The solace paradigm: an eclectic search for psychological immunity* (pp. 321–38). New York: I.U.P.

Litowitz, B. (1989). Patterns of internalization. In K. Field, B. Cohler, & G. Wool (eds.). *Learning and education: psychoanalytic perspectives* (pp. 305–28). New York: I.U.P.

Litowitz, B., & Litowitz, N. S. (1983). Development of verbal self-expression. In A. Goldberg (ed.). *The future of psychoanalysis* (pp. 397–427). New York: I.U.P.

Lucariello, J., Kyratzis, A., & Engel, S. (1986). Event representation, context and language. In K. Nelson (ed.). *Event knowledge: structure and function in development* (pp. 137–59). Hillsdale, NJ: Lawrence Erlbaum Associates.

Nelson, K. (1986). *Event knowledge: structure and function in development.* Hillsdale, NJ: Lawrence Erlbaum Associates.

Nelson, K., & Gruendel, J. (1986). Children's scripts. In K. Nelson (ed.). *Event knowledge: structure and function in development* (pp. 21–46). Hillsdale, NJ: Lawrence Erlbaum Associates.

Pea, R. (1980). The development of negation in early child language. In D. Olson (ed.). *The social foundations of language and thought* (pp. 156–86). New York: Norton.

Rogoff, B., & Wertsch, J. (eds.). (1984). *Children's learning in the zone of proximal development.* San Francisco: Jossey-Bass.

Spitz, R. (1957). *No and yes: on the genesis of human communication.* New York: I.U.P.

Verdonik, F., Flapan, V., Schmit, C., & Weinstock, J. (1988). The role of power relationships in children's cognition: its significance for research on cognitive development. *LCHC, 10*(3), 80–85.

Vygotsky, L.S. (1978). *Mind in society: the development of higher psychological processes.* Cambridge MA: Harvard University Press.

Vygotsky, L.S. (1986). *Thought and language* (A. Kozulin, trans.). Cambridge MA: MIT Press.

Vygotsky, L.S. (1989). [Concrete human psychology.] *Soviet Psychology, 7*(2), 53–77.

Wertsch, J., Minick, N., & Arns, F. (1984). The creation of context in joint problem-solving. In B. Rogoff & J. Lave (eds.). *Everyday cognition: its development in social contexts* (pp. 151–67). Cambridge MA: Harvard University Press.

Wilden, A. (1984). Montage, analytic and dialectic. *American Journal of Semiotics, 3*(1), 25–47.

Winnicott, D.W. (1971). *Playing and reality.* New York: Basic Books.

8

Vygotsky, Hymes, and Bakhtin: From Word to Utterance and Voice

COURTNEY B. CAZDEN

At the end of a course on "classroom discourse" at the Harvard Graduate School of Education, Martha Demientieff, a Native Alaskan, introduced her take-home examination with this self-reflection on her own language use:

> As I began work on this assignment, I thought of the name of the course and thought I had to use the word "discourse." The word felt like an intruder in my mind displacing my word "talk." I could not organize my thoughts around it. It was like a pebble thrown into a still pond disturbing the smooth water. It makes all the other words in my mind out of sync. When I realized that I was using too much time agonizing over how to write the paper, I sat down and tried to analyze my problem. I realized that in time I will own the word and feel comfortable using it, but until that time my own words were legitimate. Contrary to some views that exposure to the dominant culture gives one an advantage in learning, in my opinion it is the ownership of words that gives one confidence. I must want the word, enjoy the word and use the word to own it. When the new word becomes synonymous in my head as well as externally, then I can think with it. I laugh now at my discovery but realize that without it, I would still be inhibited about my writing. [March 1988]

The course Demientieff had taken was primarily about one of the ways in which mind, according to Vygotsky, is socially constituted: through the internalization and transformation of social interactions. The problem she faced, and analyzed so perceptively, is that mind is also, according to Vygotsky, socially constituted in a second way: through mediation via semiotic systems, notably language, that are themselves the expressions of sociohistorical processes.

In previous work, I have focused on implications of Vygotsky's first meaning: in analyses of parent–child and teacher–child interactions (Cazden, 1979, 1988), of peer interaction (Forman & Cazden, 1985), and most recently of one early intervention program called Reading Recovery now being imported into the United States from New Zealand (Cazden & Clay, 1990). Here I focus on implications of Vygotsky's second meaning: the speaker or writer's relation to the semiotic system or—as I argue—systems.

In Vygotsky's own writings, features of particular semiotic systems are left as unanalyzed as features of the social setting and interactions within them. We know from extensive research in sociolinguistics and the ethnography of communication that all languages are spoken in many variations— variations that have a historical development, are distributed in nonrandom ways in society, and are profoundly influenced by power relationships in both the immediate setting (the context of situation) and in society at large (the context of culture).

To oversimplify, language varieties can be grouped in two categories: *dialects,* which are distributed according to locale, ethnicity, or social class of speakers (e.g., dialects of English spoken in the South or Maine, or by lower-class black speakers); and *registers,* which are distributed according to speech situations in which people occupy particular roles (e.g., doctors speaking to patients, judges speaking in courtrooms).

Neither term—dialect nor register—fits Vygotsky's requirement that units of analysis must be "at one and the same time units of mind and units of social interaction" (Minick, 1986, p. 122). Some sociolinguistic research shows how the two dimensions interact, for example, in Labov's (1972) analyses of pronunciation features of middle versus lower class black speakers in formal versus casual speech situations. But in that literature there is no term for an integrated unit of analysis. *Dialect* pertains only to the person speaking; *register,* like the construct of "role" of which it is the verbal expression, pertains only to "normatively regulated social action" (Wertsch, 1991, Ch. 1, quoting Habermas).

One candidate term, admittedly less precise than either dialect or register but suggesting the possibility of uniting them, is the term *voice,* used by Vygotsky's contemporary, Mikhail Bakhtin.[1] *Voice* is Bakhtin's term for the "speaking consciousness": the person acting—that is, speaking or writing in a particular time and place to known or unknown others. "Voice" and its utterances always express a point of view, always enact particular values. They also are social in still a third meaning: taking account of the voices being addressed, whether in speech or writing. This "dialogic" quality of utterances Bakhtin calls "responsivity" or "addressivity."

As part of his programmatic vision for the field of ethnography of speaking, Hymes developed the construct of communicative competence (1966, 1973, 1984, 1987; there is no 1971 book, though it is frequently cited). It has been widely influential in research on language in education during the last 25 years. The related ideas of Bakhtin and his circle of Soviet intellectuals are only beginning to be considered outside the world of literary criticism. Assuming readers' greater familiarity with Hymes's ideas, I will say more about those of Bakhtin and then turn, with examples, to some implications for education.

The most relevant first-hand sources for Bakhtin's ideas are as follows.

1. "Discourse in the novel" (Bakhtin, 1981); written in 1934–35 but not published in Moscow until 1975, the year of his death at the age of 79.

2. "The problem of speech genres" (Bakhtin, 1986; and excerpts in Morson, 1986); written in 1952 but not published in Moscow until 1978.
3. *Marxism and the philosophy of language* (Voloshinov, 1973); written in 1929, published in Leningrad in 1930.

Clark and Holquist (1984) provide a detailed bibliography, and Bakhtin (1981) includes a helpful glossary.[2]

None of these works was available in English (and only one in Russian) during the 1960s, when Hymes began arguing for an ethnography of communication (1962) and first spoke about communicative competence (1966). Similarities between the two men's ideas are remarkable, generated as they were in such different sociohistorical environments; their differences combine to enrich our understanding.

Similarities

The fundamental similarity is that both Hymes and Bakhtin developed their ideas in explicit opposition to the Saussurian contrast between *langue* and *parole:* language versus speech, autonomous versus contingent, social versus individual, structured system versus unstructured variation in individual expression. Hymes's programmatic assertion that speech is structured and language variable was the basis of his call for an ethnography of communication and, derived from that, his development of the idea of communicative competence.

Bakhtin writes about *speech genres:*

> . . . the single utterance, with all its individuality and creativity, can in no way be regarded as a completely free combination of forms of language, as is supposed, for example, by Saussure (and by many other linguistics after him), who juxtaposed the utterance (*la parole*), as a purely individual act, to the system of language as a phenomenon that is purely social and mandatory for the individuum. . . . [1986, p. 96]

In another translation, Bakhtin's term becomes *discursive genres:* "Saussure ignores the fact that outside the forms of language there exist also *forms of combination* of these forms; in other words, he ignores discursive genres" (quoted in Todorov, 1984, p. 57).

Bakhtin also writes about language variation, which he terms *heteroglossia:*

> Thus at any given moment in its historical existence, language is heteroglot from top to bottom: it represents the co-existence of socio-ideological contradictions between the present and the past, . . . between different socio-ideological groups in the present, between tendencies, schools, circles and so forth, all given a bodily form. [1981, p. 291]

Hymes and Bakhtin also take a similar stance with respect to their more local opposition. For Hymes, it continues to be the Chomskyian position;

for Bakhtin it was the early Russian formalists. Both acknowledge the contributions of their opponents while asserting their limitations. Both argue against essentialism—the idea of a universal essence, unaffected by the contingencies of sociocultural history. Both oppose what Hymes calls "the rhetoric of metonomy"—considering a part (e.g., grammar) as the whole. In the first sentence of *Discourse in the Novel*, Bakhtin wrote, "The principal idea of this work is that the study of verbal art can and must overcome the divorce between an abstract 'formal' approach and an equally abstract 'ideological' approach" (1981, p. 259).

The two men are more concretely related through association with an early member of the Russian formalists, Roman Jakobson. Jakobson "played a major role in bringing Bakhtin back to scholarly attention," starting at an international meeting in Moscow in 1956 (Clark & Holquist, 1984, pp. 331–32). Two years later, Hymes heard Jakobson give his "Concluding statement: linguistics and poetics" (1960) that became "one of the ingredients of the answer I would reach . . . to the question of the relation between language and culture" (Hymes, 1984, pp. 1–2).

Although speech is structured, for both Hymes and Bakhtin it is also emergent. There is an intrinsic tension between constraint and choice, between the *given* of tradition and the *new* of responsiveness to the moment. In Bakhtin's words:

> The generic forms in which we cast our speech, of course, differ essentially from language forms. The latter are stable and compulsory (normative) for the speaker, while generic forms are much more flexible, plastic, and free. . . .
>
> The better our command of genres, the more freely we employ them, . . . the more flexibly and precisely we reflect the unrepeatable situation of communication—in a word, the more perfectly we implement our free speech plan. [Bakhtin, 1986, pp. 79–80]

These emergent qualities of interaction can be described in terms of the competence that produces them, yet they cannot be formulated into constitutive rules. Mehan's (1979) analysis of anomalous sequences of classroom interaction is a case in point.

Both Bakhtin and Hymes know literature as well as language, as did Vygotsky, who began writing about Hamlet as a schoolboy. Bakhtin's interest was in novels by Dostoevsky and Rabelais, Hymes's in the oral literature of Native Americans. All are examples of what Bakhtin calls "complex genres."

For both Bakhtin and Hymes, emergent qualities include meaning as well as form. Bakhtin contrasts the novel, where characters could act otherwise, with the epic, where they are inseparable from the plot. Hymes's book, *"In vain I tried to tell you"* (1981), takes its title from the Native American myth, "The 'wife' who 'goes out' like a man," whose theme is the conflict between maintenance of social norms and attentiveness to immediate experience (Hymes, 1981, Ch. 10). Hymes's analysis of this myth has multiple layers of linguistic, social, and literary significance that go beyond our concerns here. But because his writings on myth may be less familiar to readers than those on communicative competence, I detour briefly.

To the point here, the words of the book's title are the daughter's. She perceives an unusual sound when her uncle's 'wife' urinates. But when she tries to tell her mother, Seal, that it sounds like a man, she is shushed. Seal later discovers that her brother has been murdered, and the daughter cries, "In vain I tried to tell you." The daughter's speech preceding this remonstrance is the longest in the myth and evidently unusually long for any myth from the Clackamas Tribe. It "breaks/through into performance," emergent in response to the immediate situation, when the girl retells the whole incident, accusing her mother of responsibility for her uncle's death.

In Hymes's analysis, Seal and her daughter contrast in both speech style and world view (formal and ideological, according to Bakhtin). Using Basil Bernstein's (1971) terms, Hymes characterizes the mother's speech as positional and restricted, the daughter's as personal and elaborated:

> The mother's speech throughout the myth is a perfect example of Bernstein's "restricted code" (1971). It is positional speech in terms of her status as a mother with a certain social position. The girl's speech is not very extensive at the beginning, but the whole last part of the story is turned over to her. She retells the story metapragmatically in an elaborated code and in a burst [of] elaborated speech so that the story is, in effect, an account of her assumption of a new level of experience and understanding. [1982, p. 133]

Thus Hymes analyzes the communicative competence of both the Native American narrator, Victoria Howard, and the heroine.

The final similarity between Hymes and Bakhtin is their conception of language acquisition. Briefly, according to Hymes, "in some sense difficult to specify, children learn and use, not grammar, but ways of speaking, styles that organize linguistic means, of which the formal grammar is a precipitate" (personal communication). In similar terms, Bakhtin writes:

> We know our native language—its lexical composition and grammatical structure—not from dictionaries and grammars but from concrete utterances which we hear and which we ourselves reproduce in live speech communication with people around us. We assimilate forms of language only in forms of utterances. . . . [They] enter our experience and consciousness together. [1986, p. 95]

Differences

Like Hymes, Bakhtin acknowledges the existence of differential communicative competence (though without using that term):

> Many people who have an excellent command of a language often feel quite helpless in certain spheres of communication precisely because they do not

have a practical command of the generic forms used in given spheres. . . .
Here it is not a matter of an impoverished vocabulary or style, taken
abstractly; this is entirely a matter of the inability to command a repertoire
of genres. [1986, p. 96]

What, then, does reading Bakhtin call our attention to? First, Bakhtin
asserts the intrinsic intertextuality of all utterances. The given forms we
inherit include not only grammatical and speech structures but also words—
not because we do not create them anew, but because we do not learn them
from a dictionary. We acquire words through hearing or reading the utterances of others, and they are thereby marked with the voices of those prior
contexts. Words have not only value-free denotations but value-laden connotations; and for Bakhtin denotation is not the unmarked, privileged signification:

> We choose words according to their generic specifications. . . . Genres cor-
> respond to typical situations of speech communication, typical themes, and
> consequently also to particular contacts between the *meanings* of words
> and actual concrete utterances under typical circumstances.
>
> This typical (generic) expression can be regarded as the word's "stylistic
> aura," but this aura belongs not to the word of language as such but to that
> genre in which the given word usually functions. It is an echo of the generic
> whole that resounds in the word.
>
> Thus the expressiveness of individual words is not inherent in the words
> themselves as units of language, nor does it issue directly from the meaning
> of these words: it is either typical generic expression or it is an echo of anoth-
> er's individual expression, which makes the word, as it were, representative
> of another's whole utterance from a particular evaluative position. [1986,
> p. 97]

Bakhtin focuses on the consequences of this *heteroglossia* for writers:
"Instead of the virginal fullness and inexhaustibility of the object itself [any
referent or topic], the prose writer confronts a multitude of routes, roads and
paths that have been laid down in the object by social consciousness." But
he makes it clear that it is true for all discourse (1981, pp. 278–79).

Any speaker or writer must select among paradigmatic forms. Bakhtin
is suggesting grounds for intrapersonal conflict during the process of expression because of the "auras" that accrue to those forms from awareness of
their previous contextualized use:

> Language is not a neutral medium that passes freely and easily into the pri-
> vate property of the speaker's intentions; it is populated—overpopulated—
> with the intentions of others. Expropriating it, forcing it to submit to one's
> own intentions and accents, is a difficult and complicated process. [1981,
> p. 294]

Discussion of such conflict seems stronger in Bakhtin than in Hymes.
Although both write of the uniting of constraint and creativity, of centripetal

and centrifugal forces, Bakhtin's images suggest more intraindividual conflict among the voices internalized from a heteroglossic and stratified society (hence his interest in the novel as the richest expression of this heteroglossia).

From the beginning, Hymes has argued against the Chomskyian notion of a homogeneous speech community and for recognition of diverse ways of speaking any single language. But in his portrayal of a "community as an organization of diversity," the images of coexistence seem more peaceful and individual shifting among language varieties more painless unless access to the conditions necessary for their acquisition has been denied. For Bakhtin, the images are more of conflict than of coexistence, a conflict that continues beyond acquisition into moments of expression—not only because of the external positioning of any speaker in the social structure but because of the ideological marking of speech genres and words.

Perhaps one could say that in Hymes's writings on communicative competence the significant social problem is that of acquisition and the conditions of interaction and the attitudes of identification that influence it. Whereas for Bakhtin, who writes less of acquisition, a significant phenomenon is the intraindividual heterogeneity—and potential conflict—among whatever varieties have been acquired.

A final contrast is that such internal compositional processes are highlighted by Bakhtin, whereas Hymes focuses more on externalized performance. He mentions in passing that "communicative is a global term, encompassing indeed reflection and dialogue with oneself" and gives as an example his own additions to a previously typed paper, "interacting with myself over different points in time" (Hymes, 1984, p. 14). But his active metaphors of social life as drama are all on the external stage in which only certain parts, or certain voices, are welcome. In Bakhtin, by contrast, what Hymes calls "implicit theatre" (1984, p. 42) is internalized:

> One's own discourse and one's own voice, although born of another or dynamically stimulated by another, will sooner or later begin to liberate themselves from the authority of another's discourse. This process is made more complex by the fact that a variety of alien voices enter into the struggle for influence within an individual's consciousness (just as they struggle with one another in surrounding social reality). [Bakhtin, 1981, p. 348]

Educational Implications

If we consider Hymes's writings about communicative competence as providing an ethnographic framework for both research and practice, Bakhtin's writings call attention to particular speaking and writing situations within the total range, to the complexities of finding a voice, of being communicatively competent, in heteroglossic speech situations where voices (and the roles they express in the social structure) are felt by the speaker or writer to be in conflict.

Bakhtin makes it clear that he is talking about situations with both social heteroglossia and speaker/writer awareness of it. In an extended description of peasant life, Bakhtin contrasts heteroglossia alone, where speakers shift among varieties unconsciously, and heteroglossia with awareness, where decisions among alternatives have to be made:

> Thus an illiterate peasant, miles away from an urban center, naively immersed in an unmoving and for him unshakable everyday world, nevertheless lived in several language systems: he prayed to God in one language (Church Slavonic), sang songs in another, spoke to his family in a third and, when he began to dictate petitions to the local authorities through a scribe, he tried speaking yet a fourth (the official literate language, "paper" language). All of these are *different* languages, even from the point of view of abstract socio-dialectological markers. But these languages were not dialogically coordinated in the linguistic consciousness of the peasant; he passed from one to the other without thinking, automatically: each was indisputably in its own place, and the place of each was indisputable. He was not yet able to regard one language (and the verbal world corresponding to it) through the eyes of another language. . . . [In a footnote, Bakhtin qualifies: "We are of course deliberately simplifying; the real-life peasant could and did do this to a certain extent."]
>
> As soon as the critical interanimation of languages began to occur in the consciousness of the peasant, as soon as it became clear that these were not only various different languages but even internally variegated languages, that the ideological systems and approaches to the world that were indissolubly connected with these languages contradicted each other and in no way could live in peace and quiet with one another—then the inviolability and predetermined quality of these languages came to an end, and the necessity of actively choosing one's orientation among them began. [1981, pp. 295–96]

To bring Bakhtin's conception of these conflict situations to life, we have a few accounts by speakers and writers. First there is the dual audience that student speakers have in most classroom discourse: the audience of teacher (usually the addressee) and of peers (as ratified auditors). One acknowledgement of awareness of this duality is a brief autobiographical comment by Shuy:

> There is a natural conflict between acceptability by teacher and acceptability by peers even *within* the classroom. Personally I remember very clearly my school conflicts between peer pressure and teacher expectations. One strategy to avoid this conflict is to give the right answer to the teacher but to do so in either non-standard or informal English. [1981, pp. 170–71]

Shuy calls these dual expectations of teacher and peers "vertical" and "horizontal" acceptability, respectively. In oral lessons, his example is, "La Paz ain't the capital of Peru;" when reading aloud, the good reader reads the correct words but in an informal, peer-group style (personal communication, 1985).

Regardless of whether Shuy ever said, "La Paz ain't the capital of Peru," his point is clear. His communicative task was to produce what Bakhtin calls a "heteroglossic utterance"—one that expresses his dual identity as good student yet still one of the boys. Accomplishing this task was part of his communicative competence. It represents what Berlak and Berlak (1981) would call a "transformational solution" to an important dilemma, a solution that, if accepted by the teacher, may prevent a forced choice between peer group and school (Cazden, 1988).

Because writing is a more self-conscious activity than speaking, it is easier to find writers acknowledging problems in choosing words and finding a voice. In an essay on "Craftsmanship," Virginia Woolf writes about "one of the chief difficulties in writing them [English words] today—that they are so stored with meanings, with memories, that they have contracted so many famous marriages" (1942, p. 203).

McDermott (1988), in an article on "Inarticulateness," discusses the "creative resistance" of the writers of the Irish Literary Renaissance, for whom "The English language . . . did not come . . . as a neutral medium for expressing their thoughts." He quotes Stephen Daedalus in his conversation with an English priest (both native speakers of English) in Joyce's *A Portrait of the Artist as a Young Man:*

> The language in which we are speaking is his before it is mine. How different are the words *home, Christ, ale, master,* on his lips and mine! I cannot speak or write these words without unrest of spirit. His language, so familiar and so foreign, will always be for me an acquired speech. I have not made or accepted its words. My voice holds them at bay. My soul frets in the shadow of his language. [McDermott, 1988, p. 56, quoting Joyce]

Woolf and Joyce were professional writers. We can also reconsider in Bakhtinian terms the problems faced by student writers who are trying, or are expected to try, to enter the academic "literacy club" (Smith, 1988). Demientieff's reluctance to substitute "discourse" for "talk" is a case in point. And because she reflects on the single unit of a word, the unit of language discussed by Vygotsky, her reluctance can be analyzed to show the importance of Bakhtin's ideas as an addition to Vygotsky's.

As Vygotsky (and others) have pointed out, words have—in addition to reference—both meaning and sense. Meaning is the transsituational signification given in dictionaries. According to one dictionary, "discourse" and "talk" overlap in meaning with some distinction at the edges. Even though one word is given as a synonym for the other, the first definition for "discourse" gives as an italicized example "earnest and intelligent discourse," whereas the first meaning for "talk" (as noun) is "conversation, especially of a familiar or informal kind."

Beyond this small difference in meaning is a larger difference in what Vygotsky calls "sense"—"the sum of all the psychological events aroused in our consciousness by the word" (Vygotsky, 1986, p. 244).[3] Whereas "meaning" is stable, "sense" is "dynamic, fluid," (p. 245), shifting with contexts of interaction or of inner speech. Moreover, it is as a characteristic of inner speech, where sense predominates over meaning, that it assumes special importance in Vygotsky's theory.

What Vygotsky does not discuss but Bakhtin does is that connotations accrue to a word not only from the immediate context of situation, but from the general—and in its own way, stable—context of culture. That is what Bakhtin refers to as the word's "stylistic aura . . . [that] belongs to that genre in which the given word usually functions." It is because words are "over-populated with the intentions of others" that "Expropriating it, forcing it to submit to one's own intentions and accents, is a difficult and complicated process," especially when those "others" occupy a more powerful place in a stratified society.[4]

Demientieff's problem had nothing to do with comprehension of meaning and everything to do with "expropriating" a word that came to her laden with such alien sense that she could not yet "feel comfortable using it." Whereas "talk" could function for her as an ideologically neutral "common referring expression" (Wertsch, 1985, pp. 170–71), "discourse" came to her ideologically marked by the academic contexts in which she had encountered it.

There is educational implication to this story as well. When I named my book and my course, I could have used either "classroom discourse" or "classroom talk." The referent in either case would be the same: all the talk that goes on within the classroom walls. I did not opt for 'discourse' to select for attention only the more "earnest and intelligent" interactions that are more obviously related to the formal curriculum. I picked it because of the different connotations of the two words—"sense" as cultural rather than individual—not to make a distinction among referents but to dignify the referent by choosing a label marked for and by use in more academic or intellectual contexts.

Barnes calls these two functions of a teacher's specialized language the cognitive and sociocultural, respectively. In his words, for the student,

> Each new item must first appear to have a socio-cultural function—that is, to be "the sort of thing my physics teacher says"—and then, insofar as the pupil is able to use the item in talking, thinking, or writing, it will take upon itself a conceptual function. [Barnes, Britton, & Rosen, 1969, p. 58]

It will take on a conceptual function, that is, if there is one. In the case of "classroom discourse," none was intended. Reconsidering my choice of title now and acknowledging its purely sociocultural purpose, I realize that its effect was to make it harder for a student from outside the academic world to consider herself a member of that world in her language use.

Whereas Demientieff's problem, at least as presented in her take-home examination, was only with an individual word, for a black teacher—Nanzetta Merriman or, in pseudonym, Zan—during his work for the same master's degree in education at Harvard the conflict was over not only words but syntax and style. When Zan realized he was having trouble writing papers for his courses, a white doctoral student, Judy Diamondstone, who had been a regular observer in his 7th/8th grade social studies class (12- to 13-year-olds) the year before, agreed to help in return for permission to document his progress for one of her own courses. They did a joint presentation later in the year and, unless otherwise indicated, my excerpts are from their coauthored account (Diamondstone & Merriman, 1988).

Judy writes about Zan:

> He is about to undergo a series of accommodations to the language of the academe. . . . Zan confronts one enormous hurdle . . . : to convey his dramatic communicative style, based in oral, Black tradition, and to defend Black revolutionary ideology, in an academic discourse which he believes discriminates against his culture.

Zan writes about himself:

> During the 1950s, my time in public schools in Harlem was dotted with retentions in grades two, six and ten. My undergraduate years were clouded with failures in writing. I believe the retention and the failures are illustrative of a system which only accepts the middle caste concepts of valid knowledge and language.

They work together on one of Zan's papers, finally entitled "Vision of a Field Negro," for a course on improving schools:

> Z: (*reading aloud the sentence from his notes*) "We must realize that we are within our moral rights, when our freedom and dignity and that of others are being jeopardized, to take any means necessary "
>
> J: "To take any means necessary—"?
>
> Z: Period.
>
> J: To do what? To change the situation? To win our—to redress?
>
> Z: "To turn things around" is too weak; "redress" is too white. "To, to [*sigh*]—to end—"
>
> J: *Say* it, say it, Zan.
>
> Z: [*Seven turns later*] "We will do anything that is necessary to overcome it and to stop it."
>
> J: "To overcome." There you go.

In another session, Judy asks Zan what he has learned about his writing so far. "He answers with characteristic acuity that he had first to conquer his fear, and now has to learn the language of his audience."

> Z: I used to think writing was, as you put it, writing in a vacuum. . . . It just had to come from oneself and that's it. . . . Now I do seek out a situation of . . . you write with readers. You write with audiences. . . . I *never* wanted to use the man's words, but I did want to let the man hear. And I wanted to do in my writing what he did to us.
>
> J: You have to do it with his words.
>
> Z: I will use his words. I will use his words. *But!* I will use my words too. . . . So it's how to, not compromise, but how to have those co-mingle.

Zan's struggle is not just to learn new ways of writing, difficult as that is. Ways of writing, such as using specific words (in his case "redress," which was "too white"), are already saturated with the values of the context with which they're associated—a context, in the case of academic discourse, about which he is deeply ambivalent. So, like Shuy, he seeks the forms for creative resistance, a transformational solution in which he does not have to compromise and in which "the man's" and his own words "co-mingle."

Writing up this tutoring experience for one of her courses, Diamondstone adds a "retrospective" reconsideration of her own demands (using "sense" in its colloquial meaning):

> "To take any means necessary to overcome" is no more grammatical than "to take any means necessary." . . . The sense of the statement is already there. No more is added by completing the infinitive clause, "to take any means necessary." The real problem is one of convention—to specify the end of the means taken and to name its referent (to do *what?*). . . . If the meaning is available to the reader without completing the clause, what do such conventions afford?—those syntactic hinges that oblige the writer to say more! say more! . . . ? [Diamondstone, 1990, p. 14]

The problems of Tanya, a remedial community college student whose writing has also been analyzed by her tutors Hull and Rose (1989), exemplifies Bakhtin's ideas in a different way. Tanya wants to become a nurse's aide, and one of the assignments set by her tutors is to write a summary of a nurse's case study, "Handling the difficult patient." The result seems at first incoherent, even chaotic. Here are a few lines of the original and Tanya's summary (Hull & Rose, 1989, pp. 145–146):

Original Text	*Student Summary*
"Oh, this is going to be a great day," I said to myself. (Paragraph 4)	Oh this is going to Be a great Day I said to myself just thinking alone.
I have pride in my profession. (Paragraph 11)	I have pride In What I Do I am going to get.
But I can give the minimum, too. I can sit here most of the day and still collect my 35 bucks at the end of the shift. (Paragraph 11)	no matter what I am still am going to collect my money no matter what happen I do Believe and I no that In my mind.

Throughout her seemingly "word salad" summary, as Hull and Rose point out, Tanya copied chunks of the original, changing the order of the ideas and some of the words. When they interviewed her afterward about her composing process, they discovered her two intentions: "to display and convey knowledge. . . . [so] 'a teacher'll really know what I'm talking about' and to show she's 'not . . . that kind of student that would copy' (Hull & Rose, 1989, pp. 147–48). Their diagnosis concludes:

After wrestling with our own concerns about the errors in Tanya's written language, about all those markers of illiteracy, it struck us that something profoundly literate is going on here. A fundamental social and psychological reality about discourse—oral or written—is that human beings continually appropriate each other's language to establish group membership, to grow, and to define themselves. . . . Tanya is trying on the nurse's written language and, with it, the nurse's self. [Hull & Rose, 1989, p. 151]

For Hull and Rose, the educational implications are "to temporarily suspend concern about error and pursue, full tilt, her impulse to don the written language of another . . . [with a] free-wheeling pedagogy of imitation" (p. 151). They then comment on what Tanya's "plagiarism" can teach us:

[Our own] clearly documented writing may let us forget, or even, camouflage, how much more it is that we borrow from existing texts, how much we depend on membership in a community for our language, our voices, our very arguments. We forget that we, like Tanya, continually appropriate each other's language to establish group membership, to grow, and to define ourselves in new ways. [p. 152]

Hull and Rose do not refer to Bakhtin, but his discussion of the process by which we appropriate others' discourse fits Tanya's "plagiarism," and our own.

As with Hymes and Vygotsky earlier, Bakhtin's writings force us to confront important issues in teaching. They remind us that no text is autonomous, and that no forms of expression in natural languages are neutral referential codes. All bring with them—for all of us as speakers and writers—both pain and promise.

At the end of a personal essay, a black woman writer, Barbara Mellix, speaks to both. Like Demientieff and Merriman, she has felt the pain; and, as Hull and Rose hoped for Tanya, she has realized the promise as well:

Although as a beginning student writer I had a fairly good grasp of ordinary spoken English and was proficient at what Labov calls "code-switching" . . . when I came face to face with the demands of academic writing, I grew increasingly self-conscious, constantly aware of my status as a black and a speaker of one of the many black English vernaculars—a traditional outsider. For the first time, I experienced my sense of doubleness as something menacing, a built-in enemy. Whenever I turned inward for salvation, the balm so available in my childhood, I found instead this new fragmentation which spoke to me in many voices. It was the voice of my desire to prosper, but at the same time it spoke of what I had relinquished and could not regain: a safe way of being, a state of powerlessness which exempted me from responsibility for who I was and might be. And it accused me of betrayal, of turning away from blackness. To recover balance, I had to take on the language of the academy, the language of "others." And to do that, I had to learn to imagine myself a part of the culture of that language, and therefore someone free to manage that language, to take liberties with it. Writing and rewriting, practicing, experimenting, I came to comprehend more fully the generative power of language. I discovered—with the help of some especially sensitive teachers—that through writing one can continually bring new selves into being, each with new responsibilities and difficulties, but also with new possibilities. Remarkable power, indeed. I write and continually give birth to myself. [Mellix, 1989, p. 52]

Notes

Previous versions of this chapter appeared in *Applied Linguistics* 1989, Vol. 10, No. 2, and were presented at the 1989 meetings of the American Educational Research Association in San Francisco.

1. About the relationship between the two men, Wertsch writes: "Although some authors . . . claim otherwise, Clark and Holquist (1984) have concluded that Vygotsky and Bakhtin were neither personally acquainted nor influenced by one another's work. In my opinion, the similarities in their ideas derive from a common intellectual milieu and familiarity with many of the same works" (Wertsch, 1985, p. 237).

2. Differences of opinion among Bakhtin scholars continue over whether the writings officially authored by Bakhtin, Voloshinov, and a third colleague, Medvedev, were the work of three separable minds. Hymes himself argued that *Marxism and the Philosophy of Language* must have been written by Voloshinov on the grounds that it reads as the work of a linguist in arguments and evidence, and he was the only member of the "troika" with linguistic training (personal communication, 1988). Holquist (Introduction to Bakhtin, 1981, p. xxvi) concluded that Bakhtin wrote (or "ventriloquated") 90% of that book and one by Medvedev. Todorov and Raymond Williams believed the evidence was inconclusive.

As Wehrle, the translator of the Medvedev book, pointed out, "The works of the Bakhtin school can be seen as the realization of dialogic interaction—from which it follows that to assign the texts to Bakhtin alone is [inappropriately] to "monologize' them" (Bakhtin/Medvedev, 1978, p. xviii). Whatever the facts at the time, Williams' characterization seems right now: "The road from Vitebsk [was] that still insufficiently understood but major movement involving (uncertainly and inextricably) P. M. Medvedev, V. N. Voloshinov and M. M. Bakhtin" (Williams, 1986, p. 22).

3. At least three English editions of Vygotsky's *Thought and Language* are now in print. My page reference is to the revised translation published by MIT Press, near the end of the last chapter, simply because it was the one at hand at the moment of writing. For many readers, any edition will be fine.

4. When suggesting extensions of Vygotsky's ideas at the end of his book, *Vygotsky and the Social Formation of Mind,* Wertsch briefly discussed Bakhtin's addition to the concept of "contextualized significance, or sense" (Wertsch, 1985, pp. 224–25). Wertsch's new book (1991) includes much more on Bakhtin.

References

Bakhtin, M. (1981). Discourse in the novel. In *The dialogic imagination* (pp. 259–492). Austin: University of Texas Press.

Bakhtin, M. M. (1986). *Speech genres & other late essays.* Austin: University of Texas Press.

Bakhtin, M. M./Medvedev, P. N. (1978/1985). *The formal method in literary scholarship.* Cambridge, MA: Harvard University Press.

Barnes, D., Britton, J., & Rosen, H. (1969). *Language, the learner and the school.* Baltimore: Penguin Books.

Berlak, A., & Berlak, H. (1981). *Dilemmas of schooling: teaching and social change.* London: Methuen.

Bernstein, B. (1971). *Class, codes and control* (Vol. 1). London: Routledge & Kegan Paul.

Cazden, C. B. (1979). Peekaboo as an instructional model: discourse development at school and at home. In *Papers and reports on child language development* (No. 17, pp. 1–29). Stanford University, Department of Linguistics. Revised version in Bain, B. (ed.) (1983). *The sociogenesis of language and human conduct: a multi-disciplinary book of readings.* (pp. 33–58). New York: Plenum.

Cazden, C. B. (1988). *Classroom discourse.* Portsmouth, NH: Heinemann.

Cazden, C. B., & Clay, M. M. (1990). A Vygotskian interpretation of "Reading Recovery." In L. C. Moll (ed.). *Vygotsky and education: instructional implications and applications of sociohistorical psychology* (pp. 206–22). New York: Cambridge University Press.

Clark, K., & Holquist, M. (1984). *Mikhail Bakhtin.* Cambridge, MA: Harvard University Press.

Diamondstone, J. (1990). *Doing the do at a tete a tete: struggles over academic discourse* (technical report 4A). Newton, MA: Literacies Institute.

Diamondstone, J., & Merriman, N. (1988). To be heard, to be understood, to be believed: unpacking unpackables. Presented at the Annual Ethnography in Education Forum, University of Pennsylvania Graduate School of Education.

Forman, E. A., & Cazden, C. B. (1985). Exploring Vygotskian perspectives in education: the cognitive value of peer interaction. In J. V. Wertsch (ed.). *Culture, communication and cognition: Vygotskian perspectives.* New York: Cambridge University Press.

Hull, G., & Rose, M. (1989). Rethinking remediation: towards a social-cognitive understanding of problematic reading and writing. *Written Communication, 6,* 139–154.

Hymes, D. (1962). The ethnography of speaking. *Anthropology and Human Behavior.* Washington, DC: Anthropological Society of Washington.

Hymes, D. (1966). On communicative competence. Presented at the Research Planning Conference on Language Development in Disadvantaged Children, New York.

Hymes, D. (1973). Toward linguistic competence. In *Texas working papers in sociolinguistics.* Austin: University of Texas.

Hymes, D. (1981). *"In vain I tried to tell you".* Philadelphia: University of Pennsylvania Press.

Hymes, D. (1982). Narrative form as a "grammar" of experience: Native Americans and a glimpse of English. *Journal of Education, 164,* 121–42.

Hymes, D. (1984). *Vers la competence de communication.* Paris [page citations are to English ms.].

Hymes, D. (1987). Communicative competence. In H. von U. Ammon, N. Dittmar, & K. J. Mattheier (eds.). *Sociolinguistics: an international handbook of the science of language and society.* New York: Walter de Gruyter.

Jakobson, R. (1960). Concluding statement: linguistics and poetics. In T. Sebeok (ed.). *Style in language* (pp. 350–73). Cambridge: MIT Press.

Labov, W. (1972). *Language in the inner city: studies in the black English vernacular.* Philadelphia: University of Pennsylvania Press.

McDermott, R. P. (1988). Inarticulateness. In D. Tannen (ed.). *Linguistics in context: connecting observation and understanding.* Norwood, NJ: Ablex.

Mehan, H. (1979). *Learning lessons.* Cambridge, MA: Harvard University Press.

Mellix, B. (1989). From outside, in. In A. J. Butrym (ed.). *Essays on the essays: redefining the genre* (pp. 43–52). Athens: University of Georgia Press.

Minick, N. (1986). The early history of the Vygotskian school: the relationship between mind and activity. *Quarterly Newsletter of the Laboratory of Comparative Human Cognition, 8,* 119–25.

Morson, G. S. (ed.) (1986). *Bakhtin: essays and dialogues on his work.* Chicago: University of Chicago Press.

Shuy, R. (1981). Learning to talk like teachers. *Language Arts, 58,* 168–74.

Smith, F. (1988). *Joining the literacy club: further essays into education.* Portsmouth, NH: Heinemann.

Todorov, T. (1984). *Mikhail Bakhtin: the dialogical principle.* Minneapolis: University of Minnesota Press.

Voloshinov, V. N. (1973/1986). *Marxism and the philosophy of language.* Cambridge, MA: Harvard University Press.

Vygotsky, L. (1986). *Thought and language* (revised ed.). Cambridge, MA: MIT Press.

Wertsch, J. V. (1985). *Vygotsky and the social formation of mind.* Cambridge, MA: Harvard University Press.

Wertsch, J. V. (1991). *Voices of the mind.* Cambridge, MA: Harvard University Press.

Williams, R. (1986). The uses of cultural theory. *New Left Review,* No. 158, 19–31.

Woolf, V. (1942). Craftsmanship. In *The death of the moth and other essays.* New York: Harcourt Brace.

9

Vygotskian Perspective on Children's Collaborative Problem-Solving Activities

ELLICE A. FORMAN and JEAN McPHAIL

The everyday lives of adults are full of complex and ill-defined problems that require high-level reasoning and organizational skills. These problems are often solved in collaboration with other people. For example, a husband, wife, and babysitter may need to coordinate their weekly occupational and domestic work schedules in order to supervise one or more young children. When psychologists study problem-solving activity, however, they typically observe people while they work on well-defined problems by themselves in a laboratory environment. Only a few psychologists, educators, and anthropologists have paid much attention to the thinking activities of adults while they are engaged in naturalistic group problem-solving tasks (Gladwin, 1970; Hutchins, 1991; Lave & Wenger, 1991; Schoenfeld, 1989; Scribner, 1984). Their research shows that collaborative problem-solving activities provide a context in which supports for, constraints on, and challenges to an individual's thinking occur. In many of these situations, achieving the solution to a problem becomes secondary to negotiating a shared problem definition and a common means of communication (Schoenfeld, 1989).

School activities that employ collaborative problem solving have the potential for teaching children how to deal with complex tasks and to work with and learn from each other. One would expect that exposure to a rich array of collaborative problem-solving activities in school would help children become effective problem solvers as adults. Unfortunately, the study of peer collaboration has just begun to evaluate the short-term benefits of group work for children and has not yet assessed its long-term outcomes. In addition, when the short-term benefits of collaboration are evaluated, the criteria used are individual measures of achievement, attitudes, and problem-solving skills. Almost no attention has been paid to the value of learning to negotiate task definitions and goals or to develop a shared means of interacting and communicating. (See Forman, 1989, 1992; Newman, Griffin, & Cole, 1984; and Saxe, 1991, for exceptions.)

Educational and developmental psychologists have paid an increasing amount of attention to the use of peers as instructional resources in the classroom. Numerous articles have appeared that discuss the social, affective, and cognitive benefits of cooperative learning and collaborative problem solving.[1] (For reviews see Azimitia & Perlmutter, 1989; Brown & Palincsar, 1989; Damon, 1984; Damon & Phelps, 1989; Doise & Mugny, 1984; Slavin, 1983, 1987; Stodolsky, 1984; Tudge & Rogoff, 1989; Webb, 1982, 1989.)

Vygotsky has been cited as one of the primary theoretical sources for the developmental approach to peer collaboration (Damon, 1984; Slavin, 1987; Tudge & Rogoff, 1989). Yet Vygotsky wrote little about this topic, and until recently much of Vygotsky's work was not translated. Thus American researchers had access to a restricted number of sources for their theorizing. Because many American researchers had a limited understanding of Vygotskian theory as a whole, they tended to assume that peer tutoring and peer collaboration would be identical in a Vygotskian approach. Thus peer collaboration was viewed as a form of tutoring in which one child with task-specific expertise helps another child solve a problem through demonstration, modeling, encouragement, or explicit explanation (Azimitia, 1988; Ellis & Rogoff, 1986).

We have a number of concerns about this view of Vygotskian theory. English translations of Vygotsky's work and commentaries by American researchers (e.g., Minick, 1989; Vygotsky, 1987; Wertsch, 1985) suggest that his perspective on the teaching and learning process goes far beyond the mere transfer of knowledge from expert to novice. The purpose of our chapter is to articulate a perspective on collaborative problem solving that we believe is compatible with the broad research agenda that Vygotsky and his colleagues (e.g., Leont'ev, 1981; Zinchenko, 1981) pursued. First, we present some central concepts from Vygotskian theory and discuss the ways in which they are not consistent with current research and theory on peer collaboration or cooperative learning. Second, we illustrate our Vygotskian approach by analyzing a case study of collaborative problem solving. Finally, we address the educational implications of a Vygotskian approach to peer collaboration.

Vygotskian Approach to Peer Collaboration

What are some of the basic features of the Vygotskian research agenda, and how do they apply to the study of collaborative problem solving? First, Vygotskian theory argues for the analysis of problem solving as a culturally and historically situated activity (Leont'ev, 1981; Minick, 1989; Saxe, 1991; Scribner, 1984). That is, we need to understand the ways in which a particular problem-solving activity is embedded in a set of cultural practices and institutions at a specific point in their historical evolution. Thus the physical and institutional context of an activity, the social roles and status of the individuals involved, the cultural mediators available, and the prevalent cultural values and beliefs about the activity support and constrain the participants' attitudes, goals, understandings, and actions.

Second, in a complementary fashion, people's actions, attitudes, goals, and understandings create the cultural meaning of their activity. In other words, the cultural and historical context of an activity influences the psychological meaning of that activity; and, simultaneously, the actions of the participants in sociocultural situations can transform their institutional context, mediational means, social roles and status, beliefs, and values.

For example, two siblings who are asked to collaborate in washing the dishes at home are likely to interact in different ways from two classmates in school who are asked to collaborate in solving a mathematics problem. Despite the fact that both of these activities might involve "peers" (where peer is defined as being similar in chronological age), the feelings aroused, the mediational means employed, and the outcomes produced are likely to vary owing to differences in the two sociocultural contexts. Yet the cultural context constrains but does not determine people's goals and actions. For example, it is possible that an older sibling could transform a domestic activity such as washing dishes into a kind of academic game in which the primary goal would be to teach a younger sibling how to categorize objects. In this way, the participants' actions could change a domestic activity into a schooling activity or vice versa (Rogoff & Gardner, 1984; Wertsch, Minick, & Arns, 1984).

Therefore a Vygotskian approach to peer collaboration would require a detailed analysis of the sociocultural and historical context of a particular activity setting and of the children's goal-directed actions in order to determine how the activity was defined by the people involved. It is plausible that the results of these analyses would reveal that children engage in several alternative forms of peer collaboration. The forms that peer collaboration may take could resemble adult collaboration in an occupational setting (Hutchins, 1991; Schoenfeld, 1989) or peer collaboration in an occupational setting (Saxe, 1991) as well as the forms of peer assistance in school that Damon and Phelps (1989) have identified (peer tutoring, cooperative learning, and collaborative problem solving). Thus the activity of collaborating with a peer on a problem-solving task may have a variety of manifestations. By assuming that peer collaboration involves merely the transfer of knowledge from expert to novice, we are restricting the way we evaluate the nature and value of peer activities.

A third important factor in a Vygotskian analysis of peer collaboration would be the mediational means employed. Semiotic mediation (e.g., oral or written discourse) is the mechanism by which individual beliefs, attitudes, and goals are simultaneously affected by and affect sociocultural practices and institutions. Ochs (1990) argued that people display their affective and epistemological dispositions through their choice of lexical items, grammatical forms, and phonological and morphological structures. They do it by employing culturally specific discourse features that index social status and role (e.g., averted gaze, polite forms of address) or that indicate the sources and certainty of their beliefs (e.g., "I wonder"). Thus people select the semiotic means that enable them to express their thoughts and feelings. An analysis of the discourse features present during peer collaboration would reveal changes in children's shared task definition as well as their feelings and social relationship.

Finally, Vygotskian theory sees cognitive development as inherently integrated with social and emotional development. This view implies that fundamental changes in thinking must be accompanied by a reorganization of children's attitudes, goals, and mediational means (Minick, 1989; Saxe, 1991; Vygotsky, 1978). This aspect of the theory implies that an analysis of the potential benefits of peer collaboration must include information about changes in children's communication, goals, and social interactions over time as well as changes in their ability to solve a particular problem.

How does this broader view of Vygotskian theory compare with alternative theoretical approaches to peer collaboration? We discuss the similarities and differences between Vygotskian theory and the two theoretical approaches that have dominated the research literature since the mid-1970s. In order to be comparable with previous discussions in the literature, we identify these two approaches as the developmental and motivational (Damon & Phelps, 1989; Slavin, 1987).

Motivational and Developmental Approaches to Peer Collaboration

Robert Slavin, an educational psychologist, outlined two theoretical and empirical perspectives on cooperative learning: developmental and motivational (1987). He identified his own approach as being guided by motivational theorists (e.g., Lewin, Deutsch, Atkinson, Skinner) in contrast to the developmental theorists (primarily Piaget).

One crucial difference between the motivational and developmental approaches is the lack of attention by developmentalists to rewards or goal structures in cooperative learning activities. Slavin argued that extrinsic rewards create different types of interpersonal goal structures (cooperative, competitive, or individualistic), which in turn affect how the group responds to each others' task-related efforts. Thus children who receive rewards for their group products tend to create a cooperative goal structure "in which group members will give or withhold social reinforcers . . . in response to their group-mates' task-related efforts" (1987, p. 1163). In addition, if individual accountability is coupled with group rewards, students are motivated to learn from the group effort. According to Slavin, this combination of group rewards and individual accountability is most frequently associated with academic achievement gains as a result of exposure to cooperative learning activities.

Therefore Slavin believed that developmentalists have focused exclusively on the cognitive and social aspects of cooperative learning and have ignored subjects' motivations to interact in a cooperative manner and to learn from their peer interactions. In response, developmental researchers (Damon & Phelps, 1989; Hatano & Inagaki, 1987) have argued that intrinsic but not extrinsic rewards are an important component of cooperative learning and collaborative problem-solving activities. They believed that extrinsic rewards can be detrimental to learning because they are distracting and can mislead students into thinking that learning cannot be intrinsically rewarding.

Hatano and Inagaki (1987) proposed that motivation for comprehension should replace achievement motivation in most if not all school activities. Students demonstrate that they are motivated to comprehend when they are willing to expend the effort required to understand how and why a given procedure results in a correct answer. In contrast, students who exhibit achievement motivation merely show an interest in achieving correct solutions. Hatano and Inagaki argued that the result of academic activities that promote motivation for comprehension is learning that can be generalized to new task environments.

According to Hatano and Inagaki, motivation for comprehension cannot be elicited by providing extrinsic rewards. Instead, they argued that motivation for comprehension depends on changes in both conceptual and attitudinal conditions. First, students must experience an incongruity between their existing understandings and those required by a particular problem. Next, the students must believe that they can comprehend the problem if they expend the necessary effort. Finally, the students must believe that understanding this problem is important or valuable.

Hatano (1988) argued that students are most likely to expend the effort necessary to comprehend in their domains of expertise and interest. However, outside those domains, motivation for comprehension may require additional intrinsic rewards. These rewards, he suggested, are inherent aspects of the discussions that can occur in collaborative problem-solving activities.

In summary, Slavin (1987) argued that students' motivations to engage in cooperative interactions and to learn from those interactions must be taken into account when designing effective cooperative learning activities. He proposed that teachers manipulate group goal structures by providing extrinsic rewards for group products. He also suggested that individual achievement motivations be maintained by evaluating learning outcomes through individual testing.

Damon, Hatano, and their collaborators disagreed with Slavin about the efficacy of extrinsic rewards. Hatano and Inagaki proposed that the goal of all learning activities (both cooperative and individual) should be the achievement of genuine insight, not merely the production of correct solutions. Thus for the developmentalists, the teacher's role in fostering collaborative activities is to provide tasks that are intrinsically interesting and to encourage social interactions that can foster comprehension activity.

Comparison of the Three Approaches

Despite their disagreements, Slavin, Damon, Hatano, and their collaborators agreed that the aim of cooperative learning or collaborative problem-solving activities is individual cognitive gains. Therefore the evaluation of a successful peer instructional activity would depend on evidence that individual students increased in the number of correct solutions they produced (Slavin's approach) or in the quality of their understanding of a topic (Hatano's and Inagaki's approach).

In addition, both approaches outlined above define motivation in terms of individual beliefs, needs, and desires. Thus for Slavin, students feel the need to cooperate when the teacher provides rewards for their group products. For Hatano and Inagaki, students feel the need to understand when their previous concepts do not allow them to solve a problem and when they feel confident enough to work on an interesting problem. How do these views of peer collaboration relate to that derived from a Vygotskian perspective?

One obvious difference between a Vygotskian approach and those suggested by Slavin, Hatano, and Inagaki is that cultural and historical influences on people's motivations and understandings are missing in the developmental and motivational accounts. Instead, they locate the source of motivation and understanding primarily within or between individuals. For Slavin, teachers are capable of manipulating their students' achievement motivations through the use of rewards. When individuals see the reward-value of hard work, they spend more time-on-task, which in turn should increase their task-relevant knowledge. For Hatano and Inagaki, students are inherently motivated to understand when they are allowed to solve tasks that they value and when they are confident about their abilities. Providing individuals with these kinds of tasks and socially supportive settings in which to work should maximize the amount of individual motivation for comprehension and, subsequently, individual understanding.

In contrast, for Vygotsky, the source of individual motivation and understanding can be located in sociocultural practices. Each culture provides ample opportunities for children to observe and participate in essential economic, religious, legal, political, instructional, or recreational activities. As a result of their guided participation (Goodnow, 1990; Rogoff, 1990) in these activities, children internalize or appropriate their affective, social, and intellectual significance. For example, girls may learn that cooking and sewing are valued skills for women but that automobile mechanics is a valued skill for men. Cultural norms influence, but may not determine, individual preferences. Thus some women in any given society might learn to prefer tasks that are generally prescribed for men and vice versa. Motivations originate in cultural practices but are defined, negotiated, and modified in the context of particular interpersonal activity settings over time.

Second, for Vygotsky, cognitive, social, and motivational factors were interrelated in development. Thus it makes no sense to evaluate the benefits of peer collaboration in purely intellectual terms, e.g., via individual achievement testing. A Vygotskian perspective also implies that the outcomes of peer collaboration must be evaluated in context and over time.

Third, following Ochs' suggestion (1990), discourse features can be used to identify people's initial and subsequent epistemological and affective dispositions toward collaborative problem solving. Their discourse should reflect their individual and shared understandings and feelings about the task setting, as well as the definitions of the activity that are provided by their particular cultural and historical situation.

Application of Vygotskian Theory to a Study of Peer Collaboration

Data from a study of collaborative problem solving by children and adolescents are used here to illustrate how the expanded Vygotskian perspective can be applied to educational research. The data presented below are from two subjects, "Cindy" and "Karen," who were selected from a sample of 50 normally achieving fourth and seventh graders. In this study, subjects were observed as they worked on a scientific problem-solving task over a series of sessions. (For more details about the study, see Forman, 1989.)

We discuss our observations of Cindy and Karen in four sections: (1) by describing the task and providing some relevant background information about our two subjects; (2) by describing how each girl seemed to define the experimental task during her individual pretest; (3) by describing how these initial task definitions were negotiated during their first collaborative session; and (4) by contrasting this dynamic, descriptive approach to assessing cognitive growth in a collaborative problem-solving situation with a more traditional static assessment of individual pretest–posttest change scores.

Experimental Setting and Task

The design of the study in which Cindy and Karen were participants required that each child be seen for a total of five sessions: individual pretest and posttest sessions with an adult examiner (the second author) and three collaborative sessions supervised by the same examiner. We determined which children would work together for these three collaborative sessions based on their intellectual ability and advice from teachers. All subjects were tested in a room in their public school.

The scientific problem-solving task presented during each of the sessions involved the projection of shadows of geometric shapes onto a screen. Several geometric shapes were used. Each shape was presented with six to eight cards on which gray geometric shapes representing possible shadows were pasted. This task can be defined in one of two ways: as a science laboratory setting in which to study light and shadows or as a context in which to study transformational geometry.

Each experimental session (pretest, posttest, and collaborative sessions) followed the same format. The girls were presented with a shape (e.g., a circle) and then asked to predict, with the light off, the kinds of shadow that could be projected onto a screen from that shape. Their decisions were based on six to eight preselected shadow shapes (e.g., a variety of circles, a hexagon, a half-circle, an ellipse). Then they were told to conduct experiments to test their hypotheses with the light turned on. Finally, they were asked to draw conclusions from their experiments. The questions about their predictions and conclusions were addressed to the girls by the examiner. However, they were asked to conduct their experiments without the examiner's assistance or direction.

Background Information

Cindy and Karen were both seventh graders and were enrolled in the same advanced class in mathematics. One of their teachers reported that Cindy enjoyed the class a great deal. The girls were similar in age and intellectual ability (13 years 2 months of age and of above-average intelligence). Both girls lived in an upper-middle-class suburb in the Chicago metropolitan area. Karen's father taught engineering at a university in a neighboring suburb, and Cindy's father was an executive in a bank.

During the first collaborative session, Cindy announced to the examiner that she and Karen were both studying geometry in their mathematics class. Cindy's announcement suggested that she might have been interested in making connections between the terms and procedures that she and Karen were learning in that class and the geometric shapes of the experimental task. That is, she might have viewed the task as a context in which to study transformational geometry. Although Karen did not give us a similar clue about her initial orientation to the task, her family background might predispose her to be interested in the scientific properties of the task: the effect of placing objects between a source of light and a screen. This background information about the two girls, although limited, allowed us to interpret some of the differences in their task performance and discourse during the pretest and first collaborative sessions.

Task Definitions During the Pretest

From the very beginning of the two individual pretest sessions, the girls responded in markedly different ways to the examiner's scripted questions. For example, after the examiner demonstrated how different shadows could be produced on a screen by moving a triangular shape in prescribed directions, each girl was asked, "What do you think makes the shadow on the pad [screen] change shape?" Cindy's response to this question was brief and vague, "When you move it . . . it changes." In contrast, Karen's response was extensive and complex. For example, one part of her answer explained the result of moving a shape closer to the source of light, "When you move it closer to the light . . . more light is blocked by the shape, and so less light gets on the screen and the shape gets bigger." The remaining part of her answer addressed the effect of rotating the triangle around a line parallel to the floor which, she explained, would cause the base of the triangular shadow to lengthen.

This difference in initial task definition continued throughout their two pretest sessions. Cindy never mentioned the light during her pretest, whereas Karen discussed the blockage of light rays four times during her pretest session. Karen was much more likely than Cindy to use the past tense and first person pronoun when she explained the results of her experiments. For example, when Karen explained why it is impossible to project a rectangular shadow using a triangular shape, she said "Cause *I* couldn't get four corners." Cindy's explanation for the same rectangular shadow choice was "Because there's four points, and *you* can't make something with four points with this."

The above differences in reference to the source of light and in use of first versus second person pronouns and past versus present tense verbs seem, to us, to reflect the use of different speech registers[2]: the scientific and the mathematical. Karen's explanations appear to represent her interest in understanding how shadows are produced and how their shape changes when the experimental variables are systematically manipulated. Thus in her conclusions, she focused on reporting the results of her experiments to the examiner. In contrast, Cindy seemed to have little interest in the science of shadows. Instead, she seemed to view this situation as an opportunity to establish mathematical proofs regarding the correspondences between shapes and their shadows. Her explanations served to summarize her current understanding of the invariant features of shape to shadow correspondences. Cindy's use of the second person pronoun and present tense appeared to represent her need to speak in the mathematics register—which is impersonal and timeless (Halliday, 1975, 1978; Pimm, 1987).

Negotiation of Task Definitions

Despite these differences in initial orientation to the task, the two girls worked closely together during their three collaborative sessions. Neither girl abandoned her initial task definition but, at different times, adopted the definition of the other. To illustrate how these two definitions toward the task were negotiated, we discuss the first collaborative session. Two shapes were tested during this session, a circle and an isosceles triangle.

During the first collaborative session, the past tense dropped from Karen's explanations. However, Karen tended to employ the first person plural pronoun ("we"), whereas Cindy persisted in using the second person pronoun ("you"). Karen's use of "we" served an important social and affective function as well—that of demonstrating her interest in working with Cindy to achieve *mutual* goals. Although both girls made a conscious effort when communicating with each other and the examiner to employ technical terminology learned in their mathematics class (e.g., radius, isosceles, right angle), Cindy insisted on accurate usage of mathematical terminology.

Cindy's insistence on the precise use of technical vocabulary is best illustrated by the responses of the two girls to a question from the examiner that was posed after the conclusions about each preselected shadow shape card were justified. At this point in the session, the shadow shape cards had been sorted into two piles: those that could not be projected from a circular shape and those that could.

> **Examiner:** So, these [shadow shape cards] you can't make, and this pile you can. What would you say the Difference is? Why can you make those and not these?
>
> **Cindy:** These don't have edges.
>
> **Karen:** They're only equal from the center, they all have the same *radius*.
>
> **C:** No they don't.
>
> **K:** No, this one [the ellipse]—this one doesn't.
>
> **C:** This one's bigger . . . it has a bigger *radius*.
>
> **K:** Well, all right . . . These are all circles . . . except for this one.
>
> **C:** Curvy . . . these are oval.
>
> **E:** Alright. Then why wouldn't you be able to make those?
>
> **C:** 'Cause they're . . . not oval or *circular*.
>
> **K:** They have straight edges.

Note that Karen used the phrases "equal from the center" and "same radius" to characterize the stack of circles and ellipses that they did project. Cindy quickly corrected Karen's use of the phrase "same radius" by insisting that an ellipse does not have the same properties as a circle with respect to a term such as radius.

An example of Cindy's attempt to redefine everyday vocabulary in a mathematical manner occurred later during this same session after they had projected shadows from an isosceles triangle.

> **E:** Why can you make [the shadows in] this pile, but not that one?
>
> **C:** See, this is [an] *isosceles triangle* . . . and those aren't.
>
> **K:** These are just, you know, *right triangles*.
>
> **C:** Well, it might be, but they don't have the same *angles*.
>
> **K:** When you look at them or make shadows of them, they aren't exact, but this is pretty much, you know. . . .
>
> **C:** They're not *similar*.
>
> **K:** They aren't, yeah.
>
> **E:** Alright. Then why would you be able to make these?
>
> **C:** 'Cause they are *similar*.
>
> **K:** They're the same, they're. . . .
>
> **C:** They're *similar*.
>
> **K:** . . . pretty much the same *angles*, they're just bigger.

Cindy used the term "similar" repeatedly to emphasize to the examiner and her partner that she meant it in the mathematical sense and not in the everyday sense. Initially, Karen seemed to use "similar" to mean "alike," but finally she defined it mathematically as having the same angles but bigger (in area).

Occasionally, Karen's interest in using the scientific register reappeared when she made reference to the effect of the blockage of light. Her task definition was especially valuable during the first collaborative session when she had to explain to Cindy why shadows must be larger than the shape from which they are projected.

By the end of their first collaborative session, both girls began to incorporate the type of explanation favored by their partner.

E: What are the things that you learned about shadows from working with those shapes today?

C: You can't make a shadow that's smaller than the figure.

K: Same thing.

E: Anything else?

C: No.

K: That you can't make a shadow, like, if it's a different shape, unless it's like flat. . . .

C: Has to be *similar.*

K: Yeah.

In response to the final question from the examiner, Cindy supplied the explanation that she learned from her partner "You can't make a shadow that's smaller than the figure." In addition, Karen tried to provide an explanation that involved the concept of similarity. Cindy, however, made sure that the precise term "similar" was employed.

Contrast with the Traditional Approach to Assessment

The results from a traditional assessment of cognitive growth as a result of peer collaboration are displayed in Table 9.1. The girls' pretest and posttest sessions were coded in order to evaluate changes in each girl's ability to make accurate prediction and conclusion decisions about the projection of shadows and her ability to justify these decisions. The girls' justifications were examined in terms of their ability to explain or to demonstrate the transformations of the shape that were necessary and sufficient for producing each

Table 9.1. Summary of Pretest and Posttest Performance

Measurement	Percent of accurate decisions		Percent of adequate justifications	
	Pretest	Posttest	Pretest	Posttest
Cindy				
Predictions	43	62	28	0
Conclusions	71	71	57	14
Karen				
Predictions	50	75	12	62
Conclusions	62	100	50	62

shadow choice. It is important to note that this coding system privileged one task definition over another. That is, justifications that employed the scientific register would receive higher scores than those that employed the mathematics register.

Each girl's performance on the pretest and posttest sessions suggests that both showed some gains in their ability to make accurate decisions from pretest to posttest. However, they did not demonstrate similar gains in their ability to provide adequate justifications for their decisions. Cindy's justifications decreased in adequacy, and Karen's justifications increased in adequacy.

This lack of pretest-to-posttest gain in Cindy's ability to use adequate justifications for her increasingly accurate decisions reflects, we believe, the degree to which her task definition and goals differ from those of the experimenters. In contrast, Karen appeared to learn from her collaborative experience because her interests and goals matched those of the experimenters.

In addition, observations of Cindy's posttest session suggest that her interest in working on the task had declined during this session. For example, she conducted her experiments in a brief, perfunctory manner. In addition, her responses to the examiner's questions were terse and lacking in precision. These behaviors were unlike the ones she showed during any of the previous sessions. At the end of the posttest session, when she was asked if she had learned anything during that session, she replied, "Not really anything new." Thus it appeared that the decline in Cindy's posttest scores were a result of two factors. First, it reflected the *success* of her collaborative relationship, not its failure. Cindy's interest in understanding shape-to-shadow transformations was inherently tied to her interest in negotiating a shared task definition and means of communication with her partner. Second, the decline was the result of her unwillingness to define the task as scientific rather than mathematical.

Summary of the Case Study

Our descriptive analysis of Cindy and Karen demonstrated that young adolescents can establish, modify, reflect on, and refine their initial task goals and definitions so as to collaborate with their peers. (See Forman, 1992, for a discussion about developmental differences in peer collaboration.) Cindy and Karen consciously and voluntarily remembered and applied concepts they were studying in their geometry class to the experimental problem-solving task. They listened to each other's explanations and reflected on their logical consistency and precision. They watched each other's experiments and used their observations to modify their own task conceptions. Thus they provided a zone of proximal development (Vygotsky, 1978) for each other that facilitated the growth of higher mental functions (e.g., voluntary attention, logical reasoning).

In contrast, a traditional assessment of pretest-to-posttest gain scores was incapable of evaluating the effectiveness of this particular collaborative relationship for at least two reasons. First, quantitative gain scores, by necessity, favor one definition of a task over another. Therefore they fail to account for the ambiguous nature of goal-directed activity. Second, if attitudes, values, and goals are an inherent aspect of cognitive growth, change must be assessed within, not apart from, the specific activity setting in which the developmental change occurred.

Given the differences in their initial orientations toward the task, why were Cindy and Karen interested in working together, listening to each other, and resolving their differences? We do not have a definitive answer to that question. However, informal analyses of the videotapes suggest a number of reasons. First, the experimental task assumed an air of legitimacy, as it could be associated with their shared mathematics course. Also, that course provided a future context, apart from the experimental one, in which to continue their collaboration. Second, the personalities of the two girls seemed to be complementary. Karen seemed willing and eager to share task responsibilities with Cindy, and she expressed her sense of their mutual goals by employing the first person plural pronoun to explain the results of their joint activities to the examiner. Initially, Cindy let Karen take primary responsibility for conducting the experiments while she assumed the role of the intelligent, active listener and alert observer. Over time, each girl took turns listening, observing, explaining, critiquing, and directing their common activities. Thus their relationship had the qualities of genuine collaboration: mutuality and equality (Damon & Phelps, 1989). Obviously, the two girls recognized their differences but respected each other's intellectual abilities.

Conclusions

We have argued that Vygotskian theory both supports and extends current debates on the benefits of collaborative problem solving. It supports the research efforts of educational and developmental psychologists who have attempted to identify the kinds of social interactional processes that can be the most effective in fostering motivation to solve and comprehend complex problems. Vygotsky, however, thought that attitudes, interests, and goals are not mere facilitators of cognitive growth but are intrinsic to the nature of development. Thus the growth of higher mental functions would entail a reorganization of a child's system of goals and values.

In the case study described above, we have illustrated how an analysis of pretest-to-posttest change in cognitive performance cannot assess the intellectual and interpersonal benefits of Karen and Cindy's collaborative relationship. In order to apply Vygotskian theory to the study of the benefits of peer collaboration, we focused on the process by which children's goals, attitudes, and understandings were established, negotiated, and modified before and during their collaboration. We also examined the use of specific speech registers to indicate subjects' initial and subsequent definitions of a complex problem-solving task. Our analysis of Karen and Cindy's collaborative relationship suggests that information about children's cognitive performance that does not incorporate some assessment of their goals, interests, and beliefs provides an inadequate evaluation of the benefits of peer interaction.

Vygotskian theory suggests that higher mental functions arise when children are able to direct their own cognitive activity in a self-conscious and voluntary manner. Thus for Vygotsky, cognitive growth can be fostered under conditions in which children are given the opportunity to set their own goals and organize their own activity in the service of these goals.

Once these peer goals and incentives are recognized by researchers and teachers, successful collaborative learning activities may require teachers to give up some of their control over the determination of instructional goals as well as instructional procedures. Gilmore argued that children need to be "given room" to own at least some of their learning activities (1986). Wells, in a similar vein, proposed empowering learners to pursue their own educational aims under the indirect and supportive guidance of a sensitive teacher (1987).

Finally, peer collaboration requires children to develop a shared means of communication. Their discourse depends on the selection of appropriate semiotic devices, such as speech registers, which are supplied by particular cultural practices. School introduces children to aspects of the mathematical and scientific register (e.g., vocabulary items) but provides them with relatively few opportunities to practice these registers. It is due, in part, to the predominance of the recitation model of classroom instruction that requires students to restrict their conversation to responses to the teacher's questions (Dore, 1985; Mehan, 1979; Tharp & Gallimore, 1989). Collaborative problem solving is one activity in which children can use these academic registers in a meaningful fashion: to engage in logical arguments, to share their ideas, and to work together in the pursuit of common goals (Forman, 1992).

Vygotskian theory suggests that we pay closer attention to semiotic mediation during peer collaboration because it is seen as the mechanism of developmental change. It does not imply that children should be taught to imitate the surface forms of academic registers, but that they should be encouraged to use the semiotic devices that make up registers as a tool for solving complex scientific problems in collaboration with others. Collaborative problem solving can provide educators with an appropriate context in which to foster participation in meaningful mathematical and scientific activities and use of academic speech to accomplish problem-solving goals.

Notes

This research was supported, in part, by grants to the first author from the Spencer and Buhl Foundations and from Northwestern University and the University of Pittsburgh. We would like to thank the faculty and students of the Winnetka and Roselle, Illinois Public School Districts for their participation in this study. We would also like to thank Richard Donato, Bonnie Litowitz, Martin Packer, and Addison Stone for their comments on an earlier version of this chapter.

    1. The terms cooperative learning and peer collaboration have been used in different ways by different authors. Slavin (1987), for example, used the term cooperative learning to refer to any instructional procedure that encourages or requires students to work together and where one student is not assigned a tutoring role. In contrast, Damon and Phelps (1989) differentiated between cooperative learning and collaborative problem-solving activities. For Damon and Phelps, cooperative learning entailed an explicit, teacher-directed division of labor, whereas peer collaboration involved the mutual negotiation of task roles. For clarity, we use the two terms as they have been defined by Damon and Phelps unless we are discussing Slavin's perspective.

    2. Speech registers are a form of discourse variation that creates and reflects the sociocultural context of interaction. Halliday defined register as "a set of meanings that is appropriate to a particular function of language, together with the words and structures which express these meanings" (Halliday, 1975, p. 65). The mathematics register is comprised of new meanings for everyday words (similarity, row, column, add), new words with specific meanings (vertex, hypotenuse), phrases and compound words (right triangle), and modes of argument. Our interest in Cindy's use of the mathematics register originated in a series of informal conversations with a mathematician, Dr. Izzie Weinzweig, who was the first person to observe that, in his view, she spoke like a mathematician. Pimm argued that "part of learning mathematics is learning to speak like a mathematician" (1987, p. 76).

References

Azimitia, M. (1988). Peer interaction and problem solving: when are two heads better than one? *Child Development, 59,* 87–96.

Azimitia, M., & Perlmutter, M. (1989). Social influences on childrens' cognition: state of the art and future directions. In H. Reese (ed.). *Advances in child development and behavior* (Vol. 22, pp. 89–144). Orlando, FL: Academic Press.

Brown, A. L., & Palincsar, A. S. (1989). Guided, cooperative learning and individual knowledge acquisition. In L. B. Resnick (ed.). *Knowing, learning, and instruction: essays in honor of Robert Glaser* (pp. 393–451). Hillsdale, NJ: Lawrence Erlbaum Associates.

Damon, W. (1984). Peer education: the untapped potential. *Journal of Applied Developmental Psychology, 5,* 331–43.

Damon, W., & Phelps, E. (1989). Critical distinctions among three approaches to peer education. *International Journal of Educational Research, 13,* 9–19.

Doise, W., & Mugny, G. (1984). *The social development of the intellect.* New York: Pergamon.

Dore, J. (1985). Children's conversations. In T. A. Van Dijk (ed.). *Handbook of discourse analysis* (Vol. 3, pp. 47–65). London: Academic Press.

Ellis, S., & Rogoff, B. (1986). Problem solving in children's management of instruction. In E. Mueller & C. Cooper (eds.). *Process and outcome in peer relationships* (pp. 301–25). Orlando, FL: Academic Press.

Forman, E. A. (1989). The role of peer interaction in the social construction of mathematical knowledge. *International Journal of Educational Research, 13,* 55–70.

Forman, E. A. (1992). Discourse, intersubjectivity and the development of peer collaboration: A Vygotskian approach. In L. T. Winegar & J. Valsiner (eds.). *Children's development within social context: Vol. 2. metatheoretical, theoretical, and methodological issues* (pp. 143–159). Hillsdale, NJ: Lawrence Erlbaum Associates.

Gilmore, P. (1986). Sub-rosa literacy: peers, play, and ownership in literacy acquisition. In B. B. Schieffelin & P. Gilmore (eds.). *The acquisition of literacy: ethnographic perspectives* (pp. 155–68). Norwood, NJ: Ablex.

Gladwin, T. (1970). *East is a big bird: navigation and logic on Puluwat Atoll.* Cambridge, MA: Harvard University Press.

Goodnow, J. J. (1990). The socialization of cognition: what's involved? In J. W. Stigler, R. A. Shweder, & G. Herdt (eds.). *Cultural psychology: essays on comparative human development* (pp. 259–86). New York: Cambridge University Press.

Halliday, M.A.K. (1975). Some aspects of sociolinguistics. In *Interactions between linguistics and mathematical education* (pp. 64–73). Final report of the symposium sponsored by UNESCO, CEDO, and ICMI, Nairobi, Kenya. Copenhagen: UNESCO.

Halliday, M.A.K. (1978). *Language as social semiotic: the social interpretation of language and meaning.* Baltimore: University Park Press.

Hatano, G. (1988). Social and motivational bases for mathematical understanding. In G. B. Saxe & M. Gearhart (eds.). *Children's mathematics: new directions for child development* (No. 42, pp. 55–70). San Francisco: Jossey-Bass.

Hatano, G., & Inagaki, K. (1987). A theory of motivation for comprehension and its application to mathematics instruction. In T. A. Romberg & D. M. Stewart (eds.). *The monitoring of school mathematics: background papers. Vol. 2. Implications from psychology; outcomes of instruction* (Program Report 87-2, pp. 27–46). Madison: Wisconsin Center for Education Research.

Hutchins, E. (1991). The social organization of distributed cognition. In L. B. Resnick, J. M. Levine, & S. D. Teasley (eds.). *Perspectives on socially shared cognition* (pp. 283–307). Washington, D.C.: American Psychological Association.

Lave, J., & Wenger, E. (1991). *Situated learning: legitimate peripheral participation.* New York: Cambridge University Press.

Leont'ev, A. N. (1981). The problem of activity in psychology. In J. V. Wertsch (ed.). *The concept of activity in Soviet psychology.* Armonk, NY: M. E. Sharpe.

Mehan, H. (1979). *Learning lessons.* Cambridge, MA: Harvard University Press.

Minick, N. (1989). Mind and activity in Vygotsky's work: an expanded frame of reference. *Cultural dynamics, 2,* 162–87.

Newman, D., Griffin, P., & Cole, M. (1984). Social constraints in laboratory and classroom tasks. In B. Rogoff & J. Lave (eds.). *Everyday cognition: its development in social context* (pp. 172–93). Cambridge, MA: Harvard University Press.

Ochs, E. (1990). Indexicality and socialization. In J. W. Stigler, R. A. Shweder, & G. Herdt (eds.). *Cultural psychology: essays on comparative human development* (pp. 287–308). New York: Cambridge University Press.

Pimm, D. (1987). *Speaking mathematically: communication in mathematics classrooms.* New York: Routledge & Kegan.

Rogoff, B. (1990). *Apprenticeship in thinking: cognitive development in social context*. New York: Oxford University Press.

Rogoff, B., & Gardner, W. (1984). Adult guidance of cognitive development. In B. Rogoff & J. Lave (eds.). *Everyday cognition: its development in social context* (pp. 95–116). Cambridge, MA: Harvard University Press.

Saxe, G. B. (1991). *Culture and cognitive development: studies in mathematical understanding*. Hillsdale, NJ: Lawrence Erlbaum Associates.

Schoenfeld, A. H. (1989). Ideas in the air: speculations on small group learning, environmental and cultural influences on cognition, and epistemology. *International Journal of Educational Research, 13*, 71–88.

Scribner, S. (1984). Studying working intelligence. In B. Rogoff & J. Lave (eds.). *Everyday cognition: its development in social context* (pp. 9–40). Cambridge, MA: Harvard University Press.

Slavin, R. E. (1983). When does cooperative learning increase student achievement? *Psychological Bulletin, 94*, 429–45.

Slavin, R. E. (1987). Developmental and motivational perspectives on cooperative learning: a reconciliation. *Child Development, 58*, 1161–67.

Stodolsky, S. S. (1984). Frameworks for studying instructional processes in peer work groups. In P. L. Peterson, L. C. Wilkinson, & M. Hallinan (eds.). *The social context of instruction: group organization and group processes* (pp. 107–24). Orlando, FL: Academic Press.

Tharp, R. G. & Gallimore, R. (1988). *Rousing minds to life: teaching, learning, and schooling in social context*. New York: Cambridge University Press.

Tudge, J., & Rogoff, B. (1989). Peer influences on cognitive development: Piagetian and Vygotskian perspectives. In M. Bornstein & J. Bruner (eds.). *Interaction in human development*. Hillsdale, NJ: Lawrence Erlbaum Associates.

Vygotsky, L. S. (1978). *Mind in society*. M. Cole, V. John-Steiner, S. Scribner, & E. Souberman (eds.). Cambridge, MA: Harvard University Press.

Vygotsky, L. S. (1987). *The collected works of L. S. Vygotsky. Vol. 1. Problems of general psychology* (R. W. Rieber & A. S. Carton, eds.; N. Minick, trans.). New York: Plenum.

Webb, N. M. (1982). Student interaction and learning in small groups. *Review of Educational Research, 52*, 421–45.

Webb, N. M. (1989). Peer interaction and learning in small groups. *International Journal of Educational Research, 13*, 21–39.

Wells, G. (1987). Language in the classroom: literacy and collaborative talk. Unpublished manuscript. Ontario, Canada: Center for Applied Cognitive Science and Department of Curriculum, Ontario Institute for Studies in Education.

Wertsch, J. V. (1985). *Vygotsky and the social formation of mind*. Cambridge: Harvard University Press.

Wertsch, J. V., Minick, N., & Arns, F. J. (1984). The creation of context in joint problem-solving. In B. Rogoff & J. Lave (eds.). *Everyday cognition: its development in social context* (pp. 151–71). Cambridge, MA: Harvard University Press.

Zinchenko, P. I. (1981). Involuntary memory and the goal-directed nature of activity. In J. V. Wertsch (ed.). *The concept of activity in Soviet psychology*. Armonk, NY: M. E. Sharpe.

10

Toddlers' Guided Participation with Their Caregivers in Cultural Activity

BARBARA ROGOFF, CHRISTINE MOSIER, JAYANTHI MISTRY, and ARTIN GÖNCÜ

This chapter focuses on cultural similarities and variations in the guided participation of children in sociocultural activities. Children around the world, including middle-class U.S. children, learn and develop in situations of joint involvement with other people in culturally important activities. Caregivers and companions collaborate with children in deciding the nature of children's activities and their responsibilities for participation. In the process of collaboration children adapt their knowledge to new situations, structure problem-solving attempts, and regulate their responsibility for managing the process. This guidance and participation includes tacit forms of communication and distal arrangements of children's activities, as well as explicit verbal interaction. The mutual roles played by children and their caregivers rely on both the interest of caregivers in fostering mature roles and skills and children's own eagerness to participate in adult activities and to push their development.

Along with similarities across cultures in children's guided participation in sociocultural activities are important differences in the skills that are valued, the means of communication (e.g., dyadic conversation between adults and children versus action communication with status differences in conversation between adults and children), and the extent to which children enter into adult activity versus adults share children's activity. Middle-class children may need didactic instruction owing to their segregation from opportunities to observe and participate in important cultural activities, whereas children who have the opportunity to participate in the activities of their community may be able to shoulder the responsibility for learning themselves.

These themes are explored with illustrations from preliminary analyses of observations of eight toddlers and their caregivers from a Mayan town in Guatemala and eight toddlers and their caregivers from an urban setting in the United States (Salt Lake City). (The data are preliminary suggestions from a larger study to be reported as a monograph, involving 56 toddlers from Guatemala, India, Turkey, and the United States.) The toddlers from each setting involved an approximately equal number of boys and girls, firstborn and laterborn children, and younger (12 to 16 months) and older toddlers (20 to 23 months). Half of the Salt Lake City families were Mormon; half of the Mayan families were Catholic and the remainder Protestant. The Salt Lake City families were much more affluent, with middle-class occupations and high school or college educations; the Mayan families owned relatively little property, with most fathers in farming or labor jobs and most mothers having third-grade schooling or less.

Our observations were videotaped in a home visit involving child-rearing questions and the opportunity to observe the children and their families in everyday problem solving: exploring novel objects (which we supplied), playing social games, handling the feeding implements of their community, being dressed, and treating other people appropriately. In this chapter we focus on three episodes of interaction in which we asked mothers to get their toddlers to work a wooden nesting doll (like those from the Soviet Union) that comes apart into bottom and top halves, to make a tortilla or hamburger patty out of playdough, and to "take care of" a plastic babydoll. The toddlers interacted with their mothers; in many families fathers, siblings, and grandparents were involved as well.

The interactions were analyzed in a process of pattern analysis (Rogoff & Gauvain, 1986) that began with close ethnographic transcription of each case, attempting to portray the meanings of the events for the participants in terms that capture local family goals and practices. Then with the intimate knowledge of the data that develops from such transcription, the team developed specific categories of interaction that we thought portrayed the crucial similarities and differences across communities in terms that could abstract across the specifics of the observations while maintaining the essence. (It was a long process of dialogue across the four researchers, with all representing their knowledge of a different community, which derived from the transcriptions and from either having originated in that community or nation or having spent at least two years in the community.)

The data reported here are based on preliminary application of these analysis categories; they are preliminary in that the definitions are still in the process of being clarified, and we have not examined the extent to which two observers of the same videotape would code the events similarly. Hence we provide the observations as suggestions rather than as final findings, as a start in describing the patterns of guided participation that may be similar and those that may vary in different cultural communities.

This chapter first discusses our conceptual framework deriving from a Vygotskian sociohistorical approach to development and from the concept of guided participation (Rogoff, 1990) that focuses on the tacit and routine arrangements of children's activities and involvements. Using our observations of the eight Mayan and eight Salt Lake City toddlers, we discuss similarities as well as important differences in the children's guided participation in cultural activities. The observations are discussed as they relate to each conceptual issue, with a later section describing two contrasting cases in greater detail.

Sociohistorical Approach to Development

The influence of the sociohistorical school on conceptions of development has been marked in work on cultural psychology. Scholars interested in cognitive development in cultural context returned from fieldwork believing that views of development that assumed generic and general progress with age were not adequate to their observations that people seemed to vary in their skills according to the cultural familiarity of the context in which they were observed (Laboratory of Comparative Human Cognition, 1983; Rogoff, 1982b; Rogoff, Gauvain, & Ellis, 1984). Many researchers interested in culture and development found in the writings of Vygotsky a theory that laid the groundwork for a necessary integration of individual development in social and cultural context.

Crucial to the sociohistorical approach is the integration of individual, social, and cultural/historical levels within the analytical unit of *activity* (Cole, 1985; Leont'ev, 1981; Vygotsky, 1987; Wertsch, 1985; Zinchenko, 1985). Activity involves individuals with others in shared efforts with societal organization and tools.

In contrast with most other theories of development—which focus on the individual and the social or the cultural context as separate entities, adding or multiplying one and the other—the sociohistorical approach assumes that individual development must be understood in (and cannot be separated from) the social context. Vygotsky stressed that cognitive development involves children internalizing skilled approaches from their participation in joint problem solving with more skilled partners, who bring the intellectual tools of society within the reach of children in the "zone of proximal development."

Cole (1985) suggested that in the zone of proximal development culture and cognition create each other. Interactions in the zone of proximal development are the crucible of development *and* of culture in that they allow children to participate in activities that would be impossible for them alone, using cultural tools that themselves must be adapted to the specific activity at hand and thus are both passed along to and transformed by new generations.

Such an approach views individual development as dependent on interaction with other people in activities involving societal values, intellectual tools, and cultural institutions. Although many researchers treat the zone of proximal development as interaction between children and their social partners, such analysis is incomplete unless it also considers the societal basis of the shared problem solving—the nature of the problem the partners seek to solve, the values involved in determining the appropriate goals and means, the intellectual tools available (e.g., language and number systems, literacy, and mnemonic devices), and the institutional structures of the interaction (e.g., schooling and political and economic systems).

Ironically, the sociohistorical school's formulation of the relation between individual, social, and cultural processes is not only its strength but its weakness. Despite the theory's emphasis on context and society, it none-theless maintained assumptions regarding the contexts and societal approaches that are most valuable. Vygotsky focused on the sort of language and analysis that characterize academic learning, consistent with the agenda of his nation at the time he wrote (to establish a new Soviet nation with wide-spread literacy) and with Vygotsky's own upbringing and early career (as a Jewish intellectual and literary critic). In Vygotsky's collaboration with Luria (1976) on "cross-historical" studies in Central Asia, the bias of these views is apparent in the evaluation of the nonliterate peasants' versus the literate subjects' ways of thinking.

This unidirectional focus privileging academic, literate approaches—common to Vygotskian as well as to other major developmental theories—must be questioned if we are to understand the cultural context of devel-opment, as the goals of literacy and academic discourse are not universal. Understanding the development of children in the context of their own communities requires study of the local goals and means of approaching life. Although a cultural perspective encompassing nontechnological societies does not emerge from the work of the sociohistorical approach of Vygotsky, Leont'ev, and Luria, it is beginning to emerge in the work of current writers influenced by the sociohistorical school, such as those in this book.

From our perspective, each community's valued skills constitute the local goals of development. Societal practices that support children's devel-opment are tied to the values and skills considered important. It is not pos-sible to determine if the goals or practices of one community are more adap-tive than those of another, as judgments of adaptation cannot be separated from values. For middle-class U.S. children, the skills and patterns of social interaction practiced in school may relate closely to those necessary for eventual participation in the economic and political institutions of their society. In other communities—within the United States and elsewhere—other goals and practices take prominence.

Guided Participation and Its Similarities in Two Communities

The concept of *guided participation* (Rogoff, 1990) revises the idea of the zone of proximal development to include the developmental goals and means of communication of cultures other than those stressing literacy and academic analytical forms of discourse. The concept is also intended to address the everyday routine involvement of young middle-class children in the activities of their communities—involvement that is not captured in models of interaction based on didactic school lessons.

Guided participation stresses tacit forms of communication in the verbal and nonverbal exchanges of daily life and the distal arrangements involved in the regulation of children's activities, material goods, and companions. The notion of guided participation emphasizes the active role of children in both observing and participating in the organized societal activity of their caregivers and companions. In this more inclusive approach, the aim is to encompass more of the daily activities in which children participate and develop skill in and understanding of the valued approaches of their cultural community.

The emphasis on participation in the notion of guided participation has important implications for the question of how children gain from social interaction. With several theoretical approaches, the process is termed internalization, with the view that children bring external processes "inside." In contrast with such views, however, Rogoff (1990) suggested that the process is one of *appropriation,* emphasizing that children are already participants (either central or peripheral) in ongoing activity. As such, they already function *within* activities as they learn to manage them, rather than engaging in a two-stage process of, first, social lessons and then individual internalization in order to put the social lessons inside their heads. Children make later use of their changed understanding resulting from their contribution and involvement with joint problem-solving processes in new situations that resemble the ones in which they have participated. Rather than importing an external process to the internal plane, they appropriate a changed understanding from their own involvement and can carry to future occasions their earlier participation in and their gains in understanding of social activity. As Wertsch and Stone (1979, p. 21) put it, "the process *is* the product."

Although there are important cultural differences in valued activities and means of communication, dealt with in subsequent sections of this chapter, we believe that the processes of guided participation are widespread across differing cultural groups. In this section, we focus on processes of guided participation that we propose are similar across widely different cultural communities.

In almost all (44 of 47) of the episodes we observed involving the nesting doll, the dough, and the babydoll, the toddlers were closely involved with their parents, engaged with the same agenda (e.g., parent and child working the object together; or the parent attempting to assist the child with the object, and the child attempting to work the object with the parent's help). It is likely that if the event had not involved a focus on the toddler (due to the visitors' request to the mother to have the child work the objects), the extent of joint activity would have been much lower in both communities, a topic we will address in a subsequent report. Our point here is that in situations in which caregivers are focused on toddlers, caregivers and toddlers in both communities engaged in close communication.

Such communication between children and their caregivers involves two focal processes, discussed below, that we expect to be widespread across varying cultural communities: *creating bridges* to make connections to new ideas and skills and *structuring the children's participation* in activities through opportunities available for their involvement and through social support and challenge in activities and roles valued in their community.

Bridging to Make Connections Between Known and New

Inherent to communication is a collaborative effort of partners to find a common ground of understanding on which to base their contributions in order to ensure mutual comprehension. Partners initially have somewhat (or greatly) discrepant views of a situation but seek a common perspective or language through which to communicate their ideas. This effort to reach a common ground involves a stretch on the part of the participants. Middle-class adults often adapt their contribution to fit with what they think the children can understand, restructuring the problem definition to be within children's grasp (Wertsch, 1984). At the same time, children's efforts to participate in ongoing communication involve a stretch in the direction of a more mature definition of the situation and more skilled roles. From the collaboratively constructed common ground, which itself involves development, the participants may share in thinking as they extend their joint understanding together.

Bridging between two starting points involves emotional and nonverbal as well as verbal forms of communication. Children seek connections between old and new situations in their caregivers' emotional cues regarding the nature of a situation and how to handle it, in their interpretations of children's behavior, and in their labels for objects and events that inherently classify similarities across objects and events. All of the parents we observed indicated to the toddlers the nature of the activity with the object, orienting the children verbally in an average of 85% of the episodes and nonverbally in 91% of the episodes.

One kind of nonverbal bridging that provides young children with information about ambiguous situations is social referencing, in which infants as young as 10 months seek information from adults' expressions. They proceed to explore if the adult appears content but avoid the ambiguous situation if the adult appears fearful (Feinman, 1982; Gunnar & Stone, 1984; Sorce, Emde, Campos, & Klinnert, 1985).

An example is provided by a 20-month-old Mayan boy who attempted to gather information about an ambiguous situation: whether or not a playdough tortilla was edible. He had been skillfully patting the playdough that we had brought along into a "tortilla," with his mother's guidance:

> The baby broke off a tiny corner of the little tortilla he had made and held it up expectantly to his mother. She absently nodded to the baby as she conversed with the adults present.
>
> The baby brought the piece of play tortilla to his mouth and, looking at his mother fixedly, he stuck out his tongue and held the piece of tortilla toward it, with a questioning expression. His mother suddenly bolted out her hand and snatched his hand holding the piece of tortilla away from his mouth, blurting out "No! Not that!" The baby looked at her with a little surprise but was not disturbed by this clear message that the dough is not edible; he watched quietly as she laughingly put the little piece of dough

back on the rest of the tortilla, put it back into the baby's hand and told him that it is not to eat. He resumed patting the dough contentedly.

The mutual adjustments in communication that provide the basis of bridging between adults and children reflect adherence to principles of communication (e.g., Clark & Haviland, 1977) that a speaker be sensitive to the perspective and knowledge of the listener and that conversation focus on what is deserving of comment from the joint perspective of speaker and listener. Although there are likely to be asymmetries in responsibility for adjustment according to the status of the participants, the situation, and societal standards for responsibility for adjustment (discussed later), the phenomenon of seeking shared meaning is in the nature of human communication. Indeed, some argue that intersubjectivity between infants and their caregivers is innate—that from the earliest interactions infants are involved in the sharing of meaning (Brazelton, 1983; Luria, 1987; Newson, 1977; Trevarthen, Hubley, & Sheeran, 1975).

Collaborative Structuring of Problem Solving

Caregivers and children arrange the structure of situations in which children are involved through both distal arrangements and explicit interaction. Social activity is managed through assignment of and opportunity for participation in varying activities, such as the household chores in which 14 of the 16 toddlers were reported to engage, as well as through structuring children's responsibility for an activity through ongoing communication. Both adults and children are responsible for deciding children's activities and their role in them, often through tacit and pragmatic determination of children's skills and interests, as well as through more explicit arrangements for children's growing participation in the activities of their culture.

During caregiver–child communication, participants collaborate in structuring children's roles through division of responsibility for the activity. The more skilled partner may provide "metacognitive" support through handling higher-order goals as children handle the subgoals of which they are capable with assistance, allowing children to achieve more in collaboration than they can independently. With the nesting doll and playdough, most caregivers adjusted the object or its position to facilitate the toddlers' efforts, divided or simplified the task, and handled difficult moves for the child (in 94%, 75%, and 62% of the episodes, respectively). Such structuring was a little less frequent with the babydoll, perhaps owing to its familiarity to the children.

Children's roles in structuring an activity in social interaction may involve central responsibility for managing the situation—even when their partners have greater knowledge—and for adjusting their own level of participation. One-third of the toddlers clearly negotiated shifts in responsibility for handling the objects, seeking greater involvement or greater assistance, or resisting caregivers' suggestions. When there were tussles between caregivers and children regarding the agenda, the outcome was more likely to involve the toddlers' agenda, particularly in the Mayan community, which stresses respect for infants' autonomy. Children's interest and caregivers' constraints may ensure that young children's roles in routine activities adjust according to their interest and skills, within a dynamic zone of proximal development.

Cultural Variation in the Goals of Development

Differences across cultures in guided participation involve variation in the skills and values that are promoted according to cultural goals of maturity. Cultural communities vary in their institutions and related tools and technologies. Cultural psychologists and sociocultural theorists have argued that underlying the cognitive differences across cultural (or historical) groups are intellectual tools such as literacy and arithmetic (Cole & Griffin, 1980; Rogoff, 1981b; Rogoff et al., 1984; Scribner & Cole, 1981; Vygotsky, 1978, 1987). Communities differ in the skills considered important (e.g., reading, weaving, sorcery, healing, managing people) and approaches valued (e.g., individual achievement, speed in performance, interpersonal harmony).

Skills for the use of cultural tools such as literacy begin to be practiced even before children have contact with the technology in its mature form. Middle-class U.S. parents involve their children in "literate" forms of narrative in preschool discourse, as they embed their children in a way of life in which reading and writing are integral to communication, recreation, and livelihood (Cazden, 1988; Heath, 1982, 1983; Michaels & Cazden, 1986; Taylor, 1983).

Cultural differences in children's activities are apparent in the chores in which the mothers reported that their toddlers participated: Most of the toddlers helped with sweeping or food preparation, but most Salt Lake City toddlers also helped manage household machines such as vacuum cleaners and dishwashers; the Mayan children had less involvement with machines, but some had roles in economic activities of the adult world, such as running errands to a corner store and trying to weave.

Cultural Variation in Adult–Child Roles and Communication

There appear to be striking cultural differences in the means available for children to observe and participate in culturally important activities as well as to receive instruction outside the context of skilled activity. These differences relate to variations in the explicitness and intensity of verbal and nonverbal communication and the interactional status of children and adults (Field, Sostek, Vietze, & Leiderman, 1981; Leiderman, Tulkin, & Rosenfeld, 1977; Whiting & Edwards, 1988.) Rogoff (1990) suggested that these cultural differences fit together into patterns that vary in terms of the responsibility adults take for teaching children in cultures in which children do not participate in adult activities, and the responsibility children take for learning in cultures in which they have the opportunity to observe and participate in mature cultural activities.

Verbal and Nonverbal Communication

An emphasis on explicit, declarative statements—in contrast to tacit, procedural, and subtle forms of verbal and nonverbal instruction—appears to characterize cultures that promote Western schooling (John-Steiner, 1984; Jordan, 1977; Rogoff, 1981b, 1982a; Scribner, 1974; Scribner & Cole, 1973). The emphasis of Western researchers on talking as the appropriate means of adult–child interaction may reflect a cultural bias that overlooks the information provided by silence, gaze, postural changes, smells, and touch. Middle-class U.S. infants have been characterized as "packaged" babies who do not have direct skin contact with their caregiver (Whiting, 1981) and often spend more than one-third of their time in a room separate from any other people. U.S. infants are held approximately half the time as are Gusii (Kenyan) infants (Richman, Miller, & Solomon, 1988).

The physical separation of U.S. infants from other people may necessitate the use of distal forms of communication such as vocalizing. In contrast with U.S. children's use of distal communication, children who are constantly in the company of their caregivers may rely more on nonverbal cues, such as direction of gaze or facial expression. Infants who are in almost constant skin-to-skin contact with their mothers may manage effective communication through tactile contact in squirming and postural changes.

In our observations, almost all of the toddlers received both explanations and demonstrations of what they were to do with the nesting doll, dough, and babydoll from their caregivers. However, the amount of parental talk to the Salt Lake City toddlers was much greater, as can be seen in Table 10.1. Most Salt Lake City caregivers used many sentences, whereas most Mayan

Table 10.1. Episodes with Differing Amounts of Talk, by Toddlers' Age

	Salt Lake City		Mayan community	
	12–16 mo	20–23 mo	12–16 mo	20–23 mo
Total no. of episodes	12	12	12	11
Caregivers' talk				
Many sentences	8	8	2	4
A few sentences	4	2	6	5
Phrases at most	0	2	4	2
Toddlers' talk				
Many words; phrases	8	1	0	0
A few words	3	6	3	0
No words	1	5	9	11

caregivers spoke few sentences and some spoke none. The Salt Lake City caregivers averaged 2.0 episodes with extensive talk, whereas the Mayan caregivers averaged only 0.9 episodes with extensive talk, $F(1,14) = 4.8$, $p < 0.05$.

The Mayan toddlers, in turn, were much less talkative: Most of the older Salt Lake City toddlers' episodes involved speaking many words or phrases, whereas most of the Mayan episodes involved no talk at all by the toddler. [The community difference was significant, $F(1,14) = 24.9$, $p = 0.0003$, as was the age difference, $F(1,14) = 6.9$, $p = 0.02$.]

Caregivers' use of some forms of nonverbal communication was similar across the two communities. Most caregivers used action communication, guiding the toddlers' hands or the object or indicating with gestures.

There were differences between the caregivers from the two communities in other kinds of nonverbal communication as well. The Mayan caregivers' interactions relied more on information carried in gaze or postural or timing changes: The exchange of information by means of caregivers' gaze or by means of changes in caregivers' posture or pacing was essential for communication during an average of 1.9 and 2.2 Mayan episodes, respectively, and for only 0.5 and 0.2 Salt Lake City episodes: $F(1,14) = 6.3$, $p - 0.02$; $F(1,14) - 32.0$, $p - 0.0001$.

The Mayan babies, like the Mayan caregivers, relied more on nonverbal communication through action communication, gaze, and changes in posture or pacing. In an average of 1.6 and 1.9 Mayan episodes but only 0.5 and 0.8 Salt Lake City episodes, toddlers guided their partner's hands or the object or gestured, $F(1,14) = 7.2$, $p < 0.02$; $F(1,14) = 4.9$, $p = 0.04$. Toddlers' gaze and changes in posture or pacing were essential during an average of 1.8 and 2.1 of the Mayan episodes, respectively, but in only 0.4 and 0 of the Salt Lake City episodes, $F(1,14) = 6.9$, $p = 0.02$; $F(1,14) = 51.9$, $p = 0$.

The Mayan caregivers held their hands in readiness to assist the toddlers more frequently than the Salt Lake City caregivers [on 2.4 versus 1.1 episodes, $F(1,14) = 10.0$, $p < 0.007$], suggesting preparedness for the subtle communication of the Mayan children regarding a need for assistance.

Adult–Child Status and Locus of Responsibility for Learning

Variations in the relative status of children and adults have been noted in observations of cultural differences regarding the likelihood of adults serving as play partners with children or carrying on conversations as if children were their peers. These status variations may relate to children's opportunities to participate in adult activities and thereby learn through involvement rather than needing separate child-focused teaching situations and interactions.

Adults in Peer or Asymmetrical Roles with Children. In some communities, young children are not expected to be conversational peers with adults, initiating interactions and interacting as equals in the conversation (Blount,

1972; Harkness & Super, 1977; Schieffelin & Eisenberg, 1984). Instead, they may speak when spoken to, replying to informational questions or simply carrying out directions. Children do not converse and play with parents but with other children and kin such as older cousins, uncles, and grandparents (Farran & Mistry, personal communication; Ward, 1971).

Whiting and Edwards (1988) noted that of the 12 cultural groups they studied the U.S. middle-class mothers ranked highest in sociability with children—interacting in a friendly, playful, or conversational way, treating children at times as status equals—whereas in the other communities mothers stressed training or nurturant involvement with children, maintaining authority and dominance with respect to children.

In the Mayan community in which we carried out the research, when older children interact with adults it is in the context of adult work. Rogoff (1981a) observed that adults were as likely as or more likely than peers to be interacting with 9-year-olds when the children were doing household or agricultural work, but they were almost never involved with them when children were playing. Play is a domain for peer interaction, not adult companionship. During free time, children beyond age 3 or 4 move around town with a multi-age group of children, amusing themselves by observing ongoing events and imitating their elders in play, most of which involves emulation of adult activities.

Whereas U.S. middle-class mothers consider it part of their role to play with their children—all eight of the Salt Lake City mothers reported that they and the children's fathers often play with the baby—seven of the eight Mayan mothers reported that neither parent played with the child. Several Mayan mothers laughed with embarrassment at the idea of playing with their children, as being a playmate is the role of other children and occasionally grandparents. When a toddler is playing, reported the Mayan mothers, it is time for a mother to get her work done.

Ochs and Schieffelin (1984) contrasted two cultural patterns of speech between young children and their caregivers. In middle-class U.S. families, caregivers simplify their talk, negotiate meaning with children, cooperate in building propositions, and respond to verbal and nonverbal initiations by the child. In Kaluli New Guinea and Samoan families, caregivers model unsimplified utterances for the child to repeat to a third party, direct the child to notice others, and build interaction around circumstances to which caregivers wish the child to respond. Ochs and Schieffelin pointed to the difference in adults adapting to children versus children adapting to adults. In both of these patterns, children participate in activities of the society, but the patterns vary in terms of children's versus caregivers' responsibilities to adapt in the process of learning or teaching mature forms of speech and action.

Opportunities for Children to Participate in and to Observe Adult Activities. The adaptation of caregivers to children may be more necessary in societies that segregate children from adult activities, thereby requiring them to practice skills or learn information outside the mature context of use (Rogoff, 1981a, 1990). In the U.S. middle class, children are segregated from the work and recreational world of adults, and they learn about skills they may eventually need in order to participate in their society as adults in a separate context specialized for the purpose (i.e., school).

Young U.S. middle-class children seldom have much chance to participate in the economic functioning of the household and may be segregated from human company by the provision of separate bedrooms and a focus on attention to objects rather than people. Infants are often entirely alone for as much as 10 of 24 hours, managing as best they can to handle their hunger or thirst or comforting needs with objects (Morelli et al., 1988; Ward, 1971; Whiting, 1981). All eight of the Salt Lake City toddlers had their own separate beds, and six of the eight had their own rooms; all eight of the Mayan toddlers slept in the same room as their parents, and seven slept in the same bed with their mothers (and usually with father or siblings as well).

In communities in which children are integrated in adult activities, children are ensured a role in the action, at least as close observers. Children are present at most events of interest in the community, from work to recreation to church. They are able to observe and eavesdrop on the ongoing processes of life and death, work and play, that are important in their community. As infants, they are often carried wherever their caregiver goes, and as young children they may do errands and roam the town in their free time, watching whatever is going on. As nonparticipants in ordinary adult conversation, they may eavesdrop on important adult activities from which nonparticipant adults may be excluded.

Gaskins and Lucy (1987) noted that children's lower status and freedom to observe in a Mayan community in Mexico means that children have access to information unavailable to adults, providing extra eyes and ears for their mothers who stay at home and extract information regarding village events from the children. Mothers' questions about events focus children's attention on the relevant features of ongoing activities, guiding the children as to what aspects of events are significant. Observation and eavesdropping serve as an active method of obtaining information.

Children's Versus Adults' Responsibility for Learning and Teaching. Cultural variation in the symmetry of children's and adults' roles and in the opportunities for children to observe and participate in adult activities may relate to cultural expectations that children are responsible for learning or that adults are responsible for making children learn through teaching (Rogoff, 1990).

Eavesdropping versus peer-status conversation and language lessons. Ward (1971) offered an eavesdropping account of language learning in her description of a black community in Louisiana, in which "the silent absorption in community life, the participation in the daily commercial rituals, and the hours spent apparently overhearing adults' conversations should not be underestimated in their impact on a child's language growth" (p. 37). Small children are not conversational partners with adults, people with whom to "engage in dialogue." Children are not encouraged to learn skills in initiating and monopolizing conversation with adults on topics of their own choosing (skills useful in middle-class schooling). Questions between children and adults involve requests for information, not questions asked for the sake of conversation or for parents to drill children on topics about which the parents already know the answers. However, mothers' speech to children, although not taking the form of a dialogue, is carefully regularized, providing workable models of the language used in the community.

Heath (1983) similarly reported that working-class black Carolina adults did not see young children as conversational partners. Rather, the toddlers were always surrounded by others and moved through phases of echoing and experimenting with variation on the speech around them—at first ignored but gradually participating by making themselves part of ongoing discourse. Adults encouraged verbal facility by instigating and appreciating preschoolers' involvement in assertive challenging and scolding exchanges with adults and other children. However, because children were not seen as information givers, they were not asked test questions for which adults already had an answer, such as questions of fact or detail.

An example of instructional discourse between an adult and a toddler, with peer interactional status and test questions, appears with a 21-month-old Salt Lake City child handling the babydoll with his mother:

> The mother handed the doll to the toddler, saying, "What is it? Is that a baby? Can you take care of the baby?" with babytalk intonation. The toddler explored the doll and pointed to the eye, commenting, "Eye." His mother confirmed, "eye," and he asked "What dat?" as he pointed at the doll's face. The mother clarified and answered his question: "What's that? Her mouth." After some further interaction, the mother chirped "Where's her belly button?" When he pointed to the doll's belly button, the mother evaluated his response, "All right!" in the classic question–response–evaluation sequence that Mehan (1979) has documented as teacher-student discourse in the classroom.

In an average of 2.2 Salt Lake City episodes, parents interacted with toddlers as conversational peers, asking their opinions, responding to their vocalizations as conversation, and providing openings for equal dialogic exchanges, whereas the Mayan toddlers were treated as conversational peers in only 1 of 23 episodes, $F(1,14) = 106, p = 0$. The Salt Lake City toddlers assumed a peer role in 1.9 of the episodes, offering comments and initiating optional conversation, but the Mayan toddlers never took a peer conversational role with their parents, $F(1,14) = 22.2, p = 0.0003$. Nonetheless, the toddlers in both communities interacted reciprocally with their parents in almost all episodes with joint action and action communication. It is the presence of verbal dialogue that most differentiates the interactions of the two communities.

Many of the episodes with the Salt Lake City toddlers involved talk that can be seen as lessons in language use; such language lessons almost never occurred in the Mayan episodes. The Salt Lake City caregivers used marked babytalk intonations and speech in an average of 2.5 episodes; the Mayan caregivers did in only 0.5 episodes, $F(1,14) = 18.7$, $p = 0.0007$. The Salt Lake City caregivers used test questions, asking for information they already knew, in an average of 1.4 episodes; the Mayan parents never did, $F(1,14) = 13.4$, $p = 0.002$. The Salt Lake City caregivers labeled events or object parts didactically, produced running commentaries describing and evaluating ongoing events, and they played word games in 2.1, 2.1, and 1.0 episodes, respectively; the corresponding amounts for the Mayan caregivers were 0.4, 0.1, and 0.1 episodes, Fs = 19.6, 28.9, 8.8, ps < 0.01.

This finding does not necessarily mean that the Salt Lake City parents were self-consciously producing such "lessons"; they may have been, or they may have interacted with their children in this manner in an intuitive fashion. Whatever their explicit purpose, the differences in types of adult–toddler talk in the two communities is striking.

In communities in which children are not conversational partners of adults, they may be poorly prepared for the pattern of discourse used in school, but they become proficient in the language and other skills of their community. They are able to learn from observing and eavesdropping as ever-present members of the community, their growing participation in daily activities from an early age, the questions and directives and demonstrations of adults, and their playful talk with other children.

Observation and attention management. With opportunities to observe ongoing activity and to help when necessary, children from many cultures begin to participate in chores and other activities from age 3 or 4, when they begin to see what to do; they assume responsibilities for child, animal, and house care by age 5 or 7 (Rogoff, Sellers, Pirotta, Fox, & White, 1975; Ward, 1971; Whiting & Edwards, 1988). Their role grows and their opportunities to practice are amplified by their interest in participation and by their parents' setting them tasks within their capabilities and providing suggestions and demonstrations *in the context of joint activity.* In observations in the Mayan community, native observers identified only 6 of 1708 occasions in which 9-year-olds were explicitly being taught outside of school (Rogoff, 1981a).

An example of children's learning in the context of participation is Mayan mothers' reports of how their children learn to make tortillas. Although the Mayan mothers give pointers and structure their children's efforts, they do not regard the process as teaching; they claim that the children simply learn. They, along with researchers, seem to regard teaching as the sort of interaction that goes on in schools. According to Mayan mothers, 1- to 2-year-olds observe their mothers making tortillas and attempt to follow suit. The mothers give them a small piece of dough to use and facilitate their efforts by rolling the dough in a ball and starting the flattening process.

The toddler's "tortilla" is cooked and eaten by family members. As the child gains skill in making tortillas, the mother adds pointers and demonstrations to facilitate holding the dough in a position that facilitates smooth flattening, and the children can witness the outcome of their own efforts and contribute to making meals. The child observes carefully and participates, and the mother simplifies the task to the child's level of skill and demonstrates and gives suggestions during the process of joint activity.

Questions by children to adults are rare in some communities (Heath, 1983). Learners' questions to a teacher may be regarded as impolite challenges in that they involve a subordinate obliging a superior to respond. This exchange implies that the subordinate has the right to hold the superior responsible for the information requested, as Goody (1978) observed in the apprenticeship of Gonja youths learning to weave.

Rather than relying on questions and explanations to organize their learning, observers may be skilled in picking up information through watching, on some occasions without hands-on participation. Nash (1967) reported that the method of learning to use the footloom in a weaving factory in Guatemala is for the learner (an adult) to sit beside a skilled weaver for a period of weeks, simply observing, asking no questions and receiving no explanation. The learner may fetch a spool of thread from time to time for the weaver but does not carry out the process, until after a period of weeks the learner feels competent to begin. At that point, the learner has become a skilled weaver simply by watching and by attending to whatever demonstrations the skilled weaver has provided.

In our observations, the Mayan toddlers appeared more likely to monitor peripheral social events outside their own activity or their activity with their caregiver (doing so during an average of 2.5 episodes) than were the Salt Lake City toddlers (who monitored during an average of 1.1 episodes). The Mayan toddlers appeared to be able to attend to several events simultaneously (e.g., working the object with the caregiver and monitoring other conversation, glancing at and being involved with the flow of events, on an average of 2.1 episodes), whereas the Salt Lake City toddlers seldom appeared to attend to several events simultaneously (averaging only 0.4 episodes, $F(1,14) = 25.4$, $p = 0.0002$). The Salt Lake City toddlers were more likely to attend to one event at a time: their own activity or a joint activity, either exclusively or alternating attention between their own activity and other events.

The Mayan caregivers, like the children, appeared able to engage attention with several events simultaneously. Their timesharing of attention may have been facilitated by their reserving verbal channels of communication for adult conversation and relying heavily on nonverbal channels—gaze, posture, timing, and action communication—with the toddlers. In an average of 2.2 episodes they tracked several events simultaneously, compared with 0.5 Salt Lake City episodes, $F(1,14) = 22.9$, $p = 0.0003$. The Salt Lake caregivers usually alternated attention with other events if there were competing events that caught their attention.

In communities in which observation is possible, people may be especially active and skilled observers. Mainstream middle-class researchers, who may rely less on observation, tend to think of observation as passive. However, this research suggests that in some settings children and adults are skilled and active in attending to what they watch. In the guided participation of children in cultural communities that stress children's responsibility for learning, children may have the opportunity to observe and participate in the skills of the community and may develop impressive skills in observation, with less explicit child-centered interaction to integrate the child in the activities of society. Skilled observation may allow skilled participation by very young children, yielding impressive skill and responsibility in such activities as tending younger children (Weisner & Gallimore, 1977) or handling knives (Sorenson, 1979).

Efforts to aid children in learning may thus vary in terms of the children's responsibility to observe and analyze the task versus the caregivers' responsibility to decompose the task and motivate the child. Dixon, LeVine, Richman, and Brazelton (1984) noted that Gusii (Kenyan) mothers gave their 6- to 36-month-old infants the responsibility for learning. They used clear "advance organizers" in instruction, often modeling the expected performance in its entirety, and appeared to expect the task to be completed exactly as specified if the child attended to it. This method contrasted with the efforts of American mothers, who took the responsibility for teaching and making their babies learn. They concentrated on arousing the children's interest and shaping their behavior step by step, providing constant encouragement and refocusing.

In our observations, the Salt Lake City parents seemed to take greater responsibility for motivating their children and for managing their attention. The Salt Lake parents attempted to manage their toddlers' attention in an average of 1.5 episodes, whereas only 0.4 Mayan episodes involved parental management of the child's attention, $F(1,14) = 7.2, p < 0.02$. Consistent with the observations of Dixon et al., the Salt Lake City caregivers often tried to arouse their children's interest, showing mock excitement about an activity in an average of 2.0 episodes, compared with only 0.4 episodes with Mayan caregivers, $F(1,14) = 12.5, p = 0.003$. Consistent with teachers' efforts to motivate, half of the Salt Lake City episodes involved praise for the child's performance, but such praise occurred only once in 23 Mayan episodes, $F(1,14) = 18.7, p = 0.0007$.

Two Toddlers with their Mothers and the Nesting Doll. A contrast in verbal versus nonverbal communication, status relations of partners, and teaching versus learning emphases is apparent if we compare a 20-month-old from each community. Both are firstborn boys whose handling of the nesting doll was skilled and interested and included a counting routine with their mothers. For both communities, the interaction style was extreme in similar ways: Counting routines were not usual with this toy in either community (these two boys are the only children of the 16 who counted or were encouraged to count the nesting doll pieces), and both mothers appeared more concerned with their children's performance than most other mothers from their communities. For the Salt Lake City mother, the concern took the form of greater directiveness and of putting herself at times into a more extreme peer role with the child, acting like a child herself, than the other Salt Lake City mothers. The Mayan mother was somewhat more directive with the child than the other mothers from her community. So the style of both mothers is extreme for their communities, in the same direction.

The most important differences between these two dyads are in status roles—the Salt Lake City mother getting on the child's level and playing or teaching versus the Mayan mother assisting the child but maintaining a difference of status—and in responsivity and subtlety of their verbal and nonverbal communication. The differences are consistent with the Salt Lake City child being treated as the object of teaching and the Mayan child being responsible for learning. This example is in line with differences in the sample as a whole, in which Salt Lake City caregivers acted as teachers in an average of 1.1 episodes and as playmates in 1.1 episodes, whereas Mayan caregivers never acted as teachers or playmates with the toddlers: $Fs = 10.3$, 14.5, $ps < 0.006$. Rather, the Mayan caregivers showed readiness to aid in their children's efforts to learn.

It is important to note that although the style of the two mothers differed, each mother used both verbal and nonverbal communication adjusted to her children, and each child was comfortably engaged with his mother in handling a problem that was challenging but supported in the interaction.

The Mayan mother monitored her son's actions with the object; and though she told him clearly what to do, her moves were generally responsive rather than initiatory, and she did not overrule his agenda. The Salt Lake mother, in contrast, interrupted her child's pace and at many moves seemed to attempt to manage the agenda, even to the point of lack of coordination of the moves between mother and child. The communication between the Mayan mother and child was subtle, whereas that between the Salt Lake City mother and child involved loud and frequent talk and large movements. The Mayan mother managed to participate in adult conversation simultaneously with her support for the baby's efforts; the Salt Lake City mother focused exclusively on the child, though other adults were also present.

Salt Lake City mother and 20-month-old. The Salt Lake City mother began playing with the nesting doll as if she were herself a child, giggling and waving her hands in an animated fashion and bouncing up and down and squealing as she knelt on the floor with the child. She poked at the baby with the nesting doll and tickled him; she took pieces of the toy and made up new games with them, hiding them or putting them inside other objects. She sometimes turned the toy over to him by saying "Your turn," thereby emphasizing the equality of status.

When the baby handled the toy, she sometimes changed to an instructional tone: "*On.* Put the lid *on*" and cheered "Wonderful! Yay!" and applauded his moves, frequently gushing "Oh, you're so smaaart! You're so smaaart! I *love* you!" with a hug. The baby generally worked calmly with the object but sometimes giggled with his mother. The father sat nearby and watched placidly as if the mother's actions were not out of the ordinary.

Much later in the visit, the interviewer brought out a new version of the nesting doll, which the mother helped the baby take apart and put together, cheering "Yay! There you go, Buddy!" and jumping him up and down on her lap. When the littlest doll appeared, she gasped in exaggerated surprise and enthusiastically exclaimed, "There's three of them!" She proceeded to count them, with the child following her cues to count, but the counting efforts of the mother and child were discoordinated, with the mother both instigating and echoing with a confusion of sequence that got more complicated during the next round of counting. When the mother said "two," the baby said "one," and when she finished with "three," the baby said "two." The mother then started counting again, saying "one" before the baby said "three."

Then the mother changed the routine, holding the bottom pieces out on her flat palm and encouraging him to put the nesting doll together, "Does the lady go in there?" She encouraged in a sweet babytalk intonation, "That's right! . . . Put her in. *In*," emphasizing the term. She used a sweet voice throughout, and when he did it differently than she suggested, she emphasized his independent choice, "OK, do you want to put her that way? . . . That's fine . . . Do you choose that way?" The mother went on with the lesson in putting the pieces together, directing the baby's actions with language instruction, cheering and providing commentary on his actions, and enthusiastically marking and praising his "individual" accomplishment.

Mayan mother and 20-month-old. The playmate and teacher roles taken by the Salt Lake City mother differed from the role taken and means used by the Mayan mother, although the Mayan mother appeared to be focused on encouraging her son's performance and is a member of a family that stresses schooling; she herself has a high level of education by community standards (ninth grade, the highest in the Mayan sample).

The mother demonstrated how the nesting doll comes apart and fits together, with a few words to encourage him to look. The baby insisted on handling the toy himself; after a moment the mother took the doll back and demonstrated again, leaning over with the two halves of the big doll, saying quietly, "I'll put it together." The baby held the small inside doll and complained to get access to the big outside doll. The mother looked into the baby's eyes and pointed out "Two . . . two . . ." and handed the big doll back to the baby, repeating "two" with a significant gaze. Then she demonstrated opening and closing the small inside doll, commenting only "Look" as the baby watched her pull the big outside doll apart, saying "Put it inside." She set down the two big halves carefully in front of the baby, and set the little doll inside to demonstrate the sequence to the baby, pausing a couple of times to look at the baby to be sure he was watching. He was.

The baby went on to handle the pieces himself for a while, as his mother conversed with adults at the same time as she occasionally demonstrated the actions to the baby, using gestures and timing to emphasize the essential aspects of the action to the baby while talking and looking at the adult with whom she spoke. She thus directed the baby in an unobtrusive fashion, and when he resisted her suggestions she did not insist.

When he had trouble, the mother instantly intervened and demonstrated, commenting, "Do this one first, . . . and then cover it up with this one." The baby was attentive and attempted to work the nesting doll again, as the mother monitored his efforts and held her hands ready to help him, not interfering unless he had difficulty. This process continued until the doll was assembled, and the mother then subtly demonstrated again by carefully holding the pieces in position and making a few quiet comments. The baby watched patiently and acknowledged the demonstration with an "Okay" as if to say, "I see."

Now he could put the pieces in the right positions, and the mother merely monitored his actions as she chatted with the adults. The baby monitored the adult conversation as he worked the toy. Once the baby kissed the doll, and the mother and others encouraged him to do it again, responding with pleasure to his idea. He cheerfully continued. Then he turned and counted quietly as he put two pieces in her lap, "One . . . two. . . ." The mother repeated "two" after him, and the baby put the third piece in her outstretched hand, "three," and the mother echoed, "three." There did not seem to be further acknowledgement of the baby's counting, though he had said little else during the session.

It is notable that the Mayan baby's counting, like his kissing of the doll, was at his instigation; it received a pleasant acknowledgment but did not become a public evaluation of his intelligence or a reason for expressions of love. The baby's actions, rather than being the exclusive, individual focus of the mother, fit into the flow of ongoing social events, with both the mother and child monitoring each other and the other social activities as they handled the object. Though the child received attention, it was not exclusive; rather, the child appeared to be smoothly integrated into the social fabric, not a recipient of baby-directed play or special registers of speech.

These two examples illustrate how middle-class U.S. parents may assume didactic and dyadic roles as they rely on their own efforts to motivate children to learn, in contrast with caregivers in cultures in which children have the responsibility to learn and are involved with many other social partners in the process.

Conclusions

Children in a wide variety of cultural communities, including middle-class U.S. communities, appear to have in common opportunities to learn through guided participation in culturally arranged activities, learning and developing in situations of joint involvement with more experienced people.

Variations across communities have to do with what is being learned, with differing values and practices regarding such skills as literacy and other school-related technologies or management of people as in child care. Goals of development have local variation (along with species similarities, of course) according to local practices and values.

Related variation across communities involves contrasting means of teaching/learning, differing with children's opportunities to observe and participate in adult activities or in child-oriented instructional interactions. Differences in children's versus adults' responsibility for children's learning appear to be accompanied by variations in the interactional roles of children and adults and in reliance on explanation out of context or observation and participation in the context of important adult activities. Such differences may lead to variation in children's skill in managing their own attention and observation, and in managing verbal interactions with adults as conversational peers. These skills and interactional practices are differentially useful for participation in varying institutional contexts such as formal schooling and economic activities.

Underlying these varying circumstances, however, are similarities in guided participation: Caregivers collaborate with children in determining the nature of children's activities and their responsibilities in participation. They work together, and in the process children learn to manage new situations under collaborative structuring of problem-solving attempts and regulation of their responsibilities. This guided participation includes tacit forms of communication and distal arrangements of children's learning environments, as well as explicit verbal interaction. The mutual roles played by caregivers and children in children's development rely on both the caregivers' interest in fostering mature skills and the children's own eagerness to participate in adult activities and push their own development. Guided participation involves children's participation in the activities of their community, with the challenge and support of a system of social partners including caregivers and peers of varying levels of skill and status.

Guided participation may be universal, although communities vary in the goals of development and the nature of involvement of children and adults. Observations of variations in guided participation across cultures draw attention to:

1. Goals of mature contribution to the community that organize the skills and values that children learn
2. Opportunities available to children for learning in the arrangements made for children's activities and companions
3. Responsibility that children take for learning from the activities in which they participate and from rich opportunities for observation and eavesdropping
4. Tacit but ubiquitous nature of children's guided participation

5. Unself-conscious nature of the roles of children as well as of their social partners in day-to-day arrangements and interaction

Observations in cultures other than those of the researchers may make such aspects of guided participation more apparent. However, we suggest that these features of guided participation may also be more common for U.S. middle-class children than the explicit, didactic, self-conscious instructional interaction that has been the focus of research. The interdependence of children and their social partners in valued and routine cultural activities may be a fact of children's lives that accounts for children's rapid development as participants in the skills and understanding of their community, whether it involves learning to weave or to read, to take care of livestock or young children or homework.

Notes

The first author is grateful for the time to write and support provided by the Center for Advanced Study in the Behavioral Sciences during her fellowship 1988–89, with funding from the Spencer Foundation, the National Science Foundation (BNS87-00864), and a Faculty Fellow Award from the University of Utah. The research reported here has been supported by the University Research Committee (University of Utah) and by the National Institute of Mental Health (41060).

1. This chapter is a revision, with double the number of children, of Rogoff, B., Mosier, C., Mistry, J., & Göncü, A. (1989). Toddlers' guided participation in cultural activity. *Cultural Dynamics, 2,* 209–37. Portions of this chapter were reported at the meetings of the Society for Research in Child Development, Kansas City, April 1989.

References

Blount, B. G. (1972). Parental speech and language acquisition: some Luo and Samoan examples. *Anthropological Linguistics, 14,* 119–30.
Brazelton, T. B. (1983). Precursors for the development of emotions in early infancy. In R. Plutchik & H. Kellerman (eds.). *Emotion: theory, research, and experience* (Vol. 2, pp. 35–55). Orlando, FL: Academic Press.
Cazden, C. B. (1988). *Classroom discourse.* Portsmouth, NH: Heinemann.
Clark, H. H., & Haviland, S. E. (1977). Comprehension and the given-new contract. In R. O. Freedle (ed.). *Discourse production and comprehension* (pp. 1–40). Norwood, NJ: Ablex.
Cole, M. (1985). The zone of proximal development: where culture and cognition create each other. In J. V. Wertsch (ed.). *Culture, communication, and cognition: Vygotskian perspectives* (pp. 146–61). Cambridge: Cambridge University Press.
Cole, M., & Griffin, P. (1980). Cultural amplifiers reconsidered. In D. R. Olson (ed.). *The social foundations of language and thought* (pp. 343–64). New York: Norton.

Dixon, S. D., LeVine, R. A., Richman, A., & Brazelton, T. B. (1984). Mother-child interaction around a teaching task: an African-American comparison. *Child Development, 55*, 1252–64.

Feinman, S. (1982). Social referencing in infancy. *Merrill-Palmer Quarterly, 28*, 445–70.

Field, T. M., Sostek, A. M., Vietze, P., & Liederman, P. H. (eds.) (1981). *Culture and early interactions.* Hillsdale, NJ: Lawrence Erlbaum Associates.

Gaskins, S., & Lucy, J. A. (1987, May). The role of children in the production of adult culture: a Yucatec case. Presented at the meeting of the American Ethnological Society, San Antonio.

Goody, E. N. (1978). Towards a theory of questions. In E. N. Goody (ed.). *Questions and politeness* (pp. 17–43). Cambridge: Cambridge University Press.

Gunnar, M. R., & Stone, C. (1984). The effects of positive maternal affect on infant responses to pleasant, ambiguous, and fear-provoking toys. *Child Development, 55*, 1231–36.

Harkness, S., & Super, C. M. (1977). Why African children are so hard to test. *Annals of the New York Academy of Sciences, 285*, 326–31.

Heath, S. B. (1982). What no bedtime story means: narrative skills at home and school. *Language in Society, 11*, 49–76.

Heath, S. B. (1983). *Ways with words: language, life, and work in communities and classrooms.* Cambridge: Cambridge University Press.

John-Steiner, V. (1984) Learning styles among Pueblo children. *Quarterly Newsletter of the Laboratory of Comparative Human Cognition, 6*, 57–62,

Jordan, C. (1977, February). Maternal teaching, peer teaching, and school adaptation in an urban Hawaiian population. Presented at the meetings of the Society for Cross-Cultural Research, East Lansing.

Laboratory of Comparative Human Cognition (1983). Culture and cognitive development. In W. Kessen (ed.). *History, theory, and methods.* In P. H. Mussen (ed.). *Handbook of child psychology* (Vol. 1, pp. 294–356). New York: Wiley.

Leiderman, P. H., Tulkin, S. R., & Rosenfeld, A. (eds.) (1977). *Culture and infancy: variations in the human experience.* Orlando, FL: Academic Press.

Leont'ev, A. N. (1981). The problem of activity in psychology. In J. V. Wertsch (ed.). *The concept of activity in Soviet psychology.* Armonk, NY: M. E. Sharpe.

Luria, A. R. (1976). *Cognitive development: its cultural and social foundations.* Cambridge, MA: Harvard University Press.

Luria, A. R. (1987). Afterword to the Russian edition. In R. W. Rieber & A. S. Carton (eds.). *The collected works of L. S. Vygotsky. Vol. 1. Problems of general psychology.* New York: Plenum.

Mehan, H. (1979). *Learning lessons.* Cambridge, MA: Harvard University Press.

Michaels, S., & Cazden, C. B. (1986). Teacher/child collaboration as oral preparation for literacy. In B. B. Schieffelin & P. Gilmore (eds.). *The acquisition of literacy: ethnographic perspectives* (pp. 132–54). Norwood, NJ: Ablex.

Morelli, G. A., Fitz, D., Oppenheim, D., Nash, A., Nakagawa, M., & Rogoff, B. (1988, November). Social relations in infants' sleeping arrangements. Presented at the meetings of the American Anthropological Association, Phoenix.

Nash, M. (1967). *Machine age Maya.* Chicago: University of Chicago Press.

Newson, J. (1977). An intersubjective approach to the systematic description of mother–infant interaction. In H. R. Schaffer (ed.). *Studies in mother–infant interaction* (pp. 47–61). Orlando, FL: Academic Press.

Ochs, E., & Schieffelin, B. B. (1984). Language acquisition and socialization: three developmental stories and their implications. In R. Schweder & R. LeVine (eds.). *Culture and its acquisition.* Chicago: University of Chicago Press.

Richman, A. L., Miller, P. M., & Solomon, M. J. (1988). The socialization of infants in suburban Boston. In R. A. LeVine, P. M. Miller, & M. M. West (eds.). *Parental behavior in diverse societies* (pp. 65–74). San Francisco: Jossey-Bass.

Rogoff, B. (1981a). Adults and peers as agents of socialization: a highland Guatemalan profile. *Ethos, 9,* 18–36.

Rogoff, B. (1981b). Schooling and the development of cognitive skills. In H. C. Triandis & A. Heron (eds.). *Handbook of cross-cultural psychology* (Vol. 4, pp. 233–94). Rockleigh, NJ: Allyn & Bacon.

Rogoff, B. (1982a). Mode of instruction and memory test performance. *International Journal of Behavioral Development, 5,* 33–48.

Rogoff, B. (1982b). Integrating context and cognitive development. In M. E. Lamb & A. L. Brown (eds.). *Advances in developmental psychology* (Vol. 2). Hillsdale, NJ: Lawrence Erlbaum Associates.

Rogoff, B. (1990). *Apprenticeship in thinking: cognitive development in social context.* New York: Oxford University Press.

Rogoff, B., & Gauvain, M. (1986). A method for the analysis of patterns, illustrated with data on mother–child instructional interaction. In J. Valsiner (ed.). *The individual subject and scientific psychology* (pp. 261–90). New York: Plenum.

Rogoff, B., Sellers, M. J., Pirotta, S., Fox, N., & White, S. H. (1975). Age of assignment of roles and responsibilities to children: a cross-cultural survey. *Human Development, 18,* 353–69.

Rogoff, B., Gauvain, M., & Ellis, S. (1984). Development viewed in its cultural context. In M. H. Bornstein & M. E. Lamb (eds.). *Developmental psychology.* Hillsdale, NJ: Lawrence Erlbaum Associates.

Schieffelin, B. B., & Eisenberg, A. R. (1984). Cultural variation in children's conversations. In R. Schiefelbusch & J. Pickar (eds.). *The acquisition of communicative competence* (pp. 377–420). Baltimore: University Park Press.

Scribner, S. (1974). Developmental aspects of categorized recall in a West African society. *Cognitive Psychology, 6,* 475–94.

Scribner, S., & Cole, M. (1973). Cognitive consequences of formal and informal education. *Science, 182,* 553–9.

Scribner, S., & Cole, M. (1981). *The psychology of literacy.* Cambridge, MA: Harvard University Press.

Sorce, J. F., Emde, R. N., Campos, J., & Klinnert, M. D. (1985). Maternal emotional signaling: its effect on the visual cliff behavior of 1-year-olds. *Developmental Psychology, 21,* 195–200.

Sorenson, E. R. (1979). Early tactile communication and the patterning of human organization: a New Guinea case study. In M. Bullowa (ed.). *Before speech: the beginning of interpersonal communication* (pp. 289–305). Cambridge: Cambridge University Press.

Taylor, D. (1983). *Family literacy.* Exeter, NH: Heinemann.

Trevarthen, C., Hubley, P., & Sheeran, L. (1975). Les activités innées du nourrisson. *La Recherche, 6,* 447–58.

Vygotsky, L. S. (1978). *Mind in society: the development of higher psychological processes.* Cambridge MA: Harvard University Press.

Vygotsky, L. S. (1987). *Thinking and speech.* In R. W. Rieber & A. S. Carton (eds.). The collected works of L. S. Vygotsky (N. Minick, trans; pp. 37–285). New York: Plenum.

Ward, M. C. (1971). *Them children: a study in language learning.* New York: Holt Rinehart & Winston.

Weisner, T. S. & Gallimore, R. (1977). My brother's keeper: child and sibling caretaking. *Current Anthropology, 18,* 169–90.

Wertsch, J. V. (1984). The zone of proximal development: some conceptual issues. In B. Rogoff & J. V. Wertsch (eds.). *Children's learning in the "zone of proximal development"* (pp. 7–18). San Francisco: Jossey-Bass.

Wertsch, J. V. (1985). *Vygotsky and the social formation of mind.* Cambridge, MA: Harvard University Press.

Wertsch, J. V., & Stone, C. A. (1979, February). A social interactional analysis of learning disabilities remediation. Presented at the International Conference of the Association for Children with Learning Disabilities, San Francisco.

Whiting, B. B., & Edwards, C. P. (1988). *Children of different worlds: the formation of social behavior.* Cambridge, MA: Harvard University Press.

Whiting, J. W. M. (1981). Environmental constraints on infant care practices. In R. H. Munroe, R. L. Munroe, & B. B. Whiting (eds.). *Handbook of cross-cultural human development* (pp. 155–79). New York: Garland.

Zinchenko, V. P. (1985). Vygotsky's ideas about units for the analysis of mind. In J. V. Wertsch (ed.). *Culture, communication and cognition: Vygotskian perspectives* (pp. 94–118). Cambridge MA: Cambridge University Press.

COMMENTARY

Away from Internalization

MARTIN J. PACKER

The opportunity to review and comment on the chapters in Part II has been a welcome one. Before addressing this task, perhaps I should briefly sketch my own position. For some years I have been struggling to understand how children learn and develop in and through their social interaction with adults and other children. This topic raises numerous and complex issues of methodology and theory; practical activity is, as I have tried to describe (Packer, 1985), an odd "object" to investigate systematically. I have come to adopt a perspective I consider in two respects a "hermeneutic" one. The first way my work aims to be hermeneutic is in its method, as human activity, for a variety of reasons, requires interpretation in order to be studied. The second is that it rests on, and takes its starting point in, the "existential analytic," the phenomenological analysis of everyday human being, conducted by Heidegger (1927/1962). It is necessary here only to note that there are certain parallels between the existential analytic and Vygotsky's conception of activity as materially situated. (The general question of the similarities between existentialist and Marxist efforts to overcome the dualisms of traditional metaphysics and the debt both owe, albeit largely in opposition, to Hegel is a fascinating one that regrettably cannot be considered here.)

The Vygotskian perspective adopted by the authors of these chapters would have us direct our attention to the relations among three poles of social reality: the person, the world of objects, and the activity that binds the two (Minick, 1985, in press). The individual-in-action is the proper focus for psychological analysis. There are no universal psychological traits or characteristics; instead, a person's properties, if you like, stem from, change with, and show up in their practical involvement in action. In this way, by focusing on action as a process where person and world meet, the Vygotskian approach has a good chance of avoiding some of the problems of the Cartesian dualism between mind and world that continues to plague much psychological theory and research. There are similarities between this strategy and Heidegger's view of humans as always already situated in a world of cultural and historical possibilities. Being-in-the-world is a unitary notion that precedes, even if it is the ground for, dualisms such as those between mind and world, mind and body, reason and emotion, and person and person. In the same way, for each of the chapters in this section, interaction in a specific, concrete setting is considered the locus and carrier of learning.

Hence it has been a pleasure to read and comment on the way chapters deal with interpersonal interaction as the source of learning and development. If I am critical at times, it is because I find it impossible to resist responding to the intellectual challenge these chapters pose, and because, being inspired by the progress these chapters make toward a rethinking of development in social, cultural, and historical terms, I want to leap on board and try to leap ahead, as a result of being, because of these authors' work, better able to see where such investigations might press forward.

Barbara Rogoff, Christine Mosier, Jayanthi Mistry, and Artin Goncu take the position that we have paid too much attention to that mode of adult–child interchange where the adult engages in explicit didactic instruction. They describe the "guided participation" of toddlers by caregivers in the different cultures of a Mayan town in Guatemala and Salt Lake City, Utah. (Children in India and Turkey have also been studied, though material on these children is not reported here.) The chapter focuses on interactions that transpired when mothers were asked to help their child unpack a wooden nesting doll, make playdough food, and take care of a doll. Rogoff et al. present evidence that the didactic mode characterizes Salt Lake City caregivers but not their Mayan counterparts. They propose that even the former will use other modes regularly, so that the pedagogic mode is not as crucial as we have taken it to be. They suggest that the Mayan mode is effective, placing as it does more responsibility for learning on the child. Provocatively, they hint that the pedagogic mode approaches dysfunctionality in certain respects. The Salt Lake City caregivers were discoordinated, marking and praising " 'individual' accomplishment." They placed exclusive attention on the baby, apparently seeking to motivate their child to learn. The Mayan caregivers, in contrast, showed more demonstration, unobtrusive directing, and monitoring of the child. They employed no public evaluation of performance or public expression of love. No special speech registers were used, unlike the American mothers' baby talk. The result was that the baby's actions were fitted into the flow of ongoing events and more smoothly integrated into the social fabric.

The major point of this chapter is well taken; descriptions of scaffolding have tended to reduce the child to the role of passive recipient of an adult's didactic efforts. This picture is theoretically unconvincing; Rogoff gives us reason to think that it is, ironically, empirically accurate, given the white middle-class Western adults and children usually studied. I have two questions, however. First, as someone who has submitted parents and children to investigative procedures of varying degrees of intrusiveness, I have come to appreciate the perceived pressure on many caregivers to have their charges perform. The pride and anxiety tied up with young children and the competitive and evaluative character of our culture conspire to make the most "naturalistic," purely "observational" inquiry an occasion for caregivers to demonstrate the sincerity of their affection and involvement and to have their child demonstrate cuteness and skill. Several observations Rogoff et al. make about Mayan views of children suggest that Mayan caregivers are less likely to react this way. The didactic mode may, then, be an artifact of the way the research enterprise is construed in this culture. If so, it may help explain why American children develop social facility despite being drawn into such discoordinate exercises.

Perhaps this is just an example of something of which Rogoff and colleagues are well aware—that different cultures emphasize different goals. They point out that nontechnological societies have "local goals" that are different from those of Western technocracies, and so value different skills. Indeed, the notion of guided participation is intended to revise Vygotsky's concept of the zone of proximal development (the "Zo-ped," to cognoscenti) to take account of these variations. When talking of guided participation, Rogoff et al. drew attention to tacit forms of communication and to the distal arrangements that regulate children's lives. They are indeed important additions to those elements of the adult–child interaction to which we attend.

Each of these five chapters is concerned to avoid an appeal to a simple notion of learning as "internalization," in the sense of a simple transfer of skills and information from outside to inside the child. Rogoff et al. speak instead of children "appropriating" activities in which they are already participants. Rather than being faced with the task of taking social "information" inside their heads, they must learn to *manage* activities in which they already function. This changed involvement changes their understanding of social activity, which they can carry to new situations.

When Rogoff et al. articulate the processes at work in guided participation they make a methodological move that Addison Stone makes as well. Their focus is on processes "that we propose are similar across widely different cultural communities." They seek to describe what is *common* to the two cultures. The central processes of guided participation are assumed to be cross-cultural, although the activities, means of communication, skills, and values in which guided participation takes place differ. Although there is variation in *what* is being learned, there are common *opportunities* to learn through guided participation.

Two focal processes show up: "creating bridges" and "structuring children's participation." Creating bridges between what is known and what is new is part of an effort by child and caregiver to reach a common ground of understanding from which jointly to proceed. Both adult and child must make this effort at mutual adjustment. During collaborative structuring of problem solving, children's roles are structured by adults by such means as a division of responsibility. Children structure the interaction, too, by actively seeking greater involvement or by trying to change the agenda.

Rogoff's chapter is densely packed with measures and significance tests, yet I found myself much more informed, and more convinced, by the two narrative descriptions toward the chapter's end. Perhaps it reflects my own methodological tastes and the years I have spent trying to escape from the putative rigor and evident poverty of statistical explanations, but I think it is more. Rogoff and her colleagues are trying to capture—to observe, describe, and understand—complex and subtle patterns of interaction, and I believe these interactions inevitably escape simple quantification. Counting the number of sentences spoken can give us only a rough index of parental involvement; the significance of such an index must rest on an understanding of the culture, an understanding that is not gleaned from numbers. In particular, when appeal is made to notions such as the way responsibility is distributed between participants, a quantitative analysis is severely limited in its explanatory power. This carping aside, the work reported here is interesting and powerful.

Among these five, Addison Stone's chapter attends with the closest attention to the details of interaction. Stone addresses the question of how children learn in and through their interaction with others, especially adults, by taking as his starting point the metaphor of "scaffolding" that was introduced by Wood, Bruner, and Ross in 1976.

This metaphor was part of a move away from behaviorist conceptions of learning by means of imitation and modeling or reinforcement. (Therefore I am somewhat skeptical when Stone reintroduces these putative mechanisms later in his chapter.) Stone argues that the scaffolding metaphor is limited by the absence of specification of the "communicative mechanisms" whereby its effects are accomplished. Drawing on the work of Rommetveit and Grice, and building on Vygotsky's notion of the zone of proximal development, his chapter aims to highlight some of these mechanisms, extending a line of argument begun by Wertsch and Stone (1985).

This position is one I find convincing. I too have criticized scaffolding as too mechanical a metaphor. It seemed to me significant that

> literally, scaffolding is a framework that holds a passive structure in place until external efforts to construct it have been completed. . . . Both mechanical and biological metaphors miss the semantic character of human action. . . . An appreciation of the semantics of action, and the consequent polysemy and perspectival nature of social activity, is essential to the understanding of social development. Only when we recognize the intrinsic plurivocality of social exchanges—their necessary openness to several interpretations—can we begin to understand how the infant can appropriate and take over agency and expertise in social interaction. [Packer, 1987, p. 256]

How does Stone transform the notion of the zone of proximal development? Like Rogoff, he is dissatisfied with a simple "conduit" internalization as the account of what goes on when child and adult interact in the Zo-ped. Vygotsky talked about the mechanism of transfer of task-responsibility from the social level to the individual level. Wertsch and Stone proposed that Vygotsky meant not a literal "internalization" in the sense of a simple transfer from an external to an internal realm but, rather, a "much more subtle semiotic process, one that might be called 'appropriation of meaning,' or 'semiotic uptake.'" Stone seeks to articulate the details of this process by referring to notions whose origins are in linguistic, psycholinguistic, and speech act analyses of communication. The central semiotic mechanism is "prolepsis": "a communicative move in which the speaker presupposes some as yet unprovided information."

Following Rommetveit, Stone maintains that the use of prolepsis functions to set a challenge to the listener, as it requires "construction of a set of assumptions" before sense can be made. What counts as meeting the challenge? "When communication is successful, this set of assumptions will have re-created the speaker's presuppositions. Thus the listener is led to create for himself the speaker's perspective on the topic at issue."

I think that Stone has identified something important here, and that this level of detailed analysis is a necessary and illuminating one. The phenomena he has identified are of great interest, and his analysis moves us away from the notion of instruction as a simple conveying of information, as well as away from the Piagetian notion of individual construction of cognitive competence. It places adult and child in an active relationship and in an ongoing interrelationship. Nonetheless, I am troubled by the cognitive tone of Stone's description of how the mechanisms of prolepsis operate. First, who is in a position to judge when speaker and listener share a common perspective, or common assumptions? How can "perspectives" be compared, and how does one judge that two of them are similar or that one of them is shared by two people? The answer to these questions depends on what one means by a "perspective," and Stone never defines this animal precisely.

This worry aside, though, how is a change in perspective to be accomplished? Stone inclines to the view that a fresh perspective is achieved by inferential processes. The missing information must be inferred. Garfinkel (1967), making reference to prolepsis, calls for an empirical investigation of persons' communicative interactivity. Why should we presume that a single process is at work when people use "prolepsis"? Why should we assume that this process is a cognitive one of logical inference? Perhaps Stone is correct on both counts, but I think the case is not closed. Might not the kind of communicative work vary with the occasion in which prolepsis is employed? Indeed, there are interesting differences among Stone's examples of prolepsis, which might repay further study. The Museum Guard cracks a canny joke; the mother drops a hint; Speaker B nudges his interlocutor; Grice is ironic. In each case the effect is to make a point, to be striking, to draw attention, to make us become aware that things might be other than they seem. Something is pointed to (and pointed up)—the uninspiring crockery exhibit, a new way of categorizing, a secret liaison, a certain lack of skill despite good intentions—that we had probably not noticed before. Is it accurate to say that to notice these things now is to take on (let alone to have constructed) the other person's perspective? Why should we say that inference is involved and not that a new way of perceiving the situation has been inspired? The latter would be a more holistic reframing of the terms in which the task setting is understood and interpreted, whereas "inference" sounds more like a matter of drawing conclusions from premises.

What is needed to help answer these questions is more detail on the task in which the interlocutors are involved. If the material praxis of the concrete task is not given this kind of attention, the only candidate for the process or "mechanism" at work must seem to be a purely cognitive calculation. Yet it presupposes the very "internalization" that we are trying to understand and explain. The "work" done by prolepsis and other conversational devices must at least initially be done overtly and socially. There is some danger here of *abstracting* a semiotic mechanism from the particular situation of its concrete production. Once the rich details of specific cases are lost by combining them into a general, generic account, the mechanism can only be a covert cognitive. Rogoff et al. employ a parallel analytical strategy when they seek the features common to caregiver–child interaction in quite different cultures. It concerns me here that the "bathwater" might be playing a role in what is happening to the baby. To "abstract" what is being done from its setting is to risk losing sight of the situated character of the activity.

Courtney Cazden also broadens our understanding of what happens when people are transformed through social interaction by drawing our attention to the ways semiotic mechanisms operate beyond the here and now, by locating the local situation in broader communities. Words and phrases have "sense" that includes connotations drawn from both the immediate setting and the broader cultural context. In the notion of "voice," Cazden seeks a unit of analysis that integrates and unites two dimensions of language variation: *dialect*, which reflects the context of culture, and *register*, which reflects the context of local setting. To have a voice, or to find one's voice, is to find one's place, to make oneself at home in a cultural community, and to be able to be listened to in specific situations. It is to adopt a point of view (see Gilligan, 1982, for an example of the richness of voice in a different arena).

In drawing out the joint implications of Bakhtin's analysis of voice and Hymes' notion of communicative competence—both articulated in opposition to the structuralist distinction between speech (personal, immediate, and contingent) and language (an abstract, impersonal, atemporal system)—Cazden opens our eyes to the elements of struggle and cooption that socialization and education entail. It is this aspect of her chapter on which I wish to focus here. To come to "participate" in a linguistic community is not, she argues, a process without conflict: It involves the meeting and clash of divergent interests and the points of view to which these interests give rise.

It might be asked to what extent talk of expropriation and resistance is appropriate to a consideration of caregiver–child interaction. I think that indeed it is, if only insofar as it points out how we usually consider the infant either as a member of no group or as already somehow one with the adults around her. The adult culture embodies norms (manifest first as forms of basic bodily management) of emotionality, posture, gratification, and the delay of gratification of needs (Packer, 1983) that any child might be expected to resist. Even for the toddler, "mastery" and "maturity" are not without the costs, losses, and compromises that Cazden points out: loss of innocence, fragmentation, alienation. (Litowitz also makes this point.)

If I have a disagreement with Cazden, it is that she writes as though the conflict that is part of appropriating a cultural semiotic system is primarily an internal, private struggle, concerning ways of representing the world rather than ways of acting in and on it—connotations not consequences. I suspect that this emphasis is not a deliberate one; it reflects the way our thinking is still dominated by an emphasis on the epistemological. A similar remark can be directed at Rogoff's chapter: Rather than view gesture, facial expression, and so on as nonverbal communication (though of course they are), we could view talk as verbal action, as attempts to realize the local goals she discusses. Adults are not only *informing* children, they are *moving* them—emotionally, developmentally, literally, and figuratively. As Cazden says, quoting Hymes, children acquire not a grammar but a style, a way of speaking, of which a formal grammar is a precipitate. One might add that in doing so they also learn a way of acting, a way of socially comporting themselves. Words have meaning, reference, and sense; but they also have effects, products, and consequences. To speak is to act. At the same time, to act is to do more than speak. Thus I cannot agree that the clash that Bakhtin describes in Cazden's chapter between church, family, bureaucracy, and poetry for the Russian peasant is just a clash between languages: It is a clash between powerful social and political institutions. Thompson (1981) pointed out some of the limitations of the analogy between social structure and the structure of language: Language shows a relative absence of rapid change; it cannot easily account for the exercise of power and the occurrence of conflict, and it cannot adequately explain why disjunctive systems of signification come into existence.

It is true that academia is made up of communities where talking is the predominant mode of activity. Here the cultural possibilities are largely verbal and representational, and "voice" is the appropriate metaphor. Elsewhere metaphors of position, place, and perspective may work better, as we try to describe the ways people come to find a place to stand, from which they may act to bring about change.

Bonnie Litowitz undertakes the interesting task of fleshing out Vygotsky's account of learning with an account of motivation, in an attempt to broaden our understanding of learning from the narrow appropriation of skills to establishing a sense of self. Mastering activities and establishing a sense of self are, she suggests "entwined in complex ways." Like each of the other authors in this section, Litowitz is dissatisfied with a conduit or transfer account of what goes on in the Zo-ped. She points out that even conditioning and imitation can be described as the external and social becoming internal to the individual.

Litowitz argues that scaffolding, as the novice takes over the sequence of steps in a task so that what was performed "externally" by two people has "become internalized within one individual," involves a shift in the peoples' roles with respect to each another. It is a "shift from the reciprocity of equal partnership to the reversibility of equal responsibility." Identification and resistance are involved in the shift; identification, as Lacan and Freud have described it, can be seen when the child comes to speak the language of the adult. Adults identify with children when they organize tasks to sustain the fantasy that it is the child who is responsible. Conflicts and contradictions in language invoke resistance, and identification itself motivates resistance in the form of negation of the other in order to assume her role.

The power of Litowitz' analysis lies in her appreciation that to speak a language is to adopt "discursive positions relative to other people." Her chapter stands at a point of intersection between those of Stone and Cazden, though it lacks some of their detail and precision. She grants the way language functions as a sign system to point out, even by means of indirection and ellipsis, unnoticed features in a local situation; at the same time she acknowledges the interpersonal space of status and attachment of which and from which a "voice" speaks.

Yet there are consequences of trying to meld psychoanalytic views of the self with a Marxist account of the person. Although Litowitz speaks of child and adult ending up with "equal" responsibility, she also talks of responsibility as something the child or novice "takes." Autonomy and independence seem the unquestioned developmental goals here. The developmental outcome to be expected is one where the child is able to do the task independently; participation with others is a necessary, but only a temporary, phase in achieving autonomy. This view seems fundamentally at odds with a view of the child becoming an adult who occupies a place in a social world

Each of the four chapters we have considered so far has dealt with interaction between a child or student and a more expert adult. It is important not to overemphasize adults as the sole source of culture and learning. Once we take the step of considering culture as mediated by semiotic systems, it becomes apparent that peer interaction, because it is inevitably situated in an institutional context and supported by cultural mediators, embodies cultural values and beliefs as well as familiar social roles. (I have started to consider the kindergarten playground as a system of cultural constraints and resources—the ground from which cultural possibilities can be projected by the child, quite apart from direct interaction with adults.)

It is in this light that we can consider the chapter by Ellice Forman and Jean McPhail. Like the others, Forman and McPhail aim to go beyond thinking about the transfer of knowledge from expert to novice, and they seek to do it by studying young children's collaboration on a problem-solving task. They argue that research on collaborative peer interaction by both developmental psychologists and educational researchers has been misleading in two respects. First, evaluation of the cognitive effects of such interaction has focused on individual gains, often assessed outside the peer group and its activities. Second, in a parallel manner, evaluation of the motivational effects has construed them as individual beliefs and attitudes. The Vygotskian framework promises to correct both these prejudices by drawing our attention to the cultural and historical influences on people's interpretations and motivation and by emphasizing the interconnections among the intellectual, social, and motivational.

Forman and McPhail describe how two seventh-grade school children came to collaborate on a task (itself open to multiple interpretations) with geometric shapes projected onto a screen. The children differed in the speech register they employed (one scientific, the other mathematical), their definition of the task, their role during the experimental sessions, and their performance at a posttest assessment. Despite (or perhaps because of) these differences, they were able to "establish, modify, reflect on and refine their initial task goals and definitions in order to collaborate."

Forman and McPhail describe details of the children's collaboration, as well as their different perspectives on their common task, in a way that is illuminating. Their focus on the goals of the children themselves, rather than on imposing criteria from outside the task setting, is a salutary one. More work of this kind by educational researchers is needed. It would be interesting to conduct the same kind of analysis on interactions taking place not in an experimental setting but in the classroom as part of the regular curriculum. This method would provide more opportunity to examine the way children draw on the resources provided by teacher and materials to shape their academic interactions with peers. One would expect more complex and richer processes of mutual influence to become apparent if the children were given the responsibility to determine the topic, the location, timing, and duration of their collaborative tasks.

Let us now trace a few of the threads that run through all of these chapters and see what knots they form. Each chapter expresses dissatisfaction with the disarming simplicity of the view, attributed to Vygotsky in the past, that learning is straightforward internalization of social tools. Each shows that social interaction organizes learning in much more complex ways. Rogoff, Mosier, Mistry, and Goncu talk of the guided participation by which caregivers structure the social world for children, Stone speaks of the use of semiotic vehicles in such dyadic interaction, and Cazden makes good on the call they both issue to attend to the broader cultural and historical aspects of interaction by considering how language contains resonances to culture and time. Litowitz adds the dimension of construction of self to the appropriation of skills and values, and Forman and McPhail expand the discussion to include peer–peer collaboration.

This thread points out one of the strengths of the common perspective from which these authors speak: a perspective that centers our attention on social interaction not just as the *setting* of learning but as the *way* learning takes place. These chapters draw our attention to the fact that learning and development are not only *conceptually* problematic and difficult to understand, they are also problematic in *practice*. They thus have relevance for both researchers and educators. The first has the luxury of conceptualizing, the second must deal with practice. Educators have been reminded that learning presents practical problems, though perhaps we do not need reminding. E. D. Hirsch has called attention to how imperfectly shared background knowledge creates instructional dilemmas in what he called the "primal scene of education." What a teacher takes for granted when she gives instruction may not be known by the students, let alone understood.

Addison Stone's chapter deals with the same topic: the importance of fine-tuning prolepsis, where the adult presupposes in her speech information that has actually not yet been provided to the student. Stone suggested that in adult–child exchanges the appropriate degree of prolepsis both encourages and enables the child to construct for herself new assumptions and a new perspective on a joint task. That point raises the question of how a teacher can employ prolepsis appropriately in a class of 30 students whose familiarity with content varies widely. Teachers deal everyday with the practical problem of how to modify the kinds of information they take for granted when talking with students, and students must struggle to respond to prolepsis in their teacher's instruction. We still know little about how to help a student interpret the tacit aspects of teachers' speech. These chapters give us good reason to think that it is not simply a cognitive, logical matter; and they give us a language for talking about everyday interactional difficulties.

Researchers, too, can find much that is relevant in these chapters. Learning is conceptually problematic; in fact, learning is a much *mis*understood phenomenon. Forman and McPhail make a strong case for thinking that our typical research designs actually distort our understanding of learning. In particular, the common pretest–posttest design used to assess classroom learning is an inadequate one. Typically it focuses on *individual* learning, thereby removing the student from the activity setting, and from relationships with peers and teachers. Most achievement tests do the same thing, of course. It is striking that we hear so much about the need for learning that can be transferred to new tasks and new settings but often assess children's learning in a setting of social isolation that they are unlikely ever to experience again.

Let us return to one of the themes with which I began this discussion: the overcoming of dualistic conceptions of the person and development. Traditionally, we draw overly rigid distinctions between cognition and emotion, and between the intellectual and motivational. Each of the authors has explored ways in which the cognitive, the social, and the motivational aspects of learning and development come together; or perhaps it would be better to say the ways they have their joint origin in social interaction. Forman and McPhail describe children developing a personal relationship, a friendship, as they learn a cooperative task. Motivation, they argue, is inherent in cognitive change. Stone reconceptualizes scaffolding, generally considered in cognitive terms, as depending on a relationship of mutual trust and recognized expertise. Cazden describes the intrinsic tension between constraint and choice, and the resistance that can be part of learning. Litowitz sees identification and imitation as "kissing cousins."

Despite the strengths of these chapters and the programs of work they represent, I worry that there is still a creeping dualism at work. Descartes' ghost may be with us still: The processes and mechanisms being examined keep creeping back inside the head. Despite Forman and McPhail's timely reminder, we tend to interpret knowledge, goals, interests, and so on as *personal*. There is a temptation to view learning as *mental* change, *mental* reorganization—as change in an individual's internal capacity or competence. I have tried elsewhere to draw attention to the hegemony of the view that learning is a matter of an increase in or reorganization of knowledge (Packer & Addison, 1989). This dominant concern with epistemological issues precludes any reference to changes in practice or changes in *being* (including self-understanding and identity) to which learning might equally, or more closely, be seen as applicable.

Of course mental processes, as much as any other kind of solitary activity, can be social; but there is a temptation to interpret the internalization that results from learning in the zone of proximal development as a movement directed toward autonomy and independence—as the production of an individual who contains all the culture's tools, even though those tools have been reconstructed in the process. In such an account, the person is indeed social in *origin,* but the *outcome* is an autonomous, solitary individual. The desire to escape the clutches of such a view motivates, I think, rejection of the simple internalization theory of learning by each of these authors, but, like the return of the repressed, traces of it linger.

It would be truer to the Vygotskian framework, surely, to view learning as a change in activity, in the structure of behavior, and in a person's mode of engagement in social practices. Hence children learn when they are "empowered" in their interaction with others, when they have become effectively socialized into participating in shared cultural practices. Such practices include solitary activities (e.g., contemplation), but by and large they are interpersonal practices that require cooperation. It is for this reason that on several occasions while reviewing these chapters I have wished for a still more detailed examination of the social interchanges.

Such an analysis would need to attend to each of the three levels reflected in the organization of this book. The broad cultural and institutional context, the local setting (e.g., the classroom) as a social meeting place, and the interpersonal relationships that are played out there are not so much separate levels of analysis as they are aspects of social reality linked *in the practice* of real persons. That seems to me to be a powerful and central notion that the Vygotskian perspective must convey to the larger community of researchers and to which it must itself remain true. I have reason to think that the appropriate method for such an analysis would be hermeneutic in some respects, but I save the justification of that opinion for another place and time. It would require the recognition that researchers are situated persons too. Creeping dualism is exposed by the "lollipop test." Do we treat the people we study as lollipops: as all brain and no body? Or do they have their feet on the ground, a ground that is both epistemological and ontological, the ground that culture and tradition provide for each of us? We tend to forget this ground because it is always with us, but then we misunderstand what happens in educational settings. Similarly, we must avoid treating ourselves as lollipops, as disembodied brains who observe children in a detached manner. We have feet to move toward them and hands to help them in their practical activities. That concept is just one exciting new avenue opened up by the Vygotskian perspective.

References

Garfinkel, H. (1967). *Studies in ethnomethodology.* Englewood Cliffs, NJ: Prentice-Hall.

Gilligan, C. (1982). *In a different voice: psychological theory and women's development.* Cambridge, MA: Harvard University Press.

Heidegger, M. (1927/1962). *Being and time.* (J. Macquarrie & E. Robinson, trans.). New York: Harper & Row.

Minick, N. (1985). L. S. Vygotsky and Soviet activity theory: new perspectives on the relationship between mind and society. Unpublished doctoral dissertation, Northwestern University, Evanston, Illinois.

Minick, N. (1989). Mind and activity in Vygotsky's work: an expanded frame of reference. *Cultural dynamics, 2,* 162–187.

Packer, M. J. (1983). Communication in infancy: three common assumptions examined and found inadequate. *Human Development, 26,* 233–48.

Packer, M. J. (1985). Hermeneutic inquiry in the study of human conduct. *American Psychologist, 40,* 1081–93.

Packer, M. J. (1987). Social interaction as practical activity: implications for the study of social and moral development. In W. Kurtines & J. Gewirtz (eds.). *Moral development through social interaction* (pp. 245–80). New York: Wiley.

Packer, M. J., & Addison, R. B. (eds.) (1989). *Entering the circle: hermeneutic investigation in psychology.* Albany: State University of New York Press.

Thompson, J. D. (1981). *Critical hermeneutics: a study in the thought of Paul Ricoeur and Jurgen Habermas.* New York: Cambridge University Press.

Wertsch, J. V., & Stone, C. A. (1985). The concept of internalization in Vygotsky's account of the genesis of higher mental functions. In J. V. Wertsch (ed.). *Culture, communication, and cognition: Vygotskian perspectives* (pp. 162–79). New York: Cambridge University Press.

III

SOCIOCULTURAL INSTITUTIONS OF FORMAL AND INFORMAL EDUCATION

11

Institutional and Social Context of Educational Practice and Reform

ROLAND THARP

The conservatism, not to say fierce resistance, of schools when faced with forces of change has been both puzzle and consternation for educational reformers. Every reform theorist, regardless of the particular focus or prescription, bemoans this apparent impermeability to reason, common sense, political forces, or even budgetary variation—and it is despite a clear hunger felt by teachers for new and useful ideas. Thus schools in North America embrace wave after wave of fads; enthuse, co-opt, and trivialize them; sweep on in an inexhaustible appetite for stimulation; and—as regards fundamentals—change not at all. The most profound calls for reform appear not even to be heard, for example that of Sarason, made 20 years ago, which sadly remains as apt today as then:

> Schools are not created to foster the intellectual and professional growth of teachers. The assumption that teachers can create and maintain those conditions which make school learning and school living stimulating for children, without those same conditions existing for teachers, has no warrant in the history of man. That the different efforts to improve the education of children have been remarkably short of their mark is in part [due to] . . . ways of thinking, to a view of technology, to ways of training, and to modes of organization which make for one grand error of misplaced emphasis. . . . [Sarason, 1972, pp. 123–24]

If only for the sake of argument and demonstration, let us accept the wisdom of this statement from one of the leading educational researchers and theorists of this century. Let us take it that educational reform requires a reorganization of schools into true learning communities, in which there is provision for teachers' intellectual and professional growth, in the service of the development of the pupils' potential. If so, we must ask: Why this grand error and this misplaced emphasis? Why has there been generation after generation of failure to re-form schools into learning communities?

This question provides an opportunity to demonstrate the utility of sociohistorical, neo-Vygotskian theory for the understanding of educational problems at the institutional and cultural level. Although the most usual level of analysis in neo-Vygotskian studies of education is the teaching/

learning interaction, the concepts are by no means restricted to that level. Even though the final common pathway of all educational reform must be the teaching/learning activity between teacher and student, an institutional analysis of contemporary education can reveal the forces of stasis that hold back reformist assaults and thereby prevent the significant improvement of the teaching/learning activities themselves. Indeed, we must look to the institutional level to understand deeply ingrained patterns of teacher–student interaction.

The neo-Vygotskian structure of ideas is well suited to such an analysis because psychological and social events are discussed with the same concepts, in a shared lexicon, and in a common web of meanings. Such unities allow us to see parallels and isomorphisms, as well as discontinuities, in psychological and social structures.

In this analysis, and through these parallels, I hope to show that the processes of school instruction are reflected and supported in structures at the level of school organization, and at the community, cultural, and national levels of concept meaning. These interlocking structures provide an apparently unassailable wall of defense that helps to account for school conservatism. Although having these relationships in sight may allow us to prescribe remedies more intelligently, it is more likely that it will sober us as we plan reformist campaigns. The conclusion of this analysis provides at least one surprise. We should not be puzzled at the lack of educational reform; the wonder is that there is any change, ever.

In this analysis, I use a limited number of sociocultural concepts, namely: the zone of proximal development, assisted performance, activity setting, word meaning, and intersubjectivity. These concepts by no means exhaust the neo-Vygotskian lexicon but are sufficient for this exploratory and demonstration analysis. The concepts have been defined and used elsewhere in this volume and in the literature. With the exception of *activity setting* and *assisted performance* I depend on those previous treatments, rather than repeating them.

Recitation Script and Nonteaching

Since the last century, "teaching" in North American classrooms has consisted almost entirely of *assigning tasks,* particularly the reading of *textbooks,* and *assessing* performance—assign/assess, assign/assess—the infamous "recitation script" that has been characteristic of North American schooling, at least since the early nineteenth century (Hoetker & Ahlbrand, 1969). "Recitation" has been described in the educational literature for more than 90 years and continues today as a major portion of all student and teacher interactions (Bennett, 1986). Its basic operation is to assign a text for students to learn on their own and then assess the students to see if they learned it. It consists in a series of unrelated teacher questions that require convergent factual answers and student display of (presumably) known information, acquired almost entirely from an assigned textbook. It includes up to 20% "yes/no" questions. Only rarely during recitation are teacher questions responsive to student productions. Only rarely are questions used to assist students to develop more complete or elaborated ideas (Tharp & Gallimore, 1988).

This dismal portrait does not describe some few unlucky or deprived communities. Goodlad (1984) reported a similar picture in his broadly based survey of 38 U.S. schools. Even the contemporary enthusiasm for effective teaching "scripts" have not changed the nature of student–teacher interaction. In its worst forms, scripted teaching is little more than the recitation script of earlier eras. It emphasizes rote learning and student passivity, facts and low-level questions, and low-level cognitive functions.

The following is an excerpt from a small group reading lesson for first-grade students who have been working on a small story in a basal reader. The students have just finished re-reading a small section, and the teacher is now "teaching" them by means of the recitation script.

Teacher: Okay, Was Reggie's sister able to change his mind?

Student: No.

T: No. Why? Why was Ira going to stand firm? What did he find out?

S: [*Inaudible*]

T: He knew that Reggie wouldn't laugh at him. So did that give him the courage to go through with what he wanted to do?

S: Yes.

T: Did it matter if his sister was going to tease him?

S: No.

T: Okay. So it's not important to him anymore.

. . . .

T: Look at Ira on [this] page. What's he saying to Reggie?

S: Wake up.

T: Why does he want him to get up?

S: Because he wants to show him his teddy bear.

T: Because he wants to show his teddy bear and what else? Why else would he want him to get up? What were they doing before he fell asleep?

This dialogue is better than most recitation-script transcripts. There is at least some interaction here and some brisk talk. Sadly, it is a "better" example of conventional "teaching."

True Teaching—Responsive Teaching

My efforts in educational reform have been to change that dismaying condition. Ironic as it may be, *there is little teaching to be found in education* (Gallimore & Tharp, 1990; Tharp, 1989; Tharp & Gallimore, 1988). By that

I mean that we fail to see interactive teaching, in which the instructor assists pupils, face to face and actively, to extend their capacities for performance.

As we know from every review of teaching research, *responsive,* interactive teaching is seldom used by teachers in classrooms. This situation must be changed (Bennett, 1986): Students cannot be left to learn on their own; teachers cannot be content to provide opportunities to learn and then assess outcomes; and recitation must be deemphasized. Responsive, assisting interactions must become commonplace in the classroom.

Assisted performance is the key concept here, and by it I mean interactions that (1) begin with the child's current level of understanding; (2) consequently allow the child a meaningful role in the setting of the instructional task or goal; (3) include helping behaviors by the teacher that assist the student to pursue these goals and move from that level to the next; by (4) pulling performance from the child, so a productive communication or creation by the child is the vehicle for instantiating new knowledge. When teachers assist performance in this way, they are clearly responsive to the students' previously existing knowledge base or performance capacity and remain responsive to advances in the students' capacities. They do not work from a predefined recitation script but act responsively and flexibly to reach instructional goals.

These instructional goals themselves may be identical to those of teachers who operate a recitation script, but the responsive teacher takes a route toward those goals that is drawn in collaboration with the child and is responsive to the child's emerging capacities. The route is set by drawing the child forward into that zone just beyond current capacity.

In Vygotskian terms, teaching is good only when it "awakens and rouses to life those functions that are in a stage of maturing, that lie in the *zone of proximal development*" (Vygotsky, 1956, p. 278, quoted by Wertsch & Stone, 1985). We can therefore derive a general definition of teaching: *Teaching* consists in assisting performance through the zone of proximal development (ZPD). Teaching can be said to occur when assistance is offered at points in the ZPD where performance requires assistance. Teaching must be redefined as assisted performance. Teaching is occurring when performance is achieved with assistance.

Hence teaching is not only assessing learners, it is assisting them. Elsewhere I have discussed at length the means by which assistance is offered in teaching/learning (Tharp, 1984; Tharp & Gallimore, 1988, Tharp & Note, 1988). In brief, there are seven means of assisting performance and facilitating learning, and they have been studied with enough breadth and time that the effects are known and dependable.

1. *Modeling:* offering behavior for imitation. Modeling assists by giving the learner information and a remembered image that can serve as a performance standard.
2. *Feedback:* the process of providing information on a performance as it compares to a standard. Feedback is essential in assisting perfor-

mance because it allows the performance to be compared to the standard and thus allows self-correction. Feedback assists performance in every domain from tennis to nuclear physics. Ensuring feedback is the most common and single most effective form of self-assistance (Watson & Tharp, 1988).

3. *Contingency management:* application of the principles of reinforcement and punishment to behavior.

4. *Instructing:* requesting specific *action*. It assists by selecting the correct response and by providing clarity, information, and decision making. It is most useful when the learner can perform some segments of the task but cannot yet analyze the entire performance or make judgments about the elements to choose.

5. *Questioning:* a request for a *verbal* response that assists by producing a mental operation the learner cannot or would not produce alone. This interaction assists further by giving the assistor information about the learner's developing understanding.

6. *Cognitive structuring:* "explanations." Cognitive structuring assists by providing explanatory and belief structures that organize and justify new learning and perceptions and allow the creation of new or modified schemata.

7. *Task structuring:* chunking, segregating, sequencing, or otherwise structuring a task into or from components. It assists learners by modifying the task itself, so the units presented to the learner fit into the ZPD when the entire unstructured task is beyond that zone.

When these means are orchestrated into a flowing interaction, in which the goal of the assistor is to bring the performance of the learner through the ZPD into an independent capacity, and when the means of assistance are woven into a meaningful dialogue during joint activity, there exists the *instructional conversation,* the sine qua non of teaching. The instructional conversation is not beyond the reach of ordinary mortals; extended examples and transcripts, from kindergarten to in-service training, are readily available (Gallimore & Tharp, 1990; Tharp & Gallimore, 1988).

The following excerpt is an example of an instructional conversation between a teacher and a small group of first-grade children who are struggling to understand the plot and motivations in a piece of fiction they are reading (Tharp & Gallimore, 1988, p. 240).

Teacher: What did Cucullan say when he came over to Fin McCool's home?

Summie & Louise: Is Fin McCool at home?

Teacher: Ammm.

Kanani: She said, "No, Fin McCool is not home."

Issac: He went out to look for a giant named Cucullan.

Teacher: Ahum.

Summie: His wife said Fin McCool is stronger but he said "I'll show you who's strong."

Teacher: Okay. What could he do to show his strength?

Kanani: Lif' up the house.

Teacher: Alright. How is he going to do this?

Issac: Use his magic fingers.

Teacher: Aha. Using that . . . okay. What else could he do to show his strength?

Issac: By sweating.

Teacher: You show your strength by sweating? How do you show your strength by sweating?

Tosufa: You go like this [*child flexes her muscles*].

Teacher: Okay. What do you call it when you do that?

Louise: Show his muscles.

Teacher: Yes. Show his muscles. But does that show how strong you are?

Issac: Soft muscles.

Teacher: That you have soft or hard muscles? What could he do to show his strength?

Kanani: Lift up a tree.

Teacher: Lift up a tree. Sure. What else?

Summie: Lift up somebody's house.

Teacher: Alright. Turn to the next two pages. . . .

[*Students turn page*]

Summie: Wow. He lift up the house.

These children were assisted in their performance by a variety of means: questioning, contingency management, instructions, task structuring, and feedback. The teacher was not thinking about any formal analysis of her assistance; she was being driven by an effort to comprehend the students' thinking so she could lead them to the next level in the ZPD. There is no "telling" the students about the text; in fact, at various points in the lesson, the teacher began declarative statements and then transformed them into questions. This kind of conversation, in which topic control is shared and each participant responds to other speakers and to the text, is genuine teaching. Yet the segment is smooth and conversational. There are no abrupt changes of topic. The teacher's questions genuinely assist the children to assemble the thoughts needed to comprehend the story. It should also be noted that even such brief quality conversation is rare in classrooms because it requires the building of a set of student expectations based on reliable teacher performance of assistance, responsiveness, and respect for the gradually developing competencies of children.

We may now return to our central concern about why the school does not turn itself into a community of learners. We see that the school is neither a community of learning nor a community of teaching, in that the final common pathway of education, the teaching/learning interaction, is not one of assisting performance. Some critics seem to suggest that a dilute and lackadaisical teaching profession is enforcing, through passive resistance, some low energy performance standards. To blame teachers would be misguided indeed, however, as they are the educational product, and the supervisory responsibility, of a whole chain of educational institutions and authorities that, far from teaching teachers to teach, are teaching no one either.

No One Is Teaching Anyone

If little actual teaching occurs in schools, if teachers do not teach children, let us be clear that colleges of education are not teaching anyone either. It follows, then, that professors of education do not teach principals, principals do not teach grade-level chairs, curriculum specialists do not teach teachers. Educational administrators teach no one, and neither do educational researchers. The educational establishment is organized as a series of unconnected independent positions, each believing that somewhere below them, surely someone is teaching someone. We must grant that each position attempts to create educational opportunities for those down the chain— good textbooks, good workshops, even good performance objectives—but no one attends to assisting the performance of those objectives. By the definition of teaching we have established, instances of true teaching in the educational world are so exceptional that each of us remembers them, as small epiphanies.

So let us acknowledge that we are complicitous in this state of affairs. Educators all, and we do not teach. To lay the blame on teachers is to ignore that they are the product of the entire massive engine of education. Each of us presides over activities of learning, so that (figuratively when not literally) each professor, principal, and teacher proctors their pupils' reading of assigned texts, administers quizzes, and awards certificates to those above criterion. Learning, we say to the learners, is your problem.

We know what true teaching is—well enough to practice it, install it, study it, and continue to improve it. It is fruitless to look further into theories of teaching for an explanation of schools' resistance to this reform. To understand why we decline to do it requires another theory, a theory of schooling itself, one that treats the sociocultural organization of schools.

Analyzing Schooling: Activity Setting as Basic Unit for Analysis

The basic unit necessary for analyzing schooling and its society in neo-Vygotskian theory is the activity setting. The activity setting is a construct that unites (1) objective features of the setting and environment and (2) objective features of the motoric and verbal actions of the participants with (3) subjective features of the participants' experience, intention, and meaning. Combining these elements into a single construct is arguably the most important innovation of the neo-Vygotskian, sociohistorical movement.

Radically disconcerting to Western social science because it immediately requires discourse among the separated disciplines of semantics, sociology, anthropology, linguistics, cognitive studies, and behaviorism, it is nevertheless a new beginning of the study of life at the level and in the units in which we live and experience it.

Thus activity settings may be described in terms of the who, what, when, where, and whys of everyday life in school, home, community, and workplace. These features of personnel, occasion, motivations and meanings, goals, places, and times are intertwined conditions that together comprise the reality of life and learning. For example, the life of a school can be described in terms of its activity settings. Examples of activity settings for students would include whole-class settings, laboratory partnerships, small cooperative learning groups, debates, drama rehearsals. Activity settings for adult members of school organizations include faculty committees, peer coaching groups, workshops, individual teacher consultation by outside experts, grade-level committee meetings, or curriculum revision groups (O'Donnell & Tharp, 1990; Tharp & Gallimore, 1988; Tharp & Note, 1988).

As can be seen from those examples, it is common for activity settings to be nested. That is, depending on the purpose of analysis, one may consider a single classroom as an activity setting, or, for finer-grained analysis, several activity settings can be identified as operating, or nested, within the class—the teacher-led small discussion group, the student clean-up committee, the worktable for map-drawing. In the actual community, these levels sometimes operate in such smooth integration that boundaries are not discernible; in others the activity setting can re-form into nested components with sharp demarcations, as when the whole cooperating third-grade classroom adjourns the rehearsal of its Thanksgiving pageant and begins its science laboratory groups.

This nestedness is characteristic of all community institutions. Indeed as the community is nested within the larger context, all microsettings can be seen as nested within macrosettings.

This analysis has a profound importance, far beyond the objective mapping of schools' time and space. It is because activity settings are the events during which collaborative interaction, accompanied by speech and other semiotic events, *can* create intersubjectivity. It is through joint productive activity that shared word meanings, concepts, motivations, beliefs, and expectations are acquired. The activity setting is the social process common to the participants from which cognitive processes and structures of meaning develop, and activity settings are therefore the units by which community and cultural life are propagated.

It is also in activity settings, and only there, that assisted performance can occur; and therefore these settings are the processes that must be reorganized to allow for true teaching. Because activity settings are nested, a fundamental institutional reorganization is needed if the instructional activity settings are to be reliably produced in the classroom.

With present conditions, schools almost entirely lack these jointly productive activity settings. Reformers insistently call for peer coaching or joint problem-solving sessions because the teacher, prisoner-queen in her classroom, is isolated from opportunity for professional interaction, feedback, or shared functioning. Even schoolchildren have inadequate settings of cooperative learning, thereby necessitating the vigorous reform movement that bears that name. Joint productive activity settings, involving supervisors or consultants with teachers, are almost unheard of.

Joint productive activity settings are not guaranteed merely by having meetings. Teachers do meet informally in the teachers' lounge, but those settings do not involve production. Routine Wednesday afternoon staff meetings for all school personnel are not unusual, but those meetings are used for announcements and conducting business. "Staff development" sessions rarely involve either jointness or productivity because they are most often class-like lectures or other forms of programmed activities, not joint problem-solving, productive goal-oriented conversation-laden building of intersubjectivities during which members of a variety of administrative levels are available for mutual assistance.

Indeed, schools are not organized to assist the performance—to teach—their members; rather, they are organized up and down the line to assign-and-assess. This same pattern pervades not only the classroom but the entire educational apparatus, from the top to the bottom of its activity settings. The administrative/bureaucratic practice of assigning-and-assessing the staff's adherence to curricula, learning objectives, and regulations is organically related to the classroom practice of assigning-and-assessing the recitation script. At neither level is there sufficient assistance, responsiveness, joint productive activity, or the building of common meanings and values. Teachers have virtually no interaction with their supervisors; when they do, they are expected to "recite," be assessed, and receive directions. The recitation script is everywhere—in the classroom, the board room, and the principal's office.

Organizing Schools for Teaching

A basic condition for effective activity settings is "jointness." Without it, the supervisor cannot assist performance, affect cognitive structures of learners, or be affected by the emerging group intersubjectivity. Professors, teachers, principals, curriculum specialists, and other authorities direct their pupils/subordinates to accomplish a task but do not participate in the productive work itself. It means that they lose the opportunity to develop joint understanding, even that minimal understanding that would allow them to assess their subordinates adequately. Joint activity requires dual input, which in turn allows sharing perspectives and the emergence of shared understanding. Because intersubjectivity does not develop, the power layers of the school remain separated; because the power cannot be mobilized, the great engine puffs in place, huffing at intruders and going nowhere.

As a general rule, every member of the school community should be engaged in some setting of joint productive activity with someone at a different level of authority. This simple rule would provide for each assistor participating at all times in at least one activity setting with the assistee(s).

How could it be brought about? The responsibility of each authority in the school—professor, supervisor, principal, superintendent, principal, and teacher—should be reordered. The first priority should not be to assign-and-assess but, rather, to organize activity settings in which joint work and talk takes place, participants are assisted by other participants, and common cause can be found and made; they should also make resources of time, place, persons, and tools available to those activity settings. Supervision in schools should be redefined as assisting performance in precisely the terms we used to define teaching. Only then can schools be communities of learners. One of the duties of each individual in a school system should be to assist the performance of the person next down the line: The superintendent assists the principal, the principal assists the teacher, the teacher assists the pupils. This assistance, with its accompanying cognitive and behavioral development, should be the justifying goal of the school. All other duties should be in its service.

The basic principle for the design of effective assistance is to marshal the sources that can assist the performance of those down the supervisory chain and to eliminate the sources that hinder or obstruct that performance. Good design and management of assisted performance requires the creation of appropriate activity settings.

Schools must be organized to provide time and resources to assist teacher performance, so they may acquire the skills and knowledge needed to truly teach. It does not mean that high authority must engineer the social organization of the school from atop the tower. A community of learners is incongruent with a system that fully scripts teaching practice or fully scripts teachers' roles. Teachers must have sufficient autonomy, authority, and warrant from the school system to assist each other in their problem-solving and professional growth, as well as the authority to organize their own activities and agenda; they must also be able to spend the required joint productive time and to enlist the assistance of others with the desired knowledge. In this way, each person in the community of the school would have a part in planning for their own assistance. Administrators would have the responsibility to assist teachers to organize themselves to provide for their own assistance. In such schools each member would be engaged in joint productive activity, which includes assisted performance, and a reliable traversal of successive zones of proximal development. These conditions are necessary for learning and are the conditions required for teaching. Such schools would indeed be communities where all learn because all teach.

We have elaborated elsewhere the principles and practices of reforming schools (Tharp & Gallimore, 1988; Tharp & Note, 1988) and other institutions (O'Donnell & Tharp, 1990) through the design of activity settings. Here let us focus on the central question of resistance to change. Even if we grant the accuracy of the analysis and the warrant of the prescription, can we expect schools to adopt the modest proposals required to become communities of learners?

Schools in the Context of Society

[T]he links between dyadic or small group interactions and the broader sociocultural system must be recognized and explored . . . actions are at one and the same time components of the life of the individual and the social system. . . . No less than the action of an individual, the action of a dyad or small group is a component in the social system. Correspondingly, the intermental action and the social interaction that makes that action possible will be defined and structured in certain respects by the broader social and cultural system. [Minick, 1985, p. 257]

Schools are incorporated into the larger society and have that as their context, and many features of school social structure are conditioned by the larger society. At the simplest level, democratic America is a social context that is reflected in the school-based activity settings of student officers meeting in school government. Societal shifts bring about changes in school activity settings, for example, the disappearance of school prayer in a secularizing society.

In a more subtle sense, the activity settings of the school are conditioned by the activity settings that link schools to the social context. Consider, for example, the parallelisms among the recitation script, the assign-and-assess methods of school management, and the typical treatment of schools by their directing political bodies. Just as teachers treat students in the recitation script, schools themselves are given certain "texts" to master in the form of regulations and authorizations, and they are from time to time assessed or audited to determine if they are in compliance with those texts. Little assistance, understanding, responsiveness, or genuine dialogue occurs among policymakers and the schools. Just as the recitation-teacher responds to students, so the legislatures, school boards, and trustees respond to the administrators of their schools: If the assessment is "failed," the text is reassigned; if the assessment is satisfactory, new texts are assigned (new laws or regulations passed), and another round of assessment, reward, and punishment rolls on.

At the most fundamental level, the activity setting of "school" itself is conditioned by social context in that the very meaning of the word "school" is provided by society. Each person who touches on schools in any way, from the third-grade teacher through elected school boards and every member of the tax-paying populace, has an investment in the concept. "School" is a structure of meaning that is widely shared over all the communities and generations that have themselves been educated in the recitation script-dominated classroom. Indeed, "School" is one of the few major concepts of contemporary life whose meaning is shared by virtually all living people in

North America. Schools, consisting of assign-and-assess activity settings, were the same before the American Civil War as they are today: Everyone knows of what schools consist, and everyone knows what school means.

In the Vygotskian sense, "word meaning" provides a link between social organization and individual psychological events because the denotative, connotative, and affective components of word meaning are acquired during discourse accompanying action. Words are the stuff of the plane of consciousness. Common word meaning is the condition of intersubjectivity. When virtually an entire society is in agreement on the meaning of a major and pervasive social institution, it shall not be moved. Indeed, the individual who veers from such a widely intersubjectivized concept risks intellectual and emotional disruption and social reactions as though there were betrayal. One of the principal assessments all schools must pass is that they meet the criteria contained in the shared vision of the old-time school. For this criterion, any reform fails the assessment. Thus enormous homeostatic forces mobilize to bring a drifting school back into compliance. Any social system attempts to restore deviation from the shared internalized symbols of its meaning structures; hence schools wander off the well-worn path at their peril.

This reasoning is the basis of the arch-conservatism of schooling in America. School and society consist of an interlocking series of protocols for activity settings in which authority assigns-and-assesses, learners recite, and—by a neo-Vygotskian definition of teaching—no one teaches anyone. These nested activity settings, from classroom to whole society, have existed over a long historical period, during which common cognitive and affective meaning have become widely attached to the concept of school. Thus reformers are offensive not only to educational professionals. The conservative force that effectively blocks changes in schooling rises within the populace itself in a definitive exemplification of the power of a culturally shared intersubjectivity.

Can Schools Ever Be Reformed?

Of course, schools do change because society itself is not a stable context. Such historical changes have been documented, most ably by Reid (1987), Borrowman (1956), and Warren (1985), who have discussed the shifting social conditions during the nineteenth century that provided for changes in the roles of teachers and the physical settings for instruction. These changes, however, are attributable not to some educational reformers but to changes in the expectations of society accompanying urbanization and the Industrial Revolution. Furthermore, these shifts occur at a tectonic pace, which experienced in biographical time feels like stasis.

To observe that schools change is not the same as declaring them subject to reform. "Reform," in the sense of imposing rapid, drastic change on the schools by force of public policy or through persuasion by experts, is a far different matter and one about which we must reserve judgment. As a contemporary example, let us consider one reform movement that appears to have the brightest hope for widespread adoption. The cooperative learning movement, if it succeeds, will do so less because of the research evidence of its effectiveness than because it has some credibility with business and industry leaders who know well that teamwork is emerging as a necessary skill for corporate, managerial, and even technical success. Nevertheless, cooperative learning encounters the same massive inertia that meets all violations of the meaning of school. Our analysis here leads us to suggest that cooperative learning—so long as the management of schools continues to be in the authoritarian assign-and-assess activity settings—will be no more than a passing fad, rapidly digested and quickly expelled. We cannot expect any change in the classroom to be maintained without parallel and supporting activity-setting protocols that interweave the subjective goals, meanings, and values of the entire school. In this instance, we cannot expect cooperatively learning students to persist unless there are cooperatively learning teachers, principals, and professors.

Likewise, the rare school that might so organize itself is not allowed to persist unless the surrounding social context is involved in the learning of a new meaning of school. Whether the needs of business and industry are sufficient to change the understanding of the tax-paying public is another question, and tracking the movement of these ideas through society would provide a natural experiment of great interest to sociocultural theorists and educators. For example, there are many instances in which industry is directly relating to schools, and indeed directly supporting them, in joint efforts to improve school performance. We can also expect that the long-term effects on schools will be formed by the characteristics of the activity settings at the interface of business and school. We will see the preview of the classrooms of the future in the way those groups work together. If these activity settings—organized for problem solving and negotiation and the development of joint understandings and goals—are organized cooperatively, eventually we will see in those schools cooperative classrooms. To the extent that these initial activity settings are conducted in protocols standard for uncompetitive business and underproductive schools, little reform will trickle down, and what does will not survive.

We can thus deduce the strategy necessary for school reform, including making school into a teaching/learning community of assisting performance. It can be formulated simply: design activity settings for school and its social context that will themselves exemplify the reforms intended for the classroom, thereby building intersubjectivities among school and community members that will redefine school. Easier to propose than to do! The task requires more than rhetoric, more than demonstration data, and more than money.

Although this analysis is sobering, we may be grateful for the emergence of sociocultural theory, as it provides a conceptual structure that guides reform energy into appropriate effort. The rock that reform must roll is heavier than we thought; but it is better to push at it than to stand shouting at a brick wall.

References

Bennett, W. J. (1986). *First lessons: a report on elementary education in America.* Washington, DC: US Government Printing Office.

Borrowman, M. (1956). *The liberal and technical in teacher education: a historical survey of American thought.* New York: Teachers College, Columbia University.

Gallimore, R., & Tharp, R. G. (1990). Teaching mind and society: a theory of education and schooling. In L. Moll (ed.). *Vygotsky and education: instructional implications and applications of sociohistorical psychology* (pp. 175–205). Cambridge: Cambridge University Press.

Goodlad, J. (1984). *A place called school.* New York: McGraw-Hill.

Hoetker, J., & Ahlbrand, W. (1969). The persistence of recitation. *American Educational Research Journal, 6,* 145–67.

Minick, N. J. (1985). L. S. Vygotsky and Soviet activity theory: new perspectives on the relationship between mind and society. Unpublished doctoral dissertation, Northwestern University.

O'Donnell, C. R., & Tharp, R. G. (1990). Community intervention guided by theoretical development. In Bellack, A. S., Hersen, M., & Kazdin, A. E. (eds.). *International handbook of behavior modification and therapy,* 2nd ed. (pp. 251–266). New York: Plenum Press.

Reid, W. A. (1987). Institutions and practices: professional education reports and the language of reform. *Educational Researcher, 16*(8).

Sarason, S. B. (1972). *The creation of settings and the future societies.* San Francisco: Jossey-Bass.

Tharp, R. G. (1984). The triadic model. In J. A. Tucker (ed.). *School psychology in the classroom: a case study tutorial.* Minneapolis, MN: National School Psychology In-service Training Network, University of Minnesota.

Tharp, R. G. (1989). Culturally compatible education: a formula for designing effective classrooms. In Trueba, H. T., Spindler, G. & Spindler, L. (eds.). *What do anthropologists have to say about dropouts?* New York: The Falmer Press.

Tharp, R. G., & Gallimore, R. (1988). *Rousing minds to life: teaching and learning in social context.* New York: Cambridge University Press.

Tharp, R. G., & Note, M. (1988). The triadic model of consultation: new developments. In F. West (ed.). *School consultation: interdisciplinary perspectives on theory, research, training, and practice* (pp. 35–51). Austin: Research and Training Project on School Consultation, The University of Texas at Austin; and Association of Educational and Psychological Consultants, Austin, TX.

Vygotsky, L. S. (1956). *Izbrannie psibhologicheskie issledovania* [Selected psychological research]. Moscow: Izdateel'stro Akademii Pedagogicheskikh Nak.

Warren, D. (1985) Learning from experience: history and teacher education. *Educational Researcher, 14*(10), 5–12.

Watson, D. R., & Tharp, R. G. (1988). *Self-directed behavior* (5th ed.). Monterey, CA: Brooks/Cole.

Wertsch, J. V., & Stone, C. A. (1985). The concept of internalization in Vygotsky's account of the genesis of higher mental functions. In J. V. Wertsch (ed.). *Culture, communication, and cognition: Vygotskian perspectives* (pp. 162–79). New York: Cambridge University Press.

12

Generation and Transmission of Shared Knowledge in the Culture of Collaborative Learning: The Fifth Dimension, Its Play-World, and Its Institutional Contexts

AGELIKI NICOLOPOULOU and MICHAEL COLE

One of the most central and distinctive principles of the Vygotskian perspective is that the formation of mind is essentially and inescapably a sociocultural process; consequently, it can be grasped only by situating individual development in its sociocultural context. However, as various scholars have recently pointed out—including the editors of this volume, as well as Wertsch (1985), Goodnow (1990), and Nicolopoulou (1991, 1993)—a great deal of the research that has associated itself with the ideas of Vygotsky has focused only on certain limited aspects of the social embeddedness of thought and intellectual development. In particular, with a few exceptions—among which we include some of our own earlier work (Newman, Griffin, & Cole, 1989; Nicolopoulou, 1989; Scribner & Cole, 1981)—it has tended to conceive of the "social" or interpsychological context of development exclusively in terms of face-to-face interaction in dyadic pairs (or, rarely, in small groups).

This exclusive focus on face-to-face interaction, however, involves a truncated and inadequate conception of the sociocultural dimension of Vygotsky's theory. While the investigation of dyadic interaction accords with the primary object of analysis in most of Vygotsky's own empirical research, it taps only one element of his larger project—and, taken in isolation, does not do justice to the potential value of his theoretical perspective considered as a whole. Vygotskian research needs to move beyond this narrow focus, to address more systematically the larger institutional and cultural contexts within which face-to-face interactions occur and that structure their nature and impact. However, it is worth emphasizing that many of the key resources for doing so can be drawn from the unexplored (or underdeveloped) possibilities within the Vygotskian perspective itself.

The research presented in this chapter represents one such attempt to utilize a more comprehensive conception of the social embeddedness of thought and individual development. Furthermore, it proposes one method by which the creation and transmission of knowledge can effectively be approached as a genuinely collective enterprise, inextricably embedded in ongoing systems of shared activity. Thus it attempts to move, in two inter-connected ways, beyond the limitations we have just outlined: first, by sit-uating specific interactions in the context of a cultural and institutional framework that is understood as a genuinely *collective* reality, thereby avoid-ing the interactional reductionism implicit in much Vygotskian-inspired research; and, second, by finding a way to study genuinely *collaborative* learning, primarily by tracing the generation and transmission of *shared* knowledge.

The research is based on a close examination of the quality of the learn-ing experiences of children participating in the "Fifth Dimension," an after-school educational program in which we are involved. In particular, we focus here on one element of this program and compare its operation and consequences in two different branches of the program. Specifically, we trace the ways that two different instances of a specific task-activity—vir-tually identical in terms of their conceptual content and material equip-ment—developed very different patterns of operation and of cognitive results over the course of a year; and we show how these differences were the result of their being embedded in different sociocultural contexts. [For an elaboration of prior work on the problem of the relation between activities and their contexts, see Lave (1988) and Newman et al. (1989).]

The logic of this contextual analysis involves two (concentric) steps: (1) Most crucially, we examine the ways in which specific activities and inter-actions are embedded in, and are shaped by, the context formed by the cul-ture of each Fifth Dimension branch. The key point is that the culture of each site is a *collective* reality, not just the sum of interactions (as we explain, it is an activity *system*). The same task evolves differently and has a different meaning within two different group-cultural contexts. (2) We examine the interaction between the internal dynamics of each of these branches of the Fifth Dimension program and the larger context formed by the structure and culture of the host institution within which each was located. In partic-ular, we focus on the ways in which the culture of each Fifth Dimension site is influenced by the cultural and institutional framework of its institutional setting.

This examination of two levels of contextual embeddedness leads us to a two-step conclusion: (1) Differences in the degree of cognitive success asso-ciated with the task-activity on which we focus can be explained in large part by the different types of common culture developed at each Fifth Dimension site. Specifically, the degree of cognitive success is heavily influenced by the presence, or relative weakness, of a *culture of collaborative learning*. (2) The strength or weakness of the culture of collaborative learning developed at each site can be explained in part by the degree of affinity between the inter-nal culture of the Fifth Dimension program and the larger cultural environ-ment of the host institution. (The second conclusion is more tentative than the first; and, as we explain, the pattern of interaction between these two

Fifth Dimension branches and their respective host institutions was complex and, in some respects, even ironic.)

Before we can present and elaborate on these results, it is necessary to offer a brief overview of the Fifth Dimension program, the theoretical orientation that informs it, and the goals it is intended to accomplish.

Overview of the Fifth Dimension Program

The Fifth Dimension is an after-school educational program for elementary school children that has been a long-term project of the Laboratory of Comparative Human Cognition (LCHC) at the University of California, San Diego. Although this program has been a collective project of LCHC for a decade and many people have contributed to its present structure and organization, two people have played a central role in initiating and developing it: Peg Griffin and one of the present authors, Michael Cole. The principles that have guided this effort were drawn primarily from the approach to cultural psychology advocated by Cole. [For one formulation, with explicit reference to the Fifth Dimension, see Griffin and Cole (1984); and for elaborations, see Cole (1990a, b, c.)]

The program is designed to promote computer literacy (at a fairly basic level) and at the same time to use computer software to promote more general cognitive and social skills. It is aimed at children of elementary school age (6 to 12 years), both boys and girls. At the core of the program are a number of sites that LCHC has been running in the greater San Diego area; branches have also been set up in other cities in the United States and abroad.

The Fifth Dimension program combines two key functions (among others): (1) It is an attempt to construct workable models for developing certain forms of community-based, after-school educational activity, some elements of which can be applied in regular school settings; and (2) it provides a framework for more basic research into processes of learning and development, as the present chapter illustrates.

The most important of these research issues emerge from a central, theoretically informed question addressed by the program: how to create sustainable systems of educational activity based on a culture of collaborative learning in which play and imagination have a major role. [Griffin & Cole (1984) formulate this goal in terms of the systematic mixture of different forms of "leading activity" as a developmental strategy.] Because the attempt to pursue this goal in the Fifth Dimension makes use of computers and computer-related materials, it bears, in addition, on the question of how resources of this sort can most usefully play a role in education. In this respect, the most significant implication of the present study is to underline the message that the potential educational contributions of computer technology cannot be evaluated in isolation; rather, it is necessary to examine how computers—and other resources—can be integrated effectively into larger systems of educational practice. The experience of the Fifth Dimension, as we analyze it in this chapter, suggests some of the ways that this goal can be accomplished.

The Main Research Sites

Fifth Dimension sites are housed in a number of youth-serving institutions in the greater San Diego area. The data for this study are drawn from the sites at two of these institutions: a Boys' and Girls' Club and a community library. Before discussing these particular sites, however, it may be worth outlining more generally how each of the sites is integrated into the Fifth Dimension program as a whole. An important aspect of the program is the attempt to institutionalize a pattern of complementary and mutually beneficial interaction between the university and a variety of community institutions. Thus the operation of the program requires the cooperation of several institutions (Fig. 12.1).

The participants at each Fifth Dimension site include children and adults. In the sites under discussion, the adults directly responsible for the program come from the *University of California* at San Diego. With the exception of the site coordinator, to whom we return in a moment, they are undergraduates participating in a course entitled Practicum in Child Development offered by the university all three quarters each academic year. The students are introduced to relevant ideas from theories of child development, and they do field work at the Fifth Dimension sites. The field work consists in helping the children with the Fifth Dimension activities and writing field notes based on their site experience. Most of the undergraduates participate for one quarter, but some continue for two or even three quarters in succession.

Each site also has a coordinator, who is always present during the operation of the program and whose role is to supervise the program closely and ensure its smooth functioning. The coordinator plays a major role in training and supervising the undergraduates, facilitating the interactions between children and undergraduates, and maintaining the continuity of the site from day to day and from quarter to quarter. During the two-year introductory phase of the two sites chosen for consideration here, the coordinator at each site was a member of the LCHC research staff; and, in general, LCHC served as the liaison between the community institutions and the university.

We now turn to the two specific sites under consideration, which are, in a number of respects, exceptionally well matched for purposes of comparison. The institutions in which they are housed are located in the same community, which is a suburb of San Diego; in fact, the two are less than half a mile from each other. The programs at both sites were initiated at the same time, during the fall of 1987, and have been administered directly by LCHC. And both have drawn on essentially the same population of children, attending the same set of elementary schools; with some exceptions, the parents of

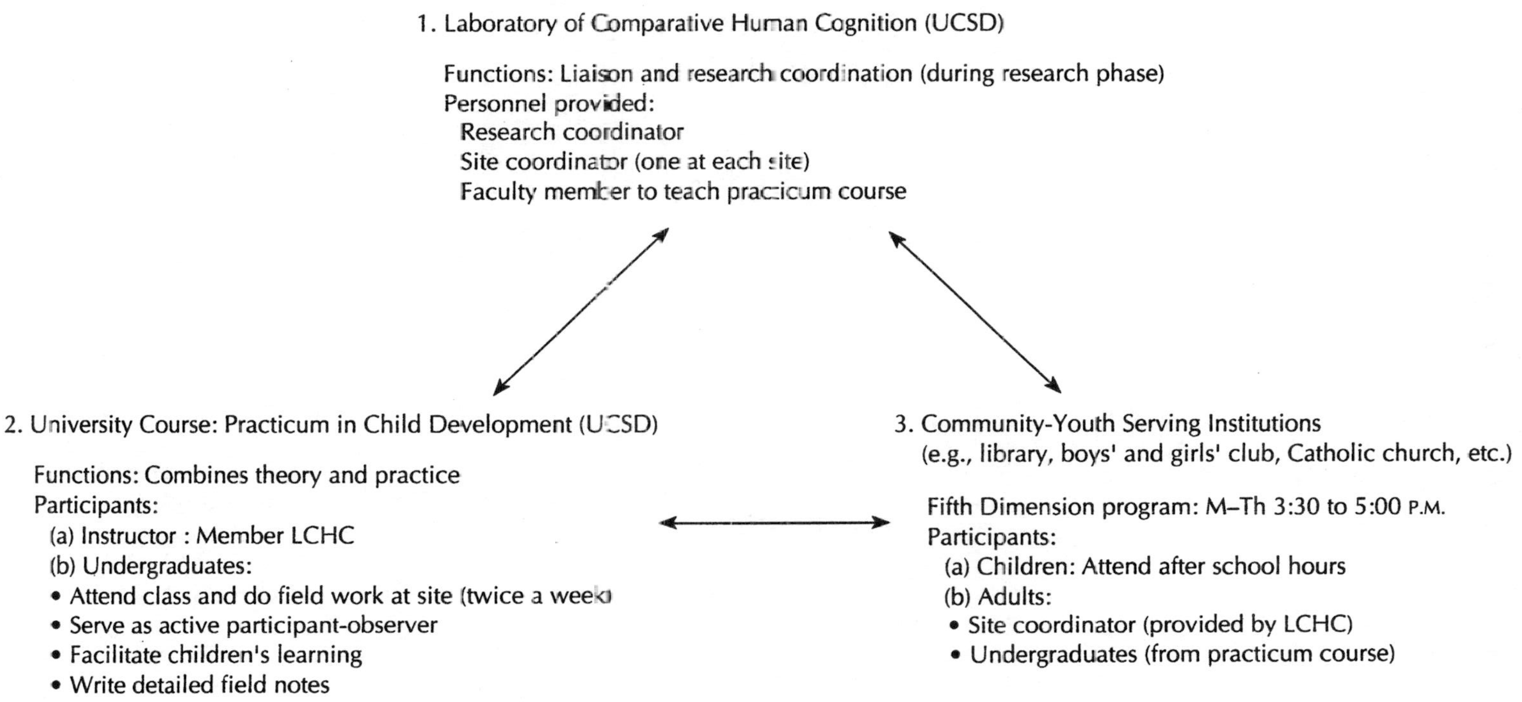

1. Laboratory of Comparative Human Cognition (UCSD)

Functions: Liaison and research coordination (during research phase)
Personnel provided:
Research coordinator
Site coordinator (one at each site)
Faculty member to teach practicum course

2. University Course: Practicum in Child Development (UCSD)

Functions: Combines theory and practice
Participants:
(a) Instructor : Member LCHC
(b) Undergraduates:
• Attend class and do field work at site (twice a week)
• Serve as active participant-observer
• Facilitate children's learning
• Write detailed field notes

3. Community-Youth Serving Institutions
(e.g., library, boys' and girls' club, Catholic church, etc.)

Fifth Dimension program: M–Th 3:30 to 5:00 P.M.
Participants:
(a) Children: Attend after school hours
(b) Adults:
• Site coordinator (provided by LCHC)
• Undergraduates (from practicum course)

Figure 12.1. Interacting institutions (university and community).

287

these children are white, middle-class, and native speakers of English. On the other hand, these two host institutions differ significantly in their organization, their orienting sense of purpose, and the overall atmosphere in which their activities are conducted. Thus they provide different institutional environments within which the operation of the Fifth Dimension could be observed.

The *Boys' and Girls' Club* is a nonprofit, privately funded youth center; it is housed in a large, well equipped building and is one of three branches that the parent club organization has founded in this community and neighboring ones. It is intended to be a place where children from elementary to middle-school age can go during after-school hours; because it is located within easy walking distance of several elementary schools and a middle school, a large number of children have ready access to it and can attend without requiring parental assistance (though they normally depend on their parents to pick them up). Every day the club provides a wide variety of social and recreational activities, ranging from indoor and outdoor games and sports to cooking classes, arts and crafts, and so on.

The club tries to be as inclusive as possible. Although there is an annual participation fee, the amount is rather low ($15) and readily affordable in a middle-class community; there are additional fees for some specific activities, but they are also low; and almost all the regular activities are offered free of charge. Furthermore, the club is self-consciously committed to maximizing the children's freedom of choice and to allowing them maximum flexibility for participating in different activities. Aside from providing the children with an extensive range of alternatives, there is a general feeling that children ought to be able to begin and end particular activities as they please.

The *Library* is a public institution, this community's branch of the county library system. It relies primarily on public funds, supplemented by voluntary contributions of time and money from a community "Friends of the Library" organization; it charges no fees. Like other local libraries around the country, it attempts to provide a range of informational and educational resources for community members. Thus, in addition to lending out books and magazines, it offers such other activities as story-reading, computer classes for adults, and so on. Its patrons range from senior citizens and parents of preschoolers to school-age children, some of whom use it as a quiet place to do their homework. The Library is housed in a brightly lit, middle-sized room, placed in a small shopping mall. Unlike the Boys' and Girls' Club, it is not within easy walking distance of most of the elementary schools in this area; thus children who come tend to be brought by their parents, though some walk or bicycle to the Library by themselves.

Both Fifth Dimension sites operated four days a week, Monday through Thursday, for an hour and a half each day, 3:30 to 5:00 PM. Children at the Boys' and Girls' Club could participate whenever they liked, on a first-come, first-served basis. At the Library site, however, for several reasons including space limitations, the program was divided into two "shifts" per week, Monday/Wednesday and Tuesday/Thursday; children had to choose one or the other and thus could participate only two days a week at most. At both sites, children had the option of beginning and ending their participation at any time during the hour-and-a-half period, but they were encouraged to stay for the entire period on any day they participated.

Although the Fifth Dimension was introduced into each of these institutions under LCHC's administration, as we have explained, the hope was that in the long run each branch would be taken up by the host institution as a self-sustaining program, without further need for direct LCHC involvement. The understanding was that after an initial trial period of two years—which corresponded with the research phase of the project—the host institution would decide if it wished to assume greater responsibility for the program in order to ensure its continuation. If so, the community institution would henceforth hire the site coordinator and provide the financial resources for such purposes as equipment repairs, software, and other supplies; the university would continue to provide the undergraduates to participate in the program, as well as some continuing assistance with telecommunications.

Structure and Practice of the Fifth Dimension Site: The Play-World

Each Fifth Dimension site had its own designated physical space. At the Boys' and Girls' Club it was housed in a single room, whereas in the Library it was located around a large table in one corner of the room. These two sites had eight and five personal computers, respectively; the children participating in the program used them for computer games and other activities (there were also some noncomputer activities, including board games such as Mastermind and Battleship).

A Fifth Dimension site has software for about 40 games and other computer-based activities. With a few exceptions, these consist of educational software in the form of games that teach children about certain content areas (e.g., history, geography, or music) while simultaneously promoting the development of cognitive skills (e.g., general problem-solving, strategic thinking, and logical reasoning). Some even introduce the children to simple computer languages such as Logo and Logowriter. There is a deliberate attempt to combine games and activities at different levels of difficulty and complexity, so that at any given moment every child has some activities that he or she can master and find satisfying.

These games and activities are organized into a complex *system,* and it is this system that is the key to what is most interesting and distinctive about the Fifth Dimension. The system is designed as a 20-room "maze" (Fig. 12.2). This maze is, of course, a *conceptual* structure; but each of the Fifth Dimension sites also has a small physical model of it. When children enter the Fifth Dimension, they move in different sequences through the maze; they choose small figurines to represent themselves, and they can mark their progress through the maze by moving their figurine around in the model.

The rules that define the maze and the ways children can move through it are therefore crucial to the program. The Fifth Dimension is a make-

_____ 's Personal Map

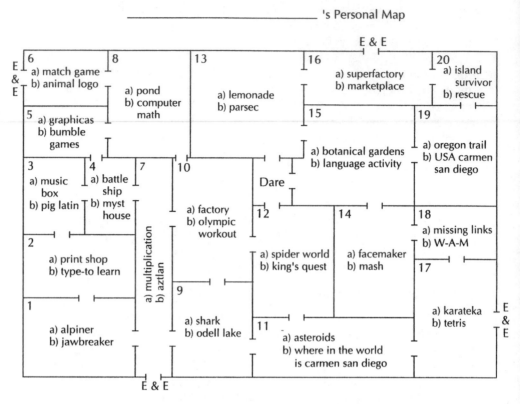

Figure 12.2. Map of Fifth Dimension maze (with games).

believe play-world constituted by its system of rules. When children join, they become "citizens"; they are given a constitution that describes the rules, and they embark on their journey through the maze that involves increasing mastery of a sequence of activities.

Children generally play the games in groups of two or three, assisted by one of the undergraduates mentioned earlier. It is important to note that the undergraduates, particularly when they begin, often do not know the games any better than the children—and sometimes they know even less than some of the children. Therefore they must learn along with the children. What they contribute are greater general knowledge and more advanced problem-solving skills. They also bring with them an awareness of the overall Fifth Dimension system and its goals.

The symbolic center of the system is the mythical figure of the Wizard, the creator and benevolent overseer of the Fifth Dimension, with whom the children are in constant communication through electronic mail. Children report regularly to the Wizard about their success or difficulties with different games and reflect on the strategies they used to master them. This activity of reflection and externalization helps children consolidate the knowledge they have gained and (among other things) promotes their meta-cognitive skills. In the process, they pass on hints about how to master the games, which the Wizard, in turn, can pass on to other children through a Hints Box, which is a computer bulletin board. The Wizard is also the final court of appeal regarding interpretations of the rules; children can send him (or her) petitions, reports of grievances, and suggestions for improving the program.

The child proceeds through the maze in a complex series of steps that are somewhat different for each child. Each "room" the child enters has two games (or other activities), and the child can choose which one to play (Fig. 12.2). Each game can be played at three possible levels of expertise; the higher the level achieved, the more choices the child is given for the next move. The general principle is that increasing mastery of a particular game opens up an increasing range of alternatives, and it is up to the child to choose which ones to pursue.

It should be noted that these three levels of expertise are not present in the computer software. For each game, on the basis of a task analysis carried out by the LCHC research staff, a task card has been constructed that defines the goals of the game and specifies these levels of mastery. The task card is given to the child to guide him or her through the activity.

The aim is that each level should represent a complete and satisfactory game in itself, clearly connected to the cognitive goals that the game as a whole is supposed to advance. This means, on the one hand, that children are introduced to the goals of the game and given some means to accomplish them, even if they do not go beyond the beginner level. On the other hand, although the higher levels provide more depth and information, they do not require the children to have completed a lower level. In most cases, the children can choose to begin at any level and can backtrack to a lower level if necessary.

The child's mission is to proceed through the maze until he or she has visited all the "rooms" in the maze and played at least ten games at the "expert" level. At that point the child can petition to become a Wizard's Assistant (a status already held by the undergraduates). In addition to the honor involved, children who become Wizard's Assistants are introduced to more complex activities and are given greater responsibilities for helping other children and for representing their Fifth Dimension site to other sites through telecommunications. These are, in broad terms, the main features of the Fifth Dimension and its play-world.

Theoretical Rationale and Significance of the Fifth Dimension

The Fifth Dimension is fundamentally an *activity system* with a certain specific inner logic. The goal is to create a context that can promote collaborative learning and within which children themselves are motivated to progress step by step, so that they are actively involved in their own development rather than simply receiving information from other people.

Three points are especially worth emphasizing in this connection: (1) The Fifth Dimension creates a make-believe world that is constituted by a *system* of shared rules. (2) It is precisely through the understanding and acceptance of this system of shared rules that children are allowed and encouraged to take an active role in their own education. (3) It is within this context that the role of the undergraduates must be understood: They are there to guide and facilitate the children's development—not to act as authoritarian figures or simply to serve as sources of information in a one-way transmission relationship. In short, what the program attempts to do is create what we will call a *culture of collaborative learning.* For creating and maintaining such a culture, the discipline provided by a system of shared and voluntarily accepted rules is crucial.

This point is of considerable theoretical importance, so it is worth spelling out. To paraphrase a comment that Peg Griffin once made, a central principle of the Fifth Dimension is that of choice within a structured context. The discipline of this structure is important. As far as possible, however, it should rest not on the authority of individuals but on the authority of an impersonal normative system: that is, a system of shared and voluntarily accepted rules that are embedded in, and constitutive of, an ongoing practice. This situation occurs at two levels in the Fifth Dimension: (1) at the level of the Fifth Dimension system as a whole; and (2) at the level of individual games, each of which constitutes an activity system of its own with its own inherent rules.

The interplay of choice and discipline brings us to another important element of the Fifth Dimension program: the attempt to integrate play and imagination into the educational process. It may seem strange to speak of play and discipline in the same breath, but we would argue that they fit together quite naturally. Play is not necessarily frivolous. On the contrary, if properly understood, it can serve precisely as a prototype of an activity constituted by shared and voluntarily accepted rules, within which people can be motivated to strive for excellence and for mastery of the possibilities inherent in that practice.

This is a key premise behind the whole Fifth Dimension program and underlies its potential implications for wider issues in education. We should therefore elaborate some of the reasoning behind this premise. The theoretical basis for this approach in the Fifth Dimension has been drawn primarily from the work of Vygotsky; one of the best examples of his way of thinking about these issues is provided by his well-known lecture on play (1933/1967), but the same approach informs his theoretical perspective more generally [see Vygotsky (1978, 1987), as well as Wertsch (1985) and Nicolopoulou (1991, 1993)]. Vygotsky himself draws importantly in this respect on the early work of Piaget, especially his book *The Moral Judgment of the Child* (1932/1965), and thus indirectly on Durkheim [in particular, Durkheim (1925/1973); see also Weintraub (1974)]. [Some formulations in the theoretical discussion that follows are adapted from Nicolopoulou (1993).]

The crucial orientation shared by Durkheim, Vygotsky, and the early Piaget can be formulated as follows: The coherence both of individual mental life and of social life is structured by systems of rules. This is true for autonomous action as well as for action performed under external constraint. Autonomy is not the same as arbitrariness; it requires a capacity for *self*-discipline and self-determination [to paraphrase one of Vygotsky's formulations (1933/1967, p. 10)]. However, to be able to think and act autonomously requires moving from dependence on the authority of particular superiors to operating within the framework of a shared and voluntarily accepted system of impersonal rules. People develop this capacity, in part, by acting within a framework of cooperative social relationships. What this kind of activity requires, and what it simultaneously helps people to grasp, is the sense that the rules are not necessarily handed down by a superior; rather, they are inherent in the structure of the activity itself and are necessary in order to be able to carry out a practice or form of activity that is valued by its participants. This is true whether the practice involved is a game, or an active collaboration, or making use of the conceptual system of mathematics in order to solve a problem—and so on.

In sum, then, the premise that these three thinkers share, and that Vygotsky emphasizes repeatedly and develops in his own way, is that thinking and cognitive development involve participating in forms of social activity constituted by systems of shared rules that must be grasped and voluntarily accepted. [To paraphrase a formulation of Giddens (1979), systems of rules are not *only* constraining but can be simultaneously constraining and *enabling*.] Rules emerge and have force within the context of a cohesive social group; and they serve, as Durkheim (1897/1951) would put it, both to regulate and to integrate the social group—that is, to *maintain* its cohesion. [These connections became clear to us through reading Weintraub (1974).]

One of Vygotsky's distinctive contributions to this shared problematic is his insistence that *play* is a crucial prototype of all such activities. Play is enjoyable, it is intrinsically voluntary, and it is at the same time an essentially rule-governed activity: Its two essential components are the presence of an imaginary situation and the rules implicit in this imaginary situation. The system of rules serves, in fact, to constitute the play situation itself; and, in turn, these rules derive their force from the child's enjoyment of, and commitment to, the shared activity of the play-world.

This discussion should help explain why Vygotsky sees play as having an important role in learning and cognitive development. The child learns that realizing the imaginary situation requires adhering to the rules implicit in that situation. This acceptance is *voluntary* but *necessary:* No one is making the child accept these rules; but, without adhering to them, one cannot play the game. Furthermore, play is always a *learning* activity because it requires learning and grasping these rules, seeing that they form a system, elaborating them, and mastering the possibilities of the form of practice they constitute. Even simple pretense play—for example, a little girl pretending to be a "mother"—requires attending to and making explicit the normally implicit rules embedded in the role of "mother." A game such as Match-23, which children play in the Fifth Dimension, requires grasping and applying fairly sophisticated principles of strategic thinking. And so on.

The relevance of this theoretical discussion to the Fifth Dimension should now be clear. The program's goal is to create a context for self-motivated learning within the framework of a voluntarily accepted system of rules. The authority of the rules is not dependent primarily on the authority of particular individuals but is embedded within the structure of collectively shared systems of activity. Incidentally, part of what contributes to the impersonal character of the system of rules is that they are, to a certain extent, built into the computer software rather than being entirely enforced by individuals. Thus we can take advantage of the possibilities offered by computer technology, even in a fairly unsophisticated form, to help create educational systems of this sort.

Comparative Analysis of Embedded Contexts

As this discussion of the Fifth Dimension and the logic behind it should make clear, a central goal of the program is to stimulate and enhance collaborative learning, and therefore it aims to foster the generation and transmission of *shared* knowledge. We might say this is the *ideal*. The analysis presented here, which is one element in an overall evaluation of the Fifth Dimension program currently in progress, undertakes a concrete assessment of how these principles have worked out in practice. We approach this problem through a comparative analysis of the sites described above and of the institutional settings in which they are located.

Methodological Approach

In the most general terms, the methodological challenge posed by this type of research is to find the most effective approach to study what is currently often called "socially situated cognition" (e.g., Lave, 1988): that is, to capture developmental patterns in real-life settings, where they are embedded in complex contexts, as opposed to experimentally designed situations. In addition, special problems arise from the attempt to study collaborative, rather than purely individual, learning.

The most crucial problem in this respect was to find the right *unit of analysis* to capture developmental changes in the context of a dynamic sociocultural system. On both theoretical and practical grounds, we argue that, to evaluate and compare programs such as the Fifth Dimension, the most appropriate unit of analysis is not the individual child or even the interactional pair.

Such an assertion may strike some people as surprising. In most developmental research, it seems almost self-evident to take the individual child as the unit of analysis. In a study such as ours, for example, we would find ways to score the cognitive abilities of children entering the Fifth Dimension, monitor changes in these scores over time, and compare these children with each other and with matched controls. If we tried to follow such a procedure in this case, however, we would encounter immediate difficulties simply on practical grounds. Children in the Fifth Dimension, as our previous discussion should have made clear, do not go through a uniform sequence of activities. In fact, no two children follow a precisely equivalent itinerary through the maze. Furthermore, the children do not travel alone but are almost always involved in *joint* activities. Thus it would be difficult to match and compare them systematically as individual units; and the attempt to do so would be, at best, strained and misleading.

On the other hand, much research in situated cognition has taken as its unit of analysis the interactional pair or trio (the mother–child dyad, for example). This move brings us closer to the solution, since children in the Fifth Dimension generally play the games in pairs or trios, along with an undergraduate. For the purposes of this analysis, however, the interactional dyad or trio is also not the most appropriate unit of analysis because the configuration of actors changes from day to day—from the most microinteractional level to the level of the site as a whole. Children and undergraduates play together in combinations that shift continuously. In addition, the overall population at each site is not stable: Children enter and leave the program throughout the year; and there is an almost complete turnover of undergraduates each quarter. This situation of flux and variability, then, means that the standard methodological approaches are inappropriate.

Therefore we decided on an alternative approach. Given the nature of the Fifth Dimension program, the most appropriate unit of analysis is a *game* conceived as an ongoing system of collective activity. It should be made clear that by "game" we do not mean a particular *occasion* when a game was played. We are referring to the game in its more encompassing sense (as in "*the* game of baseball" rather than "*a* game of baseball"); and, as we have explained, it should be understood as an ongoing *system* of activity constituted by a structure of shared and socially elaborated rules. Each game fits into the larger system of the Fifth Dimension as a whole, but it also has its own distinct characteristics (Fig. 12.3).

Taking a game as the basic unit of analysis avoids the practical difficulties we have just outlined. Examined as an ongoing activity system, it has a degree of continuity and stability that interactional pairs or the changing population of participants do not. This approach also makes the most sense on theoretical grounds, as it allows one to focus directly on a dynamic context of situated cognition and cognitive growth.

Furthermore, choosing a game that was played at both of the research sites allows for a systematic and genuinely worthwhile comparative analysis (Fig. 12.4). This comparative analysis can help to illuminate the kind of rela-

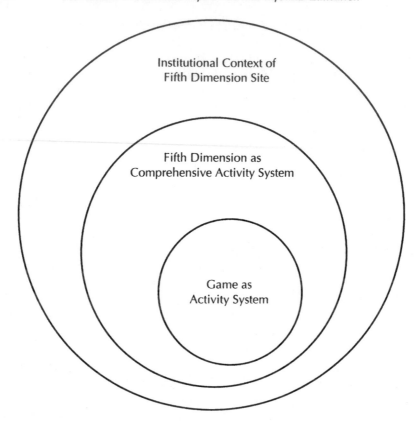

Figure 12.3. Embedded contexts of situated cognition in the Fifth Dimension program.

tionship between the game activity and its larger sociocultural context that most effectively promotes cognitive development.

Finally, it is worth noting that this sort of focus also makes sense on what might be called specifically technical grounds—having to do, in particular, with the nature of our data and the kinds of analyses for which they are best suited. Given the way that the Fifth Dimension project has been organized, our richest source of data are field notes written by the undergraduates describing, and reflecting on, their interactions with the children at site. By analyzing the whole set of field notes that deal with one particular game, one can reconstruct significant long-term patterns in collaborative activity and cognitive growth.

The Task-Activity: An Adventure Game, "Mystery House"

The activity on which we focus here is a computer game called Mystery House. It is a commercially available adventure game that follows the form of a murder mystery novel. The player enters a house in which people keep

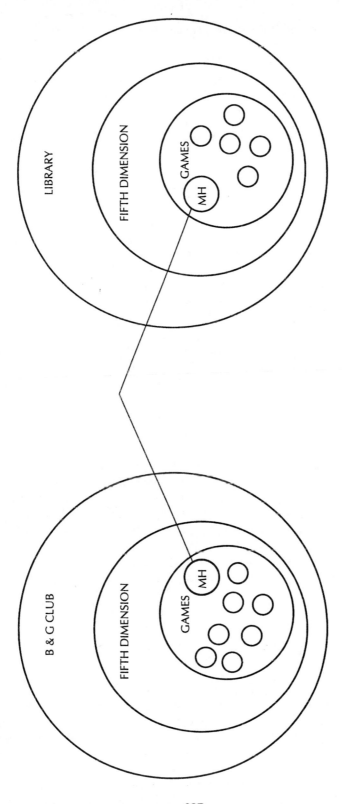

Figure 12.4. Comparative analysis of Mystery House game in different institutional contexts.

mysteriously dying and in which the player encounters both clues and dangers. The object is to unravel the clues and find the killer without getting killed, as well as to find a set of jewels hidden in the house.

Part of what makes Mystery House so useful for our purposes is that it is a complex game with a number of steps, each with its own intellectual puzzles and pitfalls. To advance in the game requires trial and error, a great deal of thought and effort, and (usually) effective teamwork. Furthermore, "success" in the game is not an all-or-nothing affair, so it can be scored at a range of levels. Thus advancing through Mystery House is a long and gradual process, involving repeated efforts—which allows long-term observation. Moreover, to advance in this game one has to maintain the previous level reached, which requires *preserving* or, in the case of a new player, *transmitting* the knowledge already attained. In short, this game is a good test of collaborative learning and problem-solving because it brings out sharply both (1) the problem of *generating* individual and shared knowledge and (2) that of *accumulating* and *transmitting* shared knowledge.

The game was played all year at both sites: at the Library and at the Boys' and Girls' Club. On any given day, the game might be played by one child or, more usually, a set of children—two or possibly three—working with an undergraduate (sometimes, but rarely, two undergraduates). We will refer to one of these groups of children and undergraduates as a team, or play-set. To score the performance of the various teams who played the game, we devised a coding scheme based on a task analysis of the game; this involved breaking the game down into its cognitive goals (and subgoals) and establishing a gradation of difficulties inherent in achieving them. Using this coding scheme to interpret the information from the field notes, we were able to calculate a total score for a team each time it played one of the games. (For Mystery House, the highest possible score in our coding scheme is 63.)

Over the course of the year, a roughly equal number of children played the game at least once at each site: 28 at the Library and 30 at the Boys' and Girls' Club. With the exception of one child at each site (both of whom joined in the fall quarter) neither the children nor the undergraduates who played the game knew anything about it in advance; they had to learn it while playing.

Results: Two Distinct Patterns of Knowledge Generation and Accumulation

For each day that a specific team played Mystery House, whether they played it once or several times in succession, we have recorded the last score they achieved (which was always the highest). Figures 12.5, 12.6, and 12.7 illustrate the pattern of scores achieved at each of the two sites over the course of the academic year. (As we explained earlier, at the Library site the program was divided into two "shifts" per week, Monday/Wednesday and Tuesday/Thursday, each with a different set of children; the patterns of scores for each of these groups are presented in Figures, 12.6 and 12.7.) A

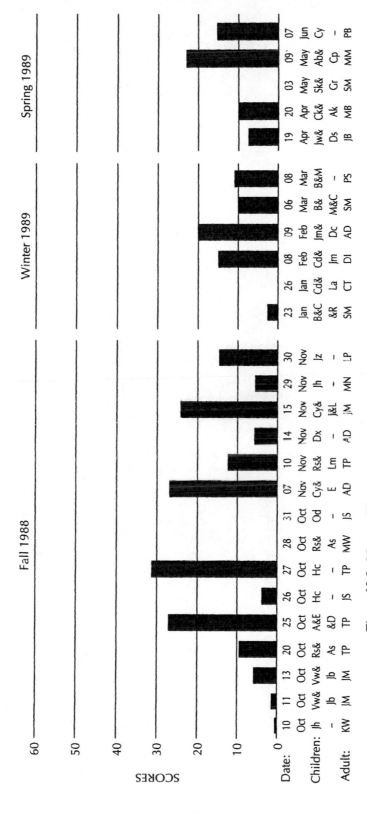

Figure 12.5. Mystery House game scores: Boys' and Girls' Club, fall 1988 to spring 1989.

299

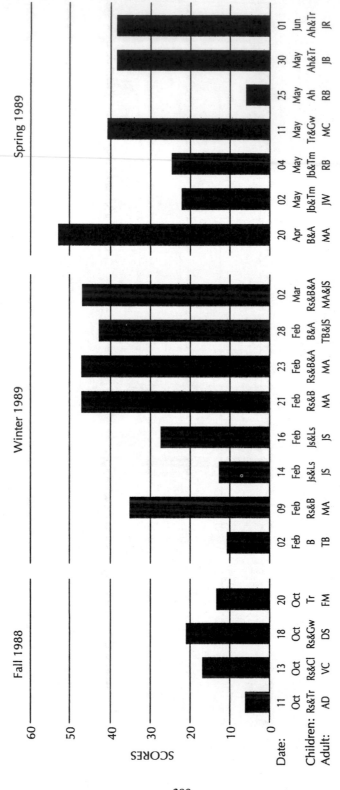

Figure 12.6. Mystery House game scores: Library (Tuesdays/Thursdays), fall 1988 to spring 1989.

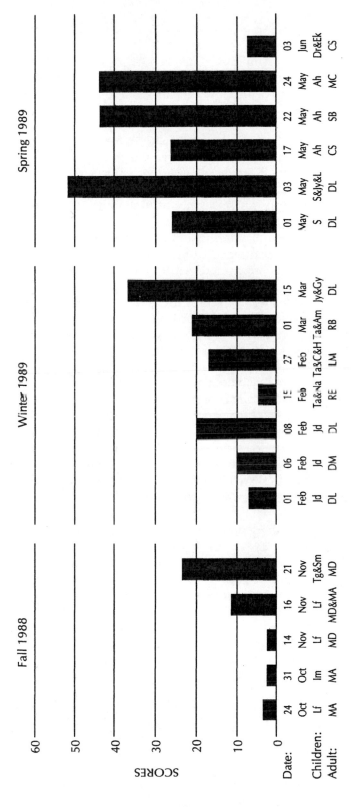

Figure 12.7. Mystery House game scores: Library (Mondays/Wednesdays), fall 1988 to spring 1989.

comparison reveals a significant difference between the two sites in this respect. Not only were the average scores higher at the Library site over the course of the year; the results show a steady accumulation of shared knowledge from quarter to quarter at the Library site, but not at the Boys' and Girls' Club site.

At the Boys' and Girls' Club site (Fig. 12.5), the highest score achieved was 32—which, as shown below, is not very high in comparison to those achieved at the Library. Even more important is the fact that this score was achieved during the fall quarter. Neither individual children nor the group as a whole improved their performance as time went on. There was some improvement during the fall, and we know from analysis of the field notes that some generation and transmission of shared knowledge took place. With the beginning of the winter quarter, however, the chain of transmission and accumulation was broken, and each new child who played Mystery House had to start from scratch.

In contrast, the pattern of scores for both groups at the Library site reveals an accumulation of shared knowledge from quarter to quarter. In the Tuesday/Thursday group (Fig. 12.6), the highest score achieved was 52, and almost half the scores recorded were over 32, the highest score at the Boys' and Girls' Club. Even more significant, the level of scores tended to increase over time, even when new children were playing the game. During the spring there was a great deal of turnover of participants, which produced some perturbations in the scores; but they remained high. And one can assume that if the new children had been able to stay another quarter the scores would have become even higher. This pattern of improvement is even more striking in the Monday/Wednesday group (Fig. 12.7). With this group we see a steady accumulation of shared knowledge from quarter to quarter. As with the Tuesday/Thursday group, the highest score (51) was achieved during the spring.

In short, these results demonstrate that the game "worked" much more successfully at the Library than at the Boys' and Girls' Club. Even though there was considerable circulation of individual participants at both sites (both children and undergraduates), the overall pattern of scores at the Library went up from one quarter to another; not only did individuals do better, but the group as a whole advanced. At the Boys' and Girls' Club, on the other hand, there was no progress of this sort. Individual children hit relatively low plateaus fairly early, and neither they nor other children were successful in building on what they had achieved.

First Level of Contextual Embeddedness: Cognitive Growth Within the Culture of Collaborative Learning

How can we account for these very different patterns of results at the two sites?

Can the difference be explained by the background characteristics of the individual children involved, which they bring to the Fifth Dimension? On the basis of the information available, it seems unlikely. Children at the two sites were similar in terms of age, gender composition, family background, ethnicity, and other standard demographic variables; they came from the same community and appeared to attend the same schools. If anything, in fact, the children who played this game were older at the Boys' and Girls' Club and had, on average, more previous familiarity with computer games.

Thus, the differences seem to have something to do with the characteristics of the Fifth Dimension sites themselves, a conclusion that is reinforced by the similarity between the patterns of results achieved by the two groups at the Library site, even though two different sets of children were involved. The next question therefore is which characteristics of the sites were critical to generating these different outcomes.

Again, some intuitively plausible factors can be ruled out. Without going into detail, let us just mention that at the Boys' and Girls' Club, as well as at the Library, there were participants who should, in principle, have been able to serve as vehicles for the accumulation and transmission of shared knowledge. Each site, for example, had a single site coordinator throughout the year; and at both sites there was some continuity of undergraduates (it was low, but the rates of turnover were about equal). Both sites had new children coming in and leaving throughout the year, so that the population was fluctuating. The Library did have a slightly higher proportion of children who stayed on for the entire year and formed a core of continuity. This circumstance can be only part of the explanation, however, as there was a continuous core of children at the Boys' and Girls' Club as well. And, to the extent that there was a larger stable core of children at the Library site, this phenomenon is part of what needs to be explained.

The explanation we would like to advance is that it was primarily the different *cultures* of the two sites that produced the difference in the outcomes. Specifically, the Library site was more successful at generating and maintaining a culture of collaborative learning. This difference was manifested in terms of two mutually reinforcing elements: (1) the pattern of interaction at the two sites; and (2) the degree of commitment to, and involvement in, the play-world of the Fifth Dimension and its system of rules. What these factors add up to is a difference between what we will call, following Durkheim (1897/1951, 1925/1973), the degree of *social cohesion* of the play-world at the two sites. The social cohesion of the Library site was demonstrably stronger, and one result was greater cognitive success.

To elaborate: Mystery House is a difficult game. At the Boys' and Girls' Club, when children encountered difficulties they were more likely to give up and do something else. As our analysis of the field notes makes clear, there was not the same degree of effort—or of cooperation. Moreover, the knowledge accumulated by individual children (or undergraduates) did not become part of a collective cultural stockpile—that is, it did not enter into the collective memory or the body of collective knowledge—so it was not effectively passed on or built upon. Thus, as we have seen, new children started from scratch, hit a low plateau early, and did not go beyond it.

Why did things work out more successfully at the Library in this respect? The crucial factor seems to be that the play-world of the Fifth Dimension, constituted by its system of shared rules, had more solidity and a stronger influence on participants. Children and undergraduates spent more time helping each other out, asked others for help more readily, and did not give up so easily. We can sum up this situation, as noted above, by saying that the *social cohesion* of the library site was stronger. The field notes provide evidence of various kinds that this was the case, but the two key indicators on which we focus here are the *quantity* and the *quality* of problem-solving interaction at the two sites.

In the first place, the Library site had a greater degree of what we will call interactional density. The rates of problem-solving interaction were higher regarding both interactions among children and among children and undergraduates. In general, there was more continuity and stability of interaction at the Library site, whereas interactional patterns at the Boys' and Girls' Club tended to be more fragmentary and discontinuous. Furthermore, there was a much more substantial transmission of shared knowledge through interactional chains at the Library site, whereas at the Boys' and Girls' Club these chains were more likely to break.

There are many aspects to this phenomenon, but let us offer one illustration. Table 12.1 measures the extent to which participants in collaborative teams—both children and undergraduates—maintained their participation from one time to the next. Specifically, what proportion of consecutive teams had overlapping membership, and how *many* of the participants overlapped? A quick glance at this table is enough to establish the difference between the two sites. At the Boys' and Girls' Club, a decisive majority of the consecutive teams (72%) showed no continuity, whereas at the Library site the opposite was the case (65% and 69%, respectively, showed continuity). The implications for the transmission of shared knowledge are obvious.

But this sort of evidence captures only part of the picture, because what is important is not only the quantitative pattern of interactions but the *quality* of interactions as well. These comparisons cannot be summarized as readily as the quantitative patterns just discussed, but it is clear from the field

Table 12.1. Proportion of Consecutive Mystery House Play-sets with Overlapping Membership

Site	Overlapping participants (%)			
	3 Part.	2 Part.	1 Part.	No Part.
B & G Club	04	04	20	72
Library (M/W)	—	12	53	35
Library (T/Th)	25	19	25	31

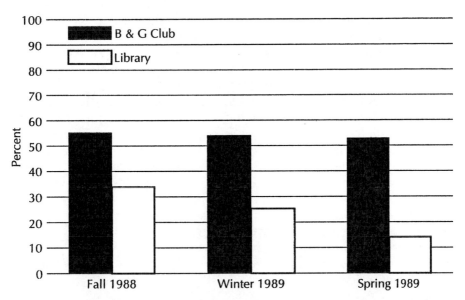

Figure 12.8. Dropout rates of children at different Fifth Dimension sites: fall 1988 to spring 1989.

notes that at the Library site there was a stronger spirit of cooperation and of commitment to the goals of the program. As we have mentioned, children there more readily asked for and offered help with the game. Moreover, various pieces of evidence suggest that, simultaneously, the undergraduates at the Library were more involved in the activities and felt a stronger bond with the children. For example, undergraduates at the Library were more likely to use the word "we" when speaking of the children; and even the quality of their field notes was better.

This analysis brings us back to the themes of our earlier theoretical discussion. These two central features of problem-solving interaction—interactional density and quality of interaction—are closely intertwined and mutually reinforcing; and each of them simultaneously *depends on* and *promotes* a sense of commitment to the goals of the play-world and to the system of rules that constitutes it. To put it in Durkheim's terms, the two crucial elements of social cohesion are integration and moral regulation; and both were higher at the Library site. Thus the Library site had a higher degree of social cohesion, which meant a stronger culture of collaborative learning.

Readers may recall that Durkheim (1897/1951), in his book on suicide, argued that integration and regulation lowered suicide rates. Suicide is not, of course, a problem in the Fifth Dimension. However, it may be of interest to note that *dropout* rates were much lower at the Library site: once children entered the program, they worked harder *and* were much more likely to stay with it the whole year (Fig. 12.8).

We can now sum up our first major conclusion: The degree of cognitive success and growth in the task-activity we have examined depended on a *collective* characteristic of the group as a whole—the strength or weakness of the culture of collaborative learning. And an effective culture of collaborative learning requires a high degree of social cohesion, which is produced by the integration and regulation of the social group.

This analysis demonstrates that the social or interpsychological context within which individual development must be understood is not limited to the immediate framework of dyadic or small-group interactions but consists, above all, in the larger sociocultural framework that shapes the meaning and impact of those interactions. In this case, the specific activities and interactions at each site were embedded in, and shaped by, the context formed by the culture of each site. The culture of the site, understood as a collective reality—as an activity *system*—is thus the key explanatory factor in accounting for the different patterns of generation and accumulation of knowledge bound up with a particular activity: The same task-activity evolves differently and comes to be imbued with different meaning within two different sociocultural contexts.

Second Level of Contextual Embeddedness: The Fifth Dimension Culture and Its Host Institution

Another question, however, remains unanswered: Why was the culture of collaborative learning stronger at the Library site? Although a number of factors are involved, the one on which we will focus is the interaction between the cultural logic of the Fifth Dimension, centered on its rule-governed activity system, and that of the host institution. For a number of reasons, the whole culture of the Library had more affinity with, and provided a more supportive environment for, the culture of collaborative learning in the Fifth Dimension than did the atmosphere and culture of the Boys' and Girls' Club.

The Library is a serious, earnest, studious, rule-governed universe. Its patrons abide by its rules and regulations, and any newcomer must learn to accept and abide by them. This rule-governed universe accorded with, and reinforced, a central feature of the Fifth Dimension program: the premise that the children will try to advance within a well-defined system of shared rules—voluntarily chosen rules, to be sure, but still a coherent structure of constraint and opportunity. Thus, as the field notes attest, the children at the Library site committed themselves rather easily and spontaneously to the framework of rules that constitute the Fifth Dimension and its play-world.

In contrast, the pervasive atmosphere of the Boys' and Girls' Club is one of deliberate lack of structure and absence of constraint. The Club prides itself on an "open door policy," whereby the children walk freely in and out of the Club, making their own decisions about what they want to do and shifting easily between different activities—whether it be the Fifth Dimension, a game of air hockey, or getting a treat from the snack bar. The Club provides a cafeteria of choices for children, who are not asked to *commit* themselves to any one of them. This context was to a certain extent at odds with the rule-governed universe of the Fifth Dimension, making it more difficult for the children to accept fully the organizing logic of its play-world; the children's inclination was to come and play only the games they liked and to leave as soon as they were done. With a few exceptions, it took much effort, continuous vigilance, and considerable persuasion on the part of the undergraduates to have the children follow their itinerary through the maze. The Fifth Dimension was a popular activity at the Boys' and Girls' Club, in terms of the number of children who wished to participate; but their involvement in, and commitment to, the play-world ran considerably less deep than at the Library site.

The differences between the atmosphere and expectations of these two institutional cultures manifested themselves in a variety of ways in the children's attitudes and behavior; but one particularly striking and significant illustration is provided by the different patterns of children's attendance at two sites. Children at both sites were encouraged, though not required, to remain for the entire hour-and-a-half period each day they participated in the Fifth Dimension. At the Library site, the children almost always did so. They generally arrived on time—even apologizing on occasion when they were slightly late—and left only at the end of the period. The children's respect for and adherence to the schedule was, admittedly, reinforced by the fact that they were usually driven to and from the site by parents or other caretakers, who did so on schedule. However, even children who walked or bicycled to the Library site almost always arrived and left on time. Thus all the participants recognized common starting and stopping times, and during the period in between they all participated in what was seen as a shared activity. At the Boys' and Girls' Club site, in contrast, everything was in relative flux. Children wandered in and out at will and rarely stayed throughout the entire Fifth Dimension period. This pattern of expectations extended to the parents as well; they picked up their children according to their convenience or the children's wishes, without regard for the schedule of the Fifth Dimension program.

These different patterns of attendance are significant as indicators of the relative strength of the children's commitment to the goals of the play-world and to the system of rules that constitutes it. But they also had important practical consequences for the degree of social cohesion at the two sites. As noted earlier, the different elements of the social cohesion of the play-world—interactional density, continuity of interaction, commitment, and so on—mutually reinforced each other. The reverse was also true: when these elements were weak, they mutually undermined each other. The steady pattern of attendance at the Library site both reflected and reinforced the solidity of the play-world and its influence on participants. On the other hand, the intermittent and fragmentary character of children's participation at the Boys' and Girls' Club site undermined the social cohesion of the play-world in a number of ways, both direct and indirect—while this pattern of attendance was in turn reinforced by the relatively weak social cohesion of the play-world.

One can begin with any one of these elements and trace a ramifying chain of mutually reinforcing effects. For example, the steadier and more continuous pattern of attendance at the Library site, both within and between sessions, encouraged more stable and engaging patterns of inter-action among the children and between children and undergraduates. The higher level of interactional density provided more opportunities for long-term collaboration and for the development of effective team groups. One way in which it supported such collaboration was by fostering closer emo-tional bonds within the group, particularly between children and under-graduates; thus when the children encountered difficulties in their Fifth Dimension activities, they were more likely to turn to other children or to undergraduates for help rather than giving up. The fact that the children and the undergraduates had a stronger sense of being involved in a shared enter-prise, and that the undergraduates were more able to be of effective assis-tance to the children in working their way through the maze, led to more satisfying relations between them. As a consequence, the undergraduates felt more committed to enhancing the children's intellectual growth, and, at the same time, the children were more willing to fulfill the intellectual demands placed on them by the play-world—and so on.

On the other hand, because children at the Boys' and Girls' Club site were less committed to steady and continuous participation, the population of the site was much more fluctuating and discontinuous, which tended to weaken both the density and the intensity of problem-solving interaction. For example, undergraduates were far less likely to work with the same child (or team) from session to session or even over the course of a single session. In combination with other factors we have mentioned, this situation con-tributed to making the interactions between children and undergraduates fragmentary and emotionally uninvolving, so that they were less likely to develop strong bonds. Because the children's involvement in, and commit-ment to, the play-world was weaker, they were more likely to give up when confronted with difficulties, rather than turning to others for help—espe-cially given the fact that at the Boys' and Girls' Club they could readily walk away from the Fifth Dimension site and engage in some other activity. And so on.

One might wonder if the atmosphere of the Boys' and Girls' Club is ever conducive to sustained intellectual effort (in playing computer games or oth-erwise). The answer is that it does sometimes seem to be so, though usually the kind of intellectual effort it stimulates is relatively individualistic. Its main thrust, however, runs counter to the cultural logic of the Fifth Dimen-sion, which is oriented to creating and maintaining a culture of *collaborative* learning. As a result, although there were certainly instances of collaborative activity at the Boys' and Girls' Club site, a *culture* of collaborative learning never took firm roots to provide a constitutive framework that would shape and permeate the activities of the participants.

In short, the key point is that the culture of the Boys' and Girls' Club and that of the Fifth Dimension were not fully integrated with each other, at least in comparison with the situation at the Library; rather than being mutually supportive, to a considerable extent the culture of the Club and that of the Fifth Dimension were working against each other. Each of these cultural systems embodies an approach to development—explicit or implicit—that might (hypothetically) have served as a basis for successful learning activity; but in practice they interfered with each other. The consequence was a weaker culture of collaborative learning than at the Library site and a correspondingly lower degree of cognitive success.

Epilogue: Financial and Organizational Constraints

One way to sum up the foregoing discussion might be to say that the culture of the Fifth Dimension had a better "fit" with the culture of the Library than with that of the Boys' and Girls' Club. To complicate matters, though, there is an ironic sequel to the picture we have presented so far. As we noted earlier, after a two-year trial period each of the host institutions was to decide whether to take up the Fifth Dimension program on a permanent basis, in the process assuming greater responsibility (financial and otherwise) for its continued operation. This goal was not met in the case of the Library, which declined to take this step. In contrast, the Boys' and Girls' Club organization not only agreed to take up the program but is in the process of completing the introduction of Fifth Dimension sites at their other two branches as well.

A number of factors contributed to this turn of events, some of them quite specific to the institutions involved. Certain of these factors are peripheral to the key analytical issues on which we have focused in our analysis, which center on the dynamics of the internal culture of the Fifth Dimension, the influence of the host institution on this culture, and the developmental consequences of the interaction between them. However, they raise issues that would evidently be important for a more comprehensive assessment of how programs of this sort can be introduced successfully into existing institutions (issues which we will address in the larger evaluation of the Fifth Dimension program). For example, one reason advanced by the Library staff for declining to continue with the program was straightforwardly financial; as a public institution with a limited budget, they thought it would be difficult to increase their financial support for the Fifth Dimension site either by obtaining new funds or by reallocating their existing resources. (The "Friends of the Library" group offered to help raise the necessary money, but it was unclear how successfully they could have done so on a long-term basis.) The Boys' and Girls' Club, on the other hand, is a more flexible and autonomous organization that could more easily shift some of its resources to support a new program.

However, some other considerations raised by the staff at the host institutions bear somewhat more directly on the question of how well a program such as the Fifth Dimension is integrated into its larger institutional environment. They bring out, in particular, how complex and ambiguous this question can be. Although a full treatment of the issues involved would take us beyond the scope of the discussion in this chapter, it may be useful to touch on some of them briefly.

One's evaluation of the degree of "success" of a program such as the Fifth Dimension—or any other educational practice—obviously depends on the criteria employed; and these criteria are shaped—in more or less subtle ways—by the orientation and priorities of the institutions involved. The goal of the Fifth Dimension is to integrate play and fantasy into the educational process in order to *use* them for the purpose of cognitive growth and development. The chief goal of the Boys' and Girls' Club is to create an atmosphere in which the maximum number of children can have fun during their after-school hours. Their outlook, as we have noted, emphasizes giving children a wide range of choice among activities—some educational, some not—and allowing them maximum flexibility in the way in which they engage in these activities. Obviously, these sets of goals overlap to a certain extent, but they are not identical.

From the point of view of the Fifth Dimension's priorities (which are the focus of this chapter) the Boys' and Girls' Club site was a more qualified success than the Library site because the environment of the Boys' and Girls' Club tended to disrupt the delicate balance between discipline and spontaneity most conducive to cognitive growth. From the perspective of the Boys' and Girls' Club, however, the program was an unqualified success. It became one of their most popular programs, as measured by the *number* of children who participated, even though their participation was more superficial and discontinuous. Thus the Fifth Dimension fit in very well, in a sense—but only by having its own culture diluted so that it was less successful in its own terms.

On the other hand, the chief priorities of the Library and of the Fifth Dimension program were much more congruent with each other, as in both cases furthering children's intellectual growth is a central goal. For this reason (among others), the Library environment was much more conducive than that of the Boys' and Girls' Club to the cohesion of the Fifth Dimension site and its culture of collaborative learning. From the point of view of the Library staff, however, the very success of the program, which kept many children involved and enthusiastic in its activities, disrupted the quiet atmosphere appropriate for a setting such as a Library. The Fifth Dimension site was a relatively quiet activity in the context of the Boys' and Girls' Club but a relatively noisy one in the context of the Library. The Library staff thought that the noise and the playful bustle of the Fifth Dimension site disturbed some of its other patrons; and because the entire Library was housed in a single room, they could not see a solution to this problem. These specific circumstances of limited space and limited (or inflexible) resources are factors that are largely "accidental" in terms of the analysis undertaken in this chapter, but in this concrete case their impact on the continuation of the program was decisive. Given these circumstances, the interaction between the Fifth Dimension site and the Library setting, which was definitely beneficial from the standpoint of the Fifth Dimension program, produced a more ambivalent reaction on the part of the host institution.

The outcome of this story serves as a reminder that the problem of integrating new programs successfully into existing institutions is complex and requires careful consideration of the often paradoxical and unanticipated outcomes of the interplay between the program and its host institution. Efforts at educational innovation of the sort discussed here pose an extensive range of theoretical and practical problems; and these can be effectively addressed only through a strategy of analysis that situates learning and development in their cultural and institutional contexts.

Some Larger Implications

In closing, we would like to suggest some further implications, both practical and theoretical, that emerge from this analysis.

In the first place, the findings reported here have important practical implications for the consideration and implementation of educational innovations. They make it clear that the effectiveness of new programs will depend, not only on their intrinsic qualities considered in isolation, but on how successfully they can be integrated into the larger framework of the educational (or other) institutions into which they are introduced. Therefore it is important to consider carefully how they can best be *situated* in these contexts, not only physically but, above all, culturally. Careful and theoretically informed comparative analysis of the concrete instantiations of such programs can play an especially useful role in this sort of consideration.

Furthermore, ensuring the *successful* introduction of educational innovations involves more than merely achieving their adoption. As we have shown, the operation and impact of a given program are significantly shaped by the interplay between its implicit cultural logic and that of the larger institution in which it is embedded, and this interplay is often complex. New programs and activities, no matter how well conceived in their own terms, do not always work equally well in all settings—nor do they necessarily work well at all if they are simply inserted into an institutional setting that remains otherwise unchanged. (This is true *a fortiori*, of course, if new hardware or equipment is simply added to existing settings.) If we want to maximize the intellectual benefits of educational innovations, it is necessary to think carefully about how this might involve *changing educational practices* and about how to create favorable conditions for such changes.

We will end on a more general theoretical note. Several writers have recently suggested that developmental psychology should draw on sociology to extend and enrich its understanding of individual development (Dannefer & Perlmutter, 1990; Dowd, 1990; Goodnow, 1990). Such cross-fertilization would certainly be useful, but many of these formulations take too much for granted the disciplinary boundaries they would like to cross. As we have tried to suggest in this chapter, one key aspect of the Vygotskian perspective is that it already transcends the apparently sharp distinction between "psychology" and "sociology" in its conception of the formation of mind as a fundamentally sociocultural process. And many of the theoretical resources for moving beyond the limitations of current Vygotskian-inspired work are available in the underdeveloped possibilities of Vygotsky's theory itself.

Furthermore, in reaching outside the Vygotskian framework to help develop and concretize these possibilities, the best way to begin is not necessarily to turn to current sociological writings for isolated elements that can be grafted onto developmental theory from the outside. Rather, we have tried to begin at a deeper level by returning to the nexus of shared premises and problems in the work of Vygotsky, Durkheim, and the early Piaget. Although it may seem surprising to those who know Durkheim only by reputation, we have found some of his contributions particularly helpful for refining and solving Vygotskian problems. This is true because of the deep affinity between certain aspects of their central theoretical projects, especially their shared conception of human nature as essentially social and their antireductionist conception of society and culture as, in Durkheim's words, realities "*sui generis.*" [In addition to Durkheim (1897/1951), to which we have referred throughout, see also Durkheim (1912/1965, 1914/1973) for especially powerful formulations.]

This shared problematic, as we have tried to show, forms a key starting point for the task of developing a conception of the "social" dimension of individual development more comprehensive than the one utilized— explicitly or implicitly—by much current research. Furthermore, we have offered one example of how such a conception, and the genuinely sociocultural perspective it embodies, can effectively be employed to address concrete issues of educational practice and cognitive development.

Note

The data on which the present study is based were collected as part of a larger project supported in part by Spencer Foundation grants B1036 and B1175 to the Laboratory of Comparative Human Cognition. A number of people aided us, in varying degrees, in collecting and preparing the data; among them we particularly want to thank Michelle Carver and Pia Bombardier for their helpful and diligent work. We are also grateful to the community institutions discussed in this chapter for their cooperation and above all for their participation in the Fifth Dimension project. Finally, the arguments developed in this chapter are indebted to the theoretical inspiration and invaluable advice of Jeff Weintraub.

References

Cole, M. (1990a). *A cultural theory of development: what does it imply about the application of scientific research?* Paper presented at the Latin American Workshop on Applied Developmental Psychology, Recife, Brazil.

Cole, M. (1990b). *Cultural psychology: some general principles and a concrete example.* Paper presented at the Second International Congress on Activity Theory, Lahti, Finland.

Cole, M. (1990c). Cultural psychology: a once and future discipline? In J. J. Berman (ed.). *Nebraska symposium on motivation, 1989: cross-cultural perspectives* (Vol. 37). Lincoln: University of Nebraska Press.

Dannefer, D., & Perlmutter, M. (1990). Development as a multidimensional process: individual and social constituents. *Human Development, 33,* 108–137.

Dowd, J. J. (1990). Ever since Durkheim: the socialization of human development. *Human Development, 33,* 138–159.

Durkheim, E. (1897/1951). *Suicide.* New York: Free Press (originally published in French).

Durkheim, E. (1912/1965). *The elementary forms of the religious life.* New York: Free Press (originally published in French).

Durkheim, E. (1914/1973). The dualism of human nature and its social conditions. In R. N. Bellah (ed.). *Emile Durkheim on morality and society* (pp. 149–163). Chicago: University of Chicago Press (originally published in French).

Durkheim, E. (1925/1973). *Moral education.* New York: Free Press (originally published in French).

Giddens, A. (1979). *Central problems in social theory: action, structure and contradiction in social analysis.* Berkeley: University of California Press.

Goodnow, J. J. (1990). Using sociology to extend psychological accounts of cognitive development. *Human Development, 33,* 81–107.

Griffin, P., & Cole, M. (1984). Current activity for the future: the zo-ped. In B. Rogoff & J. V. Wertsch (eds.). *Children's learning in the "zone of proximal development." New directions for child development, Vol. 23.* San Francisco: Jossey-Bass.

Lave, J. (1988). *Cognition in practice: mind, mathematics and culture in everyday life.* Cambridge: Cambridge University Press.

Newman, D., Griffin, P., & Cole, M. (1989). *The construction zone: working for cognitive change in school.* Cambridge: Cambridge University Press.

Nicolopoulou, A. (1989). The invention of writing and the development of numerical concepts in Sumeria: some implications for developmental psychology. *Quarterly Newsletter of the Laboratory of Comparative Human Cognition, 11,* 114–124.

Nicolopoulou, A. (1991). Play, cognitive development, and the social world: the research perspective. In B. Scales, M. Almy, A. Nicolopoulou, & S. Ervin-Tripp (eds.). *Play and the social context of development in early care and education.* New York: Teachers College Press.

Nicolopoulou, A. (1993). Play, cognitive development, and the social world: Piaget, Vygotsky, and beyond. *Human Development.*

Piaget, J. (1932/1965). *The moral judgment of the child.* New York: Free Press (originally published in French).

Scribner, S., & Cole, M. (1981). *The psychology of literacy.* Cambridge, MA: Harvard University Press.

Vygotsky, L. S. (1933/1967). Play and its role in the mental development of the child. *Soviet Psychology, 12,* 6–18 (stenographic record of a lecture).

Vygotsky, L. S. (1978). *Mind in society: the development of higher psychological processes.* M. Cole, V. John-Steiner, S. Scribner, & E. Souberman (eds.). Cambridge, MA: Harvard University Press.

Vygotsky, L. S. (1987). *The collected works of L. S. Vygotsky. Vol. 1. Problems of general psychology* (including the volume "Thinking and speech") (R. W. Rieber & A. S. Carton, eds.; N. Minick, trans.). New York: Plenum Press.

Weintraub, J. (1974). Some reflections on Durkheim's concept of human nature: preliminary expectoration. Unpublished manuscript: University of California, Berkeley.

Wertsch, J. V. (1985). *The social formation of mind: a Vygotskian approach.* Cambridge, MA: Harvard University Press.

13

Activity Settings of Early Literacy: Home and School Factors in Children's Emergent Literacy

RONALD GALLIMORE and CLAUDE GOLDENBERG

Vygotsky argued that a cognitive function appears "twice, or in two planes. First it appears on the social plane, and then on the psychological plane. First it appears between people as an inter-psychological category, and then within the child as an intrapsychological category" (Vygotsky, 1978, p. 163).

> . . . if Vygotsky's insights concerning the role of social interaction in psychological development are to be effectively incorporated . . . the links between dyadic or small group interactions and the broader socio-cultural system must be recognized and explored . . . actions are at one and the same time components of the life of the individual and the social system . . . [and] will be defined and structured in certain respects by the broader social and cultural system. [Minick, 1985, p. 257]

One set of links to be explored are the activities that mediate the impact of the "broader sociocultural system" on the life of individuals, dyads, and other social groups. Everyday activities embed opportunities to learn and develop through modeling, joint production, apprenticeship, and other forms of mediated social learning that are embedded in goal-directed interactions (Rogoff, 1982; Tharp & Gallimore, 1988; Weisner, 1984; Wertsch, Minick, & Arns, 1984; Whiting, 1980; Whiting & Edwards, 1988). Through participation in cultural activities that require cognitive and communicative functions, children are drawn into the use of these functions in ways that nurture and develop them.

Children's activity settings are the architecture of their everyday life and the context of their development. They are shaped and sustained by ecological and cultural features of the family niche. In technologically complex societies, parents and children can be co-participants in preparing meals, eating dinner, clearing up, repairing equipment, watching television, getting ready for school, doing homework, storybook time, and dozens of mundane contexts in which interaction is embedded. In subsistence agricultural societies, analogous domestic activities can be found. There are some important variants. For example, young children may spend more time in the care of siblings and other caretakers as result of parental involvement in subsistence activities (Weisner & Gallimore, 1977).

These activity settings are a perceptible *instantiation of the social system* to which Minick referred. They are the everyday conduits through which social and cultural institutions affect children's experiences and their development. Activities in which children engage as an ordinary part of their daily lives have a profound impact on the cognitive and communicative functions they develop. To study these activities is to identify the cognitive and communicative opportunities of culture (Nerlove & Snipper, 1981).

We have been part of an effort to operationalize cultural activities in ways that can guide empirical research. This effort has used five "activity setting" variables: (1) the personnel present during an activity; (2) salient cultural values; (3) the operations and task demands of the activity itself; (4) the scripts for conduct that govern the participants' actions; and (5) the purposes or motives of the participants. The activity setting concept is derivative of Soviet activity theory (Leont'ev, 1981) and the behavior setting concept of the Whitings (Whiting & Whiting, 1975), mixed with the influence of Cole (1985), Rogoff (1982), Wertsch et al. (1984), and our own investigations (Gallimore, Weisner, Kaufman, & Bernheimer, 1989; Tharp & Gallimore, 1988; Weisner, 1984; Weisner & Gallimore, 1985; Weisner, Gallimore & Jordan, 1988).

Concept of Emergent Literacy

In many societies literacy is an important subsistence tool and is a functional and embedded part of many kinds of activity setting. For children in literate cultures, literacy development begins long before formal schooling and teaching commence (Teale, 1986). In many settings and for many varied purposes, it is a means that older members of a family use to achieve long- and short-term goals. They are highly varied in terms of activities, participants, purposes, and styles of interaction, including the nature and extent of child involvement. Examples include domestic chores (writing and reading shopping lists, paying bills, making schedules), entertainment (reading television guides, game rules), school-related (homework, playing school), work (carryovers from parents' jobs), religious activities (Sunday school materials, Bible reading), communication (letters, notes, holiday cards), and storybook time.

Learning to be literate begins early for children in households that use literacy. Just as language learning begins before a child utters a word, so too does literacy begin to emerge before children can actually read or write in conventional terms (Mason & Allen, 1986). "The notion of reading preceding writing, or vice versa, is a misconception. Listening, speaking, reading, and writing abilities (as aspects of language—both oral and written) develop concurrently and interrelatedly, rather than sequentially (Teale, 1986). The recognition of this concurrency and relatedness has prompted researchers to adopt Clay's (1966) concept of *emergent literacy* to describe literacy development during a child's early years.

Mason (1977) summarized some of the emergent literacy activities that seem to be most strongly related to early reading and writing development:

> At home children have their own alphabet books, they are read to frequently and hear story records, they use the library. . . . They are encouraged to print their names, write headings on their pictures, and read labels and simple stories . . . and they enjoy demonstrating their ability to read to each other, and to adults. [p. 30]

It means that the "home curriculum" of children who learn to read early is filled not with syllable cards and phonic drills but with meaningful, communicative print and many opportunities for interacting with it. Meaningful experiences with simple texts are probably the most important influences in early literacy development.

The nature and frequency of emergent home literacy experiences such as these differ as a function of social, cultural, and economic factors. Working class families are less likely to read to their children than are middle-class families (Feitelson & Goldstein, 1986; Teale, 1986; Wells, 1985). In working class homes, fewer than 2% of all literacy activities involve story-reading (Anderson & Stokes, 1984). These differences in home literacy activities are then likely to be related to social class variations in school achievement (Adams, 1990).

However, there is considerable variability in emergent literacy experiences *within* social and cultural groups (Teale, 1986), thereby confirming White's (1982) important conclusion: *Being poor itself does not create reading problems; rather, what is critical are the kinds of literacy activities generated in the home* (Durkin, 1966; Mason & Allen, 1986).

We have been using the concept of activity setting to examine emergent literacy in the homes of low-income Spanish-speaking children. The concept suggests some promising ways for schools and teachers to have an impact on emergent literacy experiences of young minority culture children while avoiding the "shifting of blame" and related dangers of cultural imperialism of which earlier critics of "home intervention" rightly warned. To illustrate, we summarize some of our work on the emergent literacy of young Latino children at risk for poor reading achievement. Some of our work suggests an extension of Vygotskian ideas can provide a fresh look at this question. The key idea is nested in the quotation from Minick that cultural activities "are at one and the same time components of the life of the individual and the social system. . . ." (Minick, 1985, p. 257).

Activity Setting Analysis of Emergent Literacy

Our study community is located in the metropolitan Los Angeles area. It is in an extremely low-income area and has a high crime rate, drug traffic, gang activity, and heavy concentration of low-income Hispanics, almost all of whom are from Mexico and Central America.

The main street in the district is a busy urban thoroughfare lined with fast-food restaurants, Latin American bakeries and markets, and rows of apartment buildings. Children play and ride bicycles in inner courtyards of buildings. Spanish music and radio announcers can be heard blaring from radios. Young men, alone or in groups, walk or stand around, drinking, laughing, and talking; occasionally one comes up to a car and offers to sell drugs. There are also residential neighborhoods in the district that range from streets with fairly well-kept single family homes to areas with rows of dilapidated houses and apartment buildings, with old cars parked on lawns and debris scattered about.

Since 1968 the district has experienced an explosion in the student population and has also undergone fundamental changes in ethnic and socioeconomic composition. The district enrollment has gone from 2837 in 1968 to nearly 5000 students in 1988. In 1968 a high percent (81%) of the students were white; currently, 88% are Hispanic. The district's growth and transformation is a direct result of the enormous influx of Hispanic immigration into the United States, particularly southern California during the 1970s and 1980s.[1]

The population with which we are working primarily comprises American-born children of foreign-born parents. Nearly three-fourths of the parents were born in Mexico, mainly in the states of Jalisco and Michoacan. The remainder are from Central America. Approximately 90% of the kindergarten children in our studies over the past two years are U.S.-born. They attend a predominantly (88%) Hispanic, low-income elementary school district in southern California. Nearly 85% of the school population qualified for free meals during 1987–88. An additional 10% qualified for reduced-priced meals.[2]

We summarize what we learned from a series of studies of emergent literacy in this ecocultural niche in terms of the five components of activity settings mentioned earlier. We begin by focusing on the personnel available to interact with children.

Personnel Present

With rare exception, in our study community there are adults and siblings available in every household to supervise and interact with children everyday after school and in the evenings. Case studies of ten families provided a glimpse of household variability (Reese, Goldenberg, Loucky, & Gallimore, 1989). For these case studies, ten children were selected at random from four kindergarten classrooms. In each of the ten families at least one parent was employed, and in six cases both parents worked outside the home. Jobs included work in hotels, factories, maintenance, mechanics firms, and garbage collection. No family received welfare support, although eight of the ten children received free or reduced-price meals at school.

Parental employment ensured that no family was destitute, but the economic circumstances of most of the families were relatively precarious. In four families parents were laid off work during the course of the study. In another an aunt who worked as a maid in a hotel was occasionally sent home without pay when not needed. Some families supplemented their income by collecting aluminum cans and cardboard. Others worked out of their homes, doing welding, selling jewelry and clothing, and selling illegally copied cassettes (an activity halted by a police raid).

Parents' educational levels were generally low, even in comparison to the overall education level of Mexican-origin adults in the United States, who in 1988 had a median of less than 11 years of schooling (U.S. Department of Commerce, 1988). The median for parents in the case study sample was seven years of schooling for mothers and five years for fathers (overall mean 6.5 years; range 1 to 12 years). In other samples we have used for a series of different studies, the mean years of schooling was 6.4 (SD 3.1) for mothers and 6.3 (SD 3.0) for fathers. Spanish was the language of all of the homes studied. All children participated in a bilingual instructional program in which literacy instruction for the first few years is in Spanish.

Salient Cultural Values

Parents in our study community have expressed uniformly high aspirations for their children's education. For example, 93% of the parents of 30 kindergarten children we surveyed said they wanted their son or daughter at least to finish high school; 87% of the same parents wanted their child to go on to college.

Our findings are consistent with another group of investigators who surveyed recent Mexican immigrant parents (all from our study community). Nearly all 100 parents questioned wanted their children to complete high school, with 93% wanting their children to continue beyond high school, either in college or a vocational school (McLean-Bardwell, Bryan, Baca, & Gomez, 1987).

For the parents in our study community, education is a means toward economic security, the attainment of professional status, or both. Its necessity for social mobility and economic success was unquestioned. In this regard, there was no doubt among any of the parents that they wanted their children to go as far as possible in their schooling. Many spoke explicitly of professional careers they hoped their children would pursue:

> After she [his daughter] finishes secondary [high] school, I'd like her to study medicine, law, engineering . . . a major career . . . [but if I can't afford that] then she can study to be a nurse; if she can't be a doctor or a lawyer, then a nurse or a dentist . . . so that she can make a good living, do well on her own. . . . If it's too expensive here [we are thinking] we would send her to Mexico to finish her studies. Where I work, I am saving for that. She is 5 years old and I have already begun to save. I want to give my children something for their education, for when they finish high school.

Parents drew a stark contrast between their own educational experiences and opportunities and those they wish for their children. In particular, parents expressed the view that education would permit their children "to be somebody" (*ser alguien en la vida*), something they believe was denied to them because of the limited education they had received themselves.

In this regard, literacy was seen as playing a key role. One mother, who herself had attended only a few weeks of school in her native Mexico, said she had not paid sufficient attention to her older children's literacy development. She expressed her commitment to doing things differently with her youngest:

> These [her older children] are children who don't like to pick up a book. That's why I am trying to induce this little one into reading [*inducirlo a la lectura*], because I have had a lot of problems with the others. . . . They have had problems in school with reading and writing.

[Quotations have been translated from the original Spanish.]

In sum, there is a clear sense among the parents with whom we have been working that educational attainment in general and the acquisition of literacy in particular are essential for their children's social and economic advance. Moreover, parents explicitly repudiate what they perceive to be their own parents' failure to help them obtain a higher level of formal education. They attribute their own low social and economic status to their lack of formal education and their failure to acquire sufficiently high levels of literacy and other academic skills.

Task Operations and Demands

The third of the five activity components introduces topics that are more traditionally associated with "activities," that is, what people actually do and the kinds of operations and demands a task imposes. Ours is a broad definition of "literacy activities"—an inclusive definition of the ways reading and writing play a part in the lives of children and their parents (see also Anderson and Stokes, 1984; Teale, 1986).

Household Literacy Activities and Tasks. With almost no exception, parents in our study community are literate, at least at a rudimentary level. Most of the Spanish-speaking parents write letters at least occasionally (Goldenberg, 1989b). According to parents' reports, households send and receive an average of three or four letters per month. We also have direct observational evidence of letter-writing in the homes, often in the presence of children (Reese et al., 1989). In fact, the kindergarten children in our studies often express an interest in writing and reading letters themselves.

Most of the homes we have visited over the past five years of research have one or more books, although not necessarily books for children. In a few cases, families have one or more bookcases containing encyclopedias they have bought for their children, nature books, Bible stories, discarded schoolbooks, dictionaries, comic books, and textbooks parents use in their English classes. Parent reading of newspapers or magazines has rarely been observed, but most parents report having them in the home at least occasionally; many parents say they read them at least weekly, often at work. Printed advertisements are delivered regularly to homes, and children appear interested in the pictures and descriptions of advertised specials.

Despite the low educational and socioeconomic status of these families, therefore, the homes are not devoid of printed material, as is often assumed. Nonetheless, it would be equally incorrect to assume they are infused with literacy or "filled with print," as Auerbach (1989) concluded about other inner-city households.

Children's Literacy. According to parents' reports and to observational data gathered during 1988–89, all children express an interest in interacting with print in some way. For example, virtually all parents reported that their children would ask what street signs or other written materials said. All parents reported some instances of children attempting—or pretending—to read or write. One mother said, for example:

> About two or three times a week he gets a book and leafs through it. According to him, he's reading. . . . It's as if he were reading. He moves his hand as if he were reading. [Goldenberg, 1989b, p. 10]

Direct observations confirmed this portrait.

Other parents reported their children attempted or pretended to read magazines, advertisement flyers, notes and letters from school, and street signs. Children also attempted to write, most often while older siblings were doing homework but also on occasions when parents or others wrote letters.

However, 77% of the kindergarten parents interviewed shortly after the middle of the school year reported that their child had not been taken to the library (outside of school hours) since the beginning of kindergarten. Another 8% reported that their child had been to the library only once. Children's books were also noticeably absent from many of the homes. Sixty percent of the parents reported having fewer than five children's books in the homes; more than 40% reported none at all (Goldenberg, 1989b).

Other sorts of literacy activities have been reported by parents and observed by field workers: reading and writing letters from cereal or cake mix boxes; parents reading and explaining to the child notes sent home by the teacher; and children asking visitors and family members how to write their names, then trying to write them themselves. In several homes children had small chalkboards they used when playing alone, with their parents, or when playing school with siblings and friends. Some parents reported teaching their children some letters and sounds, although reading was not a part of the kindergarten curriculum at the time. One parent, for example, specifically said that she was beginning to teach her child how to read because she thought her older children had not made satisfactory progress in reading. In many cases the presence of an elementary school-age sibling seemed to increase the frequency and nature of children's home literacy experiences.

In each of the ten homes studied by Reese et al. (1989), the school had a major impact on the children's home literacy experiences and was largely responsible for the consistency in types of task observed. More than 40% of all observed learning activities involved use of materials from school. In two families the flyers, calendars, homework, and booklets sent home by the school accounted for virtually all of the printed material in the home. Homework and homework-like drill initiated by parents were part of the literacy experience of all target children and accounted for most of the learning activities in certain households. Paper and pencil activities reflecting activities taking place at school were also common. Indeed, several parents reported that they had waited to teach their child certain skills until the child went to school.

At least as early as kindergarten, therefore, children in our study community have some literacy experiences at home and have at least some knowledge about how print functions, how it is produced, and that a relation exists between print and meaning. Moreover, according to parents and to our observational data, children clearly have an interest in interacting with print. In other words, the children show many signs of being ready to learn to read. However, they are lacking many experiences most closely associated with children's early and sustained literacy growth: children's books in the home, an abundance of meaningful, age- and developmentally appropriate reading experiences, verbal interactions around meaningful texts with more competent readers, and being encouraged to read and write or to pretend to read and write.

Scripts for Conduct and Individual Purposes and Motives. In our sample families, young children's attempts at reading and writing are considered amusing, at best. In the parents' minds, children are not doing anything meaningful or important when they scribble or talk to themselves as they leaf through printed matter. They are simply pretending. Children's attempts to practice writing their names or writing recognizable letters are taken more seriously, but anything else is considered "pure scribbling" ("*puros garabatos,*" parents frequently said). One mother said her daughter pretended to read, "although she doesn't know anything." The mother said her daughter would get the older sister's school books and "read" them: "She talks to herself and makes it up," the mother said, laughing.

In another instance a fieldworker in the study reported by Reese et al. observed a mother writing a letter to her family of origin in Mexico. A five-year-old kept intruding and asking to participate. The mother suggested drawing some pictures to be included in the letter to grandmother in Mexico. Eventually, after continuing overtures by the child, the mother wrote out two sentences in Spanish for the child to copy. The sentences were copied and included in the letter. This classic example of an emergent literacy event—a child who cannot read or write in the "schooled sense" participating in a literacy event—was lacking an important element: The mother never read the sentences to the child, and they were copied without the child ever knowing what was being communicated.

Summary of the Argument So Far

For two of the five activity setting components—personnel and cultural values—the necessary conditions for emergent literacy events are present. Despite generally low educational levels among parents, they value schooling, are available to the children, and are interested in and capable of providing literacy-enhancing experiences.

Actual literacy tasks—the third component of activity settings—are more frequent than some stereotypes of low income Spanish-speaking families suggest, but they are not optimal for literacy development. Children were either seen or reported to have relatively few experiences of the sort most conducive to early literacy growth: hearing, reading, and pretending to read children's books; and writing or trying to write words, messages, or even stories in the presence of more competent individuals who attempt to render meaningful these immature attempts at literate behavior.

In terms of the fourth and fifth activity components (scripts and purposes), what we observed was also not optimal. When children attempted to use or create "texts," parents did not seem to consider what the children were doing to be an important step in "emerging literacy." They did not use such events as occasions for "talk" about texts, reading, and the like. Opportunities for meaningful oral interchanges about texts were present, but they were not exploited.

Yet many believe it is just such opportunities for "pretend reading" or "pseudoreading," preferably in the presence of a responsive, more competent individual, that represent an important step in young children's early literacy acquisition (Chall, 1983; Teale, 1978). More generally, literacy development is profoundly affected by the opportunities children have at home to hear and use language in its many forms and functions (e.g., Chall, 1983; Feagans & Farran, 1982; Heath, 1983; Olson, Torrance, & Hildyard, 1985).

Let us examine the question of nonoptimal emergent literacy opportunities from the perspective of the activity setting concept. Beyond the mere existence of at least some literacy tasks, the single most critical component in most emergent literacy activities is the personnel present. Someone has to be available and capable of assisting a child if we are to see "literacy-promoting" interactions. Given the personnel and at least some literacy tasks, what aspect of an activity setting is likely to have the greatest impact on a child's experience? Probably, it is the purpose that the more capable individuals see in the task they are jointly performing with the emerging literate. On the surface, a task may seem the same, and the personnel may appear similar; but depending on the purpose in the minds of the participants, a child's experience can vary greatly. In other words, what the participants "think" they are doing affects how they go about it, and that determines how the event contributes to emerging literacy skills.

A classic demonstration of how purpose can affect interaction was provided in the Wertsch et al. (1984) comparison of Brazilian mothers and teachers interacting with children. Although the task (a puzzle) and the personnel (a child and an adult woman) were identical, the nature of the interaction that occurred was entirely different. Teachers perceived the puzzle as a "teaching opportunity" and used a scaffolding script to assist the children but without actively participating. Mothers, however, treated the puzzle as a "job to be finished" and actively collaborated with the children to find a solution. *What the women believed about the purpose of the activity determined the behavioral script they employed.*

With this perspective, consider the literacy activities observed in the Spanish-speaking homes of our study community. Literacy events were relatively infrequent. When they did occur, parents did not treat them as opportunities to talk about, encourage, support, and reinforce child literacy experiences. But they could, and they occasionally do. They just do not do it often enough or take full advantage when they do.

Given the families' values, we wondered what would happen if teachers regularly sent home "little books"[3] and asked parents to let the child read to them? It is possible that the mere addition of a supply of "literacy tasks" plus a "purpose" suggested by a high status individual (teachers) might produce a substantially different picture than our observations and interviews have revealed. Would the books lead parents to imbue "reading together" with a *purpose* that leads to "scripts" associated with emergent literacy opportunities? Would a teacher-prompted "read together" activity increase the kind of "talk" said to be optimal for literacy development?

Effect of Task on Scripts in Home Literacy Activity Settings

In one completed study (Goldenberg, 1989a), we examined the effects of two different activity settings on children's home literacy experiences. Each activity setting was prompted by a different type of literacy material teachers sent to the homes of their Spanish-speaking kindergartners. Our hypothesis was that differences in one activity component (*task demand*) would lead to differences in another (language use, or the "*scripts*" used by parents and their children). We expected that the differences in task demands of the two activity settings would lead parents to infer a different *purpose* for engaging their children in early literacy interactions.

The scripts parents use in their interactions with children are important in terms of contemporary theories of early literacy development. Previous research has suggested that low economic status Mexican-American mothers, compared to higher status Mexican-American or Anglo mothers, ask fewer questions. They also use relatively more directives and nonverbal modeling cues when teaching their young children (Laosa, 1978, 1980).

Because of the overwhelming importance of language in U.S. classrooms, these differences in language use during learning episodes could put young, lower socioeconomic Hispanic children at a disadvantage when they enter school. Teachers tend to ask many questions during the course of instruction, so that children who are not accustomed to "didactic questioning" (Edwards & Furlong, 1978) or "known information questions" (Heath, 1982; Mehan, 1979) are less likely to respond quickly and effectively.

Activity theory suggests it might be possible to influence the scripts parents use in their interactions with children by manipulating the nature of the task and the purposes participants infer. To this end, the two groups of kindergarten children participating in this study received contrasting materials to take home. One group of children received conventional beginning reading or reading readiness materials—for practicing the child's name, writing and naming letters, and learning letter-sound correspondences. These materials were what the kindergarten teachers normally sent home for children to practice.

In the second group, children received short, simple, but meaningful texts (*libritos*) developed by a kindergarten teacher in the district where we have been working (Mark, 1986). Children were shown the books at school and asked to read at home with parents or siblings. When they came for the fall conference, attended by nearly 100% of kindergarten parents, the parents were also shown sample booklets. They were encouraged to read the *libritos* with their children and to concentrate on the story content. Teachers expressly encouraged parents *not* to focus on word recognition per se or to dwell on sounding out syllables or words. Rather, parents were told that the goal was to read for enjoyment of the story and to give the child the opportunity to hear, learn, and possibly "read" (i.e., pretend-read) entire little books. Sample texts are provided in Table 13.1.

To test the impact of *libritos* on children's emergent home literacy experiences, we collected home data on Spanish-speaking children in two groups

Table 13.1. Sample Texts from *Libritos*

Qué tiene la mamá osa? [*What does the mother bear have?*]	
Page	
1	*La mamá osa tiene una taza.* [The mother bear has a cup.]
2	*La mamá osa tiene uno mono.* [The mother bear has a monkey.]
3	*La mamá osa tiene un perro.* [The mother bear has a dog.]
4	*La mamá osa tiene un elefante.* [The mother bear has an elephant.]
El niño elefante [The little (boy) elephant]	
Page	
1	*El niño elefante es un amigo.* [The little (boy) elephant is a friend.]
2	*Es el amigo de un perro.* [He is the friend of a dog.]
3	*y de un oso* [and of a bear]
4	*y de un mono* [and of a monkey]
5	*y de una mula* [and of a mule]

Source: Mark (1986). Reprinted by permission.

of classrooms. In four classrooms, teachers used and sent home a new *librito* every month of the school year. In four comparison classrooms, teachers followed the district curriculum, which emphasized a combination of reading readiness activities followed by instruction in vowels and a few consonants. We videotaped children and parents (and on some occasions older siblings) as they engaged in whatever literacy activities the teacher had sent home.

Language and Meaning in Home Literacy Interactions

The activity setting concept guides us to examine various issues in children's home literacy experiences and, more specifically, how different materials sent by the teacher have different effects on these experiences.

For example, the nature of the activity (what parents and children engage in) should influence *how* an activity is carried out, that is, the scripts and language used by participants. Parents of children given the *libritos* should have more chances to use questions and related language forms, given the scarcity of books and other reading materials observed in the households (Goldenberg, 1989b; Reese et al., 1989). In contrast, simple rote tasks such as copying letters or names should create fewer such opportunities. Hence this study explored the possibility that by manipulating activity setting components—in this case, the materials children use—conditions can be created that encourage and support beneficial language use during parent–child teaching/learning interactions.

We found that *the use of the* libritos *greatly increased language use during home literacy activities.* Although the two types of material yielded episodes almost identical in length, parents spoke with their children much more during book reading than did the parents whose children received more conventional copying and letter-learning activities. More specifically, parents gave children more positive feedback, asked more questions, and made more modeling statements (Goldenberg, 1989a). In other words, the meaningful texts led to increasingly elaborate verbal scripts during literacy episodes.

However, these changes in amount of language were true only for *parents.* The texts produced no increase in spontaneous child language production relative to the conventional materials group.

In the book reading interactions, parents asked their children far more questions than those doing more conventional kindergarten "reading readiness" homework. This effect is important, given previous findings that young Latino children experience fewer opportunities to answer parents' questions during learning episodes (Laosa, 1978, 1980).

However, the *libritos produced relatively few interactions focusing on the meaning of the text.* Under both home literacy conditions, parents' overwhelming emphasis was on children's correct performance of the given task at the most superficial level, either writing or naming letters correctly or reading a text accurately. Utterances focusing on "surface associations" (letter-, word-, or phrase recognition with no reference to meaning) constituted by far most of the utterances—more than 90%. Despite the fact that the simple books we had sent home contained stories and various meaningful elements and parents were explicitly encouraged to focus on these elements, they did not prompt more meaning-oriented interactions between parents and children.

Parents' Purposes and Interactional Scripts

Although there might be several reasons parents attended almost exclusively to the surface features of the texts, our activity setting model suggests that one explanation lies in the *participants' immediate purposes and motives*. Purposes and motives, together with broader cultural values and goals, influence how tasks are carried out, that is, what scripts participants use.

The parents attended to surface features of the text because doing so is consistent with their conception of how children learn to read—through repetitious and accurate practice of letters, syllables, or words (Goldenberg, 1988a; Reese et al., 1989) This conception of the purpose of the early literacy activity—correct and precise word and letter recognition at the most literal and concrete level—is consistent with their own experiences. Spanish reading is taught in the United States and elsewhere as a matter of "code breaking." Virtually without exception, Spanish-speakers are taught to read in formal school settings where learning the phonetic rules is the primary focus. From what we know of the parents in our cohort, this method is how they learned to read (Reese et al., 1989) and it is what they presume to be the purpose of their children's homework, whether it is ditto sheets or little books. Their preoccupation with surface features of even meaningful texts is therefore entirely reasonable.

Furthermore, given the importance these parents attach to their children's academic achievement and specifically their learning to read (i.e., the broader cultural values and goals previously discussed), they treat materials or "homework" sent by the teacher as highly consequential. These activities are to be completed correctly and precisely, *in accordance with their view of how children learn to read*. Parents attend conscientiously to what *they* see as the main purpose of the activity, and they give children little latitude for incorrect responses.

At the level of immediate purposes and motives, the fifth facet of the activity setting, parents are therefore likely to construe the tasks sent home by teachers in a way that leads them to focus on what they view as critical for learning to read. The "idea" of pretend-reading, discussing the relations between texts and pictures, and relating a child's previous experience to what he or she is reading probably support early literacy development. However, these factors appear to be meaningless abstractions to the parents, in comparison to their definition of "real" reading, that is, correctly recognizing words in a written text.

Implications for Educational Practice

It would be wrong to conclude that parents in this study, or low-income Spanish-speaking parents more generally, are unique in their preoccupation with the most superficial aspects of texts and materials sent from the school. Teachers often behave in similar ways: They frequently interrupt oral reading to correct trivial mistakes, interfering with the flow of the reading and preventing students from dealing with more substantive features of the text (Anderson, Hiebert, Scott, & Wilkinson, 1985).

Parents and teachers may both have a tendency to overcorrect misreadings or mispronunciations for precisely the same reasons: Reading is seen as an important skill, and therefore there is little tolerance for errors in performance. Reading is defined principally in terms of its most immediately observable and salient features, namely, accurate and fluent identification of words in a text. As many reformers have found to their dismay, simply changing textbooks has little impact on instruction and never will so long as the teachers see reading as "cracking the code" rather than extracting meaning.

The conventional solution to the problem of too few home literacy events and less-than-optimal language-use opportunities has been parent training. Attempts have been made to train parents to use new scripts. Henderson and Garcia (1973), for example, trained Mexican-American mothers to teach and reinforce question-asking by their first-grade children. More recently, Edwards (1989) has attempted to train low-income black mothers to read and interact verbally around storybooks with their preschool children. Some attempts to promote low-income children's language opportunities through "parent training" have had at least short-term success (Topping, 1986).

However, other reviewers have been skeptical. Farran (1982), for example, expressed doubt about attempts to "remediate . . . deficiencies in the parent by attempting to make the parent behave like middle-class parents" (p. 271). Perhaps, as Heath argued, many of these efforts are unlikely to have long-term effects because "trying to impose external values [in this case, linguistic or interactional ones] on preschool home life is not likely to bring any significant internal change to families" (Heath, 1986, p. 181).

In the terms we use here, Heath's comment can be recast in this way: No intervention is sustained unless it is fitted to the ecocultural conditions of the family and to the activity settings for children that are part of a family's everyday routine. This assertion is consistent with our studies of emergent literacy in Latino households. Simply providing books and encouragement to "read together" does not produce conversation about meaning and text beyond the accurate decoding and pronouncing words. A change in the *task operations and demands* has some effect on the *scripts* parents use, but it does not guarantee it will change the *purpose* they see for doing the task. As soon as the parents construe an activity as the "teaching of literacy," their prevailing conception of literacy development is activated, driving the interaction and determining the script-in-use.

Is there no way to assist these parents to broaden their children's home literacy experiences? After all, our activity setting analysis suggests that many of our Spanish-speaking parents have in place the conditions necessary to assist their children's literacy development. The personnel necessary are present and available. They have values congruent with this intervention scheme; they value education. They are receptive to teacher-provided books and suggestions. Moreover, we found that the kindergarten books did in fact promote important kinds of language-use at home—usages not prompted by traditional readiness-type "homework."

Our data suggest that one way to assist parents requires a major shift in many school districts' early literacy practices: Schools should find ways to provide meaningful texts for children to read (or "pretend-read") at home with adults or other, more competent individuals. These materials should be seen as part of a comprehensive effort to create, both at home and at school, more exposure to and more talk about meaningful texts.

Although our results suggest it would be naïve to expect such a change in practices to alter radically children's home literacy interactions and opportunities, we *can* expect such a change to provide children with important home literacy experiences they otherwise would not receive. The sort of changes we are advocating here have the added virtue of being fairly simple and cost-effective. They do not require major infusions of time and resources, yet they hold considerable promise for helping to create home conditions that are conducive to early literacy development.

Such increased exposure to meaningful text must occur in schools as well as in homes, however. It is absurd to criticize families when study after study documents the limited use in schools of meaningful text and the prevalence of limited forms of communication. The importance of certain types of language-use for school success requires an increase in children's exposure to language as a medium for displaying what is known and for seeking and integrating knowledge (Tharp, 1989; Tharp & Gallimore, 1988). In-school curricula and methods are available, and there is some evidence of emerging effective methodologies for instruction in both first- and second-language development (Hart, 1982; Krashen & Terrell, 1983; Tough, 1982; Ward & Kelley, no date).

This much is certain: If reading books and talking with children helps them succeed in school, the material prerequisites should be available to every parent, regardless of their social, economic, or cultural circumstances. Most schools can help stimulate such home activities at little cost, and our findings suggest that the activities stimulated by such simple texts are potentially valuable.

In an ideal form, the parents need receive no training, thus making the intervention not only more economical but also at less risk of cultural intrusion. Such a strategy makes no demand for value or role changes. If it is a culture in which parents do not do things such as read with children, it can be siblings or whomever assumes caregiver functions (Gallimore, Boggs, & Jordan, 1974; Weisner & Gallimore, 1977; Weisner et al., 1988). Indeed, we have observed just such arrangements in our case studies (Reese et al., 1989).

Families are not hapless victims. They are guided by beliefs and cultural tools to modify and accommodate to ecological constraints and pressures (Gallimore et al., 1989). For these Latino families, one such accommodation involves doing what is needed to assist their child adapt to U.S. society, schools, and available adult roles, all of which are greatly influenced by access to literacy of a certain kind. How the parents respond to their child's initiations of literacy events is left to them in regard to what they choose as important and to what they see as purposes of interactions with their children.

An intervention strategy with the focus we propose here is different from those that assume parents must acquire new values or be "trained" to use specific scripts. The approach we suggest requires only that teachers regularly and systematically send home literacy materials that can create desired activity settings. In effect, merely providing more meaningful texts and the invitation to use them makes the child the agent or vehicle of intervention. By arming the child with a task (books) and a purpose (reading for meaning), the intent is to increase child-initiated emergent literacy events.

Such an approach capitalizes on a pattern of child initiation and structuring of literacy events that already is present in some Latino households. Reese et al. reported that in some of our study families 80% of all learning activities observed over the course of a year were initiated by kindergarten children. Particularly in homes where parents exhibited a more laissez-faire attitude to children's learning and attempts at literacy, the degree of child initiation became a key factor in determining the frequency of literacy activities. These data contradict the common assumption of family literacy programs that "the 'natural' direction of literacy learning is from parent to child" (Auerbach, 1989).

Some families might not want to respond to child-initiated or school-provided literacy activities. Others might not be able to. We have not experienced such obstacles. On the contrary, parents are delighted when teachers send home literacy materials or homework, and they express some dissatisfaction when teachers do not send home academic activities for children (Goldenberg, 1988b).

Nevertheless, parents cannot and should not be coerced. No program should violate the principles of a pluralistic society. What parents might and can do with the information is separate from whether appropriate information and materials are made available to them. Sending books and telling parents about the potential benefits of reading and listening to their young children runs no risk. It does offer some hope that it will assist the parents as they construct activity settings that suit their means and ends.

Conclusions

> Almost every major theory of development accepts the premises of individualism and takes the child as the unit of study. . . . There are signals now aloft that the dogma of individualism, both in its claim of lifelong stability of personality and in its claim that human action can be understood without consideration of context or history, is under severe stress. The story that Vygotsky (1978) told 50 years ago, *the story of the embeddedness of the developing mind in society,* has finally been heard. [Kessen, 1979, pp. 819–20, emphasis added]

The evolution in perspective that Vygotsky's ideas have brought represent a formidable challenge to traditional research methods and procedures. How are we to conceive of and study "components of the life of the individual and social system at one and the same time" (Minick, 1985, p. 257)? A major challenge is to find a practical way to study cultural experiences in the everyday life of individuals and to understand how they shape their cognitive and communicative development.

Culture is not a nominal variable equivalent to nationality. Treating the concept in this way assumes that everyone in a group receives an equal dose of a uniform thing called "culture." The cross-cultural evidence does not warrant such an assumption (Weisner et al., 1988; Whiting & Edwards, 1988; Whiting & Whiting, 1975). Variance within groups means that "culture" cannot be controlled for or measured as a *trait* equally applicable to all members of a group if the goal is meet the challenge of Vygotsky's ideas.

One solution is to construe *culture as the shaper and sustainer of activity settings*—contexts for individual action, teaching, learning, and task competence (Whiting, 1980; Whiting & Edwards, 1988). Activity settings identify the constituent elements through which culture affects the individual. The constituent elements—personnel, motives, tasks, scripts, goals/beliefs—represent the instantiation of culture at the individual level. The elements reflect evolved, adapted responses to opportunities and constraints of the local niche. Activity elements are "the links between dyadic or small group interactions and the broader sociocultural system . . . [and] are at one and the same time components of the life of the individual and the social system. . . ." (Minick, 1985, p. 257) They are the "contexts of culture."

Notes

This research was supported by a National Academy of Education Spencer Fellowship to C. Goldenberg and a grant from the Spencer Foundation to R. Gallimore and C. Goldenberg. Additional support was provided by the Linguistic Minority Research Project of the University of California. Our thanks to Leslie Reese and James Loucky, who gathered ethnographic data and provided invaluable assistance for this research, and to Jane Mark, who developed the kindergarten books and accompanying materials used in a study reported here.

This chapter is a revised version of a paper delivered for a symposium on Vygotsky and education at the annual meeting of the American Educational Research Association, San Francisco, March 1989. Unless otherwise noted, the data reported here come from a two-year study of the home literacy experiences of Hispanic kindergarten children (Goldenberg, 1988a, 1989a, b) and a study of home and school literacy currently under way (Gallimore & Goldenberg, 1988). Both studies are with children attending a small elementary school district in the metropolitan Los Angeles area.

1. From Goldenberg (1984) and more recent district records.

2. To qualify for free meals, the gross yearly income of a family of five cannot exceed $17,030; to qualify for reduced-price meals, family income must be $24,235 or less (1987 dollars).

3. Our work has been influenced by that of Mason, McCormick, and Bhavnagri (1986), although at the time our study began we were not aware of the "Little Books"—since renamed "Predictable Books"—developed by Mason et al.

References

Adams, M. (1990). *Beginning to read: thinking and learning about print*. Cambridge, MA: MIT Press.

Anderson, A. B., & Stokes, S. J. (1984). Social and institutional influences on the development and practice of literacy. In H. Goelman, A. Oberg, & F. Smith (eds.). *Awakening to literacy* (pp. 24–37). Portsmouth, NH: Heinemann.

Anderson, R. B., Hiebert, E. H., Scott, J. A., & Wilkinson, I.A.G. (1985). *Becoming a nation of readers: the report of the Commission on Reading*. Champaign, IL: Center for the Study of Reading.

Auerbach, E. (1989). Toward a social-contextual approach to family literacy. *Harvard Educational Review, 59*, 165–81.

Chall, J. S. (1983). *Stages of reading development*. New York: McGraw-Hill.

Clay, M. (1966). Emergent reading behavior. Unpublished doctoral dissertation, University of Auckland, New Zealand.

Cole, M. (1985). The zone of proximal development: where culture and cognition create each other. In J. V. Wertsch (ed.). *Culture, communication, and cognition: Vygotskian perspectives* (pp. 146–61). Cambridge: Cambridge University Press.

Durkin, D. (1966). *Children who read early: two longitudinal studies*. New York: Teachers College Press.

Edwards, A. D., & Furlong, V. J. (1978). *The language of teaching: meaning in classroom interaction*. London: Heinemann.

Edwards, P. (1989). Supporting lower SES mothers' attempts to provide scaffolding for book reading. In J. Allen & J. M. Mason (eds.). *Risk makers, risk takers, risk breakers: reducing the risks for young literacy learners* (pp. 222–50). Portsmouth, NH: Heinemann.

Farran, D. (1982). Intervention for poverty children: alternative approaches. In L. Feagans & D. Farran (eds.). *The language of children reared in poverty: implications for evaluation and intervention* (pp. 269–71). Orlando, FL: Academic Press.

Feagans, L., & Farran, D. (eds.) (1982). *The language of children reared in poverty: implications for evaluation and intervention.* Orlando, FL: Academic Press.

Feitelson, D., & Goldstein, Z. (1986). Patterns of book ownership and reading to young children in Israel school-oriented and non-school-oriented families. *Reading Teaching, 39,* 924–30.

Gallimore, R., & Goldenberg, C. (1988). The social context of emergent Spanish literacy among Hispanic children. Grant proposal funded by the Spencer Foundation.

Gallimore, R., Boggs, J. W., & Jordan, C. (1974). *Culture, behavior and education: a study of Hawaiian-Americans.* Beverly Hills, CA: Sage Publications.

Gallimore, R., Weisner, T., Kaufman, S., & Bernheimer, L. (1989). The social construction of ecological niches: family accommodation of developmentally delayed children. *American Journal of Mental Retardation, 94,* 216–30.

Goldenberg, C. (1984). Roads to reading: studies of Hispanic first graders at risk for reading failure. Unpublished doctoral dissertation, Graduate School of Education, University of California, Los Angeles.

Goldenberg, C. (1988a). Methods, early literacy, and home-school compatibilities: a response to Sledge et al. *Anthropology and Education Quarterly, 19,* 425–32.

Goldenberg, C. (1988b). Improving the early reading achievement of Hispanic children learning to read in their native language: research activities and findings, 1986–1988. Unpublished report to the Superintendent of Lennox, California, School District.

Goldenberg, C. (1989a). Language use in two home literacy events: the effect of activity setting on Spanish-speaking parents' language. Unpublished manuscript.

Goldenberg, C. (1989b). The home literacy experiences of low-income Hispanic kindergartners whose parents are recent arrivals from Latin America. Presented at the annual meeting of the American Educational Research Association, San Francisco.

Hart, B. (1982). Process in the teaching of pragmatics. In L. Feagans & D. Farran (eds.). *The language of children reared in poverty: implications for evaluation and intervention* (pp. 199–218). Orlando, FL: Academic Press.

Heath, S. B. (1982). Questioning at home and at school: a comparative study. In G. Spindler (ed.). *Doing the ethnography of schooling: educational anthropology in action* (pp. 102–31). New York: Holt, Rinehart & Winston.

Heath, S. B. (1983). *Ways with words: language, life, and work in communities and classrooms.* Cambridge: Cambridge University Press.

Heath, S. B. (1986). Sociocultural contexts of language development. In *Beyond language: social and cultural factors in schooling language minority students* (pp. 143–86). Los Angeles: Evaluation, Dissemination and Assessment Center, California State University.

Henderson, R., & Garcia, A. (1973). The effects of parent training program on the question-asking behavior of Mexican-American children. *American Educational Research Journal, 10,* 193–201.

Kessen, W. (1979). The American child and other cultural inventions. *American Psychologist, 34,* 815–20.

Krashen, S., & Terrell, T. (1983). *The natural approach: language acquisition in the classroom.* Hayward, CA: Alemany Press.

Laosa, L. (1978). Maternal teaching strategies in Chicano families of varied educational and socioeconomic levels. *Child Development, 49,* 1129–35.

Laosa, L. (1980). Maternal teaching strategies in Chicano and Anglo-American families: the influence of culture and education on maternal behavior. *Child Development, 51,* 759–65.

Leont'ev, A. N. (1981). The problem of activity in psychology. In J. V. Wertsch (ed.). *The concept of activity in Soviet psychology* (pp. 37–71). Armonk, NY: M. E. Sharpe.

Mark, J. (1986). Fostering early reading through parent involvement in the use of little books. Unpublished paper, Loyola Marymount University.

Mason, J. M. (1977). *Reading readiness: a definition and skills hierarchy from preschoolers' developing conceptions of print* (T.R. No. 59). Urbana-Champaign: Center of the Study of Reading, University of Illinois.

Mason, J. M., & Allen, J. (1986). A review of emergent literacy with implications for research and practice in reading. *Review of Research in Education, 13,* 3–48.

Mason, J. M., McCormick, C., & Bhavnagri, N. (1986). How are you going to help me learn? Lesson negotiations between a teacher and preschool children. In D. Yaden & W. S. Templeton (eds.). *Metalinguistic awareness and beginning literacy: conceptualizing what it means to read and write* (pp. 159–72). Exeter, NH: Heinemann.

McLean-Bardwell, C., Bryan, D., Baca, R., & Gomez, F. (1987). Mexican immigration in a port-of-entry school: an advance report from the La Entrada Research Group. Unpublished manuscript, Immigration & Education Institute, California State University, Dominguez Hills.

Mehan, H. (1979). "What time is it, Denise?": asking known information questions in classroom discourse. *Theory into Practice, 28*(4), 285–94.

Minick, N. J. (1985). L. S. Vygotsky and Soviet activity theory: new perspectives on the relationship between mind and society. Unpublished doctoral dissertation, Northwestern University.

Nerlove, S. B., & Snipper, A. S. (1981). Cognitive consequences of cultural opportunity. In R. H. Munroe, R. L. Munroe, & B. B. Whiting (eds.). *Handbook of crosscultural human development* (pp. 423–74). New York: Garland Press.

Olson, D., Torrance, N., and Hildyard, A. (eds.) (1985). *Literacy, language, and learning: the nature and consequences of reading and writing.* Cambridge: Cambridge University Press.

Reese, L. M., Goldenberg, C. N., Loucky, J., & Gallimore, R. (1989). Ecocultural context, cultural activity, and emergent literacy: sources of variation in home literacy experiences of Spanish-speaking children. Presented at the Annual Meeting of the American Anthropological Association.

Rogoff, B. (1982). Integrating context and cognitive development. In M. E. Lamb & A. L. Brown (eds.). *Advances in Developmental Psychology* (Vol. 2, pp. 125–70). Hillsdale, NJ: Lawrence Erlbaum Associates.

Teale, W. (1978). Positive environments for learning to read: what studies of early readers tell us. *Language Arts, 55,* 922–32.

Teale, W. H. (1986). Home background and young children's literacy development. In W. H. Teale & E. Sulzby (eds.). *Emergent literacy: writing and reading* (pp. 173–206). Norwood, NJ: Ablex.

Tharp, R. (1989). Psychocultural variables and constants: effects on teaching and learning in schools. *American Psychologist, 44,* 349–59.

Tharp, R., & Gallimore, R. (1988). *Rousing minds to life: teaching, learning and schooling in social context.* Cambridge: Cambridge University Press.

Topping, K. (1986). *Parents as educators: training parents to teach their children.* Cambridge, MA: Brookline Books.

Tough, J. (1982). Language, poverty, and disadvantage in school. In L. Feagans & D. Farran (eds.). *The language of children reared in poverty: implications for evaluation and intervention* (pp. 3–18). Orlando, FL: Academic Press.

United States Department of Commerce (1988). *The Hispanic population in the United States: March 1988 (advance report).* Bureau of the Census Current Population Reports, Series P-20, No. 431. Washington DC: U.S. Government Printing Office.

Vygotsky, L. S. (1978). *Mind in society: the development of higher psychological processes.* Cambridge, MA: Harvard University Press.

Ward, B., & Kelley, M. (no date). *Developing children's oral language: teacher's handbook.* Berkeley, CA: Far West Laboratory for Education Research and Development, Macmillan Educational Services.

Weisner, T. S. (1984). Ecocultural niches of middle childhood: a cross-cultural perspective. In W. A. Collins (ed.), *Development during middle childhood: the years from six to twelve* (pp. 335–69). Washington, DC: National Academy of Sciences Press.

Weisner, T. S., & Gallimore, R. (1977). My brother's keeper: child and sibling caretaking. *Current Anthropology, 18*(2), 169–90.

Weisner, T. S., & Gallimore, R. (1985). The convergence of ecocultural and activity theory. Presented at the annual meeting of the American Anthropological Association, Washington, DC.

Weisner, T. S., Gallimore, R., & Jordan, C. (1988). Unpackaging cultural effects on classroom learning: Hawaiian peer assistance and child-generated activity. *Anthropology and Education Quarterly, 19,* 327–53.

Wells, G. (1985). Preschool literacy-related activities and success in school. In D. R. Olson, N. Torrance, & A. Hildyard (eds.). *Literacy, language, & learning: the nature and consequences of reading and writing* (pp. 299–355). Cambridge: Cambridge University Press.

Wertsch, J. V., Minick, N., & Arns, F. J. (1984). The creation of context in joint problem-solving. In B. Rogoff & J. Lave (eds.). *Everyday cognition: its development in social contexts* (pp. 151–71). Cambridge: Harvard University Press.

White, K. R. (1982). The relation between socioeconomic status and academic achievement. *Psychological Bulletin, 91,* 461–81.

Whiting, B. (1980). Culture and social behavior: a model for the development of social behavior. *Ethos, 8*(2), 95–116.

Whiting, B., & Edwards, C. (1988). *Children of different worlds: the formation of social behavior.* Cambridge: Harvard University Press.

Whiting, B., & Whiting, J. (1975). *Children of six cultures.* Cambridge, MA: Harvard University Press.

14

A Sociocultural Approach to Agency

JAMES V. WERTSCH, PEETER TULVISTE, and FRAN HAGSTROM

In his review of the history of "psychological science and ideologies," Joravsky (1989) argued that a great deal of contemporary research in psychology rests on implicit assumptions that were once the topic of overt reflection and controversy. He pointed out that we now gloss over many issues, such as volition and the role of aesthetics in human thought, that were once at the center of inquiries into human nature. It is not because these issues have been adequately defined, let alone resolved, but because historical trends such as disciplinary fragmentation function to keep them out of view. The result is that psychology rarely addresses such matters. Instead, "Sophisticated people have learned to evade questions that seemed urgent a century ago," and "articulate prisoners" of the current *Zeitgeist* "shrug indifferently" when asked about troubling assumptions that underlie their research (Joravsky, 1989, pp. 3 and 4).

In this chapter, we address an assumption that has a strong grip on Western, especially U.S., psychology. This assumption concerns the nature of human *agency*. Agency and the associated issues of voluntary and involuntary action have been the focus of extended debate in philosophy (e.g., Davidson, 1971), but in psychology they rarely emerge in any form other than implicit assumptions. To the extent that agency is explicitly addressed in contemporary studies in psychology, it arises in connection with issues such as moral reasoning, where topics such as responsibility and free will are unavoidable.

In our view, however, basic assumptions about agency underlie most studies in psychology. As evidence, consider the now standard claim that perception, memory, and cognition cannot be understood without taking into account the active, and often purposeful, agent; or consider the focus of many psychological theories on purposeful and voluntary self-regulation. Such claims rest on basic assumptions about agency. If these assumptions are denied, we are left with unsatisfactory accounts such as those that invoke the picture of "thoughts thinking themselves" (Vygotsky, 1987, p. 50).

The most basic, underlying assumption made in Western psychological theories about agency is that *agency is a property of the individual.* Furthermore, studies typically proceed as if this individual existed in a cultural, historical, and institutional vacuum. Of course it is not to say that investigators deny the existence of sociocultural factors. Indeed, many investigators focus explicitly on them. However, studies in psychology typically approach this issue on the assumption that sociocultural factors can somehow be appended onto a preexisting, "basic" account of the individual.

In our view, attempts grounded in the assumption that the individual has this kind of "analytical priority" (Wertsch, 1991) cannot capture certain basic facts about the relation between psychological and sociocultural processes. The kind of "methodological individualism" they reflect results in a situation in which psychology not only does not, but cannot, address certain essential aspects of this relation. As we argue, there is much to suggest that this form of individualism is grounded in unexamined cultural beliefs held by contemporary Western psychologists. It has become entrenched as one of the seemingly obvious and natural bedrock assumptions that guides our inquiry.

In what follows, we outline a sociocultural approach to agency that addresses this problem. The essence of our argument is, to paraphrase Bateson (1972), that agency "extends beyond the skin." Human agency extends beyond the skin first of all because it is frequently a property of dyads and other small groups rather than individuals. In Vygotsky's (1987) terminology, agency exists at the "intermental"[1] as well as at the "intramental" plane of functioning. It extends beyond the skin in a second way owing to the involvement of cultural tools, or "mediational means," such as language in human action. In addition to arguing for the need to examine mediation in general, we argue that an essential property of mediational means is that they are inherently tied to historical, cultural, and institutional settings. It follows, then, that the analysis of agency takes us beyond intermental, or social, interactional processes. It must be tied to a broader sociocultural milieu.

Theoretical Foundations

The roots of our argument can be found in the ideas of contemporary philosophers such as Taylor (1985, 1989). In his analysis of Western social science, Taylor has argued that its theory and method are fundamentally grounded in a certain tradition of individualism that permeates our personal and professional lives. This form of individualism, which he called "atomism," can be traced at least to the writings of Locke. From Locke we have inherited the notion that

> the human agent was no longer to be understood as an element in a larger, meaningful order. His paradigm purposes are to be discovered within. He is on his own. . . . this yields a picture of the sovereign individual, who is "by nature" not bound to any authority. The condition of being under authority is something which has to be *created*. [Taylor, 1989, pp. 193–94]

Taylor argued that our general cultural view of the sovereign individual has resulted in a social science that takes the atomistic agent as its basic building block. This view in turn has led to accounts of human mental functioning in which such agency is viewed as being analytically and developmentally prior to sociocultural life. The view of the individual at issue is grounded in a "typically modern notion of freedom, as the ability to act on one's own, without outside interference or subordination to outside authority" (Taylor, 1985, p. 5). This underlying notion has shaped inquiry in psychology such that it is difficult, if not impossible, to deal adequately with how sociocultural forces shape or constitute individuals.

In contrast to the tenets of atomism, the ideas of Vygotsky (1978, 1981a,b 1987) and Bakhtin (1981, 1986; Voloshinov, 1973) provide the foundations for an alternative view of human agency. The starting point for this view is Vygotsky's claim that "the social dimension of consciousness is primary in time and in fact. The individual dimension of consciousness is derivative and secondary" (Vygotsky, 1979, p. 30). Like Mead (1934), who was developing a similar position in the United States at the same time, Vygotsky was therefore arguing for the analytical and genetic priority of social life when trying to understand psychological processes in the individual.

One of the formulations in which the analytical priority given to social processes emerged most clearly was in Vygotsky's "general genetic [i.e., developmental] law of cultural development."

> Any function in the child's cultural development appears twice, or on two planes. First it appears on the social plane, and then on the psychological plane. First it appears between people as an interpsychological category, and then within the child as an intrapsychological category. This is equally true with regard to voluntary attention, logical memory, the formation of concepts, and the development of volition. . . . [I]t goes without saying that internalization transforms the process itself and changes its structure and functions. Social relations or relations among people genetically underlie all higher functions and their relationships. [Vygotsky, 1981b, p. 163]

The claims involved in Vygotsky's general genetic law of cultural development are more radical than are often recognized. He was not simply asserting that mental processes in the individual somehow emerge out of participation in social life. Instead, he was making the much stronger claim that the specific structures and processes of intramental functioning can be traced to their developmental precursors on the intermental plane. It does not mean that higher mental functioning in the individual can be viewed as a direct and simple copy of social processes; the point Vygotsky made in his formulation about the transformations involved in internalization warn against any such interpretation. However, it does mean that there is a close connection created by genetic transitions between the specific structures and processes of intermental and intramental functioning, which in turn implies that different forms of intermental functioning give rise to related differences in the forms of intramental functioning.

A second, related claim entailed in the general genetic law of cultural development concerns an assumption about the definition of higher mental functions such as thinking, or reasoning, and voluntary attention. Vygotsky did not assume that these terms apply only to processes of individuals, a point reflected in his claim that a mental function (i.e., one and the same mental function) appears first on the intermental and then on the intramental plane.

This idea contrasts with the use of terms such as "memory" and "cognition" in the discourse of contemporary psychology in the West. In this discourse assumptions about atomistic agency are reflected in the fact that such terms automatically apply to processes carried out by an individual unless explicitly marked to the contrary. Investigators who have wished to examine ways in which groups carry out cognitive or memory processes or can be characterized with regard to intelligence have been compelled to use new terms, usually derived by adding a modifier to the "basic," unmarked term. As a result we have seen the appearance or reappearance of interest in "socially shared cognition" (Resnick, Levine, & Teasley, 1991), "collective memory" (Middleton, 1987; Middleton & Edwards, 1990), and "group intelligence" (Williams & Sternberg, 1988).

Agency "Beyond the Skin"

Intermental Functioning

The view we have begun to outline challenges basic assumptions psychologists have tended to make about agency, that is, about who it is who carries out mental processes. As we shall see, instead of an isolated individual, it is often a group that provides the appropriate locus of evaluation. The kind of group performance we have in mind has been examined by investigators such as Hutchins (1991).

In Hutchins' analyses of how crews of naval vessels organize their activity so they can guide a ship into a harbor, cognition is "socially distributed." A team of individuals must function together effectively if the task is to be carried out efficiently and safely. Hutchins has documented the complex communicational, computational, and organizational processes required for the group to function effectively and argued that the appropriate unit of analysis in such cases is not the individual but the group. Furthermore, the whole of socially distributed cognition is greater than, or at least qualitatively different from the sum of the individuals' cognitive processes that constitute it. There is no way to reduce the analysis of socially distributed cognition to a set of individuals' processes, and as a result a type of agency is attributed to the group rather than to the individual.

An analysis such as that carried out by Hutchins of cognitive tasks that are carried out on the intermental plane does not mean that the investigation of mental functioning of the individuals involved is deemed unworthy of study. However, it does mean that intermental functioning is given analytical priority, and hence the nature of individuals' mental functioning can be understood only by beginning with a consideration of the social system in which it exists. Attempts to understand the processes involved by starting with atomistic agency are doomed to miss this point.

In addition to redefining the boundaries of agency, approaches that focus on socially distributed cognition, socially shared cognition, and other such notions have important implications for the *development* of individual mental functioning. The point we have in mind here follows directly from Vygotsky's general genetic law of cultural development. Although it certainly need not be true in all cases, it is often the case that socially shared (i.e., intermental) processes are mastered and internalized to form intramental processes. The resulting picture is one of "individual as group," which contrasts with the "group as individual" (e.g., Williams & Sternberg, 1988). Vygotsky clearly had something along the lines of the former in mind when he wrote that "humans' psychological nature represents the aggregate of internalized social relations that have become functions for the individual and form the individual's structure" (1981b, p. 164).

A specific application of the general genetic law of cultural development that has received a great deal of attention in the West (e.g., Brown & Ferrara, 1985; Brown & French, 1979; Cole, 1985; Rogoff & Wertsch, 1984) is Vygotsky's notion of the "zone of proximal development." He defined this zone as the distance between a child's "actual developmental level as determined by independent problem solving" and the higher level of "potential development as determined through problem solving under adult guidance or in collaboration with more capable peers" (1978, p. 86).

Vygotsky devised his account of the zone of proximal development in order to address two practical issues. First, he argued that it can serve as a productive tool when trying to understand the nature of psychological assessment. In this connection he argued that measuring the level of potential development is just as important as measuring the actual developmental level, a claim that has been explicated by investigators such as Brown and Ferrara (1985). Second, Vygotsky argued that understanding the level of potential development is crucial for formulating approaches to learning and instruction. In contrast to approaches that are based on assessments of the actual developmental level, he asserted that the organization of teaching should be tied more closely to the level of potential development.

All this reasoning amounts to saying that the boundary between individual (i.e., intramental) and group (i.e., intermental) mental processes is often much more difficult to maintain than we tend to assume in the discourse of Western psychology. Correspondingly, the assumption that agency automatically attaches to the individual comes into question. Whereas it may be relatively easy to determine if an individual is functioning in physical isolation from others, it is often much more difficult to specify if the individual is operating in a kind of "psychological isolation." Instead, it is often obvious that intramental "dialogic" processes (Wertsch, 1991) such as "self-interrogation" (Brown, Campione, & Barclay, 1979) are best understood in terms of how social processes have been "imported" into the individual's mental functioning.

Mediated Agency

We have just outlined one way in which "agency extends beyond the skin." Instead of assuming that agency applies only to individuals, it is seen as properly attaching to groups functioning on the intermental plane. A second way in which agency extends beyond the skin can be seen in Vygotsky's treatment of "mediation" (Wertsch, 1985, 1991). In Vygotsky's view, a criterial feature of human action is that it is mediated by tools ("technical tools") and signs ("psychological tools"). His primary concern was with the latter, and for that reason we are concerned primarily with "semiotic mediation" here.

Basic to all his work on this issue was the insight that the inclusion of psychological tools, or signs in human functioning, fundamentally transforms this action. In this view, the incorporation of mediational means does not simply facilitate the functioning that could have occurred without them. Instead, "by being included in the process of behavior, the psychological tool alters the entire flow and structure of mental functions. It does this by determining the structure of a new instrumental act, just as a technical tool alters the process of a natural adaptation by determining the form of labor operations" (Vygotsky, 1981a, p. 137). As Wertsch (1985, 1991) has argued, Vygotsky's account of mediation provides the theoretical underpinning for the rest of his approach and is what distinguishes this approach from those of others such as Piaget, Mead, and Janet.

In Vygotsky's view, "the following can serve as examples of psychological tools and their complex systems: language; various systems for counting; mnemonic techniques; algebraic symbol systems; works of art; writing; schemes, diagrams, maps, and mechanical drawings; all sorts of conventional signs; and so on" (1981a, p. 137). In all cases, these mediational means are the products of sociocultural evolution and are appropriated by groups or individuals as they carry out mental functioning.

To understand how these mediational means function in human action the boundaries of agency once again need to be clarified. Instead of the individual in isolation, the agent is viewed as being an irreducible aggregate of individual (or individuals in intermental functioning) *together with mediational means.* This position is not unique to Vygotsky-inspired approaches. For example, building on a theoretical tradition different from that of Vygotsky, Bateson argued that it often makes little sense to assume a boundary between the individuals and the mediational means they employ.

> Suppose I am a blind man, and I use a stick. I go tap, tap, tap. Where do *I* start? Is my mental system bounded at the handle of the stick? Is it bounded by my skin? Does it start halfway up the stick? Does it start at the tip of the stick? But these are nonsense questions. The stick is a pathway along which

transformations of difference are being transmitted. The way to delineate the system is to draw the limiting line in such a way that you do not cut any of these pathways in ways which leave things inexplicable. [Bateson, 1972, p. 459]

Like Bateson, we believe that in order to avoid posing "nonsense questions" the notion of mediation must be taken into consideration in order to account for the agent responsible for mental functioning.

One of the clearest ways to recognize the importance of mediation is to consider an interesting modern addition to Vygotsky's list of mediational means—the computer. It is now widely recognized that the use of computers has changed many aspects of our lives. Discussions of how this situation has come about seem to lead inexorably to issues of agency. For example, we often speak of how many tasks that formerly were carried out by humans have now been taken over by computers, which has led to arguments about whether computers have consciousness, are agents, and so forth (e.g., Dennett, 1981).

For our purposes, the more relevant concern is with ways in which humans solve problems by incorporating computers into their activity (e.g., Tikhomirov & Klochko, 1981). Even simple applications of computers such as the use of word processing and spreadsheet programs typically result in reports of how one's thinking, writing, and problem solving change. Furthermore, when we reflect on who was responsible for carrying out certain aspects of a task, we often attribute agency to computers or computer programs.

Such issues raise fundamental questions about whether an individual or computer is responsible for carrying out a particular action. In our view, to assume that these two alternatives exhaust the range of possibilities for answering this question is to fall into a trap. A third alternative has not been considered. It is that the appropriate unit of analysis for understanding agency is an individual or individuals functioning together with mediational means. In this view the individual(s) involved certainly continues to bear the major responsibility for initiating and carrying out an action, but the possibilities for formulating certain problems, let alone the possibilities for following certain paths of action are shaped by the mediational means employed. The resulting picture is one in which the irreducible unit of analysis for agency is "individual(s)-operating-with-mediational-means." Rather than trying to employ this cumbersome hyphenated term, we shall refer to it as "mediated agency."

Mediated agency has been the object of analysis for several socioculturally oriented studies. For example, Belyaeva and Cole (1989) have examined it in connection with a kind of intermental functioning that emerges when parties in various locations in the world communicate with one another through the medium of electronic mail, and it has been examined in the case of face-to-face intermental functioning by Wertsch (1991). An underlying assumption in all these studies is that in order to analyze mental functioning or to assess levels of performance or intelligence it is essential to recognize that agency does not reside in the individual in isolation. Instead, mental functioning is viewed as "extending beyond the skin" by virtue of the mediational means employed.

Sociocultural Situatedness of Intermental Functioning and Mediational Means

We have outlined two ways in which agency extends beyond the skin: (1) Agency may be attributable to groups rather than individuals; and (2) agency is an attribute of the individual(s)-operating-with-mediational-means. In the end, of course, these two ways of redefining the notion of agency such that it is not viewed as an attribute of the isolated individual are intertwined. The reason is that one of the criterial properties of the intermental functioning is that it is mediated by signs.

Vygotsky's great contribution was to recognize these two ways in which agency extends beyond the individual. However, he did relatively little to specify how intermental functioning and mediational means fit into a broader framework of sociocultural processes. This shortcoming is reflected at several points in his writing. For example, in an account of the intermental foundations of intramental functioning, Vygotsky limited his analysis of social processes primarily to dyads or other small groups. In a way much like Mead (1934), he focused on the dynamics of small group interaction that play an essential role in the formation of psychological processes in the individual.

Although not wishing to deny the importance of examining such forms of intermental functioning and the mediational means they employ, we think it is essential to recognize that, in isolation, a concern with this level of social process suggests a kind of universalism that is antithetical to the argument for sociocultural situatedness that Vygotsky himself was pursuing. This is because it fails to specify any reason to expect semiotically mediated intermental functioning to vary as a function of cultural, historical, and institutional setting. In order to avoid this shortcoming, a sociocultural approach must posit some concrete mechanism for connecting cultural, historical, and institutional processes with mediated intermental and intramental processes. As Minick (1985, p. 257) has noted:

> [T]he links between dyadic or small group interactions and the broader socio-cultural system must be recognized and explored. . . . [A]ctions are at one and the same time components of the life of the individual and the social system. This point is as crucial for the analysis of the development of intermental actions as it is for the analysis of the development of intramental actions. No less than the action of an individual, the action of a dyad or small group is a component in the social system. Correspondingly, the intermental actions and the social interaction that makes that action pos-

sible will be defined and structured in certain respects by the broader social and cultural system.

We believe that the key to extending Vygotsky's approach such that it takes into consideration the sociocultural situatedness of agency is to be found in the account of mediational means one provides. The line of argument we pursue is that the mediational means that shape human mental functioning reflect and are fundamentally involved in creating and maintaining cultural, historical, and institutional contexts. Mediational means such as language in its various uses do not emerge de novo in small groups or individuals; instead, they are embedded in a sociocultural milieu and are reproduced across generations in the form of collective practices. By "appropriating" (Leont'ev, 1959; Newman, Griffin, & Cole, 1989) them in the process of carrying out intermental and intramental functioning, human mental functioning is shaped in socioculturally specific ways.[2]

Vygotsky seemed to be coming to recognize this issue near the end of his life. It is reflected in the difference between Chapters 5 and 6 of *Thinking and Speech* (1987). Both chapters deal with the ontogenetic transition from "complexes" to "genuine," or "scientific," concepts. However, the two chapters differ markedly in what they see as relevant developmental forces. In Chapter 5 [based on research with Shif (1935) and written during the early 1930s), concept development is treated primarily in terms of intramental processes, that is, children's conceptual development as they move from "unorganized heaps" to "complexes" to "concepts."

In Chapter 6 (written in 1934), there is an essential shift in the way Vygotsky approached these issues. He clearly continued to be interested in intramental functioning, but he shifted to approaching concept development from the perspective of how it emerges in institutionally situated activity. Specifically, he was concerned with how the forms of discourse encountered in the social institution of formal schooling provide a framework for the development of conceptual thinking. He did it by the teacher–child intermental functioning found in this setting.

This is an essential shift in Vygotsky's focus for two reasons. First, it was a move toward analyzing conceptual thinking in terms of its intermental precursors, which is in line with the argument he had employed all along in connection with issues such as inner speech; and, of course, it follows naturally from his general genetic law of cultural development. Second, and more important for our purposes, it was a move toward recognizing that an account of the social origins of intramental functioning cannot stop with the intermental plane. Instead, the point is that the forms of mediated intermental functioning involved must themselves be recognized as being socioculturally situated.

To say that Vygotsky was beginning to take sociocultural situatedness into account does not mean that he provided anything approximating a complete account of it. He did make some initial steps in identifying the semiotic mechanisms that mediate mental functioning in formal instruction, but he provided little detail on this issue, and he said nothing about why these mediational means should take the form they do. In order to address these issues, it is useful to turn to the theoretical constructs of a "social language" and "speech genres" as outlined by Bakhtin (1986).

As Wertsch (1985, 1991) has outlined, there are several important respects in which Bakhtin's ideas complement those of Vygotsky. In the case of a social language, Bakhtin's ideas make it possible to clarify some of the ways in which semiotic mediation is socioculturally situated. For Bakhtin, a social language is "a discourse peculiar to a specific stratum of society (e.g., professional, age group) within a given social system at a given time" (Holquist & Emerson, 1981, p. 430). In his terminology, a social language differs from a "national language" such as Russian or Thai.

Bakhtin's ideas about social languages have much in common with contemporary sociolinguistic notions such as code (Bernstein, 1975) or language variant (Heath, 1983). However, in contrast to most other treatments, his notion of a social language was inherently linked with a particular kind of dialogicality, or multivoicedness, namely, "ventriloquism." This idea follows from Bakhtin's claim that:

> The word in language is half someone else's. It becomes "one's own" only when the speaker populates it with his own intention, his own accent, when he appropriates the word, adapting it to his own semantic and expressive intention. Prior to this moment of appropriation, the word does not exist in a neutral and impersonal language (it is not, after all, out of a dictionary that the speaker gets his words!), but rather it exists in other people's mouths, in other people's concrete contexts, serving other people's intentions: it is from there that one must take the word, and make it one's own. [Bakhtin, 1981, pp. 293–94]

The implication here is that any utterance involves at least two voices: that of the speaker producing the concrete utterance and that of another speaker or other speakers who have used the same words or, more generally, patterns of discourse. This view, in turn, implies that an account of utterance meaning must be grounded in the analysis of a specific kind of dialogicality, namely, "double voicedness." From the perspective of how children come to be socialized such that they can function successfully in particular sociocultural settings, then, the issue is one of learning how to ventriloquate through new social languages.

For our purposes some of Bakhtin's most relevant comments in this connection can be found in his account of the related notion of "speech genre." Speech genres such as military commands, everyday greetings, farewells, congratulation and the genres of table conversation and intimate conversations among friends are typical forms or types of utterances.

> In the genre the word acquires a particular typical expression. Genres correspond to typical situations of speech communication, typical themes, and consequently, also to particular contacts between the *meanings* of words

and actual concrete reality under certain typical circumstances. [Bakhtin, 1986, p. 87]

According to Bakhtin the production of virtually any utterance involves ventriloquating through, or populating the form of, a speech genre.

> We speak only in definite speech genres, that is, all our utterances have definite and relatively stable typical *forms of construction of the whole.* Our repertoire of oral (and written) speech genres is rich. We use them confidently and skillfully *in practice,* and it is quite possible for us not even to suspect their existence *in theory.* Like Molière's Monsieur Jordain who, when speaking in prose, had no idea that was what he was doing, we speak in diverse genres without suspecting that they exist. [Bakhtin, 1986, p. 78]

Thus in Bakhtin's view it is no more possible to produce an utterance without invoking some speech genre than it is possible to produce an utterance without using some national language such as Russian or English.

By incorporating Bakhtin's notion of social language into the basic sociocultural approach we have outlined, it is possible to expand Vygotsky's notion of a mediational means in a useful and much needed way. Because social languages are "peculiar to a specific stratum of society . . . within a given social system at a given time" (Holquist & Emerson, 1981, p. 430), they provide an essential construct in a sociocultural approach for connecting intramental functioning with social life as organized by institutional, cultural, and historical forces.

Mediated Agency in Sociocultural Context: An Illustration

The notions of ventriloquism and social languages as mediational means have several implications for an account of mediated agency. Ventriloquism is a useful construct because it reveals how agency cannot be reduced to an attribute of either the individual or the mediational means in isolation. The notion of ventriloquating through, or populating, a social language entails the idea that the basic, irreducible description of agency is the individual(s)-operating-with-mediational-means. The notion of social language is useful because it is a mediational means that is inherently tied to sociocultural setting. In appropriating the social language of a socioeconomic class and culture (e.g., see Heath, 1983, on "language variants") or the social language of formal schooling (e.g., see Wertsch & Minick, 1990, on "text-based realities"), one is appropriating a mediational means for communicating and thinking that is inherently situated with regard to cultural, historical, and institutional context.

By way of explicating these claims, consider the practice of "reciprocal teaching" outlined by Palincsar and Brown (Brown & Palincsar, 1982; Palincsar, 1987; Palincsar & Brown, 1984, 1988). With this procedure, students are required to lead a dialogue (i.e., pose questions usually reserved for the teacher) in a reading task. In their analyses Palincsar and Brown have focused particularly on "the active strategies the reader employs to enhance understanding and retention, and to circumvent comprehension failures" (1984, p. 118).

On the basis of a review of major processes that must be carried out for successful reading to occur, Palincsar and Brown identified four concrete activities in which to engage students as they attempt to learn the strategies of comprehension skills: *summarizing* (self-review), *questioning, clarifying,* and *predicting*. Noting that these activities are precisely the kinds that many poor readers do not carry out, Palincsar and Brown devised a set of training and assessment procedures for students at various grade levels who had been identified as having major problems in developing reading skills. The core of these procedures revolve around reciprocal teaching in which students and teachers take turns leading dialogues about texts, generating summaries and predictions, and clarifying misleading or complex sections of the text.

The procedure of reciprocal teaching has produced some striking results. Palincsar and Brown reported that at the end of a relatively small number of sessions poor readers showed remarkable improvement.

> Gradually, the students became much more capable of assuming their role as dialogue leader and by the end of ten sessions were providing paraphrases and questions of some sophistication. For example, in the initial sessions half of the questions produced by the students were judged as nonquestions or as needing clarification; however, by the end of the sessions, unclear questions had dropped out and were replaced with questions focusing on the main idea of each text segment. A similar improvement was found for summary statements. At the beginning of the sessions, only a few summary statements captured main ideas, whereas at the end, the majority of the statements were so classified. [Palincsar & Brown, 1984, p. 125]

From the perspective of the general genetic law of cultural development the most important result was that student improvement was not limited to performance in the reciprocal teaching sessions. It extended to intramental functioning as well.

> Each day, before (baseline), during, and after (maintenance) training, the students took an unassisted assessment, where they read a novel passage and answered ten comprehension questions on it from memory. From their baseline performance of 15% correct, they improved during training to accuracy levels of 85%, levels they maintained when the intervention was terminated. Even after a 6-month delay, the students averaged 60% correct without help, and it took only 1 day of renewed reciprocal teaching to return them to the 85% level achieved during training. [Palincsar & Brown, 1984, p. 125]

From our perspective, the method of reciprocal teaching raises interesting questions about agency. In one sense, of course, we can point to the individual student as the agent. After all, it is the performance of the individual students that has been shown to have benefited from the procedure. In another sense, however, this individual performance is best understood in terms of a conceptualization of "individual as group," a point reflected in Palincsar and Brown's (1984, p. 125) comment:

> Remember that these scores [on unassisted assessment measures] were obtained on *privately read* assessment passages, that is, different texts that the students read independently after their interaction with the instructor. *What was learned during the instructional sequence was used independently by the learners.* [emphasis added]

In terms of the general genetic law of cultural development, the point is that processes and structures that had initially occurred on the intermental plane have been mastered and internalized to form intramental functioning. Thus the origins and structure of agency on the intramental plane can be understood only by turning to the group.

Up to this point we have considered reciprocal teaching primarily from the perspective of how it involves the mastery and internalization of intermental functioning. Of course such mastery and internalization also involve mediational means. After all, they are processes comprised of particular patterns of intermental and intramental discourse. To consider reciprocal teaching strictly in terms of mediated intermental and intramental processes, however, is to produce a truncated view, in our opinion. The method and its success cannot be adequately understood without taking into account some essential sociocultural factors. Specifically, we believe that the source of reciprocal teaching's success is its employment of a social language that is seldom found in the institutional setting of formal schooling.

The social language we have in mind and the other social languages with which it contrasts can be characterized in terms of one of the criterial properties Bakhtin (1986) used to characterize utterances: the relationship between a speaker and other speakers. One of the fundamental properties of most classroom discourse is that the teacher controls the topic and flow of discourse. This relationship has been characterized in many ways. For example, Mehan (1979) analyzed it in terms of the prototypical exchange pattern of: (1) teacher *initiation* with the help of an instructional question (e.g., Teacher: "Who was the main character in this story?"); followed by (2) pupil *response* (e.g., Pupil: "George."); followed in turn by (3) teacher *evaluation* (e.g., Teacher: "Good."). This "I–R–E" pattern is one in which the teacher controls the topic, the specific questions to be asked, and the evaluation of responses.

For many pupils, participation in this pattern of discourse seems to foster some kind of cognitive growth. In such cases the process is probably one in which the pattern of teachers' questions is taken over and mastered by pupils. These successful pupils incorporate the pattern of intermental functioning in which they have participated in their functioning on the intramental plane. However, for other pupils, such as the poor readers studied by Palincsar and Brown, the procedure has obviously not had the intended effect. In the terminology we outlined above, we argue that the strategy involved in reciprocal teaching is one of creating a new social language for pupils and instituting a procedure in which they are explicitly required to ventriloquate through it. It is this procedure that leads to their mastery of the discourse patterns that are adaptive in the classroom setting.

The verity that a new social language is involved for the pupils derives from the fact that the relationship between the pupil speaker and other speakers has been fundamentally changed. In contrast to normal classroom discourse, where the teacher alone occupies a position of authority, reciprocal teaching entails the pupil being given responsibility for formulating and initiating the communicative sequence. For example, pupils are encouraged to employ instructional questions (i.e., questions to which they know the answer) and are thereby put in the position of judging the appropriateness of others' responses.

With normal classroom discourse, unless pupils spontaneously begin to pose the same questions to themselves that are posed by the teacher, they are left in a position where passive responses are all that is required. It is this situation that indeed appeared to have occurred in the case of the poor readers studied by Palincsar and Brown. In contrast, the procedures employed with reciprocal teaching challenge the basic authority structure of classroom discourse. Instead of leaving the teacher in the position of ultimate "cognitive authority," pupils are required to appropriate this social language.

The role ventriloquism plays in the procedures of reciprocal teaching is striking. Although Palincsar and Brown did not use this term, several of their comments attest to its importance. For example, when describing their procedure Palincsar and Brown noted that poor seventh-grade readers in a pilot study they conducted initially "had great difficulty assuming the role of dialogue leader when their turn came"; and as a result, "The adult teacher was sometimes forced to construct paraphrases and questions for the pupils to *mimic*" [italics ours] (p. 125). Such a procedure might at first glance seem to be of questionable utility because, as Palincsar and Brown themselves noted, "the pupils were relatively passive observers" (p. 125) in such a process. Furthermore, Palincsar (1987) demonstrated that simple imitation of appropriate questions in isolation from actual dialogue with other students did not have the strong positive effect on pupil's subsequent intramental functioning. However, the procedures of reciprocal teaching are such that pupils are not allowed to remain in a passive role. They are required to take on an increasingly active responsibility for the strategic processes involved in reading comprehension precisely because they are required to participate in intermental functioning by ventriloquating through a social language that presupposes their taking on cognitive authority.

The process of taking on cognitive authority and hence responsibility for a task by actively appropriating others' mediational means is basic to the formation of mediated agency. From the perspective of how agency is defined, it suggests that individual-operating-with-mediational-means is the appropriate description. Studies such as those carried out by Palincsar and Brown indicated that at least in some cases major changes in performance can be produced through "re-mediation," that is, by reequipping people with new mediational means. A key to such changes seems to be to create settings in which people are encouraged or required to appropriate different mediational means (e.g., social languages) than the ones they otherwise would employ.

One of the reasons it often proves to be so difficult to do in practice has to do with the sociocultural situatedness of the processes at issue. A shift in the assignment of who is to ask questions or pose tasks is typically not governed by cognitive considerations alone. Instead, it almost always must occur in a context where some kind of institutional order (e.g., formal schooling) exists and where there are strong interests for maintaining and reproducing this order. Especially when mental processes are first played out on the intermental plane, it can cause major challenges to such an order. For example, it is difficult in many classroom settings, at least as they are currently organized, to imagine how one could give pupils the kind of cognitive authority, even temporarily, suggested by the procedure of reciprocal teaching. The transformations required would often result in a process that is alien to the ordered activity we are used to seeing and valuing in such settings.

In cases where this problem has been successfully addressed, the key has usually *not* been to turn over all authority and decision-making processes to the pupils. Instead, the key has been to create well organized "institutional spaces" in which pupils are given the chance to ventriloquate through social languages that foster their mental growth in institutionally adaptive ways. In addition to the procedure of reciprocal teaching, instructional approaches motivated by this general set of assumptions can be found in the work of Itakura (1986) and Hatano and Inagaki (1991) in the area of scientific reasoning and in the work of Tharp and Gallimore (1988) in the area of reading.

Cultural Activities and Heterogeneity

In our examples up to this point, we have focused on forms of agency that are valued in formal schooling—an activity setting that plays an important role in contemporary psychological studies of cognition, learning, and instruction. With a sociocultural approach such as the one we have outlined here, however, it is essential to view this setting and the forms of intermental and intramental mediated functioning associated with it as one of several possible foci. By doing so we avoid the temptation to give the cognitive practices of formal schooling the kind of privileged, "basic" status they often implicitly enjoy. This point is closely tied to the claims of such authors as Gardner (1985), Rogoff and Lave (1984), and Sternberg (1985), who have argued that constructs such as intelligence and cognition are best understood in terms of an array of abilities. This array includes, but goes beyond the list of, abilities typically required in formal schooling.

Not surprisingly, from the perspective of a sociocultural approach to agency, the key to understanding this array, or this "heterogeneity," is to be found in socioculturally situated, mediated functioning on the intermental and intramental planes. The ideas of Vygotsky (1978, 1987), Leont'ev (1959, 1975, 1981), and Luria (1976, 1981) provide a foundation for our account of heterogeneity.

Building on this foundation, Tulviste (1975, 1987, 1988) has argued that various modes of thinking correspond functionally to an array of "cultural activities" and are created by them. Each cultural activity (e.g., science, arts, everyday life, religion) poses specific tasks that can be solved only by using the corresponding mode of thinking. For instance, practical thinking or common sense is not sufficient to solve scientific tasks, whereas scientific thinking is of little use when writing a poem or sermon or when solving most everyday practical problems. Although the same words are often used in different sociocultural settings, their meanings vary substantially from one activity to another. For instance, the term "force," when used in a discussion among physicists, may contrast markedly with its use in everyday life; and the word "salt," when used in the kitchen, contrasts with its use in a chemical laboratory.

Furthermore, mental actions surrounding the different meanings of these terms also vary. When used in physics, the term "force" can be employed in a precise way to construct formulas and carry out computations, whereas this application is typically not the case for the everyday use of this term. The general picture is one in which various cultural activities make use of different internal and external sign systems. Furthermore, it is a picture in which the sociocultural history as well as the ontogenesis of sign systems and their associated activities are understood in terms of differentiation (Vygotsky, 1987; Werner & Kaplan, 1963). Hence development is viewed as occurring in several different (though interdependent) directions simultaneously and resulting in a structure best represented by a branching tree rather than a ladder.

The upshot is that mental functioning and the mediational means it employs are viewed as being domain-specific in the sense that they occur according to the cultural activities in which humans participate. Such an approach is different, for example, from that outlined by Piaget in that it does not focus on the development of a form of intelligence that is assumed to apply across domains. Leont'ev's theoretical formulation encourages the investigation of intermental and intramental functioning in specific sociocultural settings and views the ideal as being the person who has at his or her disposal a wide range of the mediational means associated with a culture and knows which of them must be applied in any particular situation.

It is not to say that different forms of thinking are somehow hermetically sealed off from one another. Although certain modes of thinking correspond to certain kinds of activities, it is clear that modes related primarily to one cultural activity are often used for other activities as well. Thus in the actual process of solving scientific problems, creative solutions often are found not when relating concepts to each other in a strictly logical way or using formulas but, rather, when using modes of thinking associated with common sense. Therefore the ability to use different modes of thinking flexibly and adequately at different stages of solving a task belonging to a certain activity must be considered an important metacognitive element of mental functioning.

Conclusion

The sociocultural approach to agency we have outlined is grounded in a few basic assumptions. The most important is that agency is not automatically attributed to the isolated individual. Instead, it "extends beyond the skin" in two interrelated ways. First, agency is often socially distributed or shared. This view takes on particular significance in connection with Vygotsky's general genetic law of cultural development. His formulation of this law entails the claim that different intramental outcomes may be fundamentally shaped by their differing intermental precursors.

Second, human agency involves mediational means. Even when an individual acts in physical isolation from others, the action continues to be socioculturally situated because it typically has its roots in intermental functioning and because the mediational means employed (be they computers, social languages, or whatever) are provided and constrained by cultural, historical, and institutional context. In an important sense, individuals can be no more intelligent than the psychological tools they employ. Indeed, it is not individuals, but individuals-operating-with-mediational-means, who define the basic unit of agency.

In our view the notion of mediational means provides the key to specifying how human intelligence and mental processes are situated in cultural, historical, and institutional contexts. This idea follows from that fact that these means reflect and constitute such contexts. Furthermore, we have stressed that humans function in a range of sociocultural contexts and are hence required to carry out a range of cultural activities. The result is that mental functioning is most appropriately viewed as being inherently heterogeneous rather than monolithic.

A final, general point we raise is that an adequate account of mediated agency cannot be grounded in the perspective of any single academic discipline. In order to recognize and describe the various sociocultural settings suggested by the notion of heterogeneity, psychology must work together with anthropology, sociology, and other disciplines. To understand how reciprocal teaching works, let alone to establish it in new settings, researchers concerned with learning and instruction must recognize the cultural and institutional forces that are the focus of study for scholars from other disciplines. Much in the tradition of Vygotsky and Bakhtin, contemporary studies of mediated agency must be willing to travel freely across the barriers that characterize our contemporary academic scene.

Notes

The writing of this chapter was assisted by Spencer Foundation grants to the first and second authors, and a grant from National Medical Enterprises, Inc., to the third author. The statements made and the views expressed are solely the responsibility of the authors.

1. Following the practice used by Minick in Vygotsky (1987), we employ the terms "intermental" and "intramental" as translations for the Russian terms *interpsikhicheskii* and *intrapsikhicheskii,* respectively. This usage contrasts with the use of "interpsychological" and "intrapsychological" in other translations of Vygotsky's works but is more consistent with the use of "mental" as a translation for *psikhicheskii* in Vygotsky's writings.

2. Of course, to argue that the mediational means that shape mental functioning reflect their sociocultural setting does not mean that they are not shaped by requirements imposed by their need to serve as psychological tools as well. However, the approach we are suggesting challenges an underlying assumption often held by psychologists that the mechanisms that mediate human mental functioning somehow exist solely for that purpose. In our view, the psychological tools that mediate thinking, memory, and other mental functions are typically shaped strongly by forces distinct from the dictates of mental functioning and for this reason import "foreign" structures and processes into this functioning.

References

Bakhtin, M. M. (1981). *The dialogic imagination: four essays by M. M. Bakhtin* (M. Holquist, ed.; C. Emerson & M. Holquist, trans.). Austin: University of Texas Press.

Bakhtin, M. M. (1986). *Speech genres and other late essays* (C. Emerson & M. Holquist, eds.; V. W. McGee, trans.). Austin: University of Texas Press.

Bateson, G. (1972). *Steps to an ecology of mind: a revolutionary approach to man's understanding of himself.* New York: Ballantine.

Belyaeva, A. V., & Cole, M. (1989). Computer-mediated joint activity in the service of human development: an overview. *Quarterly Newsletter of the Laboratory of Comparative Human Cognition, 11*(3), 45–57.

Bernstein, B. (1975). *Class, codes, and control. Vol. 3. Toward a theory of educational transmission* (2nd ed.). London: Routledge & Kegan Paul.

Brown, A. L., & Ferrara, R. (1985). Diagnosing zones of proximal development. In J. V. Wertsch (ed.). *Culture, communication, and cognition: Vygotskian perspectives.* New York: Cambridge University Press.

Brown, A. L., & French, L. A. (1979). The zone of proximal development: implications for intelligence testing in the year 2000. In R. J. Sternberg and D. K. Detterman (eds.). *Human intelligence: perspectives on theory and measurement.* Norwood, NJ: Ablex.

Brown, A. L., & Palincsar, A. S. (1982). Inducing strategic learning from texts by means of informed, self-centered training. *Topics in Learning and Learning Disabilities, 2*(1), 1–17.

Brown, A. L., Campione, J. C., & Barclay, C. R. (1979). Training self-checking routines for estimating test readiness: generalization from list learning to prose recall. *Child Development, 50,* 501–12.

Cole, M. (1985). The zone of proximal development: where culture and cognition create each other. In J. V. Wertsch (ed.). *Culture, communication, and cognition: Vygotskian perspectives.* New York: Cambridge University Press.

Davidson, D. (1971). Agency. In R. Binkley, R. Bronaugh, & A. Marras (eds.). *Agent, action, and reason.* Toronto: University of Toronto Press.

Dennett, D. C. (1981). *Brainstorms: philosophical essays on mind and psychology.* Cambridge, MA: MIT Press.

Gardner, H. (1985). *Frames of mind: the theory of multiple intelligence.* New York: Basic Books.

Hatano, G., & Inagaki, K. (1991). Sharing cognition through collective comprehension activity. In L. A. Resnick, R. Levine, & S. Teasley (eds.). *Perspectives on socially shared cognition.* Washington, DC: American Psychological Association.

Heath, S. B. (1983). *Ways with words: language, life, and work in communities and classrooms.* Cambridge: Cambridge University Press.

Holquist, M., & Emerson, C. (1981). Glossary. In *The dialogic imagination: four essays by M. M. Bakhtin.* Austin: University of Texas Press.

Hutchins, E. (1991). The social organization of distributed cognition. In L. A. Resnick, R. Levine, & S. Teasley (eds.). *Perspectives on socially shared cognition.* Washington, DC: American Psychological Association.

Itakura, K. (1986). Hypo-experience-instruction method of learning: "springs and force" and "magnets." Presented at the International Conference on Trends in Physics Education, Tokyo.

Joravsky, D. (1989). *Russian psychology: a critical history.* Oxford: Basil Blackwell.

Leont'ev, A. N. (1959). *Problemy razvitiya psikhiki.* Moscow: Moscow University Press. Published in English (1981) as *Problems in the development of mind.* Moscow: Progress Publishers.

Leont'ev, A. N. (1975). *Deyatel'nost', soznanie, lichnost'.* Leningrad: Izdatel'stvo Politicheskoi Literaturi. Published in English (1978) as *Activity, consciousness, personality.* Englewood Cliffs, NJ: Prentice Hall.

Leont'ev, A. N. (1981). The problem of activity in psychology. In J. V. Wertsch (ed.). *The concept of activity in Soviet Psychology.* Armonk, NY: M. E. Sharpe.

Luria, A. R. (1976). *Cognitive development: its cultural and social foundations.* Cambridge, MA: Harvard University Press.

Luria, A. R. (1981). *Language and cognition* (J. V. Wertsch, ed.). New York: Wiley Intersciences.

Mead, G. H. (1934). *Mind, self, and society from the standpoint of a social behaviorist.* Chicago: University of Chicago Press.

Mehan, H. (1979). *Learning lessons.* Cambridge, MA: Harvard University Press.

Middleton, D. (1987). Some issues and approaches. *Quarterly Newsletter of Comparative Human Cognition* (Special Issue: Collective Memory and Remembering), *9*(1).

Middleton, D., & Edwards, D. (1990). *Collective Remembering.* London: Sage.

Minick, N. (1985). L. S. Vygotsky and Soviet activity theory: new perspectives on the relationship between mind and society. Unpublished doctoral dissertation, Northwestern University.

Newman, D., Griffin, P., & Cole, M. (1989). *The construction zone working for cognitive change in school.* New York: Cambridge University Press.

Palincsar, A. S. (1987). An apprentice approach to the instruction of comprehension skills. Presented at the symposium: Perspectives on Expert Learning: An Integrative Examination of Theoretical and Empirical Issues, American Educational Research Association.

Palincsar, A. S., & Brown, A. L. (1984). Reciprocal teaching of comprehension-fostering and comprehension-monitoring activities. *Cognition and Instruction,* *1*(2), 117–75.

Palincsar, A. S., & Brown, A. L. (1988). Teaching and practicing thinking skills to promote comprehension in the context of group problem solving. *RASE,* *9*(1), 53–59.

Resnick, L. B., Levine, R., & Teasley, S. (1991). *Perspectives on socially shared cognition.* Washington, DC: American Psychological Association.

Rogoff, B., & Lave, J. (eds.). (1984). *Everyday cognition: its development in social context.* Cambridge, MA: Harvard University Press.

Rogoff, B., & Wertsch, J. V. (eds.) (1984). Children's learning in the "zone of proximal development" (no. 23). In *New directions for child development.* San Francisco: Jossey-Bass.

Shif, Zh. I. (1935). *Razvitie nauchnykh ponyatii u shkol'nika: issledovanie k voprosu umstvennogo razvitiya shkol'nika pri obuchenii obshchestvovedeniyu* [The development of scientific concepts in the school child: the investigation of intellectual development of the school child in social science instruction], Moscow-Leningrad. Gosudarstvennoe Uchebno-Pedagogicheskoe Izdatel'stvo.

Sternberg, R. J. (1985). *Beyond IQ: a triarchic theory of human intelligence.* London: Cambridge University Press.

Taylor, C. (1985). *Human agency and language: philosophical papers 1.* Cambridge: Cambridge University Press.

Taylor, C. (1989). *Sources of the self: the making of modern identity.* Cambridge, MA: Harvard University Press.

Tharp, R. G., & Gallimore, R. (1988). *Rousing minds to life.* Cambridge: Cambridge University Press.

Tikhomirov, O. K., & Klochko, V. E. (1981). The detection of a contradiction as the initial stage of problem formation. In J. V. Wertsch (ed.). *The concept of activity in Soviet psychology.* Armonk, NY: M. E. Sharpe.

Tulviste, P. (1975). O sotsial'no-istoricheskom razvitii poznavatel'nykh protsessov (na materiale zarubezhnikh eksperimental'no-psikhologicheskikh issledovanii) [The social-historical development of cognitive processes. (material based on foreign experimental-psychological research)]. Dissertation, Psychology, Moscow.

Tulviste, P. (1987). L. Levy-Bruhl and problems of the historical development of thought. *Soviet Psychology, 25*(3), 3–21.

Tulviste, P. (1988). *Kul'turno-istoricheskoe razvitie verbal'nogo myshlenie (psikhologeskoe issledovaniya)* [The cultural-historical development of verbal thinking (psychological research)]. Tallin: Valgus.

Voloshinov, V. N. (1973). *Marxism and the philosophy of language* (L. Matejka & I. R. Titunik, trans.). New York: Seminar Press.

Vygotsky, L. S. (1978). *Mind in society: the development of higher psychological pro-*

cesses (M. Cole, V. John-Steiner, S. Scribner, & E. Souberman, eds.). Cambridge, MA: Harvard University Press.

Vygotsky, L. S. (1979). Consciousness as a problem in the psychology of behavior. *Soviet Psychology, 17*(4), 3–35.

Vygotsky, L. S. (1981a). The instrumental method in psychology. In J. V. Wertsch (ed.). *The concept of activity in Soviet psychology.* Armonk, NY: M. E. Sharpe.

Vygotsky, L. S. (1981b). The genesis of higher mental functions. In J. V. Wertsch (ed.). *The concept of activity in Soviet psychology.* Armonk, NY: M. E. Sharpe.

Vygotsky, L. S. (1987). *Thinking and speech* (N. Minick, ed. & trans.). New York: Plenum

Werner, H., and Kaplan, B. (1963). *Symbol formation.* New York: Wiley.

Wertsch, J. V. (1985). *Vygotsky and the social formation of mind.* Cambridge, MA: Harvard University Press.

Wertsch, J. V. (1991). *Voices of the mind: a sociocultural approach to mediated action.* Cambridge, MA: Harvard University Press.

Wertsch, J. V., & Minick, N. (1990). Negotiating sense in the zone of proximal development. In M. Schwebel, C. A. Maher, and N. S. Fogley (eds.). *Promoting cognitive growth over the life span.* Hillsdale, NJ: Lawrence Erlbaum Associates.

Williams, W. M., & Sternberg, R. J. (1988). Group intelligence: why some groups are better than others. *Intelligence, 12,* 351–77.

COMMENTARY

Interface between Sociocultural and Psychological Aspects of Cognition

ROBERT SERPELL

The mental act of knowing is a personal condition, a relationship between an individual and some aspect of the world. As Wittgenstein (1958) succeeded in demonstrating to the satisfaction of many, however, it cannot be considered a private condition, isolated from the rest of society. What we mean when we say that someone knows something has to do with regularities in his or her speech and other observable behavior. Cognition is a dimension of experience we infer from consistency in the ways in which people behave toward one another. The knowledge of one person is therefore, by definition, accessible to others, and many of society's institutions are based on the premise that knowledge is shared. No laws, or schools, or libraries would make any sense in the absence of this premise. No communication could take place.

The enduring coherence of individual persons is central to the "primary theory" shared by all human cultures (Horton, 1982). The borders between individuals "emerge" from everyday experience as sharply defined (Lakoff & Johnson, 1980). Yet the minds that apprehend this segmented world of persons are by their very nature bound into a communicative interdependence that leads us to perceive ourselves through the eyes of others.

This socially constructed nature of human self-understanding has proved difficult to reconcile with the objectivist philosophical premises on which the physical and biological sciences are built (Lakoff & Johnson, 1980; Taylor, 1971). A loosely formulated notion of social context as the meeting point between psychology and the other social sciences tends to be unsatisfactory for two reasons. First, its lack of operational concreteness leads many psychological researchers simply to ignore it when designing their experiments. Second, the parameters of interest to sociologists and economists are often treated as based on a radically different kind of logic from that of psychological theorizing, and taking account of context is treated as somewhat analogous to washing one's hands before sitting down to eat: a necessary prerequisite that has no direct bearing on the next and more intrinsically interesting task.

One of the major attractions of Vygotsky's theoretical perspective for an analysis of the interaction between sociocultural factors and psychological factors is often said to be its provision of a repertoire of two-sided constructs to bridge the two domains of analysis. Tharp, in his chapter, for instance, explicitly claims that in

> ... the neo-Vygotskian structure of ideas psychological and social events are discussed with the same concepts, in a shared lexicon, and in a common web of meanings. Such unities allow us to see parallels and isomorphisms, as well as discontinuities, in psychological structures and social structures.

Articulating the Nature of the Interface

Probably the best known of Vygotsky's bridging constructs is the zone of proximal development (the Zo-ped, or ZPD), where, as Cole (1985) has put it, "culture and cognition create each other." How should we interpret this metaphor of mutual creation? Culture may be said to create cognition in the Zo-ped by structuring the practices in which adults engage with their children, so that the cognitive growth of the child within his or her Zo-ped is steered toward a set of goals specified by the culture, which is shared by the adult and other members of the cultural group, and into which the child is being socialized. Cognition, on the other hand, may be said to create culture by structuring the social interaction between adult and child, who together generate new practices and ideas for inclusion in the cultural group's repertoire.

Each of the chapters in this section of the present book seeks to extend further the claim that neo-Vygotskian theory is well equipped to capture the essential features of this interface and, in the process, to explicate its structure and dynamics.

Tharp's "exploratory and demonstration analysis" of "the institutional and social context of educational practice and reform" describes two theoretical facets of the interface: (1) layers and levels of embeddedness; and (2) modes of interaction and forms of accountability.

Nicolopoulou and Cole use two additional constructs to explain the interaction between the two "institutional contexts" in which they situated their educational "play-world," the Fifth Dimension, and the "culture of collaborative learning" the participants "generated": (3) constitutive rules and scripts; and (4) degree of fit.

Wertsch, Tulviste, and Hagstrom develop their "sociocultural approach to agency" by proposing a refined version of Vygotsky's account of the "internalization" of overt speech during the course of development, using Bahktin's (1981, 1986) notions of: (5) appropriation and ventriloquism.

Gallimore and Goldenberg center their account of "home and school factors in children's emergent literacy" around the construct of (6) activity settings, which they explicitly "operationalize" in terms of five dimensions of variation:

1. Personnel present
2. Cultural values
3. Task demands
4. Scripts
5. Purposes and motives of actors

The diversity of these formulations illustrates the fertility of this field of research and the exploratory nature of the explanations it offers. In this brief commentary, I attempt to synthesize these various accounts of the interface between sociocultural and psychological aspects of cognition and in the process highlight some unresolved problems and challenges for future research on this topic.

What Is Embedded in What?

The simplest account of culturally embedded human development is compatible with an objectivist mode of description: *the individual is embedded in a niche.* Yet, as Super and Harkness (1986) have pointed out, the niche of human development is structured by culture in three complementary ways: (1) physical and social settings; (2) customs of child care and child rearing; and (3) the psychology of the caretakers (by which the authors referred to the implicit psychological theories that inform the caretaking activities). This "ecocultural" structure has been described by Gallimore, Weisner, Kaufman, and Berheimer (1989, p. 224) as follows:

> Ecology is not only a matter of toting up material resources or constraints. . . . The social constructions of families . . . can have a powerful impact on the daily activities of children, and thus on developmentally significant experiences.

The interactive nature of the ecocultural embeddedness of human development may in fact be better captured by describing the child as a member of a system. In Bronfenbrenner's (1979) formalization of this approach, dyads (e.g., a mother and her infant) are described as *microsystems, which are embedded in larger-scale mesosystems* (e.g., a family or a neighborhood), *which in turn are embedded in an overarching macro system* (e.g., a cultural group or a nation-state). Unlike the niche in which the individual is embedded, these larger systems can be regarded as formally isomorphic with the smallest unit of analysis, the micro system. As my analysis proceeds it will become apparent that this concept may be an important theoretical gain—but one that is purchased at the price of losing sight of the individual person as a unit of analysis, which is (to say the least) radically counterintuitive for most psychologists.

In Gallimore and Goldenberg's analysis, individuals, dyads, and other social groups participate in *activities* (e.g., literacy) *which are embedded in activity settings,* which in turn are "shaped and sustained by ecological and cultural features of the family niche." Facing inward, "children's activity settings are the architecture of their daily life"; facing outward, they are "a perceptible instantiation of the social system." Classroom lessons, shopping in a supermarket, and playing a computer game are familiar examples of such socioculturally structured settings in which American children of the late twentieth century engage in activities conducive to the development of specifiable aspects of their cognition.

Yet a closer examination of the cognitive processes that occur in the context of such activities suggests that it is often difficult to attribute responsibility for separate elements to different individuals (Cole, Hood, & McDermott, 1982; Rogoff & Lave, 1984). As with Hutchins' (1991) example of "how crews of naval vessels organize their activity so that they can guide a ship into a harbor," much of the cognition involved in everyday activities such as cooking, shopping, or playing a ballgame is "socially distributed" (Wertsch, Tulviste, & Hagstrom, this volume). Thus a further variation on the theme of cultural embedding is that cognition is embedded in social activities, mediated by a cultural meaning-system.

What Constitutes Embeddedness?

Each of the formulations discussed above lends itself to more than one account of the relation termed embedded. The metaphor of the niche borrowed from ecological analysis suggests a basic image of *location and timing*. Nicolopoulou and Cole's computer play-world the Fifth Dimension, for instance, was embedded in two preexisting sociocultural contexts: an afterschool social club and a public library service, each of which had specific premises and hours of operation within which the computer games were played.

Their embeddedness was further defined by a *structure of participation,* such that certain clients and officers of the "host institution" played particular roles in the embedded activity. The concept of participation has also been applied in illuminating ways to the socialization of children's cognition through the mechanism of apprenticeship (Lave, 1990; Rogoff, 1990). Children's opportunities to learn adult skills at a rate compatible with their stage of development in the context of everyday activities can be construed from a social perspective as "legitimate, peripheral participation" under the supervision and guidance of their more expert elders. As socialization proceeds, the character of the child's participation in the social activity changes: the progress from novice, though apprentice and deputy, to expert is marked by increasing autonomy, representing an increase in the individual's cognitive power, which is acknowledged socially by the withdrawal of guiding support.

Participation in a socioculturally structured activity involves adherence to the rules specifying correct performance. Another dimension of embeddedness is thus *regulation.* But whereas during the early stages of peripheral participation this is experienced by the agent as a constricting, if not outright oppressive, influence from the outside, later the competent expert adheres to the rules effortlessly. As Nicolopoulou and Cole put it:

> To be able to think and act autonomously requires moving from dependence on the authority of particular superiors to operating within the framework of a shared and voluntarily accepted system of impersonal rules.

These rules are another construct that faces both ways: for the individual they are a source of structured guidance for behavior; for the culture they are "constitutive" (Searle, 1965) of the activities it encodes.

Although external guidance is no longer required, the adherence of a competent individual to the constitutive rules of culturally structured activities is monitored indirectly by other members of the cultural group. If she does not follow the rules of grammar, her speech becomes unintelligible. If her performance of the culturally "scripted" activities that constitute a social practice (e.g., greeting, purchasing) deviates too far from social norms, she will be held accountable by others whom the practice affects. *Accountability* is thus another facet of regulation. Tharp describes the hierarchical interlocking of systems within the formal educational bureaucracy of the American public school system as follows:

> Just as teachers treat students in the recitation script, schools themselves are given certain "texts" to master in the form of regulations and authorizations, and they are from time to time assessed or audited to test whether they are in compliance with those texts.

On a more subjective plane, another measure of embeddedness is variously termed *membership,* or *ownership.* Although Tharp argues cogently for the radical view that the only "true teaching is responsive teaching . . . that is, assisting performance of [students] by teachers," he acknowledges the paradoxical phenomenon that over the ages and across many cultures a much commoner paradigm for school instruction has been what he calls "the recitation script": assigning tasks and assessing performance, a discourse pattern described by Mehan (1979) as teacher initiation–pupil response–teacher evaluation (I–R–E). As Wertsch, Tulviste, and Hagstrom point out:

> For many pupils, participation in this pattern of discourse seems to foster some kind of cognitive growth. In such cases the process is probably one in which the pattern of teachers' questions is taken over and mastered by pupils.

Others, failing to make this connection, "are left in a position where passive responses are all that is required." A highly efficacious mode of remedial intervention was designed by Palincsar and Brown (1984), in which poor readers were engaged in "reciprocal peer-teaching," taking turns as dialogue leaders and in this teaching role generating summaries and predictions, and clarifying misleading or complex sections of text. The theoretical basis for the success of this method is explained by Wertsch, Tulviste, and Hagstrom as follows:

> The pupil is given responsibility for formulating and initiating the communicative sequence . . . and thereby put in the position of judging the appropriateness of others' responses. . . . Instead of leaving the teacher in the position of ultimate "cognitive authority," pupils are required to appropriate this social language.

The process of appropriation, or "taking on cognitive authority," imparts to the developing individual not only confidence in her competence to act autonomously but also a sense of membership in the group and corresponding ownership of its cultural resources. The authority of the claim "this is my language, my culture, my community" is simultaneously based in a sense of belonging (of being owned and accepted by the group) and in a sense of control (of owning the medium and hence having the power to use it skillfully and innovatively).[1]

Criteria of Fit

Given that the context in which a psychological process is embedded has its own sociocultural properties, the question arises as to how well the two fit. The Fifth Dimension play-world described by Nicolopoulou and Cole is an innovatory educational program, packaged within a computer game format that can be inserted as a module into a variety of host settings. The authors report an ironic contrast between the degree of fit between this curriculum module and the two activity settings (ecocultural niches) into which it was embedded and the eventual outcome in the larger sociocultural arena. From the perspective of the theorists, focusing on learning outcomes, the Library, with its orderly, studious atmosphere, was clearly a more appropriate and successful niche than the Club, with its emphasis on fun and unstructured freedom to switch between activities. As the authors put it, "the cultural logic" of the Fifth Dimension found in the library "a more supportive environment." Yet from the perspectives of their own institutional concerns, the host organizations perceived the Fifth Dimension as less compatible with the goals of the Library than with those of the Club. "The library staff felt that the noise and playful bustle of the Fifth Dimension site disturbed some of its patrons," whereas at the Club the Fifth Dimension "became one of their most popular programs, measured by the number of children who participated—even though their participation was more superficial and discontinuous."

It is tempting to dismiss these considerations, as well as the financial constraints that contributed to the Library's decision to discontinue the program, as "peripheral to the key analytical issues" or "accidental." But, as the authors acknowledge, they played a decisive part in the "real world" outcome of this planned intervention. Such paradoxical divergences between theoretical concerns and sociocultural decision making are common in applied psychology: What "ought to fit" in theory often fails to do so in practice.

A well-known example in the recent educational history of the United States was the resistance of many African-American parents to the proposal to introduce Black English Vernacular forms into the elementary school curriculum. The theoretical rationale for this proposal centered on the principle that children should be afforded opportunities in the classroom to deploy skills they had acquired in their preschool, home, and community environment as a source of confidence, a cognitive foundation on which to build new learning, a linking mechanism to facilitate out-of-school rehearsal of school-learned behaviors, and a demonstration of the direct relevance of school activities to the demands of everyday life in the community by way of guaranteeing its appropriateness as a preparation for the future challenges of adult life.

Thus on theoretical grounds we would expect that the most receptive sections of the population to such a curriculum innovation would be those families in which Black English Vernacular is most widely used relative to "standard English" in home and community contexts, as it is children from this section of the society for whom the discontinuity between a standard English school curriculum and the preschool, out of school, and after school home and community environments would be greatest.

Yet as far as we are able to reconstruct the sociology of the resistance to these curriculum innovations, it appears that the most pronounced resistance to the innovation came precisely from that section of society that on theoretical grounds would have been expected to welcome it most enthusiastically. What happened was that parents with low incomes and low levels of formal education construed the innovation as a strategy to "keep our children back," to prevent them from using formal education as a route for upward social mobility. They argued that Standard English was, in practice in "the real world", a major entry criterion for selecting a small number of young people born into the lower income strata of society—a kind of passport to successful participation in the higher echelons of society. A curriculum that reduced the emphasis on this key survival skill in the competitive market for jobs was thus not only not helpful to their children but denied them one of the most important practical advantages their parents were seeking for them from school (Smitherman & McGinnis, 1980).

Dissonance of this kind between two estimates of the fit between a psychological process and a sociocultural context can be interpreted in a variety of ways. It may be attributed to (1) differences in the time frame over which the adequacy of the fit is judged; (2) conflict among vested interests that systematically distort the judgments of observers; or (3) different configurations of essentially the same set of variables.

One estimate may be attuned to a shorter time frame than the other. For example, in the short term, "giv[ing] pupils the kind of cognitive authority, even temporarily, suggested by the procedure of reciprocal teaching" would "cause major challenges" to the existing "institutional order" of contemporary classroom settings and might for that reason be rejected as impractical (Wertsch, Tulviste, and Hagstrom, this volume). Yet despite the apparently overwhelming conservatism of the educational hierarchy, "schools will change . . . [but] these shifts occur at a tectonic pace, which [for a critical participant] experienced in biographical time, feels like stasis" (Tharp, this volume). That which seems impractical in the short term may be instrumental in promoting what in the longer term is seen as progressive change.

A second possibility is that the estimates are biased by vested interests that seem extrinsic to the central purpose of the project. Some teachers, for instance, might resist the introduction of a curriculum innovation because it would require them to work longer hours or because it might reduce employment opportunities for teachers. Some parents might resist such an innovation because they believe it would intrude on their domestic privacy. Conversely, some researchers and administrators may seem to advocate the innovation because it would advance their personal careers.

More theoretically challenging is the possibility that both estimates are based on considerations of equally genuine and immediate relevance to the project, but they represent different configurations of a multiplicity of variables. For instance, to the librarian the Fifth Dimension appears to be an instance of the category "opportunities for learning to read," whereas to the research psychologist the library is an instance of the category "sites for collaborative learning." The relation between collaborative learning and learning to read is theoretically complex, requiring an analysis not only of the dynamics of cognitive development but also of the ecocultural patterning of literacy events.

According to Heath (1989), collaborative reading may be more characteristic of the literacy practices of some traditional, low-income, African-American communities on the one hand and of modern workplaces on the other relative to those represented in the prevailing pattern of mainstream American schooling. Thus the political economy of this distribution of a particular form of social practice across contexts might be of great importance for reaching an administrative decision on whether the Fifth Dimension should take priority in the design of a local library over opportunities for silent browsing among books. Psychological considerations of transfer of learning from the home to school and from the school to the workplace would also have a bearing on such a decision, but only when combined with information about the social and cultural composition of the population within the catchment zone served by the library.

Interactional Complexities among Levels of Structure

One of the dangers of the double-sided character of much of the neo-Vygotskian terminology is that it tends to invite the exaggeration of analogies.

Groups as well as individuals engage in activities, make use of texts and scripts, have repertoires of signs, and experience gradual change over time that is sometimes called development. Tharp's account of administrative practices in education treats them as isomorphic "qua" activity settings with the activity setting of classroom instruction. This concept does not stand up to close examination, however; for example, it is highly improbable that a legislator ever asked an administrator to recite the text of the law as evidence of conformity with it. In fact, the accountability of a school system to the state legislature is an institutional relationship, quite different from the negotiated, interpersonal accountability some schoolteachers feel toward the parents of their pupils. [Elliott (1980) offered an illuminating account of the differences between these two types of accountability in the relationship between schools and parents in one section of English society.]

Wertsch, Tulviste, and Hagstrom repeatedly assert that the form of intramental cognitive processes is structured by their intermental, social precursors such as genres of discourse. It is not clear, however, that the interactional aspect of discourse (e.g., in Mehan's I–R–E) is what makes it work intramentally. Rather, the interactional form seems to be conducive to appropriation of the tools by some subjects and not others.

Processes of change in sociocultural arrangements are controlled by a different set of variables from those that impinge directly on psychological change in the context of instruction or ontogenetic development (Scribner, 1985). Historical analysis of the origins of the age-graded curriculum that has become standard in contemporary schools all over the world reveals that this institutional pattern evolved gradually over several centuries in western Europe in response to a complex of pedagogical, administrative, and ethical considerations (Aries, 1962; Serpell, in press).

Likewise, the differentiation of language varieties within a speech community is a complex phenomenon with its own social and political dynamics, which are distinct from those impinging on an individual's bilingual repertoire (Fishman, 1967; Gumperz, 1968). The effective environment of children such as those born into first-generation immigrant families from Mexico studied by Gallimore and Goldenberg is characterized by the coexistence of two different systems of socialization, marked among other signs by differences in language. The bilingualism and biculturation that typically emerges in such a situation involves a differentiated cognitive repertoire through which the individual expresses different dimensions of intersubjectivity.

Bahktin's analysis of genres, cited by Wertsch, Tulviste, and Hagstrom, evokes not only Bernstein's but also Gumperz's (1982) notion of code and Halliday's (1970) use of register. What children internalize is not a fixed set of context-bound behavioral routines but, rather, a differentiated set of semantic resources whose connotations are defined by their location within the web of associations. We can think of these resources as tools, but they are constantly being redeployed in new ways (Ochs, 1990).

Individual Cognitive Development and Cultural Change

When trying to understand the behavior of a schoolchild, analytical priority must be given to a definition of the activity. It is this contextual framework that specifies the dimensions of meaning in terms of which the behavior must be assessed. But task demands and scripts are only seldom fully determined in advance of the activity itself, for example, when a computer game allows only certain moves or a routine stipulates a particular sequence of ritualized acts. For most activities, including any school lesson worth its salt, the particular personnel present, their purposes, and their motives specify the particular behaviors that will occur within this context. The shared web of meanings informs (rather than determines) the interpretations placed by each participant on the other's provisional moves; and as interaction proceeds, an agreed definition of the task demands and script are defined through negotiation (Serpell, 1977).

It is this open-ended creativity of individual behavior within the framework of a set of constitutive rules that ensures that the culture will not be static but will change over time.

The mutual interdependence of individual mind and sociocultural system poses two complementary paradoxes of cognitive development.

1. As the individual's mind develops, it becomes increasingly powerful by virtue of a growing stock of cognitive resources. Yet ipso facto it also becomes increasingly committed to that particular way of thinking which is shared among members of the sociocultural group from which those resources were learned.
2. As the child develops toward adulthood, the sociocultural group that takes responsibility for her socialization and enculturation strengthens its claims on her as a member through an increasingly internalized awareness of her obligations to conform with social and cultural norms. Yet this shift of emphasis toward internal self-control is precisely what enables the individual to legitimate her nonconformity.

The resolution of each of these paradoxes throws light on the other. The possibility of psychological empowerment through cultural commitment arises from the fact that society values most highly those of its members who innovate. Moreover the need for society to tolerate nonconformity in its young arises from the fact that the most effective method for recruiting a new member is to assign them responsibility for participation.

Note

1. Since this is a significant phenomenological aspect of enculturation, I find the term appropriation to be much more apt than "ventriloquism," which seems to connote a quite different kind of agency. In appropriating a cultural resource, I claim to be responsible and intelligible by virtue of shared participation in and ownership of

a system of meanings (D'Andrade, 1984). A ventriloquist, on the other hand, pretends not to be responsible for the utterance he generates.

References

Ariès, P. (1962). *Centuries of childhood* (R. Baldick, trans.). London: Cape.
Bakhtin, M. M. (1981). *The dialogic imagination* (C. Emerson & M. Holmquist, trans.). Austin: University of Texas Press.
Bakhtin, M. M. (1986). *Speech genres and other late essays.* Austin: University of Texas Press.
Bronfenbrenner, U. (1979). *The ecology of human development.* Cambridge, MA: Harvard University Press.
Cole, M. (1985). The zone of proximal development: where culture and cognition create each other. In J. V. Wertsch (ed.). *Culture, communication, and cognition: Vygotskian perspectives.* Cambridge: Cambridge University Press.
Cole, M., Hood, L., & McDermott, R. (1982). Ecological niche-picking. In U. Neisser (ed.). *Memory observed: remembering in natural contexts.* San Francisco: Freeman.
D'Andrade, R. G. (1984). Cultural meaning systems. In R. A. Shweder & R. A. Levine (eds.). *Culture theory: essays on mind, self and emotion* (pp. 88–119). Cambridge: Cambridge University Press.
Elliot, J. (1980). Teachers' perspectives on school accountability. In J. Elliot, D. Bridges, D. Ebbutt, R. Gibson, & J. Nias (eds.). *School accountability.* London: Grant McIntyre.
Fishman, J. A. (1967). Bilingualism with and without diglossia; diglossia with and without bilingualism. *Journal of Social Issues, 23*(2), 29–38.
Gallimore, R., Weisner, T. S., Kaufman, S. Z., & Bernheimer, L. P. (1989). The social construction of ecocultural niches: family accommodation of developmentally delayed children. *American Journal on Mental Retardation, 94*(3), 216–30.
Gumperz, J. J. (1968). The speech community. In *International Encyclopedia of the Social Sciences.* (pp. 381–86). New York: Macmillan. Reprinted (1972) in Giglioli, P. (ed.). *Language and social context.* Harmondsworth: Penguin.
Gumperz, J. J. (1982). *Discourse strategies.* Cambridge: Cambridge University Press.
Halliday, M. A. K. (1970). Language structure and language function. In J. Lyons (ed.). *New horizons in linguistics.* Harmondsworth: Penguin.
Heath, S. B. (1989). Oral and literate traditions amoung black Americans living in poverty. *American Psychologist, 44*(2), 367–73.
Horton, R. (1982). Tradition and modernity revisited. In M. Hollis & S. Lukes (eds.). *Rationality and relativism.* (pp. 201–60). Oxford: Blackwell.
Hutchins, E. (1991). The social organization of distributed cognition. In L. B. Resnick, J. M. Levine, & S. D. Teasley (eds.). *Perspectives on socially shared cognition* (pp. 283–307). Washington, DC: American Psychological Association.
Lakoff, G., & Johnson, M. (1980). *Metaphors we live by.* Chicago: University of Chicago Press.
Lave, J. (1990). The culture of aquisition and the practice of understanding. In J. W. Stigler, R. A. Shweder, & G. Herdt (eds.). *Cultural psychology* (pp. 309–27). Cambridge: Cambridge University Press.

Mehan, H. (1979). *Learning Lessons.* Cambridge, MA: Harvard University Press.

Ochs, E. (1990). Indexicality and socialization. In J. W. Stigler, R. A. Shweder, & G. Herdt (eds.). *Cultural Psychology* (pp. 287–308). Cambridge: Cambridge University Press.

Palincsar, A. S., & Brown, A. L. (1984). Reciprocal teaching of comprehension-fostering and comprehension-monitoring activities. *Cognition and Instruction, 1*(2), 117–75.

Rogoff, B. (1990). *Apprenticeship in thinking: cognitive development in social context.* New York: Oxford University Press.

Rogoff, B., & Lave, J. (eds.) (1984). *Everyday cognition: its development in social context.* Cambridge, MA: Harvard University Press.

Scribner, S. (1985). Vygotsky's uses of history. In J. V. Wertsch (ed.). *Culture, communication, and cognition: Vygotskian perspectives.* Cambridge: Cambridge University Press.

Searle, J. (1965). What is a speech act? In M. Black (ed.). *Philosophy in America* (pp. 221–39). Ithaca, NY: Allen Unwin and Cornell University Press.

Serpell, R. (1977). Context and connotation: the negotiation of meaning in a multiple speech repertoire. *Quarterly Newsletter of the Institute for Comparative Human Development, 1*(1), 10–15.

Serpell, R. (in press). *The significance of schooling.* Cambridge: Cambridge University Press.

Smitherman, G., & McGinnis, J. (1980). Black language and black liberation. In R. L. Jones (ed.). *Black psychology* (2nd ed.). New York: Harper & Row.

Super, C., & Harkness, S. (1986). The developmental niche: a conceptualization at the interface of child and culture. *International Journal of Behavioural Development, 9*(4), 545–69.

Taylor, C. (1971). Interpretation and the sciences of man. *Review of Metaphysics, 25,* 3–51.

Wittgenstein, L. (1958). *Philosophical investigations* (2nd ed.) (G.E.M. Anscombe, trans.). Oxford: Blackwell.

AFTERWORD

Direction of Post-Vygotskian Research

JACQUELINE J. GOODNOW

The chapters in this book are well served by the Introduction and the commentaries on each part. To say something new in an Afterword is a challenge.

To meet it, I shall concentrate on some aspects of what gives rise to the particular topics and questions the chapters in this book consider. I do not include the rereading of Vygotsky and the increased attention to other Soviet scholars that many of the chapters have noted as part of the background. Instead, I concentrate on the general state of discussions about cognition and context and on the studies that preceded this volume. The present concerns have a past, and there are several ways to tackle the same issue. A brief look at the past and at some cohorts can provide a setting for the present work and a base for suggesting where the next lines of research may lead.

I start with a minimal history, inevitably selective and seen from one person's perspective. Let us suppose, however, that during the 1950s or 1960s you were interested in the issues of context and cognition or of culture and thought. You would have encountered in the psychological literature some dominant ways of defining context. It was most often considered in terms of large variables such as "culture" or "schooling" accompanied by research formats that varied these subjects in the way independent variables are supposed to be varied. Cognition was most often regarded in terms of structures that were both general (cutting across situations) and logical. The desirable endpoint of development was the competent scientist or the effective processor of information. The connections between cognition and context would often be phrased in terms of stimulation, deprivation, amplification, or, more insightfully, the presence of discrepancy and challenge. For the latter, the prime example was Piaget's insistence that, at least in the area of moral reasoning, interactions between peers facilitated cognitive development by presenting a difference in perspectives, a demand to state one's point of view, and a demand for resolution. Both demands were seen as increasing the likelihood of reflection and the achievement of a less simplistic outlook.

These dominant ways of thought gave rise to both a great deal of research and a number of misgivings. As Rogoff and colleagues put it in this book, many scholars have returned from fieldwork with the feeling that the pre-

vailing views did not fit their observations. To take myself as an example, I
started a research project in Hong Kong with the goal of exploring the effects
of schooling on a range of Piagetian tasks (Goodnow, 1962). Hong Kong at
the time contained both schooled and unschooled children, providing a way
to disentangle the lack of schooling from a peasant or rural existence. I
returned with a strong sense of the importance of daily activities (shopping
for rice, for instance, was often the referent used when asked to think about
conservation of the weight of two balls of clay) and—an especially lasting
effect—a respect for cultural differences in what was regarded as the intelligent or "smart" way to behave in various situations (e.g., Goodnow, 1976,
1984). I also returned, as many have, with the sense that more thought
needed to go into what was meant by "context" or "culture," into the nature
of cognition, the connection between the two, and the processes involved in
any connection.

Additional giving-of-thought marked much of the writing and research
beginning around 1970. As a way of breaking out of their usual ways of
thinking and their usual research formats, some developmental psychologists turned toward other disciplines (social psychology, anthropology, and
sociology). Others turned instead (or in addition) to a developmental theory
that gave social factors a central theoretical slot, revived interest in the
nature of education or instruction, and pointed to some novel ways of doing
research. This theory was the one contained in writings by Vygotsky and
other Soviet psychologists.

A number of themes marked the rethinking, and I shall be referring to
several of them. At the start, however, I wish to note one theme that has had
a particular influence on this book. It has to do with the integration of
"micro" and "macro" approaches. Developmental psychology has long
contained an emphasis on "micro" analyses. Close attention has been given,
for instance, to the way individuals construct schemes, solve problems, and
acquire cognitive styles. In addition, there has been an emphasis on influences in the form of face-to-face interactions (mother–child interactions,
teacher–pupil exchanges, peer conflicts). Far less attention has been paid to
influences from the larger setting: the quality, for instance, of the extended
family, the neighborhood, the school, or, as in Elder's (1974) classic study,
the nature of the economy.

As that position began to change, however, another problem emerged:
How could one simultaneously pay attention to both "micro" and "macro"
factors? How could one combine, for instance, a concern with face-to-face
interactions with a concern for the effects of the neighborhood or the economy?

One approach lay in dissecting psychological theory and psychologists'
practices to reveal the way in which these reflected the values of the society
to which psychologists belonged. In an early example, Looft (1971) pointed
out the similarity between a society that emphasized the accumulation of
goods and the scoring of tests in such a way that "more" meant "better" (the
more correct the answers, the higher was the achievement considered to be).

A more widespread approach took the form of regarding parents as reflecting the larger society. In other words, they act as "agents of society." They are conduits or buffers, the routes by which effects "trickle down" or "bubble up." They present in concrete or "instantiated" fashion the knowledge, values, or ways of thinking that are present in the larger society. Thus when we describe these measures for parents, we might be absolved from the task of describing them for any other part of the social system.

It takes little reflection to realize that this solution is simply not good enough. Nor can we make much progress if we use completely different dimensions or terms to describe "society" and "individuals," making any cross-mapping impossible (Goodnow, 1987). To use an argument from Minick cited by several authors in this book, we need some common units of analysis. We need, as the title of the introduction to this volume makes clear, to bring together "institutional, social, and individual processes."

With this rough sketch in hand, let us turn to some of the revisionist approaches. I shall note in each case the way in which the approach prompts or frames many of the questions addressed in this book.

Nature of Context

One of the first moves was to take apart large variables such as "schooling." As Scribner and Cole (1981) pointed out, it was essential first to distinguish schooling from literacy. It was also necessary to ask: How is literacy being taught? What exactly is happening in this setting called "school"? In what ways is it similar to, or different from, other settings? It is a setting, people observed, where children were taught in places isolated from daily activity, by words rather than by actions, and with a high value placed on "decontextualized" knowledge (e.g., Bruner, 1972; Donaldson, 1978). It is also a place where people learn to be competent members of a classroom: They learn their place in a particular social group, acquire its rituals and its scripts, and become acceptable to others in the group (Mehan, 1979). These arguments were certainly interesting. They were also—as the authors themselves recognized—far from complete answers. Many of the chapters in this volume continue with the same questions.

Why should schools and classroom continue to serve as a major focus in the search to delineate what is meant by context? One reason is that Vygotsky's emphasis on the social bases of knowledge was seen as restoring the importance of instruction, an importance diminished somewhat by an emphasis on processes such as biological unfolding, discovery, and individual constructions. A second reason, more conceptual in style, is that schools offer a particular opportunity to observe events at individual, interpersonal, and institutional levels. It is here—as the title of the Introduction suggests—that the opportunities exist to see how several forms of influence combine or conflict. It is here also, to take a concrete example from Tharp and Gallimore (1988), that one can ask about the extent to which teachers assist the performance of pupils and that of each other.

Classrooms or learning sites of various kinds also offer a way of working with a description of context as activity settings. "Activity setting" is currently a popular term, and it is helpful to note Tharp's definition (this volume): "The activity setting is a construct that unites (1) objective features of the setting and environment; (2) objective features of the motoric and verbal actions of the participants; with (3) subjective features of the participants' experience, intention, and meaning." Gallimore and Goldenberg (this volume) added still other features. Their list covered "(1) the personnel present . . . ; (2) salient cultural values; (3) the operations and task demands of the activity itself; (4) the scripts for conduct that govern . . . actions; and (5) the purposes or motives of the participants."

The idea that one might break contexts into settings is not completely new. Ecological descriptions of environments, noting the places where children are to be found and the people who are also present, go back at least to Barker and Wright (1955). Settings are also a major part of Beatrice Whiting's (1980) proposal that parents influence children not only by way of face-to-face interactions but also by their assignment of children to activities and places that allow or close off opportunities. Being assigned to herd sheep, for instance, means that a child misses both schooling and time with peers.

What was new was the description of settings in terms of some specific features. They had a spatial location. They contained activities, tasks, and practices. They contained people who, as Super and Harkness (1986) pointed out, also had a "psychology," which gave rise to some particular expectations about the nature of children and development. As Serpell pointed out (this volume), their description was often accompanied by references to embeddedness.

Each of the several features has attracted attention either in its own right or in combination with others. For some scholars, for instance, the feature of most interest has been the nature of the "ethnotheories" or the "cultural models" held by parents or others in charge of developmental settings (e.g., Goodnow & Collins, 1990; Quinn & Holland, 1987; Reid & Valsiner, 1986).

For others, the intriguing aspect of settings has been the possibility that one may be "embedded" in another. This direction, for instance, is the one taken by Bronfenbrenner (1979) in his description of children as contained in dyads, which are in turn part of mesosystems (e.g., a family or neighborhood), which are in turn part of macrosystems (e.g., a cultural or national group). It is also the direction taken by Tharp (this volume) in his description of activity settings as "nested" within one another. Both the potential and the limitations to the metaphor, as Serpell (this volume) pointed out, require further consideration.

Among a third set of scholars—especially those with a direct interest in Vygotsky—the feature that was picked up most strongly was "activity." Giving particular attention to this feature fits with the sense that what counts most in a culture is what people do. It fits also with the sense that learning is functional (it is for some purpose) and is active rather than passive in form. It makes learning more observable: It is, for instance, easier to study people "doing mathematics" than coming to understand mathematics. Moreover, it has the potential of moving toward a state where the same unit of analysis, or the same kind of discourse, can be used to refer to institutions, small groups, and individuals.

In their wake, however, the concepts of "activities" and "activity settings" brought a new set of questions, which have been a focus of this book. What exactly is the nature of an activity? How is one activity different from another? Is it possible to speak of types of activity, or is each unique? These questions, one may note, are similar to those asked by Newman, Griffin, and Cole (1989) about the concept of a "task." Are activities best described by what is done, by what is aimed for, or by what is achieved? Is there a way, as Griffin and colleagues (this volume) asked, to talk about boundaries between one activity and another (or, to quote them more accurately, between one context and another)? Would we do best—to take another question made explicit in the same chapter—to observe naturally occurring activities or to create them? How well, as Serpell asked, does an activity fit a setting? What is the fit, for instance, between Nikolopoulou and Cole's computer games and the settings of a library or an after-school club? Does a question about the fit between the activity and the setting divorce "activity" and "setting" in a way not originally intended?

The minor theme in all this research had to do with the presence of people. There was some recognition, within the Vygotskian-based research, that settings involve people who are related to one another in ways other than being the givers and receivers of skills or knowledge. For example, Verdonik and his colleagues pointed to the presence of power relationships and their impact on the way interactions proceeded on a teaching/learning task (Verdonik, Flapan, Schmit, & Weinstock, 1988). The significance of the relationships among the people involved, however, was given far less attention than it was given, for instance, in analyses that started with Moscovici's theory of social representations. (For developmental applications, a 1990 book edited by Duveen and Lloyd, is the best source.) In that type of theory, the critical feature to any setting is the nature of one's position with the group it contains. One may be part of the mainstream, on the margins, a member only of this group, or a participant in several groups with ideologies not always compatible. In each case, it is the nature of one's positions, of one's participation in the social life of the group, that influences the extent to which one picks up, and appropriates as one's own, the skills and ways of thinking valued by the group.

The relationships among the people involved in teaching/learning settings clearly cannot be ignored. The challenge has been to find ways to include them within descriptions focused on the nature of activities. It is interesting to see that this challenge has been taken up in several chapters of this book. Stone, for instance, commented on the need for mutual trust if learning is to take place, and Litowitz underlined issues of identification between teacher and learner. Finding other ways to merge interest in these two features of settings—activities and relationships among the people involved—is a challenge I would expect to receive continued attention.

The likelihood of attention to another feature—the way in which people enter settings—is less clear-cut. The nature of access and of progression through settings was an aspect of settings raised by Barker and Wright (1955). Outside of Vygotskian research, it appears to be reemerging in studies such as that of Ogbu (1991) in terms of the impact of whether one is a member of a minority group by choice or by social exclusion, in discussions of access to the settings where knowledge may be gained (e.g., Bourdieu & Passeron, 1979), and in arguments about research on what people regard as the feasible or legitimate ways to gain knowledge in various situations (e.g., Goodnow, 1988; Stodolsky, 1988). An interest in access and entry patterns seems to be highly compatible with an interest in activities. One hopes also to see it integrated into the discussion of other features of activity settings as Vygotskian scholars move toward an increasingly enlarged and thoughtful view of activities, tasks, settings, and contexts. Griffin and her coauthors (this volume) are undoubtedly right in saying that we "still encounter difficulties accepting Vygotsky's invitation to attend to context. . . . There is no accepted consensus about what to focus on for a sufficient study of context." There is, however, clearly no lack of interest and no lack of momentum in work on the problem.

Nature of Cognition

At the same time the nature of context or culture was coming under scrutiny, so also was the nature of cognition. The scrutiny came from several sources, with the scholars interested in "mind and society" one of the interested parties.

Briefly, people came to ask whether differences in intellectual performance were the result of differences in competence or in production, if standardized tasks were appropriate measures of intellectual development, and whether it was reasonable to describe cognition as (1) based on general factors, (2) logical, or (3) the property of an individual rather than shared among individuals. Some of the push toward rethinking this area derived from the tension between a belief in the equality of people and the observations of "poor" performance on the part of people from non-Western countries when presented with Western tasks. Some of it came from research on cognition that emphasized its pragmatic properties and its reliance on heuristics. Some came from the recognition that when two people worked on the same task, whether by talking to one another or solving the same spatial problem, the critical issue was not so much the individual's understanding as the presence of shared meanings, of "intersubjectivity."

Some of these background debates appear to have had more impact than others on the chapters herein. For instance, for some time the most prominent debate was the discussion about whether cognition is "general" (e.g., takes the form of an intellectual skill that cuts across situations) or "specific" (displaying little or no transfer but also displaying a good fit to the demands of the situation in which it is learned). Such debate underlies much of the interest in the way arithmetical skills arise over the course of particular activities and fit the demands of the activities, e.g., as in the research of Carraher, Carraher, and Schliemann (1985), Lave (1988); Saxe (1991), and Scribner (1986). To judge from the chapters in this book, the debate over generality no longer holds the fire it once did. Specificity now seems to be taken for granted by scholars working from a Vygotskian base; or perhaps a return to the issue of "transfer" waits for a satisfactory definition of differences among tasks and activities. What appears instead is a strong concern with getting down to the specifics of what learning involves and what is needed for a successful ending to a problem; a prime example is an analysis of the precise parts of a learning activity that reciprocal teaching affects (Palincsar et al., this volume).

Within this book there is more evidence that researchers have taken to heart the need to find measures of competence or of development that are not in the form of tasks expected to be applicable to every group and in any situation. There is also clear evidence, as in the chapter by Forman and McPhail, that they have begun to accept the need to consider situations where people work together rather than struggle alone with a problem.

There is also evidence of extended response to the challenge of attending to the nonlogical characteristics of cognition and of going beyond a view of development as taking the form of an increasing use of logic. That view of cognition came under fire because of an array of evidence to the effect that logic was often resorted to only in unfamiliar situations or under duress. In everyday life, thinking was found to be marked by shortcuts and a great reliance on what usually happens. Moreover, thinking was often value-laden. From one social group to another, one could find variations in what was regarded as intellectual good form or good "taste" (Bourdieu, 1979), in "cognitive values" (Goodnow, 1990a), in the "esthetics of thought" (Wertsch, Tulviste, & Hagstrom, this volume). Concern with the normative or evaluative aspects of cognition is elaborated by Moll and Whitmore in their attention to the normative aspects of an activity (e.g., what counts as a problem or a solution), in the attention given by Wertsch and coauthors to "cognitive authority" and accountability, and in Cazden's emphasis on the importance of coming to believe that particular ways of speaking and acting are one's "own" rather than imposed by others. These points are much needed extensions of what was earlier the rather baldly stated proposal that what is being transferred from expert to novice is not only "expertise" and a capacity for "self-regulation" but also "responsibility" for a task.

Context/Cognition: Connections and Processes

This book takes up in a variety of ways the challenge to move beyond framing the issue of context in x or y terms: the effect, for instance, of culture or context on cognition. There seems, in fact, to be a consensus that the problem is not solved by a change in preposition (mind *and* society, mind *in* society) or by the simple assertion that both are "socially constructed" or "socially structured."

The way in which processes are to be considered is far less clear. The present volume comes at a time when no one finds it satisfactory to attribute development to either "discovery" or "transmission." The grossness of the latter term was especially underlined in this volume by Hatano. How has that general difficulty been taken up?

I shall concentrate on what has happened to "transmission," a term Hatano singled out as in great need of dissection and clarification. As a step in those directions, I shall note a number of ideas about the nature of: (1) adult assistance or guidance; (2) the learner's participation; and (3) the interaction or coordination of the two.

Nature of Adult or Expert Assistance

Some concern in the past had to do with specifying and comparing forms of assistance in terms of their relative effectiveness. Formal teaching, scaffolding, apprenticeship, proleptic instruction: Which of these factors produced increased understanding or competence on the part of the novice? Could it be demonstrated that a particular form of assistance produced lasting or transferable results? Could a mother who demonstrated effective methods with her own child use them also with another child?

In the early studies, the primary description of assistance—as I read the literature—was in terms of the way the expert's actions were tailored to the competence of the novice and shifted with changes in competence. In effect, the learner's competence and the expert's sensitivity provided the major constraints on the expert's actions. At the same time, however, there existed an accompanying literature on cultural variations in the way people were supposed to teach children, dealing especially with appropriate forms of verbal communication (e.g., Heath, 1983, 1989; Ochs & Schieffelin, 1984; Rogoff, 1990). There were also analyses of communication (e.g., Wertsch, 1985) that pointed to still further constraints. In effect, here was a range of constraints on what adults might do or say. One would expect these lines of thought to come increasingly together. They do so in this book in several places: in the chapters by Rogoff et al., Cazden, and Stone. They do so also in the concern shown by Cobb, Wood, and Yackel (this volume) with institutional constraints on what a teacher may do or say, and the attention given by Chang and Wells (this volume) to the impact (on what is said) of both the teachers' and the students' assumptions about appropriate statements.

In contrast, there is less of an impact from an aspect of background that concentrates on the motivation and the goals of the expert. D'Andrade (1981) particularly took studies of cognition to task for proceeding as if cognition took place in neutral settings. Most skills and most knowledge, he pointed out, were acquired under conditions where the guiding hand had a vested interest in seeing that particular skills or particular ways of looking at the world were acquired. The goal was what one might call "selective uptake" or appropriation of ideas, and the guidance was highly directive. Sociologists such as Bourdieu and Foucault, as I have discovered in a search for additional literature on directiveness and access (Goodnow, 1990b), take it for granted that the expert may have no wish to share knowledge, except perhaps with a privileged few. Perhaps it is only the educated middle class who see it as their role to teach all the time and who turn every event into an opportunity to present children with a new word or a new fact.

Attention to the motives of the expert is not missing in Vygotskian-based studies. Wertsch, Minick, and Arns (1984), for instance, noted the importance of whether a mother sees it as her role to teach and whether she sees the pressure for performance as falling on her ("I need to demonstrate what an effective mother I am") or on the child. Rather, the goals of the adult seem still to be treated as a relative constant (a competent, self-regulating child), leaving the child's capacity to use assistance as the major source of constraints on the adult's activity. That this condition need not be so, however, is a point made by several: by Wertsch, Tulviste, and Hagstrom in their chapter, for instance, by Litowitz in another chapter, and by Packer in his commentary. Perhaps I am biased by a particular interest in the topic, but I certainly see as an emerging theme—both here and in the future—the attention to motives (combined with attention to relationships and to institutional factors) as constraints and influences on the assistance adults provide.

Nature of the Learner's Input

Part of the general background to the current studies is the widespread view of the learner as "active," a participant in the process. Whereas the early Vygotskian studies tended to emphasize what the adult did, this book emphasizes participation. That emphasis is prominent also in Rogoff's (1990) book and in the present chapter by Rogoff and her colleagues.

"Participation," however, leaves much to be filled in. The present chapters have responded to the problem in several ways. One is by distinguishing among forms of participation. Is it in the form of a "recitation script" (Tharp, this volume)? Is it in the form of "ventriloquism" (Wertsch et al., quoting Bakhtin) or in a form directed more toward being innovative and accountable (Wertsch et al., this volume)?

A second response is by asking about the motives and goals of the learner. As several have pointed out here (e.g., both Litowitz and Cazden), people cast in the role of learners are not always enthusiastic receivers of knowledge, and resistance may be more prominent than a rapid and willing appropriation of ideas as one's "own."

As I have already commented on motivation with reference to adults (treating them as the holders of knowledge), let me give short shrift at this point to the motives of learners and raise instead an issue that seems more strictly cognitive. It occurs particularly in the chapters on which Hatano commented.

In the area of cognitive development, we have seen two strong lines of research: one emphasizing the individual as actively constructing schemes and meanings, the other emphasizing social or guided constructions. These two lines of research need not become opposed orthodoxies. On the contrary, they need to strengthen each other. There are also points where the two overlap. The starting point for effective action within the zone of proximal development, for instance, is the capacity to operate with assistance. The starting point for accommodation in Piagetian theory is the presence of schemes that make it possible to see new information as relevant. We are now, Hatano argues, at a point where the several interests in construction may begin to work together, giving a particular interest to the chapters on which he comments, and to future mergers.

Evaluating the Actions of Two or More People

A challenge that faces every analyst of interactions are the interactions that occur between peers and those between experts and novices. Finding effective ways to describe how the two mesh or collide is no easy task. It is, for instance, the task recognized by Rogoff (1990; Rogoff et al., this volume) in her term "guided participation." It is the essence of the attention given, outside this book, to the impact on cognitive development of "social conflict" (discrepancies between the viewpoints of two people who are required to come up with a common answer) (e.g., Doise & Mugny, 1984). It is present in every description of interactions as involving synchrony or asynchrony (e.g., Kaye, 1982).

The problem has not been solved. Note, however, that there is a common line of attack emerging from both outside and within this book. It is an approach that emphasizes development as taking the form not simply of some acquisition by one individual (e.g., self-regulation, or an understanding of conservation) but as the acquisition of shared meanings. Light and Perret-Clermont (1989) took this approach toward interactions between any interviewer or tester and any child. Wertsch et al. (this volume) raised it with reference to situations where the adult's goal is more explicitly one of teaching. It may well be that Vygotskian analysis has always had a theoretical place for shared meanings (and for mutual accommodations), but it is interesting to see that theoretical possibility taking clearer shape and offering a base for integrating theories rather than discarding one as incompatible with the other.

Final Comment

If I were to select a single theme for my comments, it would be along the lines of the phrase, "a problem solved is a problem created." Each new step we take, in theoretical or research format, means that we move forward and at the same time face new questions. The chapters in this book provide a rewarding approach to both old and new questions: rewarding for readers deeply immersed in Soviet theory, readers sympathetic to it but not aficionados, and readers interested in the way thinking is shaped, to quote the Introduction's title, by "individual, social, and institutional processes."

References

Barker, R. G., & Wright, H. F. (1955). *Midwest and its children: the psychological ecology of an American town.* New York: Harper & Row.

Bourdieu, P. (1979). *Distinction: a social critique of the judgment of taste.* London: Routledge & Kegan Paul (translated by R. Nice).

Bourdieu, P., & Passeron, J. C. (1979). *Reproduction in education, society and culture.* Beverly Hills, CA: Sage.

Bronfenbrenner, U. (1979). *The ecology of human development.* Cambridge, MA: Harvard University Press.

Bruner, J. S. (1972). The nature and uses of immaturity. *American Psychologist, 27,* 687–716.

Carraher, T. N., Carraher, D., & Schliemann, A. D. (1985). Mathematics in the streets and in the schools. *British Journal of Developmental Psychology, 3,* 21–19.

D'Andrade, R. G. (1981). The cultural part of cognition. *Cognitive Science, 5,* 179–195.

Doise, W., & Mugny, G. (1984). *The social development of the intellect.* Oxford: Pergamon Press.

Donaldson, M. (1978). *Children's minds.* New York: Norton.

Duveen, G., & Lloyd, B., eds. (1990). *Social representations and the development of knowledge.* Cambridge: Cambridge University Press.

Elder, G. H., Jr. (1974). *Children of the great depression.* Chicago: University of Chicago Press.

Goodnow, J. J. (1962). A test of milieu effects with some of Piaget's tasks. *Psychological Monographs, 76*(36, whole no. 555).

Goodnow, J. J. (1976). The nature of intelligent behavior: questions raised by cross-cultural studies. In L. Resnick (ed.). *The nature of intelligence* (pp. 169–188). Hillsdale, NJ: Lawrence Erlbaum Associates.

Goodnow, J. J. (1984). On being judged intelligent. *International Journal of Psychology, 19,* 391–406.

Goodnow, J. J. (1987). Cultural conditions and individual behaviors: conceptual and methodological links. *Australian Journal of Psychology, 38,* 231–244.

Goodnow, J. J. (1988). Children, families and communities: ways of viewing their relationships to one another. In N. Bolger, A. Caspi, G. Downey, & M. Moorehouse (eds.). *Persons in context: developmental processes* (pp. 50–76). Cambridge: Cambridge University Press.

Goodnow, J. J. (1990a). The socialization of cognition: what's involved? In J. Stigler, R. Shweder, & G. Herdt (eds.). *Cultural psychology* (pp. 259–286). Chicago: University of Chicago Press.

Goodnow, J. J. (1990b). Using sociology to extend psychological accounts of cognitive development. *Human Development, 33,* 81–107.

Goodnow, J. J., & Collins, W. A. (1990). *Development according to parents: the nature, sources, and consequences of parents' ideas.* London, Lawrence Erlbaum Associates.

Heath, S. B. (1989). Oral and literate traditions among black Americans living in poverty. *American Psychologist, 44,* 367–373.

Heath, S. G. (1983). *Ways with words: language, life and work in communities and classrooms.* Cambridge: Cambridge University Press.

Kaye, K. (1982). *The mental and social life of babies: how parents create persons.* Chicago: University of Chicago Press.

Lave, J. (1988). *Cognition in practice: mind, mathematics and culture in everyday life.* Cambridge: Cambridge University Press.

Light, P., & Perret-Clermont, A. N. (1989). Social context effects in learning and testing. In A. Gellatly, D. Rogers, & J. A. Sloboda (eds.). *Cognition and social worlds* (pp. 99–112). Oxford: Oxford University Press.

Looft, W. (1971). The psychology of more. *American Psychologist, 26,* 561–565.

Mehan, H. (1979). *Learning lessons.* Cambridge, MA: Harvard University Press.

Newman, D., Griffin, M., & Cole, M. (1989). *The construction zone: working for cognitive change in school.* Cambridge: Cambridge University Press.

Ochs, E., & Schieffelin, B. B. (1984). Language acquisition and socialization: the developmental stories and their implications. In R. Shweder & R. LeVine (eds.). *Culture and its acquisition.* Chicago: University of Chicago Press.

Ogbu, J. (1991). Presented as part of a discussion session, "Roundtable in social construction and psychological development" (W. Damon & J. Youniss, chairmen), at the Biennial Meeting of the Society for Research in Child Development, Seattle.

Quinn, N., & Holland, D. (1987). Culture and cognition. In D. Holland & N. Quinn (eds.). *Cultural models in language and thought* (pp. 3–42). Cambridge: Cambridge University Press.

Reid, B. V., & Valsiner, J. (1986). Consistency, praise, and love: folk theories of American parents. *Ethos, 14,* 1–15.

Rogoff, B. (1990). *Apprenticeship in thinking: cognitive development in social context.* Cambridge: Cambridge University Press.

Saxe, G. (1991). *Culture and cognitive development: studies in mathematical understanding.* Hillsdale, NJ: Lawrence Erlbaum Associates.

Scribner, S. (1986). Thinking in action: some characteristics of practical thought. In R. Sternberg & R. Wagner (eds.). *Practical intelligence* (pp. 13–30). Cambridge: Cambridge University Press.

Scribner, S., & Cole, M. (1981). *The psychology of literacy.* Cambridge, MA: Harvard University Press.

Stodolsky, S. (1988). *The subject matters: classroom activity in mathematics and social studies.* Chicago: University of Chicago Press.

Super, C. M., & Harkness, S. (1986). The developmental niche: a conceptualization of the interface of child and culture. *International Journal of Behavioral Development, 9,* 546–569.

Tharp, R. G., & Gallimore, R. (1988). *Rousing minds to life: teaching and learning in social contexts.* Cambridge: Cambridge University Press.

Verdonik, F., Flapan, V., Schmit, C., & Weinstock, J. (1988). The role of power relationships in children's cognition: Its significance for research on cognitive development. *LCHC Newsletter, 10,* 80–85.

Wertsch, J. V. (ed.) (1985). *Culture, communication, and cognition: Vygotskian perspectives.* Cambridge: Cambridge University Press.

Wertsch, J. V., Minick, N., & Arns, F. J. (1984). The creation of context in joint problem-solving. In B. Rogoff & J. Lave (eds.). *Everyday cognition: its development in social contexts* (pp. 151–167). Cambridge, MA: Harvard University Press.

Whiting, B. B. (1980). Culture and social behavior: a model for the development of social behavior. *Ethos, 8,* 95–116.

NAME INDEX

SUBJECT INDEX

Accountability. *See also* Institutions
  as societal means of regulation, 358, 361, 365
Activity settings, 270, 284, 358
  accessibility of, 374
  as basic unit of analysis for study of learning, 232, 295–96, 306, 359, 372–73
  components of, 316, 318, 323–24, 329–30, 372
    cultural activities, 316
    cultural values, 316, 319, 323, 327
    demands, 328
    goals/beliefs, 331
    motives, 316, 327, 331
    operations, 316, 328
    personnel, 316, 318, 323–24, 331
    scripts, 193, 316, 322–29, 331, 358, 361
    social relationships, 373–74. *See also* Social interactions; Social relationships
    surface features, 327
    tasks, 316, 322–28, 330–31
  as conceptual tool in educational reform, 275–81
  definition of 275–77, 315–16
  for mathematics instruction, 94, 98, 100, 110. *See also* Mathematics
  purposes of, 291–92, 316, 322–24, 327–28, 330
  role of children in, 231–33
  theoretical derivations of, 316, 325, 372–73
Affect. *See also* Motivation; Negation; Resistance
  conflict, 189, 202–4
  desire—as factor in learning, 187–90, 194
  emotional acts, 107
  in group work, 67–68, 78
  and learning, 10, 85
  role in scaffolding, 179. *See also* Scaffolding
Agency, human, 13, 336, 338, 352
  analysis of, 337, 342
  distributed, 13, 339–44, 360
  individual, 336, 342
  intermental and intramental, 337. *See also* Intermental and intramental functioning

mediated, 341–42, 346, 349, 354. *See also* Mediation
  sociocultural approach to, 337. *See also* Sociocultural
Analytical unit, for study of behavior, 198, 232, 294–95, 337–40, 359, 373. *See also* Activity settings
Anthropological perspective, 106. *See also* Culture
Appropriation, 40, 358, 362. *See also* Internalization
  of child's meaning by teacher, 109
  distinguished from internalization, 170–71, 234
  of mediational means, 341–42, 344–46, 349. *See also* Mediation
  relation to identification, 6, 362
  role of inference in, 171, 173–74, 178, 180
  role of social relationships in, 6. *See also* Scaffolding
  of sense, 206
  of voice, for creating identity, 209, 218, 362. *See also* Voice
Assessment. *See also* Dynamic assessment
  listening comprehension, 46
  reasoning by analogy, 47, 49–51
Assisted performance, 270, 272, 276, 278. *See also* Guided participation; Interpsychological; Mediation; Scaffolding
Attention
  management of, 243–45
  time-sharing of, 244, 248
Audience, needs of, 66–67, 73
Authority, cognitive, 349–50
Autonomy, 261, 264

Behaviorism, 257
Beliefs, 106, 113
Bilingual classrooms, 19–22, 37. *See also* Bilingualism; ESL learners
  instruction in, 319
  literary materials, 30
  reading, 29, 32
  writing, 28–29, 32
Bilingualism, 21. *See also* Bilingual classrooms
  additive conditions, 21
  as differentiated cognitive repertoire, 365
  as resource for learning, 37
Black English. *See* Dialect

389

Sociocultural systems (*continued*)
ecological constraints and pressures, 330.
See also Accountability
family niche, 315
literacy development, 316
practices within, 214, 218
social system, 316
subsistence, 315–316
values, 328
Sociocultural theory, 231–32, 337–52. *See
also* Sociohistorical theory
and constructivism, 9, 154, 159, 169
contexts, 352
forces, 338
history, 351
process, 337, 343, 351
recent developments in, 3–7
settings, 351–52
situatedness, 343–45, 350–52
Vygotsky's general genetic law, 338–40,
344, 347–48, 352
Sociogenesis, 120, 164–65
Sociohistorical theory, 231–32. *See also*
Sociocultural theory
extensions of, 3–6, 11
limitations in interpretations of, 3–5
role of culture in, 3–5
Speech, 184, 188–89. *See also* Conversation;
Discourse; Language; Talk, Voice
dialogic, 189. *See also* Dialogue
and gestures, 184
heteroglossic, 189. *See also* Voice
vs. language, 199
social, egocentric, inner, 188–89
Speech genres, 199–200. *See also* Social
language
as mediators of cognition, 6, 345–
56
as sources of conflict, 202
Speech registers. *See* Discourse
Strategies, 43–44, 52–53
metacognitive, 55
principled use of, 52–53
Structuralism, 259
Subjectivity, role in learning, 188, 190, 193–
94
Symbolic interactionism, 91, 100

Talk. *See also* Conversation; Discourse
collaborative, 66
and epistemic literacy, 72, 83, 86
teacher's role in, 66, 82–84
about texts, 63
tutorial, 66, 84
Tasks, structuring, 273–74
Teacher assistance. *See also* Assisted
performance; Classroom practices;
Reciprocal teaching; Talk,
collaborative
in learning-directed activities, 84
multifaceted nature of, 84–85

Teacher training
staff development, 277
supervision, 278
Teaching. *See also* Classroom practices;
Education
definition of, 270, 272
and learning, 269–70, 272
reciprocal. *See* Reciprocal teaching
responsive, 272
as scaffolding. *See* Scaffolding
scripts in, 271
Text. *See also* Literacy; Talk, about texts
artifacts as extension of, 79
not autonomous, 209
Textbooks, 162
Thinking. *See also* Cognitive processes
modes of, 351
Topic, choice of, 73–77
connecting to existing interests, 75
strategies for, 74–75
Transfer of knowledge. *See* Appropriation;
Internalization; Knowledge, transfer
of

Unit of analysis. *See* Analytical unit

Voice, 10, 176, 259
adoption of, as source of self, 192–93
appropriation of, 206–9
conflicts among, 189, 202–4, 259
definition of, 198
multiple-voiced utterance, 189–90
programmer's, 162. *See* Computers
single-voiced utterance, 189
ventriloquation, 345–46, 349–50, 358

Writing. *See also* Literacy
academic, 197, 205–9

Zone of proximal development, 53, 60,
122, 155, 185, 224, 256–57, 260, 270,
278. *See also* Guided participation;
Scaffolding
active role of child in, 39, 105, 160, 358
child's motivation for participation in,
187–91, 194
collective zones, 20–21, 37
discourse in, 64, 83, 171–78
individualistic bias in discussions of, 11,
264, 340–41
and language acquisition, 62
mediated assistance in, 39–41. *See also*
Mediation
as more than assisted performance, 11,
19–20, 39, 232–33
prolepsis in. *See* Prolepsis
teaching viewed as, 8, 272. *See also*
Reciprocal teaching
Vygotsky's definition of, 44–45, 124, 170,
340

Printed in the United Kingdom
by Lightning Source UK Ltd.
106583UKS00002B/5

9 780195 109771